ALABAMA

Contact

Dear Readers:

Every effort was made to make this the most accurate, informative, and easy-to-use guidebook on the planet. Any comments, suggestions, and/or corrections regarding this guide are welcome and should be sent to:

Outside America™
c/o Editorial Dept.
300 West Main St., Ste. A
Charlottesville, VA 22903
editorial@outside-america.com
www.outside-america.com

We'd love to hear from you so we can make future editions and future guides even better.

Thanks and happy trails!

HIKE AMERICA™ GUIDES

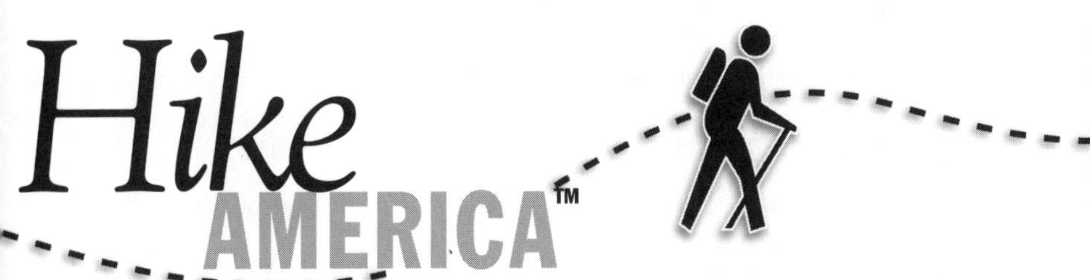

ALABAMA

An Atlas of Alabama's Greatest Hiking Adventures

by Joe Cuhaj

Guilford, Connecticut

Published by
The Globe Pequot Press
P.O. Box 480
Guilford, CT 06437
www.globe-pequot.com

Produced by
Beachway Press Publishing, Inc.
300 West Main St., Ste A
Charlottesville, VA 22903
www.beachway.com

Cover Design Beachway Press

Photographer Joe Cuhaj

Maps designed and produced by Beachway Press

Find Outside America™ at **www.outside-america.com**

Cover Photo: An autumn hike along Deep Creek Trail near Telluride, Colorado. Wilson Peaks in the background. Photo by Amanda Williams

Library of Congress Cataloging-in-Publication Data is available.

ISBN 0-7627-0843-3

Printed in the United States of America
First Edition/First Printing

Acknowledgments

The completion of this book is the culmination of a dream of mine, but it could not have happened without a supporting cast, and to them I am greatly appreciative. First and foremost, thanks goes to my wife, Maggie, for being a part-time hiking partner, knee-mender, driver, and for keeping me on track during this process, and for forgiving me for not mowing the lawn for weeks on end. Thanks also go out to my daughter Kellie for being a part-time photographer, hiking partner, proofreader, and best of all, comic relief on the trail, especially during "The Great Flood."

A big thank you is also in order for Pastor Tony LaGear, his family, and all of our friends at the Eastern Shore Christian Center for their thoughts, prayers, and words of encouragement.

As for writing the book itself, I need to thank Scott Adams, Ryan Croxton, Bryan Kelley, Don Graydon, and the staff at Beachway Press for all of their help, guidance, and especially patience. Special thanks also go to the many clubs throughout the state who were kind enough to give guidance and suggestions, including the Alabama Trail Association; the Vulcan Trail Association; the Cahaba, Coastal, East Alabama, Mobile, and North Alabama chapters of the Sierra Club; and the dozens of cyberbuddies who made trail suggestions.

The research for this book could not have been completed without the help of a variety of people from around the state and the South including Frank Lepore from the National Hurricane Center, Barry Gooden with the National Weather Service, and of course, all of the staff and rangers at the state parks and national forests, too many to mention here, but thank you for your advice!

Finally, thanks to the members and friends of the "Mahwah Hiking Club," Gary, Tom, Jay, Mark, Kevin, Terri, Debbi, Debbie, and Steve, for being with me when the hiking bug first hit so many years ago.

Table of

Contents

Northern Alabama

HIKES AT A GLANCE

1. Pine Beach Trail

Length: 4-mile out-and-back
Difficulty Rating: Easy
Time: 1–2 hours
Nearby: Gulf Shores, AL

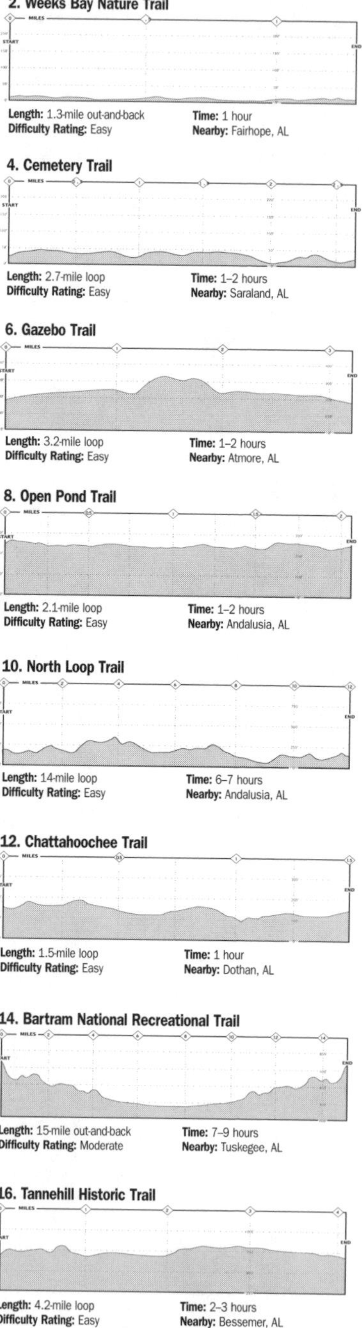

2. Weeks Bay Nature Trail

Length: 1.3-mile out-and-back
Difficulty Rating: Easy
Time: 1 hour
Nearby: Fairhope, AL

3. USS Alabama Historical Trail

Length: 6.5-mile loop
Difficulty Rating: Easy
Time: 3–4 hours
Nearby: Mobile, AL

4. Cemetery Trail

Length: 2.7-mile loop
Difficulty Rating: Easy
Time: 1–2 hours
Nearby: Saraland, AL

5. CCC Trail

Length: 1.5-mile loop
Difficulty Rating: Easy to Moderate
Time: 1 hour
Nearby: Atmore, AL

6. Gazebo Trail

Length: 3.2-mile loop
Difficulty Rating: Easy
Time: 1–2 hours
Nearby: Atmore, AL

7. Redoubt Trail Loop

Length: 6.1-mile loop
Difficulty Rating: Easy
Time: 3 hours
Nearby: Spanish Fort, AL

8. Open Pond Trail

Length: 2.1-mile loop
Difficulty Rating: Easy
Time: 1–2 hours
Nearby: Andalusia, AL

9. Five Runs Loop Trail

Length: 3.2-mile loop
Difficulty Rating: Easy
Time: 2 hours
Nearby: Andalusia, AL

10. North Loop Trail

Length: 14-mile loop
Difficulty Rating: Easy
Time: 6–7 hours
Nearby: Andalusia, AL

11. Conecuh Trail

Length: 19.2-mile point-to-point
Difficulty Rating: Easy grade
Time: 10–12 hours
Nearby: Andalusia, AL

12. Chattahoochee Trail

Length: 1.5-mile loop
Difficulty Rating: Easy
Time: 1 hour
Nearby: Dothan, AL

13. Wildlife Drive

Length: 7-mile loop
Difficulty Rating: Easy
Time: 3–4 hours
Nearby: Eufaula, AL

14. Bartram National Recreational Trail

Length: 15-mile out-and-back
Difficulty Rating: Moderate
Time: 7–9 hours
Nearby: Tuskegee, AL

15. Horseshoe Bend Trail

Length: 2.8-mile loop
Difficulty Rating: Easy
Time: 2 hours
Nearby: Alexander City, AL

16. Tannehill Historic Trail

Length: 4.2-mile loop
Difficulty Rating: Easy
Time: 2–3 hours
Nearby: Bessemer, AL

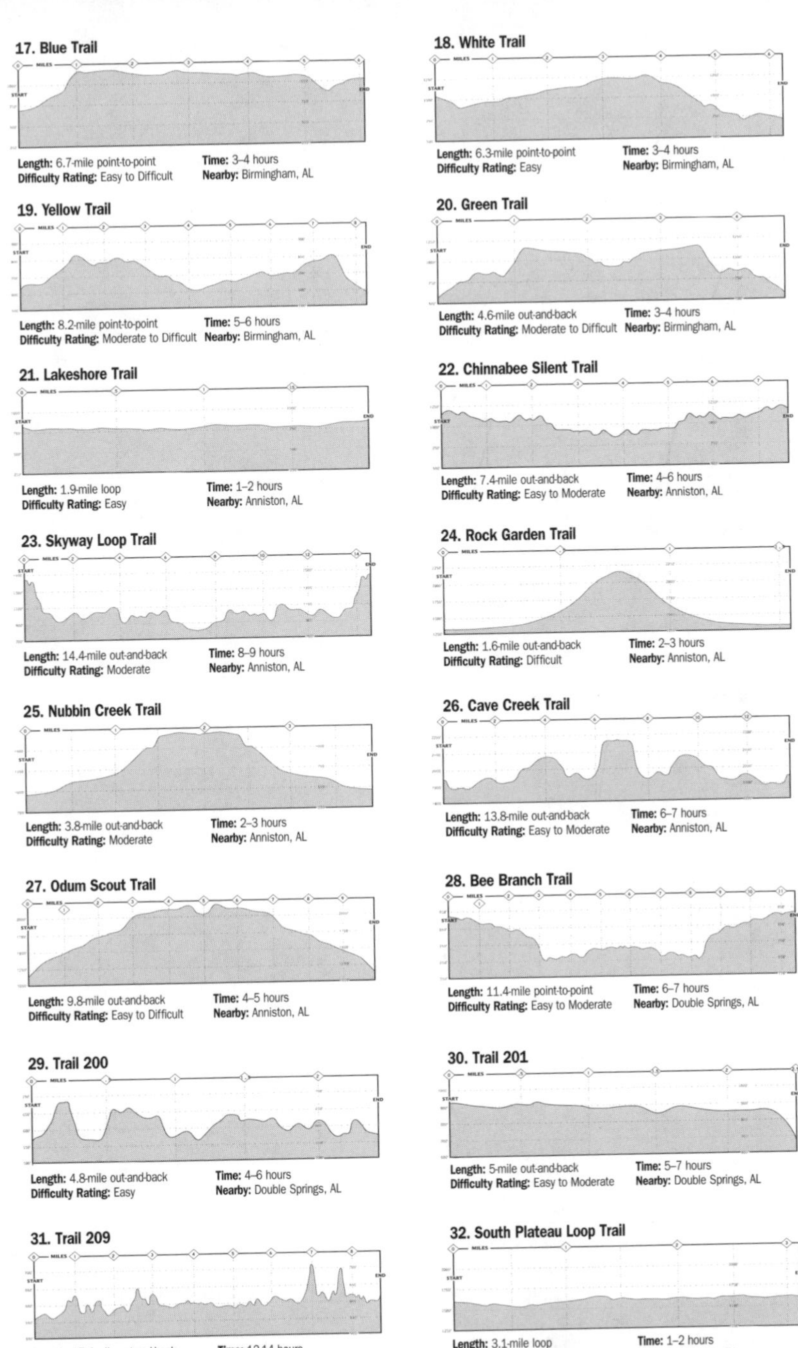

17. Blue Trail

Length: 6.7-mile point-to-point
Difficulty Rating: Easy to Difficult
Time: 3–4 hours
Nearby: Birmingham, AL

18. White Trail

Length: 6.3-mile point-to-point
Difficulty Rating: Easy
Time: 3–4 hours
Nearby: Birmingham, AL

19. Yellow Trail

Length: 8.2-mile point-to-point
Difficulty Rating: Moderate to Difficult
Time: 5–6 hours
Nearby: Birmingham, AL

20. Green Trail

Length: 4.6-mile out-and-back
Difficulty Rating: Moderate to Difficult
Time: 3–4 hours
Nearby: Birmingham, AL

21. Lakeshore Trail

Length: 1.9-mile loop
Difficulty Rating: Easy
Time: 1–2 hours
Nearby: Anniston, AL

22. Chinnabee Silent Trail

Length: 7.4-mile out-and-back
Difficulty Rating: Easy to Moderate
Time: 4–6 hours
Nearby: Anniston, AL

23. Skyway Loop Trail

Length: 14.4-mile out-and-back
Difficulty Rating: Moderate
Time: 8–9 hours
Nearby: Anniston, AL

24. Rock Garden Trail

Length: 1.6-mile out-and-back
Difficulty Rating: Difficult
Time: 2–3 hours
Nearby: Anniston, AL

25. Nubbin Creek Trail

Length: 3.8-mile out-and-back
Difficulty Rating: Moderate
Time: 2–3 hours
Nearby: Anniston, AL

26. Cave Creek Trail

Length: 13.8-mile out-and-back
Difficulty Rating: Easy to Moderate
Time: 6–7 hours
Nearby: Anniston, AL

27. Odum Scout Trail

Length: 9.8-mile out-and-back
Difficulty Rating: Easy to Difficult
Time: 4–5 hours
Nearby: Anniston, AL

28. Bee Branch Trail

Length: 11.4-mile point-to-point
Difficulty Rating: Easy to Moderate
Time: 6–7 hours
Nearby: Double Springs, AL

29. Trail 200

Length: 4.8-mile out-and-back
Difficulty Rating: Easy
Time: 4–6 hours
Nearby: Double Springs, AL

30. Trail 201

Length: 5-mile out-and-back
Difficulty Rating: Easy to Moderate
Time: 5–7 hours
Nearby: Double Springs, AL

31. Trail 209

Length: 17.4-mile out-and-back
Difficulty Rating: Easy to Moderate
Time: 12-14 hours
Nearby: Double Springs, AL

32. South Plateau Loop Trail

Length: 3.1-mile loop
Difficulty Rating: Easy
Time: 1–2 hours
Nearby: Huntsville, AL

HIKES AT A GLANCE

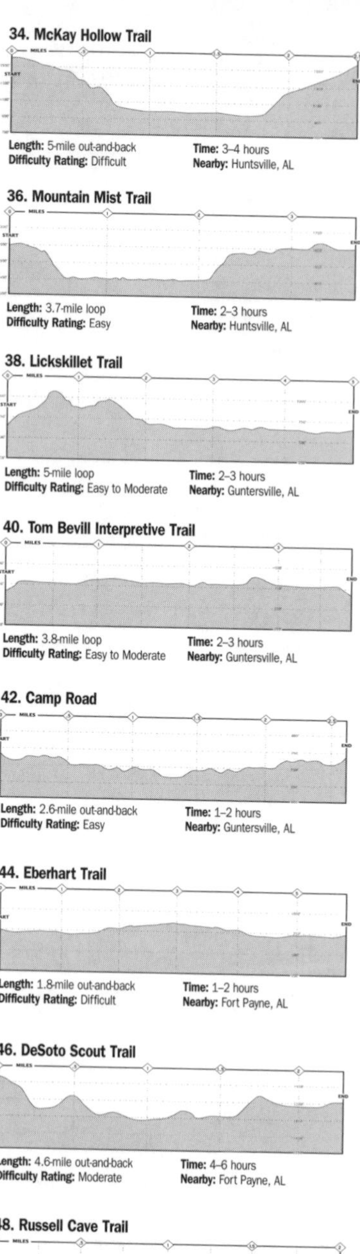

33. North Plateau Loop Trail

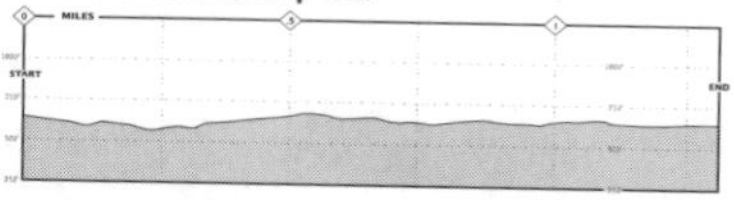

Length: 1.3-mile loop
Difficulty Rating: Easy
Time: 1 hour
Nearby: Huntsville, AL

34. McKay Hollow Trail

Length: 5-mile out-and-back
Difficulty Rating: Difficult
Time: 3–4 hours
Nearby: Huntsville, AL

35. Stone Cuts Trail

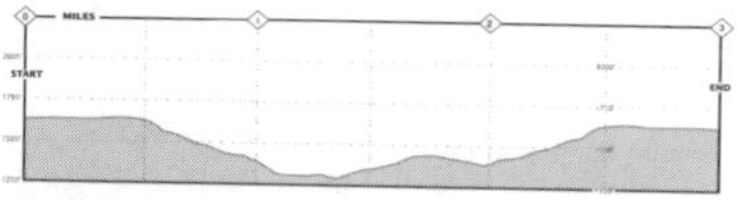

Length: 3-mile loop
Difficulty Rating: Moderate
Time: 3–4 hours
Nearby: Huntsville, AL

36. Mountain Mist Trail

Length: 3.7-mile loop
Difficulty Rating: Easy
Time: 2–3 hours
Nearby: Huntsville, AL

37. Land Trust Loop

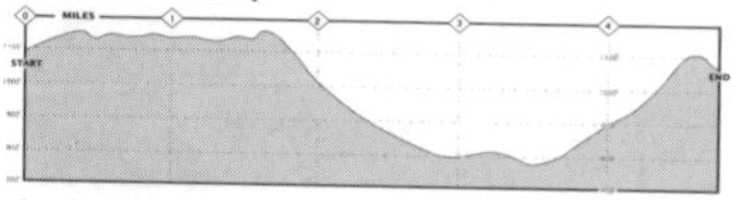

Length: 4.7-mile loop
Difficulty Rating: Difficult
Time: 3–4 hours
Nearby: Huntsville, AL

38. Lickskillet Trail

Length: 5-mile loop
Difficulty Rating: Easy to Moderate
Time: 2–3 hours
Nearby: Guntersville, AL

39. Cascade Loop Trail

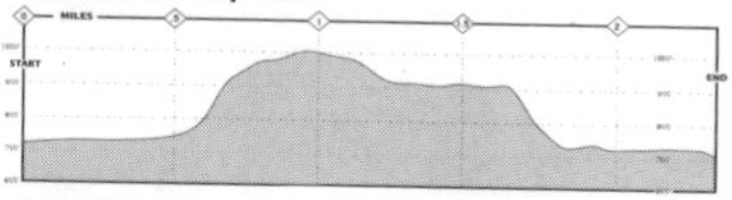

Length: 2.3-mile loop
Difficulty Rating: Moderate
Time: 2–3 hours
Nearby: Guntersville, AL

40. Tom Bevill Interpretive Trail

Length: 3.8-mile loop
Difficulty Rating: Easy to Moderate
Time: 2–3 hours
Nearby: Guntersville, AL

41. Cutchenmine Trail

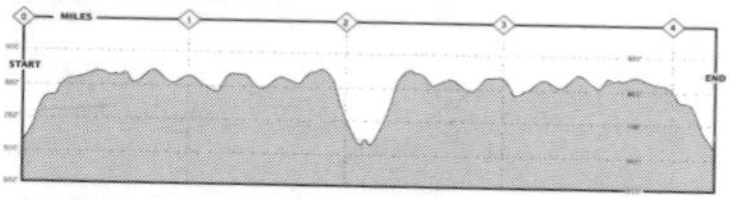

Length: 4.2-mile out-and-back
Difficulty Rating: Easy
Time: 2–3 hours
Nearby: Guntersville, AL

42. Camp Road

Length: 2.6-mile out-and-back
Difficulty Rating: Easy
Time: 1–2 hours
Nearby: Guntersville, AL

43. Point Rock Trail

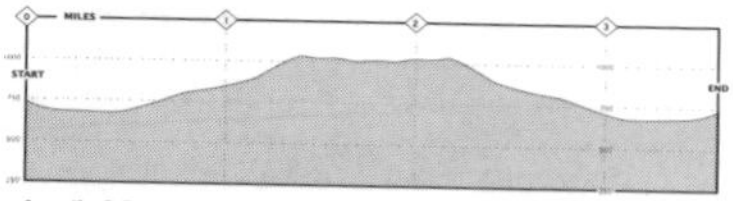

Length: 3.5-mile out-and-back
Difficulty Rating: Moderate
Time: 2–3 hours
Nearby: Guntersville, AL

44. Eberhart Trail

Length: 1.8-mile out-and-back
Difficulty Rating: Difficult
Time: 1–2 hours
Nearby: Fort Payne, AL

45. Rhododendron Trail

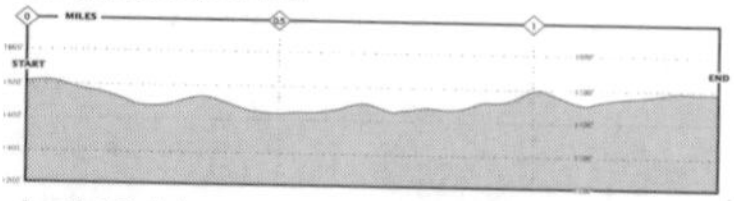

Length: 1.3-mile loop
Difficulty Rating: Easy to Moderate
Time: 2 hours
Nearby: Fort Payne, AL

46. DeSoto Scout Trail

Length: 4.6-mile out-and-back
Difficulty Rating: Moderate
Time: 4–6 hours
Nearby: Fort Payne, AL

47. Lost Falls Trail

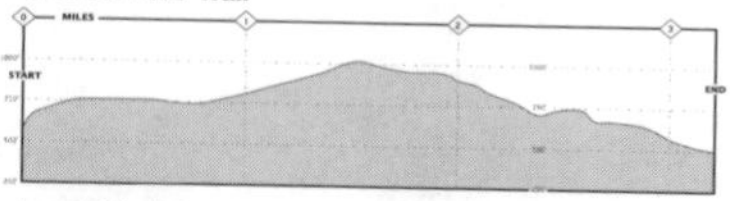

Length: 3.2-mile loop
Difficulty Rating: Easy
Time: 2–3 hours
Nearby: Fort Payne, AL

48. Russell Cave Trail

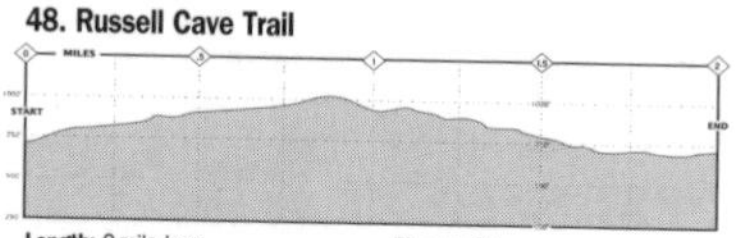

Length: 2-mile loop
Difficulty Rating: Moderate
Time: 1–2 hours
Nearby: Bridgeport, AL

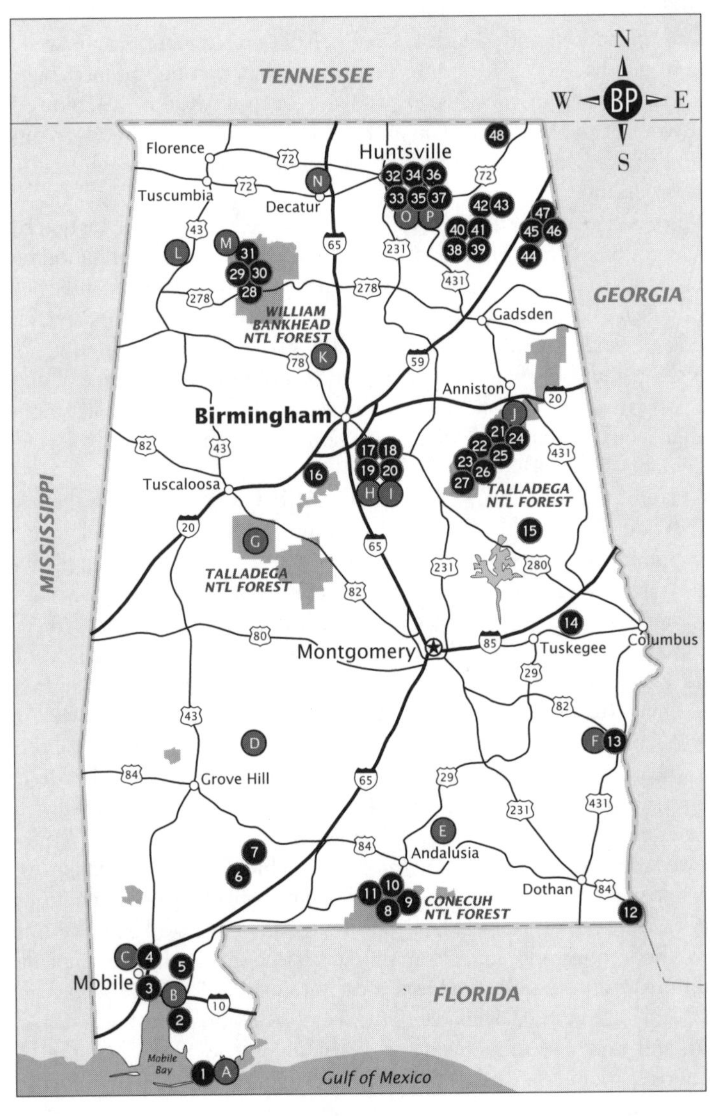

TENNESSEE
GEORGIA
MISSISSIPPI
FLORIDA
Gulf of Mexico
Mobile Bay
N
S
E
W
BP
Florence
Tuscumbia
Decatur
Huntsville
Gadsden
Anniston
Birmingham
Tuscaloosa
Montgomery
Tuskegee
Columbus
Grove Hill
Andalusia
Dothan
Mobile
WILLIAM BANKHEAD NTL FOREST
TALLADEGA NTL FOREST
TALLADEGA NTL FOREST
CONECUH NTL FOREST

HOW TO USE THIS BOOK

Take a close enough look and you'll find that this little guide contains just about everything you'll ever need to choose, plan for, enjoy, and survive a hike in the state of Alabama. We've done everything but load your pack and tie up your bootlaces. Stuffed with 368 pages of useful Alabama-specific information, *Hike America: Alabama*™ features 48 mapped and cued hikes and 17 honorable mentions, as well as everything from advice on getting into shape to tips on getting the most out of hiking with your children or your dog. And as you'd expect with any Outside America™ guide, you get the best maps man and technology can render. With so much information, the only question you may have is: How do I sift through it all? Well, we answer that, too.

We've designed our Hike America™ series to be highly visual, for quick reference and ease-of-use. What this means is that the most pertinent information rises quickly to the top, so you don't have to waste time poring through bulky hike descriptions to get mileage cues or elevation stats. They're set aside for you. And yet, an Outside America™ guide doesn't read like a laundry list. Take the time to dive into a hike description and you'll realize that this guide is not just a good source of information; it's a good read. And so, in the end, you get the best of both worlds: a quick-reference guide and an engaging look at a region. Here's an outline of the guide's major components.

WHAT YOU'LL FIND IN A *HIKE AMERICA*™ GUIDE. Let's start with the individual chapter. To aid in quick decision-making, we start each chapter with a **Hike Summary**. This short overview gives you a taste of the hiking adventure at hand. You'll learn about the trail terrain and what surprises the route has to offer. If your interest is peaked, you can read more. If not, skip to the next Hike Summary. The **Hike Specs** are fairly self-explanatory. Here you'll find the quick, nitty-gritty details of the hike: where the trailhead is located, the nearest town, hike length, approximate hiking time, difficulty rating, type of trail terrain, and what other trail users you may encounter. Our **Getting There** section gives you dependable directions from a nearby city right down to where you'll want to park. The **Hike Description** is the meat of the chapter. Detailed and honest, it's the author's carefully researched impression of the trail. While it's impossible to cover everything, you can rest assured that we won't miss what's important. In our **Miles/Directions** section we provide mileage cues to identify all turns and trail name changes, as well as points of interest. Between this and our Route Map, you simply can't get lost. The **Hike Information** box is a hodgepodge of information. In it you'll find trail hotlines (for updates on trail conditions), park schedules and fees, local outdoor retailers (for emergency trail supplies), and a list of maps available to the area. We'll also tell you where to stay, what to eat, and what else to see while you're hiking in the area. Lastly, the **Honorable Mentions** section details all of the hikes that didn't make the cut, for whatever reason—in many cases it's not because they aren't great hikes, instead it's because they're over-crowded or environmentally sensitive to heavy traffic. Be sure to read through these. A jewel might be lurking among them.

We don't want anyone, by any means, to feel restricted to just the routes and trails that are mapped here. We hope you will have an adventurous spirit and use this guide as a platform to dive into Alabama's backcountry and discover new routes for yourself. One of the simplest ways to begin this is to just turn the map upside down and hike the course in reverse. The change in perspective is fantastic and the hike should feel quite different. With this in mind, it will be like getting two distinctly different hikes on each map.

For your own purposes, you may wish to copy the directions for the course onto a small sheet to help you while hiking, or photocopy the map and cue sheet to take with you. Otherwise, just slip the whole book in your backpack and take it all with you. Enjoy your time in the outdoors and remember to pack out what you pack in.

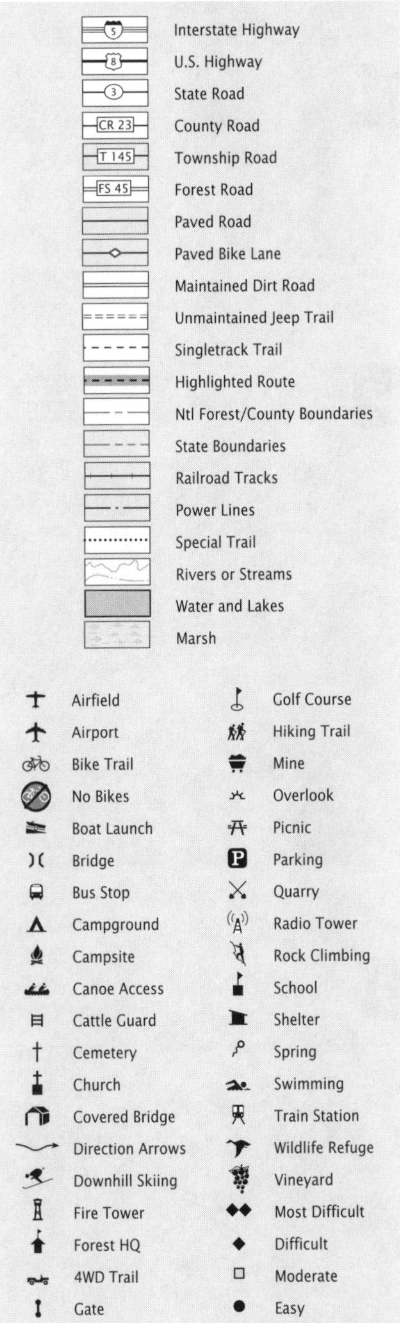

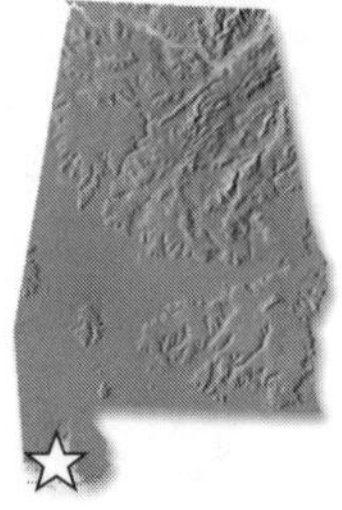

1 Area Locator Map

This thumbnail relief map at the beginning of each hike shows you where the hike is within the state. The hike area is indicated by the white star.

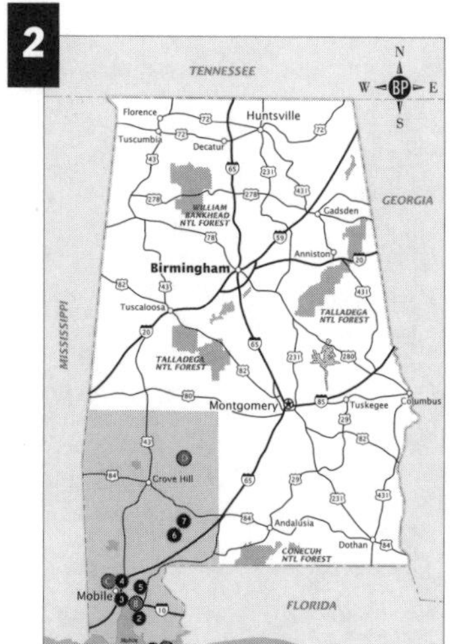

2 Regional Location Map

This map helps you find your way to the start of each hike from the nearest sizeable town or city. Coupled with the detailed directions at the beginning of the cue, this map should visually lead you to where you need to be for each hike.

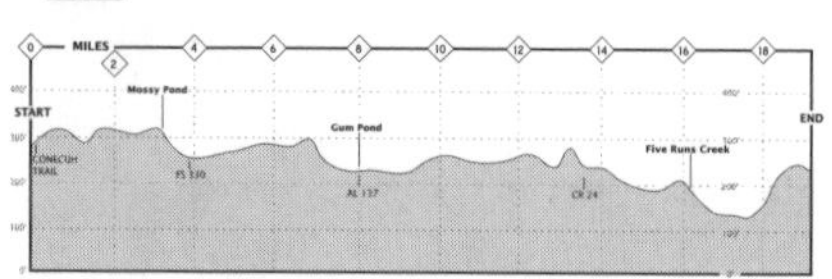

3 Profile Map

This helpful profile gives you a cross-sectional look at the hike's ups and downs. Elevation is labeled on the left, mileage is indicated on the top. Road and trail names are shown along the route with towns and points of interest labeled in bold.

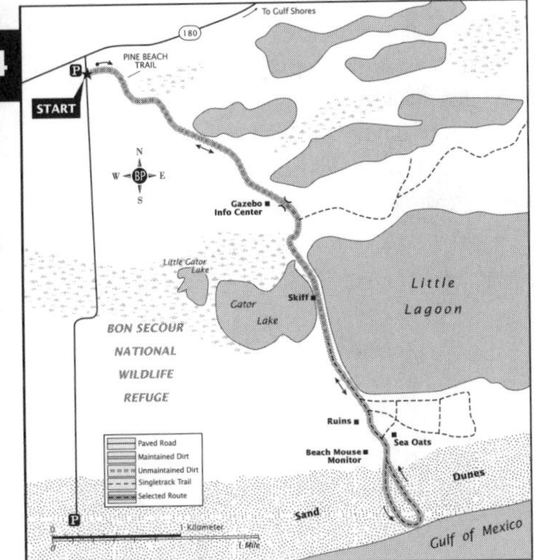

4 Route Map

This is your primary guide to each hike. It shows all of the accessible roads and trails, points of interest, water, towns, landmarks, and geographical features. It also distinguishes trails from roads, and paved roads from unpaved roads. The selected route is highlighted, and directional arrows point the way. Shaded topographic relief in the background gives you an accurate representation of the terrain and landscape in the hike area.

Hike Information *(Included in each hike section)*

Trail Contacts:
This is the direct number for the local land managers in charge of all the trails within the selected hike. Use this hotline to call ahead for trail access information, or after your visit if you see problems with trail erosion, damage, or misuse.

Schedule:
This tells you at what times trails open and close, if on private or park land.

Fees/Permits:
What money, if any, you may need to carry with you for park entrance fees or tolls.

Maps:
This is a list of other maps to supplement the maps in this book. They are listed in order from most detailed to most general.

Any other important or useful information will also be listed here such as local attractions, outdoor shops, nearby accommodations, etc.

A note from the folks behind this endeavor...

We at Outside America look at guidebook publishing a little differently. There's just no reason that a guidebook has to look like it was published out of your Uncle Ernie's woodshed. We feel that guidebooks need to be both easy to use and nice to look at, and that takes an innovative approach to design. You see, we want you to spend less time fumbling through your guidebook and more time enjoying the adventure at hand. We hope you like what you see here and enjoy the places we lead you. And most of all, we'd like to thank you for taking an adventure with us.

Happy Trails!

Introduc

Introduction

I'll be honest; I'm a Jersey boy, born and raised. So what would possess me to move from the Yankees, Egg Creams, and traffic jams to the land of Bear Bryant and cheese grits? My wife for one, a Mobile native and New Jersey transplant. After we married, we decided to try life along the Gulf Coast and headed to the "Heart of Dixie." And was I in for a surprise.

If all you know about an area is based on hearsay and casual history, chances are your understanding is warped, if not blackened. For example, New Jerseyans see Alabama as being full of lazy hills and backward hillbillies. Conversely, people from Alabama think of New Jersey as a dumping ground for New York City.

A former governor once referred to Alabama as "The State of Surprises." As it turned out, this Northerner's opinion would change quickly.

The first surprise was the state's terrain. Alabama is divided into four distinct regions: the Highland Rim, the Piedmont Plateau, the Black Belt, and the Coastal Plain. To the extreme north is the Highland Rim. Thousands of years ago the entire region was covered with a shallow ocean. As the waters receded and the land began to rise, ancient shell banks and coral reefs dried out and died forming the limestone bedrock that is the mountains of north and northwest Alabama. Over the years the action of the elements on the soft rock created huge crags, cliffs, and caves. Areas such as the Stone Cuts in Monte Sano State Park near Huntsville are the result and provide excellent caving and climbing opportunities. To the west, this same action combined with the flow of dozens of rivers has created the canyons of the Sipsey Wilderness, with spectacular waterfalls and again plenty of caves.

Just as the receding ocean created the Highland Rim, so to did unveil the Piedmont Plateau. As the land thrust upward, forming the southern-most end of the Appalachian mountain chain, it created the highest peaks in the state. It's in this region that you'll find the state's highest point, Cheaha Mountain, which stands just over 2,100 feet above sea level. You'll also encounter the largest canyon east of the Mississippi, Little River Canyon, carved by the Little River, the longest mountain top river in the country.

The fertile Black Belt, the land from Montgomery to just above the coast, has gently rolling hills and notoriously rich soil, which makes this region prime agricultural territory. Here, rivers flow and create sanctuary for birds and wildlife, like at Eufaula National Wildlife Refuge along the Chattahoochee River.

Finally, there is the Coastal Plain. This region has some of the most pristine white beaches to be found along the Gulf of Mexico, in addition to the second largest delta in the country. The Tensaw River Delta encompasses one of the largest protected areas for wildlife in the state with a multitude of endangered species calling the area home. Such locations as Bon Secour National Wildlife Refuge and the Weeks Bay National Estuarine Research Reserve allow us the opportunity to visit this wildlife first hand.

Another surprise is the amount of history that can be found in Alabama. Native American history can be traced back to 7,000 BC at Russell Cave National Monument in Northeast Alabama. Europeans came to the region in the 1500s, first the Spanish, then the French, and then the British. The United States finally took control in the early 1800s, following such bloody engagements as the Battle of Horseshoe Bend where General Andrew Jackson took down the last of the Creek Indian defenses, ushering in the tragic mass-relocation of Natives along what was dubbed the "Trail of Tears."

Time and time again, the Civil War pops up in our travels. The last major battle of the war was fought near Mobile in what is today the Blakeley Historic State Park. Tannehill State Historic Park is the site of a major foundry, rebuilt to its original operating condition, where munitions for the Confederacy were forged. The first capital of the Confederacy was Montgomery. And don't think that all of Alabama was behind the succession of the south. Winston County where the Sipsey Wilderness is located actually declared itself a free county and backed the Union.

And history continues to be made in the state. As humans reach for the stars, the city of Huntsville is home to NASA's Marshall Space Flight Center, where the Saturn V moon rocket was designed and built and the modules for the international space station Freedom are being constructed.

The biggest and best surprise about Alabama is the people. The state may be known as the "Heart of Dixie," but it is also the heart of Southern hospitality. The people make this state as great as it is.

Each and every time I travel and hike the state, I can truthfully say that I uncover more and more surprises. New adventures and beautiful scenery are always just a hill or turn away. Hopefully the trails and experiences described in this guide will help you appreciate all that Alabama has to offer and help you discover your own surprises.

Alabama Flora and Fauna

Over two-thirds of Alabama is covered in forest. On the whole these forests are largely Southern yellow, red, white, loblolly, and slash pine forests, though red cedar is also prevalent. Of the deciduous trees, you'll likely encounter hickory, sweet gum, and several varieties of oaks including live oaks. Some of the favorite aromatic and blooming trees in the state include the magnolia and dogwood.

Alabama is blessed with a wide variety of wildflowers along the trails and roadways. Some of the more interesting varieties include bollworms, also known as merry bells, which bloom in the spring throughout the state. These flowers are part of the lily family and bloom from April to June. The plant has very thin and delicate stems topped with hay-yellow bells.

Along the marshes and streams the cardinal flower blooms into a bright scarlet color in late summer. In early March, the vines of the Carolina jessamine will be found clinging to fences and trees. These vines with yellow flowers can be found throughout the state.

Another quite common wildflower is the yellow orchid. This flower blooms in late summer through early fall and can be found along just about any trail. From late July through September the yellow fringed orchid can be found in roadside ditches, bogs, woods and fields.

And of course, rhododendron and a variety of azaleas line most of the trails through the state, adding bright colors and fragrances to the hikes.

Alabama has a varied wildlife population. While the hiker is more apt to find white tail deer and gray squirrels along the trail, the state hosts many other species of animals. Black bears roam from one end of the state to the other, with the largest concentration found in the Tensaw River Delta of the Gulf Coast. Bobcat (or lynx) are also quite common throughout the state, but are rarely seen.

From north to south, wild turkey scurry along the trails of the state. The turkey population was once on a dangerous decline but made an astounding recovery in the middle of the 20th Century. Farmers used the Eastern wild turkey to develop all current domestic varieties of turkeys. Armadillos can frequently be seen foraging through the leaves along trails. Although cute, their bite is nasty. I'll confess, 10 armadillos chased me down the Skyway Loop Trail in the Talladega National Forest, so don't doubt their ability to get angry.

The American alligator, one of only two species of alligators in the world, can be found in the southeast and gulf coast regions. Alligators tend to feed on fish, frogs, snakes, turtles, birds, and small mammals. Luckily they're naturally afraid of humans, but feeding them or harassing them in any manner changes the rules. The alligator was declared an endangered species in 1967 due to over hunting, but the species has made a strong comeback and some states have allowed them to be hunted once again (Alabama is not one of them).

Several species that are currently considered endangered have found sanctuary within the state, such as the Beach Mouse, the Logger-head Sea-Turtle, and the Brown Pelican. The American bald eagle has also found a new refuge in Alabama.

Alabama Weather

The range of weather in Alabama is striking—from its sub-tropical climate in the south to the cold and snowy winters of the north. In general, the weather for hiking Alabama is near perfect. Even in the northern part of the state in the higher elevations, winters are generally short-lived with frequent spring-like days scattered throughout January and February.

In the north, temperatures on average range from 46 degrees Fahrenheit in January to 80 degrees Fahrenheit in July. Colder temperatures are more frequent in the north, and yes, significant accumulations of snow can occur, though rarely.

In the southern portion of the state, temperatures on average range from 52 degrees in January to 85 degrees in July. Cold snaps of below 30 degrees, even below zero, do occur, but seldom, and they only last a day or two.

Though the weather in Alabama is generally ideal for hiking, there are exceptions. Usually in the months of June through August, the mix of heat and 100 percent humidity can make a deadly combination with heat indexes that frequently soar well into the hundreds. On these days, outdoor activity of any kind is discouraged by weather services and state officials.

Also during the summer, extremely heavy and severe late-afternoon thunderstorms can pop up without warning. Although they are widely scattered and short in duration, the large amount of rain and dangerous lightning can make outdoor travel a challenge.

Finally, May through November is hurricane season in Alabama. Though a hurricane will only hit a relatively small area with its full fury, the surrounding areas, some hundreds of miles from the storm, can still feel its effects. As a matter of fact, most injuries and deaths resulting from hurricanes come from flash flooding in areas that are not even in the storm's center.

When hiking during hurricane season, especially in September when most of the storms in the Atlantic Ocean make their way into the Gulf of Mexico, check the weather and be alert for any tropical disturbances before heading out. If there are any storm reported, keep tabs on their progress to determine if hiking is a good idea at that time or not. There is typically plenty of advance warning to react to a storm, so don't let hurricanes discourage you from coming to Alabama to hike!

Alabama Wilderness Restrictions/Regulations

Alabama has 26 state parks, five national forests, and a national monument and preserve. With the exception of high altitude mountain climbing, these protected lands offer every type of hiking experience imaginable, from a short walk with endangered species through preserves to true wilderness hiking. As is the case across the country, the number of people hitting the trail is ever increasing. Fortunately, the state and federal agencies tasked with manning these facilities do an excellent job of maintaining the balance between use and preservation.

Alabama's state parks provide an ideal setting for families looking to get away to the great outdoors, or for those seeking a bit more of an adventure. Generally speaking, camping is not allowed on state park trails due to the short length of the trails. Trailside camping is allowed in some parks and is noted in the trail descriptions in this book. All state parks have primitive camping areas for tents, which usually only run $8 a night (this includes those with trailside camping). Most also have what is called "improved campsites" that have their own water spigot and electrical outlets. These usually run $14 a night.

Reservations are not required for primitive campsites at the state parks. Reservations are recommended for improved sites and are accepted up to 12 months in advance of a visit. A maximum of eight people are allowed per site. Additional regulations may apply, so be sure to check at the ranger station of each park.

Within the state's national forests, camping is permitted along the trails at no cost. The rangers only ask that you follow the policy of dispersal camping in which campsites are spread far apart and at least 100 feet from the trail. In some areas, others have set up campsites close to the trail. If this is the case, rangers suggest using these sites to minimize any further impact of camping on the location. Some of the national forests have recreational areas set up for camping. Again, these have both primitive and improved campsites ranging in price from $6 a day to $12, respectively.

Most of the trailheads described in this book at the national forests do not charge for parking. There are some, noted within the trail descriptions, that charge a day-use fee of $3.

Since you'll almost always be within a stone's throw of a lake, river, or ocean, you may want to try your hand at fishing. A seven-day freshwater or saltwater fishing license is $6 for residents, $11 for non-residents. Dogs are usually welcomed at the state parks, but a leash is required unless otherwise noted. Also keep in mind that hunting is allowed in national forests. Contact the national forest or district forest ranger about the dates for hunting season, which can restrict camping locations and hiking trails. Permits are not required for hiking the national forests; however, they do ask that you register at the trailheads in case of an emergency.

Now that all the loose ends are tied up, it's time to get outside and hit the trails of Alabama!

Joe Cuhaj

Getting Around Alabama

Area Codes

The area code **256** covers Huntsville and northern Alabama. For Birmingham and central Alabama the area code is **205**. The area code for Mobile and the Gulf Coast is **334**.

Roads

For road conditions, contact the Alabama Department of Transportation. Call **1–334–242–4128** or visit *www.dot.state.al.us* for current road closings and openings, traffic updates, and road construction plans and timetables.

By Air

Birmingham Airport (BHM) is Alabama's main point of entry, *www.bhamintlairport.com.* Your travel agent can best advise you on the least expensive and/or most direct way to connect from wherever you're departing.

Mobile Regional Airport (MOB) serves greater Mobile and the Gulf Coast, and can be found on the internet at *www.mobairport.com.* Shared ride vans and taxi's serve Mobile and the surrounding areas.

To book reservations on-line, visit your favorite airline's website or search one of the following travel sites for the best price: *www.cheaptickets.com*, *www.expedia.com*, *www.previewtravel.com*, *www.priceline.com*, *http://travel.yahoo.com*, *www.travelocity.com*, *www.trip.co*—just to name a few.

By Bus

Greyhound serves all major towns and cities in Alabama. Greyhound also carries connecting Amtrak passengers to off line cities (see below). Schedules and fares are available online at *www.greyhound.com* or by phone at 1–800–231–2222.

By Train

Amtrak has two routes that serve Alabama. The Crescent train runs daily to Anniston, Birmingham, and Tuscaloosa from Atlanta, New Orleans, and New York. A bus transfer in Atlanta connects the Crescent to Mobile and Montgomery. The Sunset Limited train serves Atmore and Mobile three times a week from Orlando, New Orleans, and Los Angeles. On days when the Sunset Limited does not run, Amtrak offers bus service to the New Orleans Amtrak station to connect with the City of New Orleans train to Memphis and Chicago. Amtrak information and reservations are available online at *www.amtrak.com* or by phone at 1–800–872–7245.

Visitor Information

For visitor information or a travel brochure, call the Alabama Office of Tourism at **1–800–252–2262 (ALABAMA)** or visit their website at *www.alabama.com.*

The Hikes

1. Pine Beach Trail
2. Weeks Bay Nature Trail
3. USS Alabama Historical Trail
4. Cemetery Trail
5. CCC Trail
6. Gazebo Trail
7. Redoubt Trail Loop

Gulf

Honorable Mentions

A. Black Willow Trail
B. Nature Trails of Gulf State Park
C. Beach Loop Trail
D. Roland Cooper State Park

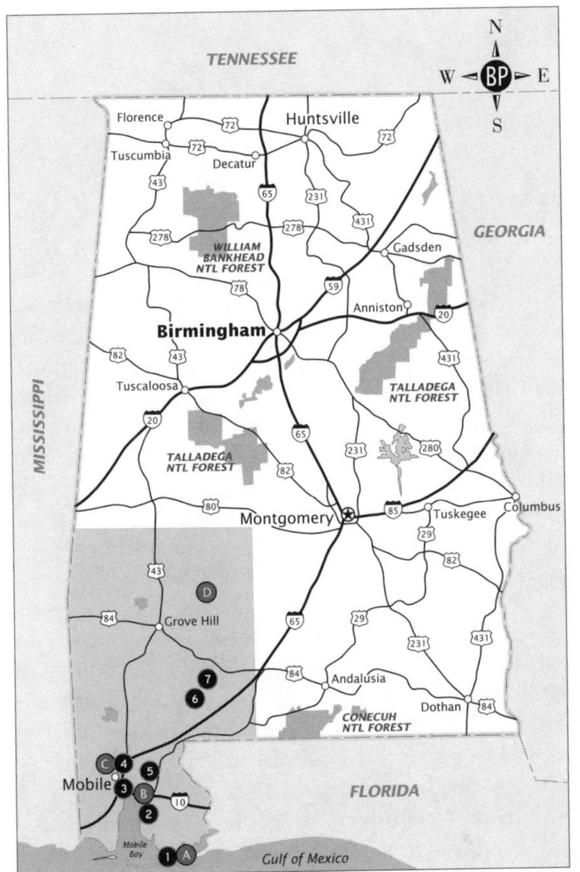
TENNESSEE
N
W
BP
E
S
Florence
Huntsville
Tuscumbia
Decatur
WILLIAM BANKHEAD NTL FOREST
GEORGIA
Gadsden
Anniston
Birmingham
Tuscaloosa
MISSISSIPPI
TALLADEGA NTL FOREST
TALLADEGA NTL FOREST
Montgomery
Tuskegee
Columbus
Grove Hill
Andalusia
Dothan
CONECUH NTL FOREST
Mobile
Mobile Bay
FLORIDA
Gulf of Mexico

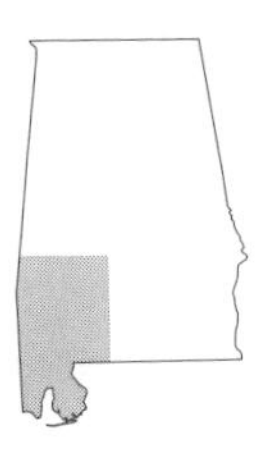

Coast

Gulf Coast

The Gulf Coast region of Alabama supports not only a wide variety of endangered wildlife but also countless perches from which to view them.

The traveling by foot in this region is rarely strenuous. Elevations range from sea level to around 100 feet. It's in this region that the Mobile and Tensaw rivers converge to form the Tensaw River Delta, and ultimately empty into the Gulf of Mexico. The Tensaw River Delta has the distinction of being the second largest river delta in the country—second only to the Mississippi Delta. The American alligator calls this area home, as do the largest population of black bear in the state and the endangered brown pelican.

This region is also the home to the white sand beaches of Gulf Shores and Orange Beach. The Pine Beach Trail Bon Secour National Wildlife Refuge takes hikers directly to the beach. The refuge protects such endangered species of animals as the beach mouse and the loggerhead sea turtle.

History abounds in the region, as well, with the centerpiece being the city of Mobile, the state's second largest city. Mobile is known as the "Mother of Mystics" and is recognized as the birthplace of Mardi Gras in the United States. Hiking along the USS Alabama Historic Trail is a good way to soak in the 300-year history of the city.

It is also in this area that the famous "Battle of Mobile Bay" occurred during the Civil War. It was in this battle that Admiral David Farragut uttered the immortal words, "Damn the torpedoes, full speed ahead!" Speaking of the Civil War, just across the Mobile River in Spanish Fort is Blakeley Historic State Park, site of the Battle of Blakeley, the last major battle of the Civil War.

The weather in the region is sub-tropical. Late summer heat is accentuated with high humidity that often hits 100 percent, making outdoor activity a bit uncomfortable and sometimes not recommended. The warm air and its location on the Gulf of Mexico mean that sudden and very heavy rainfall can be expected without warning. The storms are short, but the rain plentiful. In fact, Mobile has held the National Weather Service title of "wettest city in America" a number of times.

Perhaps the worst weather system you'll see in the summer is a hurricane. Mobile and Baldwin counties have been hit by several large and devastating hurricanes in the past, but an eye on the weather forecast will keep you safe. Hurricane season "generally" runs between May and November.

Fall and winter along the Gulf Coast is wonderful, to say the least. Most of the time, moderate temperatures averaging in the low-to-mid 70s last well into the fall. During this time, the humidity is quite low, making hiking a real pleasure. Temperatures in January average around 52 degrees. Now don't get me wrong; it does get cold in Dixie. Temperatures have dropped to below zero on occasion, but those days are few and are usually short lived.

Pine Beach Trail

Hike Summary

This is one of those surprising trails—a simple walk down a forested nature trail that unfolds to reveal the sand dunes and pristine white beaches of the Gulf of Mexico. As the trail meanders to the sea, you're treated to a close look at the marshes of southern Alabama, where American alligators may be found.

Hike Specs

Start: From the southeast end of the Pine Beach parking area at Bon Secour National Wildlife Refuge
Length: 4-mile out-and-back
Approximate Hiking Time: 1½ hours
Difficulty Rating: Easy, along flat roadways
Trail Surface: Dirt and sand service road; fine beach sand
Lay of the Land: Forest of slash pine, dotted with sawgrass and live oak; sea oats and scrub pines along the dunes; marshes and beaches
Land Status: National wildlife refuge
Nearest Town: Gulf Shores, AL
Other Trail Users: Service vehicles on service-road portion of trail
Canine Compatibility: Not dog friendly—due to wildlife and the fragile nature of the preserve; if you do take a dog, leash required

Getting There

From Mobile: Take I-10 west to AL 59 (Exit 44). Head south on AL 59 toward Gulf Shores. Travel 0.5 miles past the Intracoastal Waterway to the intersection with AL 180. Follow AL 180 west 9.0 miles to the refuge headquarters on the right. To get to the trailhead, continue past the refuge headquarters another mile. The parking area is on the left side of the highway and marked with a large wooden sign that reads "PINE BEACH TRAIL." The trailhead is at the southeast end of the parking lot. ***DeLorme: Alabama Atlas & Gazetteer:*** Page 65 F1

Along a stretch of highway at the extreme southern tip of Alabama, a peninsula stretches westward along the Gulf of Mexico to form the mouth of the Mobile Bay delta. On this spit of land, between outcroppings of beachside condominiums, lies Bon Secour National Wildlife Refuge.

The refuge encompasses more than 6,500 acres of fragile landscape and is home to more than 500 species of animals and birds—which provide hikers with endless photo ops. The key to viewing this wide variety of animal life is to take the time to sit quietly on one of the many benches situated just off the trail. Patience will be rewarded each and every time.

End of the trail at the Gulf of Mexico.

The Pine Beach Trail is the longest in the refuge. Early in the hike, the trail crosses a marshy area as it works its way between Little Lagoon and Gator Lake. This is the best vantage point for viewing alligators. Many visitors leave disappointed because they didn't see an alligator—but they are there. Most of the time, they lie just below the surface of the water, looking like submerged logs. Stay quiet and be patient and you'll see them. Alligators are naturally wary of humans; do not feed them or approach them in any way.

Saltwater fishing is allowed along the banks of Little Lagoon—of course, a saltwater fishing license is required. Across the trail from Little Lagoon is Gator Lake—a 40-acre freshwater lake known for its largemouth bass and catfish. It's open for fishing year-round, with a freshwater fishing license required.

Among the rare animals in the refuge is the Alabama beach mouse. Although you'll probably never see one, you can tell they're here from the numerous burrows and mouse trails near the beaches. Avoid disturbing the burrows.

Another unusual animal that visits the refuge is the loggerhead sea turtle. The loggerhead species made its first appearance on Earth more than 200 million years ago and has remained virtually the same ever since. The loggerhead population has declined due to habitat loss along the coastlines.

MilesDirections

0.0 START from the end of the Pine Beach Trail parking area at the cable gateway.

0.2 As the trail heads southeast, the first of 15 numbered markers indicate the flora of the area—be sure to pick up a brochure at refuge headquarters to follow along.

0.3 Here you encounter the toughest gradient—a gradual downhill jaunt of about 10 feet as the trail heads toward sea level. At the bottom of this hill is a small sign marking an abandoned route.

0.4 The trail begins to curve to a more southerly direction and comes to a gazebo. Notices and additional information are posted here, and there are benches to sit and view the marsh and its inhabitants. A few feet further, the trail crosses a 10-foot wooden footbridge over a small canal that feeds the marsh. Evidence of hurricane Frederic from 1979 and the debris from its 150-mph winds can still be seen here.

0.5 The trail heads due south. A brown directional sign points to Little Lagoon on the left, Gator Lake to the right, and the beach one mile straight ahead. Just a few feet farther and there are excellent views of Little Lagoon. The condominiums of Gulf Shores are in the distance. The trail travels the banks of Little Lagoon. You'll likely see muscle and clams and small schools of fish.

0.6 A sign marks the beginning of the Gator Lake Trail to the right. This 0.8-mile trail is used to portage boats to the lake

View from the footbridge toward Gator Lake. The Debris is from Hurricane Frederic.

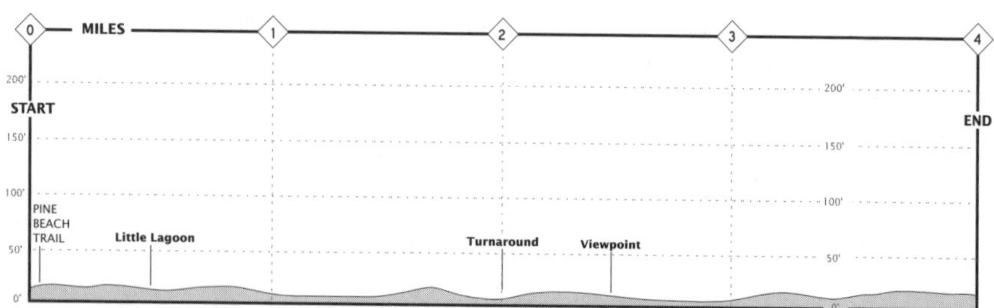

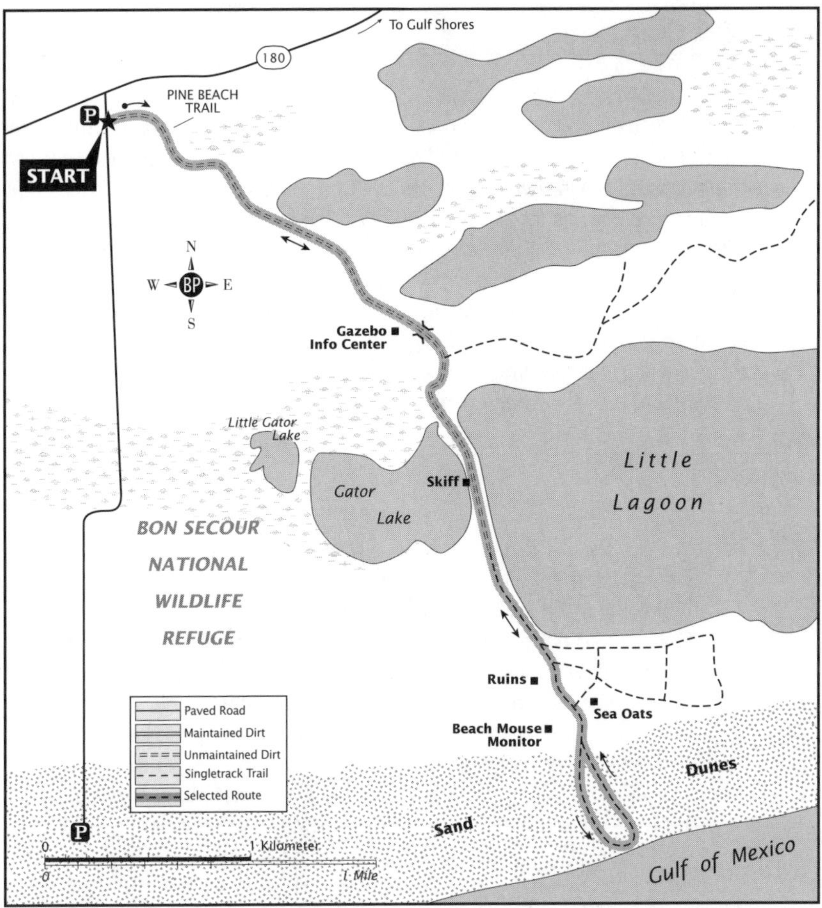

for fishing. There is also a small skiff here that the refuge allows visitors to use to float around the 40-acre lake. At this point, the trail becomes progressively more sandy, all the way to the Gulf.

1.0 Reach a Y-intersection and continue on to the right. A "BEACH" sign points you in the right direction.

1.3 The trail now passes by the ruins of a beach house that was destroyed by hurricane Frederic. Notice the Alabama beach mouse holes along the sides of the trail in the sand. Also, the Gulf's sea oats begin to line the trail. The waters of the Gulf of Mexico can be seen straight ahead.

1.5 The trail crests a sand dune and you can see a beautiful panoramic of the Gulf as well as the skyline of Gulf Shores. Continue another 0.5 miles along the dunes and take in the sea breeze and views. In the summer months, you can see the tracks of nesting loggerhead sea turtles.

2.0 Turn around and retrace your route back to the trailhead.

4.0 Arrive back at the trailhead.

Mullet Over

The Flora-Bama Lounge in Perdido Key, Florida, on the Gulf of Mexico, directly on the Florida-Alabama border, is renowned not only for its annual National Songwriter Festival, but also for its mullet. And not just for eating. Each winter, this bar and restaurant hosts the National Mullet Tossing Championships. Participants toss mullet (dead, of course) as far as they can across the border for cash and prizes.

Each year, people flock to the Flora-Bama to compete in the contest. For the past several years, South Alabama native and former NFL quarterback Kenny Stabler has tossed out the first mullet to get the event under way. The event became so popular that at Mobile Mysticks hockey games, instead of throwing octopus like they do in Detroit when a goal is scored, fans began throwing mullet—a practice that has since been banned by the East Coast Hockey League.

At Bon Secour, loggerheads have a safe nesting area. From May through September, they make their way unobtrusively to the dunes at night, lay their eggs, and then crawl back into the sea.

Wildlife is not the only striking feature of the trail. The flora in the refuge is just as fascinating. Blueberries and huckleberries grow along the trail, though berry picking isn't allowed in order to preserve the feeding plots for the wildlife. Among other plant life is the hairy wicky (no kidding)—a plant similar to mountain laurel, with white blooms in the summer.

Marshy areas support floating bladders—aquatic plants with yellow flowers. Trees include live oaks, myrtles, dwarf sand oaks, and several varieties of pine. Along the beach, the tall, golden grasses known as sea oats wave in the sea breeze—but again, no picking!

The trail culminates in a breathtaking view and walk along white beaches on the Gulf of Mexico. You can fish in the surf here (as long as you have a saltwater license). Swift currents and an undertow mean that swimming is not allowed, but only a few highway miles away, Gulf State Park offers swimming.

If you decide to bushwhack off the designated trails, it's best to wear boots for thicker brush areas and waders through the marshes. Otherwise a good pair of sneakers will work fine along the service road, with either sandals or bare feet on the sandy parts of the trail.

Among the wildlife you'll wish to avoid are mosquitoes and sand gnats. Rather than rely on luck, bring bug spray. The swampy marsh, combined with high humidity, make this a fertile environment for these formidable pests.

Hike Information

Trail Contacts:

Bon Secour National Wildlife Refuge, Gulf Shores, AL; (334) 540–7720 or http://*southeast.fws.gov/bonsecour*

Schedule:

Trails are opened year round 7 A.M.–sunset. Refuge headquarter hours are M–F, 7 A.M.–4 P.M.

Fees/Permits:

No fees charged. No camping is allowed.

Local Information:

Alabama Gulf Coast Convention and Visitor's Bureau, Gulf Shores, AL; 1–800–745–7263 or *www.gulfshores.com*

Local Events/Attractions:

National Shrimp Festival, first weekend of October, Gulf Shores, AL; (334) 968–6904 or *www.alagulfcoastchamber.com—This is the biggest shrimp festival in the country featuring live bands, arts and crafts, and plenty of delicious Gulf Shrimp.* • **Gulf State Park**, Gulf Shores, AL; (334) 948–7275 or *www.dcnr.state.al.us—[Refer to the "Gulf Coast Honorable Mention" section for a description.]*

Accommodations:

Acadian Inn, Orange Beach, AL; (334) 981–6710 • **Romar House Bed and Breakfast**, Orange Beach, AL; (334) 978–1625 or *www.bbonlin.com/al/romarhouse*

Restaurants:

Original Oyster House, Gulf Shores, AL; (334) 948–2445 • **Sea-N-Suds**, Gulf Shores, AL; (334) 948–7894

Organizations:

Mobile Sierra Club, Mobile, AL; *www.sierraclub.org/chapters/al/mobile.html*

Local Outdoor Retailers:

Smith Outdoors, Gulf Shores, AL; (334) 981–1855

Maps:

USGS maps: Bon Secour Bay, AL • **Pine Beach Trail Map, Bird List, & Refuge Pamphlet**—*available at the Bon Secour Wildlife Refuge headquarters.*

Weeks Bay Nature Trail

Hike Summary

This trail provides a short and very easy walk at the Weeks Bay Estuary. The estuary, home to a wide variety of birds and other plant and animal life, offers an interesting, enjoyable experience for all members of the family.

Hike Specs

Start: From the Weeks Bay Estuary office
Length: 1.3-mile out-and-back
Approximate Hiking Time: 1 hour
Difficulty Rating: Easy, over level paths
Trail Surface: Dirt path and boardwalks
Lay of the Land: Magnolias and cypress trees
Land Status: National estuarine research reserve
Nearest Town: Fairhope, AL
Other Trail Users: None
Canine Compatibility: Dog friendly—leash required

Getting There

From Fairhope: Take U.S. 98 south 10 miles. Come to a stop sign and turn left (AL 42 and U.S. 98 now head to the east). Travel five miles. The estuary is clearly marked on the right. If you cross over the Weeks Bay Bridge, you've over shot the turn. ***DeLorme: Alabama Atlas & Gazetteer:*** Page 63 G6

This is not a high-tech, high-altitude, three-day backpacking trip. In fact, it's just the opposite. This short and simple nature path is included here for the purposes of spotlighting an endangered habitat and providing the perfect hike for couples looking to take the kids—and who knows, the children just might learn something in the process.

Weeks Bay National Estuarine Research Reserve is one of 26 estuaries administered by the National Oceanic and Atmospheric Administration. An estuary, by definition, is as a semi-enclosed body of water where freshwater from rivers mixes with saltwater from the ocean. It is because of this merger of diversity that estuaries are generally teeming with a wide variety of plant and animal life.

The Weeks Bay reserve, established in 1986, protects land that was once at high risk of development—Baldwin County, in which the reserve is situated, is the fastest growing county in the state of Alabama. The reserve maintains for posterity 3,000 acres along Weeks Bay and Mobile Bay and is fed by the Magnolia and Fish rivers.

The reserve's nature trail utilizes a combination of vegetation-friendly boardwalks and dirt paths to lead you through the forested swamps, along the banks of salt and freshwater marshes, and through the tidal flats. Signs along the boardwalks identify animals and plants—the same information is also provided in a brochure available at the reserve office. Among the animals that live here are blue crabs, red-bellied turtles, and American alligators. More than 350 species of birds are found at Weeks Bay, either permanently or during migration periods. Among them are the black needlerush, the great blue heron, and the once-endangered brown pelican.

The first place to visit is the estuary office, where you'll find displays that describe the estuary and its plants and animals. At the back of the office building, where the trail begins, is a mini-zoo with fish, blue crabs, and an alligator.

MilesDirections

0.0 START from the rear of the estuary office and head south onto the boardwalk. The path turns to the southeast in about 200 feet.

0.1 The boardwalk comes to a Y-intersection. Take the right fork and continue to the south.

0.2 Come to the banks of the bay. There are binoculars here for you to use. Turn right and head to the east. The path winds to the northwest and in 300 feet, returns to the previous Y-intersection. Turn left and head north back toward the office.

0.3 When you arrive back to the office, follow a sidewalk around to the right side of the building—between the office and conference building—and arrive at the front parking lot. Turn left and head west. In 200 feet, come to a large wooden sign that reads "Nature Trail." Take the dirt path into the woods.

0.4 Head to the southwest over this flat, wide path. Downed trees surround the area, but the path is well cleared. In 200 feet, come to a wooden footbridge over a small creek. Cross the bridge to the west. In 100 feet, cross another footbridge to the southwest. Along this section, diamond "WB" markers lead the way.

0.5 Cross another bridge to the west. *[**Option.** To the right, a short side trail leads to a picnic area near U.S. 98.]* Make a left turn and head southwest. The trail narrows somewhat but is still level and dirt.

0.8 The trail comes to a boardwalk that leads to the banks of the bay with great views of the waterway. Turn right and in 50 feet, come off the footbridge and travel on a dirt path to the northwest until you reach another boardwalk that gives you another perspective of the bay. Turn around here and follow the trail and boardwalk back to the parking lot.

1.3 Arrive back at the trailhead.

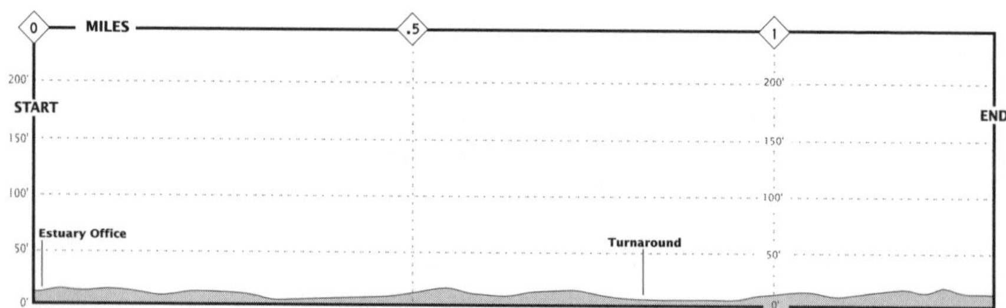

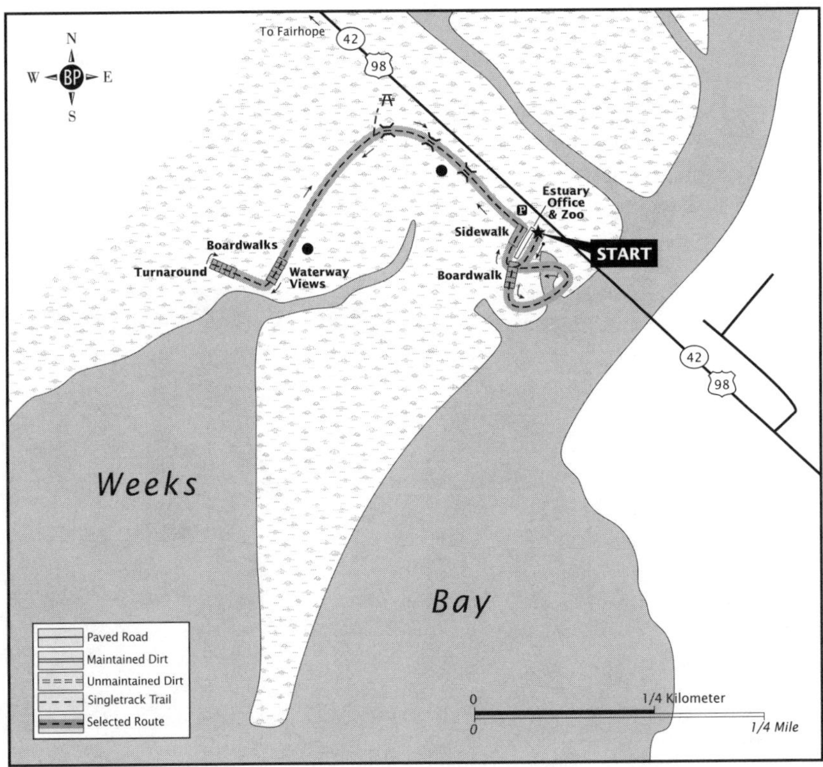

The Jubilee City

It's a phenomenon that occurs only once or twice a year between June and September, if at all, and only occurs in a few rare places on earth. It's a time after the sun sets when the breeze is still, the water of Mobile Bay is calm, and the residents of the Eastern Shore of Mobile Bay in the city of Daphne wait for the call.

What happens is hundreds of thousands of fish, crabs, and other marine life swim right up to the shores of the bay and end up on the sandy beaches. The cry goes out around town, "JUBILEE!"—that's what this phenomenon is known as. Residents pick up buckets full of fresh seafood for their tables. But just as quick as it starts, the Jubilee is over.

No one is exactly sure what causes the Jubilee, but it's believed that a seasonal drop in the water's oxygen level draws both prey and predator to the surface looking for food and air.

While you're in the neighborhood, be sure to head down to the Weeks Bay Pitcher Plant Bog. (Take U.S. Route 98 over the nearby Weeks Bay Bridge and turn left onto County Road 17.) The curious pitcher plant is worth the visit. This wily carnivore feasts on insects and other tiny creatures—so watch the ankles (just kidding). The Wintermeyer Nature Trail guides visitors easily through the bog—which, contrary to what you might think, is a relatively dry environment.

Another boardwalk takes hikers to the banks of Weeks Bay.

Hike Information

Trail Contacts:

Weeks Bay National Estuary, Fairhope, AL; (334) 928–9792 or *inlet.geol.sc.edu/WKB/home.html*

Schedule:

Open 9 A.M.–5 P.M. Monday–Saturday, 1 P.M.–5 P.M. Sunday, closed for state and federal holidays.

Local Information:

Eastern Shore Chamber of Commerce, Daphne, AL; (334) 621–8222 or *www.siteone.com/towns/chamber* • **City of Fairhope**, Fairhope, AL; (334) 928–2136 or *www.cofairhope.com*

Local Events/Attractions:

Fairhope Arts and Crafts Festival, 2nd weekend of March, Fairhope, AL; (334) 621–8222—*One of the largest such events on the Gulf Coast with lots of music, food, and of course, arts and crafts.* • **Fairhope Municipal Pier**, Fairhope, AL; (334) 928–2136—*A one-quarter-mile long pier jutting into beautiful Mobile Bay. The pier is open for fishing and walks 24-hours. The beach next to the pier for swimming is open from 9 A.M.–5 P.M. The city holds an impressive Fourth of July fireworks over the bay with music provided by the Eastern Shore Symphony.*

Accommodations:

The Parker House, Fairhope, AL; (334) 928–8472

Restaurants:

The Yardarm, Fairhope, AL; (334) 928–0711—*Fresh gulf seafood is the fare at this restaurant located right smack dab in the middle of the Fairhope Municipal Pier.*

Hike Tours:

Weeks Bay National Estuary, Fairhope, AL; (334) 928–9792—*Contact the estuary office to set up times for a guided tour of the research facility and the estuary.*

Organizations:

Weeks Bay Watershed Project, Fairhope, AL; (334) 928–9792 • **Weeks Bay Reserve Foundation**, Fairhope, AL; (334) 990–5004

Other Resources:

Alabama Department of Environmental Management, Montgomery, AL; (334) 271–7710 or *www.dcnr.state.al.us*

Maps:

USGS maps: Magnolia Springs, AL • Brochures are available at the estuary office

USS Alabama Historical Trail

Hike Summary

The city of Mobile is justly proud of its history and heritage, from the early Native Americans to the Europeans' first exploration of the region in 1528, through the Civil War, and into the city's present-day rejuvenation. This trail allows you to experience this history firsthand as you stroll by antebellum homes, historical museums, and old cemeteries. The route passes under towering live oaks draped in Spanish moss, making an archway above the road. Azaleas, blooming fiery red each spring, line the streets.

Hike Specs

Start: From the Fort Conde Museum
Length: 6.5-mile loop
Approximate Hiking Time: 3–4 hours
Difficulty Rating: Easy, on sidewalks
Trail Surface: Concrete sidewalks and paved road
Lay of the Land: Historical sites and museums; ancient oak trees
Land Status: City streets
Nearest Town: Mobile, AL
Other Trail Users: Cyclists and pedestrians
Canine Compatibility: Dog friendly—leash required; bring water; dogs not permitted in homes or museums

Getting There

From Mobile: From I-65 in Mobile, take U.S. 90 east 15 miles to downtown Mobile. Turn right onto South Royal Street at the Bankhead Tunnel. Travel down the brick roadway 0.3 miles. Fort Conde, the starting location, is on the right with parking on the left. ***DeLorme: Alabama Atlas & Gazetteer:*** Page 62 D4

It's time to get off the beaten path and hit the pavement with this city excursion created by the Boy Scouts as a badge and medal hike. The path travels the streets of Mobile, passing through centuries of history.

This history begins with the Maubilian, Choctaw, and Alibamu Indians who occupied this region for centuries. The first Europeans to visit and eventually settle the area were the Spanish in 1528, followed by the French in 1699, then the British in 1763. Finally the United States seized control in 1812.

Many of the events in Mobile history may amaze the average person. For example, forget what New Orleans says about Mardi Gras. That city's Mardi Gras may be bigger, but Mobile is the birthplace of this carnival celebration in the United States—beginning in 1830.

Mobile Bay was the site of the naval battle in which Union Admiral David Farragut uttered the famous words, "Damn the torpedoes! Full speed

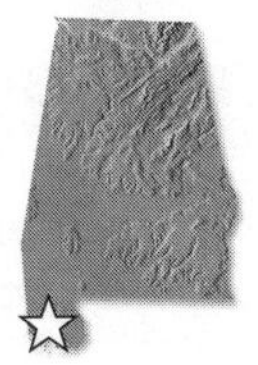

ahead!" It was also here that William A. Alexander built the world's first successful submarine, the *Hunley*. It was eventually used to sink a federal ship off the coast of South Carolina.

This trail through time—named for the USS *Alabama* battleship, which is on display nearby—begins at the Fort Conde Welcome Center and Museum. This re-creation of the 1711 fort built by the French is only a third the size of the original but is located on the exact site of the old fort. A tour of the museum's pictures and artifacts offers a taste of what's in store on the walk. While at the fort, be sure to catch the musket firings by people dressed in early French marine uniforms, and the cannon firings from the ramparts.

From the fort, the trail swings past the original 1865 city hall, which is seeing renewed life as the new city museum. Next door are the J.L. Bedsole Imax Theater and the Gulf Coast Exploreum. The Exploreum features hands-on science activities, especially attractive to children. Just past the Imax Theater is a statue honoring Admiral Raphael Semmes, commander of the warship *Alabama* during the Civil War.

Fort Conde—the starting point for this trail.

Local Events/Attractions:

Mardi Gras, two weeks prior to Ash Wednesday, Mobile, AL; 1-800-252-3862 or *www.mobile.org* • **First Night Mobile**, December 31st, Mobile, AL; 1-800-252-3862 or *www.mobile.org—This celebration is a non-alcoholic family festival celebrating the New Year with fireworks, live bands, and family activities.* • **Mobile Mysticks / East Coast League Hockey**, Mobile, AL; (334) 208-7825 or *www.mysticks.com—Ice Hockey is now a "Southern thing" as the Mysticks skate in to town. Catch the up and coming players of the NHL each year between the months of October and April.* • **J.L. Bedsole Imax Theater**, Mobile, AL; (334) 208-6873 or *www.exploreum.net —The theater is open in the summer Monday–Wednesday 9 A.M.–5 P.M., 9 A.M.–8 P.M. Thursdays, 9 A.M.–9 P.M. Friday and Saturday, 12 P.M.–5 P.M. Sunday. Fall and winter hours are 9 A.M.–5 P.M. Monday–Thursday, 9 A.M.–9 P.M. Friday and Saturday, 12 P.M.–5 P.M. Sunday. Admission is $7 adults, $6 for youths and seniors, and $5.50 for children.* • **Gulf Coast Exploreum**, Mobile, AL; (334) *208-6873 or www.exploreum.net—The museum is open in the summer Monday–Wednesday 9 A.M.–5 P.M., 9 A.M.–8 P.M. Thursdays, 9 A.M.–9 P.M. Friday and Saturday, 12 P.M.–5 P.M. Sunday. Fall and winter hours are 9 A.M.–5 P.M. Monday–Thursday, 9 A.M.–9 P.M. Friday and Saturday, 12 P.M.–5 P.M. Sunday. Admission is $7 adults, $6 for youths and seniors, and $5.50 for children.*

The trail travels down to the Mobile River, which made Mobile a thriving seaport second only to New Orleans. At the riverfront you'll see the modern spire of the Mobile Convention Center, and coming soon is the Gulf Coast Maritime Museum.

Looping back around to the southwest, the trail passes a series of historic buildings, including the Catholic Basilica of the Immaculate Conception (built in 1835) and the Berstein House (built in 1872), which up until 2000 housed the city museum. The trail passes Magnolia National Cemetery, named a national cemetery in 1866, which holds the remains of soldiers from the War of 1812 and the Civil War. Among those buried here are members of the first crew of the Civil War submarine *Hunley*, who died during sea trials of the warship.

You can also visit Church Street Cemetery, first set up in 1819 for victims of a yellow fever epidemic. Since then, many area notables have been laid to rest here, including Joe Cain, the man who brought Mardi Gras back to the South after the Civil War.

A word of caution about the weather: Bring a raincoat or umbrella if you visit in the summer. Heavy afternoon downpours are not uncommon.

Hike Information

Trail Contacts:
Fort Conde Visitor Center, Mobile, AL; (334) 434–7304—*Open seven days a week 8 A.M.–5 P.M., closed Christmas and Mardi Gras Day*

Schedule:
Open year round. One of the best times to take in the trail is the two weeks prior to Ash Wednesday (Mardi Gras).

Fees/Permits:
No fee is charged for hiking the trail or visiting the city museums.

Local Information:
City of Mobile Department of Tourism, Mobile, AL; 1–800–252–3862 or *www.mobile.org* • **Mobile Transit Authority**; (334) 344–5656—*All bus routes serve Bienville Square. The Highway 90 bus travels the main route of this trail, Government Street. Buses run down Government Street every 30 minutes. Service runs Monday through Saturday until 6:30 P.M.*

Accommodations:
Adam's Mark Hotel, Mobile, AL; (334) 438–4000 or *www.adamsmark.com/mobile* • **Radisson Admiral Semmes Hotel**, Mobile, AL; (334) 432–8000 or *www.rdadmsemmes.com*

Restaurants:
Port City Brewery, Mobile, AL; (334) 438–2739 • **Rousso's**, Mobile, AL; (334) 433–3322

Local Outdoor Retailers:
Academy Sports, Mobile, AL; (334) 344–0047 • **Ward's Army /Navy Stores**, Mobile, AL; (334) 479–9058

Maps:
USGS maps: Mobile, AL • **USS Alabama Historical Trail Map and assorted city brochures**—*available at Fort Conde Welcome Center and Museum, Mobile, AL*

Raising Cain in Mobile

The term "raising cain" takes on a new meaning in Alabama's southernmost city, Mobile. The city was the scene of the first Mardi Gras celebration in the United States, back in 1830. The annual event was prohibited by Union troops during their occupation of the city following the Civil War.

One Mobilian, Joe Cain, brought the celebration back to life one evening when he and fellow revelers dressed as Indians and paraded through the streets of the city. Following Cain's death, a tradition began in which townspeople honored Cain by gathering around his grave during Mardi Gras and partying in an attempt to "raise Cain." The tradition continues to this day.

MilesDirections

0.0 START from the Fort Conde Welcome Center and Museum. Be sure to pick up the trail pamphlet and while there, spend a few minutes browsing the exhibits. Head north on South Royal Street.

0.1 Pass the former city hall. This building was built in 1856 as a city fish market, and later became the city hall/marketplace. In 1999, the city government moved to their new building and renovation is now underway to make this building the new home of the city museum, set to open in 2001. Next to the city hall is the Gulf Coast Exploreum and the J.L. Bedsole Imax Theater. Both are fantastic stops if you are traveling with children. Just past the theater is a statue honoring Admiral Raphael Semmes, the commander of the Civil War warship *Alabama*. Turn right onto Government Street (U.S. 90 east).

0.5 The trail heads to the waterfront. It was here that Mobile became a booming port city. Paddle boats and steamers would move cotton to ports all over North America. Today, the waterfront is being revitalized. The Cooper Riverside Park allows visitors to sit and take in the ships moving in and out of the harbor. The modern spire of the Mobile Convention Center is here, as well as a new attraction, the Cotton Blossom, an authentic Southern riverboat. In late 2000, a new maritime museum will be opened here. The trail loops here and then heads southwest back down Government Street.

0.7 The trail passes a marker indicating the boundary of the city limits back in 1711—the year Fort Conde was constructed—and then turns right onto South Joaquim Street. Travel one city block and then turn left onto Conti Street.

0.9 To the right at the intersection with Claiborne Street sits the Catholic Basilica of the Immaculate Conception. This cathedral was built in 1835 and features beautiful ornate statues and stained glass. Every statue has a story and the staff is more than happy to tell them. The trail now turns left down Franklin Street.

1.0 At the corner of Franklin and Government streets is the home of Confederate Major William Ketchum—now the home of the Archbishop of the Mobile Catholic Church. The home has 23 rooms and a 60-foot drawing room. Directly across the street is the Bernstein House, the former home of the Mobile City Museum. From here, turn right heading southwest once again back onto Government Street. Just next door to the museum is Spanish Plaza, built in honor of the relationship between Spain and Mobile. The statue of Queen Isabella in the plaza was a given to Mobile from the Spanish exhibit at the 1965 World's Fair in New York.

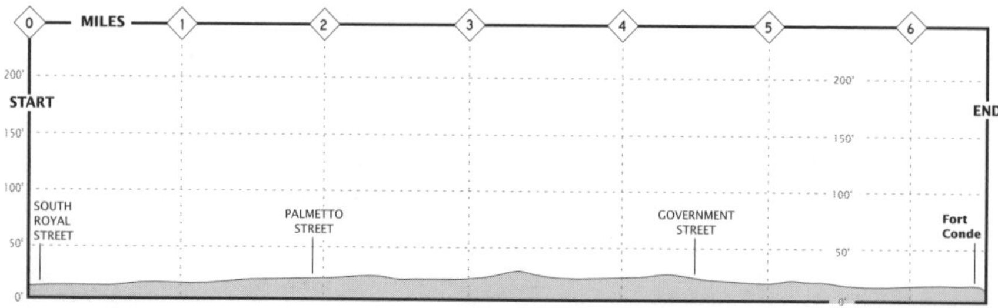

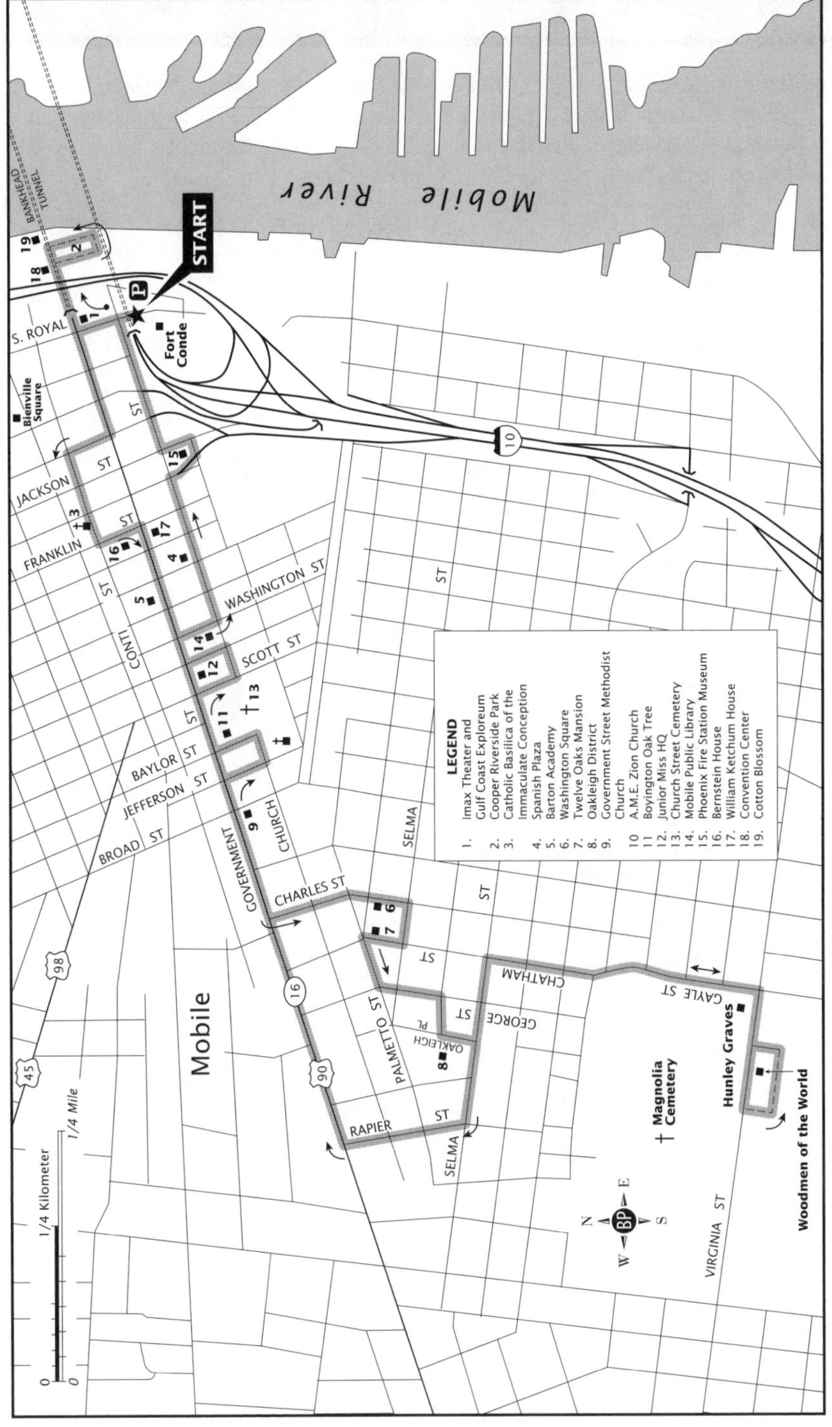
Mobile River
BANKHEAD TUNNEL
START
Fort Conde
Bienville Square
S. ROYAL
JACKSON ST
FRANKLIN ST
CONTI ST
WASHINGTON ST
SCOTT ST
BAYLOR ST
JEFFERSON ST
BROAD ST
GOVERNMENT
CHURCH
CHARLES ST
SELMA ST
PALMETTO ST
OAKLEIGH PL
GEORGE ST
CHATHAM ST
GAYLE ST
RAPIER ST
VIRGINIA ST
Mobile
Magnolia Cemetery
Hunley Graves
Woodmen of the World
1/4 Kilometer
1/4 Mile
LEGEND
1. Imax Theater and Gulf Coast Exploreum
2. Cooper Riverside Park
3. Catholic Basilica of the Immaculate Conception
4. Spanish Plaza
5. Barton Academy
6. Washington Square
7. Twelve Oaks Mansion
8. Oakleigh District
9. Government Street Methodist Church
10 A.M.E. Zion Church
11 Boyington Oak Tree
12. Junior Miss HQ
13. Church Street Cemetery
14. Mobile Public Library
15. Phoenix Fire Station Museum
16. Bernstein House
17. William Ketchum House
18. Convention Center
19. Cotton Blossom

MilesDirections (Continued)

1.2 Barton Academy is on the right. Built in 1836 and now the home of the Mobile County Board of Education, this building served as a hospital during the Civil War.

1.5 Continuing southwest, the trail passes the home of Admiral Raphael Semmes. This home was given to Semmes by the city in honor of his service to the Confederacy during the Civil War.

1.7 Turn left onto Charles Street.

1.9 The trail comes to Washington Square. This small park area was deeded to the city in 1859 for use as a promenade. Decorated with statues and fountains, the park was occupied by the Union Army during the Civil War and relieved of everything but the iron statue of a deer that still remains. The trail turns right on Augusta Street for one block. Turn right on Chatham Street and head north for one city block to Palmetto Street.

2.0 At the intersection of Palmetto Street and Chatham Street is Twelve Oaks Mansion, built in 1867. Travel to the southwest on Palmetto Street.

2.1 Take a left turn and head south on George Street. In about one block, George Street intersects Savannah Street. Make a right turn onto Savannah and continue until it intersects Oakleigh Place.

2.3 Turn south onto Oakleigh Place. Be sure to pay a visit to Oakleigh Mansion. Built in the 1830s, this house is now the home of the Historic Mobile Preservation Society and is a museum of the beautiful historic homes of the city. Admission is $1 adults, 50 cents for students. Travel past Oakleigh one block and turn east onto Selma Street.

2.4 Follow Selma Street two blocks and turn right onto Chatham Street. In three blocks, Chatham turns into Gayle Street. Magnolia Cemetery, established in 1866, is on the right. There is a Confederate cemetery here.

2.8 Turn west onto a short, unnamed street that runs from the southeast to southwest corner of Magnolia Cemetery. At this turn, the graves of the first crew of the Confederate submarine *Hunley* can be seen.

3.0 Turn left and head south a short distance on another unnamed street. The Woodmen of the World building is here.

3.1 Turn east onto a third unnamed street.

3.3 Turn north onto one final unnamed road, completing a circle of the Woodmen of the World building. The trail intersects the first street (at the 2.8-mile mark) near the *Hunley* graves. Make a right heading north on Gayle Street. Travel three blocks and Gayle Street again becomes Chatham Street. Continue another two blocks and make a left onto Selma Street.

3.7 Take a left turn (westward), on Selma Street.

4.0 Turn right on Rapier Street.

4.5 Turn right and head northeast onto Government. *[**Option**. For a longer trip, turn left (southwest) here onto Government Street (U.S. 90 west). The longer trip is detailed in the literature provided at the fort and passes by an original eleven inch cannon used at Fort Morgan during the Battle of Mobile Bay. Also along this route is Murphy High School, the oldest high school in Alabama and the only high school listed on the National Register of Historic Places. This longer trip is 11 miles in total length.]*

Statue of Admiral Raphael Semmes.

5.0 At the corner of Government Street and Broad Street, the trail passes the Government Street Methodist Church, built in the 1890s and patterned after Spanish Baroque architecture of the 17th Century. The building was known as the "Beehive" because of the bustle of activity that occurred there day and night. Visitors are welcome. Special services are held each day at noon. From the church, continue northeast across Broad Street one block. Turn southeast onto Jefferson Street. Follow Jefferson one block to Church Street. Turn left onto Baylor Street, passing the AME. Zion Church, built in 1860.

5.2 As you head northwest on Baylor, pass the Boyington Oak Tree. On November 16, 1834, John Boyington was hanged on this site for murder. Before the execution, Boyington said, "I am innocent, but what can I do? From my grave shall grow a tree of many branches that will prove my innocence." Years later, an oak tree, the Boyington Oak, began to grow on this site as the real murderer turned himself in. A few short feet past the tree, the trail turns right onto Government Street, heading northeast, and passes the home of America's Junior Miss. This national competition is held every June in Mobile and awards scholarships to the brightest and most outstanding high school students in the country.

5.5 Turn right and head southeast on Scott Street. After a block, make a left onto Church Street. This is the site of the Church Street Cemetery, established in 1819 for victims of a yellow fever epidemic. The cemetery is divided into several sections including veterans, strangers, Catholics, and Protestants. Many Mobile notables are buried here including Joe Cain. Just past the cemetery is the Mobile Public Library, housed in a building constructed especially for the facility in 1928. Make a left turn onto the unnamed side street and continue 50 feet to Government Street where the trail turns right and continues northeast.

5.6 Take a right on Washington Street and proceed 0.1 miles. Take a left onto Church Street and continue heading northeast. The Church Street East District—where you are— is the second oldest neighborhood in the city with many of the houses dating back to 1850.

6.2 Turn right on Claiborne Street and head southeast for about 100 feet when you come to the Phoenix Fire Station. This 1838 building was the original home of fire station number 6 of the Phoenix Steam Fire Company. Today, it is a museum dedicated to to the city's history of fire fighting. The station is open Tuesday–Saturday 10 A.M.–5 P.M., Sunday 1 P.M.–5 P.M. Admission is free. From the fire station, turn left on Jackson Street and return to Church Street. Make a right here and continue 0.3 miles to return to Fort Conde.

In Addition

Back to the Future in Mobile

Mobile, Alabama, one of the oldest cities along the Gulf Coast, may be a perfect example of the New South—preserving its past while moving aggressively into the future.

The annual Mardi Gras celebration demonstrates this mix of old and new. Mobile is the birthplace of the Mardi Gras carnival season in the United States. About 1830, Mobile resident Michael Kraft formed a secret society that attracted prominent citizens as members. One night after a bit of drinking, the group began parading in the streets. The revelry drew a lot of attention, some of it from spectators who wanted to join in the fun.

The celebration caught on. Soon other societies were formed and likewise began showing off with parades, music, and dancing. By 1840, the parades included floats depicting special themes, and participants rode the floats in costume. Word of the celebration spread, and New Orleans began its own Mardi Gras festivities after seeing the work of the Mobile societies.

With only a short cessation during and just after the Civil War, Mardi Gras has continued and thrived in Mobile. The original parades were held on New Year's Eve, but after the Civil War, they became synonymous with the religious season of Lent and began two weeks prior to Ash Wednesday.

The Mobile celebration has since become known more as a family event. Each night parades fill the streets, and people turn out to catch the beads, candy, and marshmallow pies thrown by parade participants.

While respecting the past, the downtown area has seen an extraordinary revitalization in the past few years. A museum dedicated solely to Mardi Gras is set to open in 2001. Also there is the Exploreum, with its hands-on science activities, and the J.L. Bedsole Imax Theater. A nautical museum is taking shape on the waterfront. On Dauphin Street, nightclubs, comedy venues, and restaurants keep the city electric.

Mobile is a big sports town, and the folks here love their football. Each Friday night, thousands of people flock to high school football games, whether or not they follow the teams playing. Each January the city hosts the Senior Bowl, a game showcasing the best professional football prospects among the nation's graduating seniors. A recent addition to the scene is the Mobile Alabama Bowl, a new event on the NCAA holiday schedule.

Baseball is a tradition in the city. From the 1930s to the 1950s, the Mobile Bears played here. A legend of the Negro League, Satchel Paige, was born in Mobile, as were other notable professional baseball players such as Tommy Agee and Cleon Jones of the 1969 Miracle Mets, the "Wizard of Oz" Ozzie Smith, and home run king Hank Aaron. The new Mobile Bay Bears are now playing here as part of Major League Baseball's Southern AA minor league.

An unusual sports addition is the Mobile Mysticks of the East Coast Hockey League. Yes, ice hockey in the Deep South. The East Coast Hockey League is a developmental arm of the National Hockey League. The Mysticks, first ice hockey team on the Gulf Coast, headed into their sixth season in the year 2000.

Cemetery Trail

Hike Summary

An interesting trail within Chickasabogue Park, the Cemetery Trail is used by both hikers and cyclists, with hikers heading in one direction, cyclists the other. The directions are reversed each month. The trail is ideally located for family hiking, with plenty to do at the park, and it provides easy trekking for young hikers.

Hike Specs

Start: From the parking lot at the northwest side of the sports field at Chickasabogue Park
Length: 2.7-mile loop
Approximate Hiking Time: 1½ hours
Difficulty Rating: Easy, on level and well-maintained trail
Trail Surface: Dirt and sand path; gravel in washout-prone areas
Lay of the Land: Slash pine forest; many fern-lined creeks
Land Status: County park
Nearest Town: Saraland, AL
Other Trail Users: Cyclists
Canine Compatibility: Dog friendly—leash required; bring water as sources are seasonal; dogs are not allowed at the pavilion at the beach along the creek

Getting There

From Saraland: Take the Saraland exit (Exit 13) from I-65. Head west on Shelton Beach Road for 0.1 miles to the intersection of AL 213 south. Make the left turn onto AL 213 and travel three miles to Whistler Street (a sign for Chickasabogue Park will be seen on the right). Take a left onto Whistler Street and follow it 0.7 miles to Adlock Street. Turn left onto Adlock Street and follow it one mile. Adlock Street runs straight into the main gate of the park. The park information center is located next to the gate. Trail parking is available by making a right turn from the information center and continuing down Adlock Street for 0.2 miles. A large playing field is on the right. Parking spots run alongside the playing field. This is also where the hike will begin. ***DeLorme: Alabama Atlas & Gazetteer:*** Page 62 B3

Owned and maintained by the Mobile County Commission, Chickasabogue Park encompasses more than 1,100 acres of forest, wetlands, and creeks. In addition to preserving the natural environment, the commissioners have made it their mission to provide a quality family getaway—and they have succeeded.

Chickasabogue features easy trails over lightly rolling hillsides, just right for children. The trails are mostly sandy and cross several creeks. The wildlife, including white-tailed deer, gives parents plenty to talk about with their children as they spend an afternoon together.

In addition to superb hiking and cycling trails, the park offers ball fields, a swimming beach along Chickasaw Creek, playgrounds, and picnic areas.

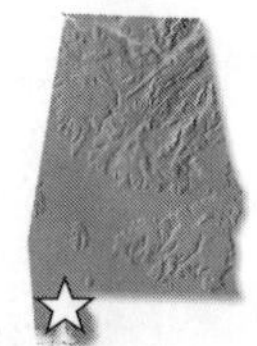

The information center at Cickasabogue Park.

The park is also home to an 18-hole disc golf course that is sanctioned by the Professional Disc Golf Association. Located in one of the state's bigger counties, the park can get crowded on weekends, so try to arrange your visit during the week if at all possible.

A little history education is also part of the Chickasabogue experience. At the entrance to the park, next to the information center, is the former Eight Mile AME Church. This small structure, built in 1879 in the neighboring town of Eight Mile, was moved to the park to serve as a museum. The museum features artifacts of Native American culture from as far back as 1500 BC. The museum, open to the public without charge, also displays photos of old Mobile.

The explorer Hernando de Soto first visited the area around 1540. Pirates also ventured through the region, using Chickasaw Creek as a their primary point of entry. The outlaw Cooper Gang, who roamed the Southeast robbing stagecoaches and businesses, lived here in the late 1800s. This rugged band helped runaway slaves flee the area, only to then sell them to plantations in other states.

Chickasabogue Park provides three walking routes: Cemetery Trail, Indian Loop Trail, and Beach Loop Trail. The Cemetery Trail, used by both hikers and cyclists, incorporates portions of the Indian Loop Trail. The trail is marked with small wooden planks that can be a bit confusing to a first-timer. In one direction they are painted red, in the other direction yellow—a way to help hikers and cyclists stay in opposite directions and thus see each other coming. Check with the information center to confirm which direction you're meant to travel.

The Cemetery Trail begins at the parking area next to the playing field. As the trail meanders away from the parking area, it runs parallel

MilesDirections

0.0 START from the grass parking area at the northwest side of the sports field. Head across the field to the southeast. The woods of Chickasabogue can be seen at the opposite side of the field. Just before entering the woods is a nature study pond. Beautiful water lilies float at the top of the pond with small fish schooling under the surface. A small gazebo sits at the end of a pier that protrudes into the pond. No fishing is allowed here! Continue south along the right or east bank of the pond toward the woods.

0.2 A sign marking the Cemetery Trail appears as the trail ducks into the woods heading west. There are very few trail markers along this portion of the route, but early in the hike, several trees are marked with white blazes. As the trail sinks a few hundred feet into the woods, a campground appears through the trees on the left.

0.4 The trail takes a turn to the south and heads down into a ravine. At the bottom, the trail crosses one of several small streams and creeks over wooden footbridges.

0.6 Cross a larger 50-foot long footbridge.

0.8 After leveling off at the top of a ridge and traveling about 30-yards, the path takes a turn to the east and then makes a steep descent once again about 100 feet to the bottom of another ravine. At the bottom, a 20-foot footbridge crosses another stream. If the crowds are small, whitetail deer may be seen foraging and drinking nearby. Off through the trees, a picnic area can be seen to the left. Follow the trail a few more feet and it makes a hook to the south and then to the east where there is another footbridge. In the distance you can hear the sound of I-65.

1.0 Trail signs become more frequent. Don't be confused about the Red and Yellow trail signs. Remember, they are both part of the Cemetery Trail. A chicken coup can be seen off to the northeast just off the trail. In about 50 feet, the trail comes to the paved park road. Cut

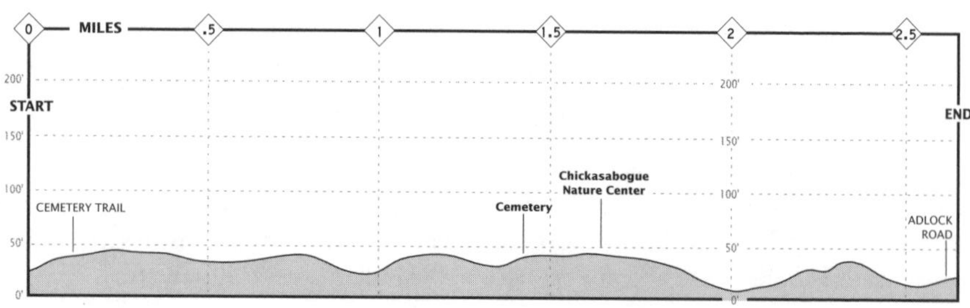

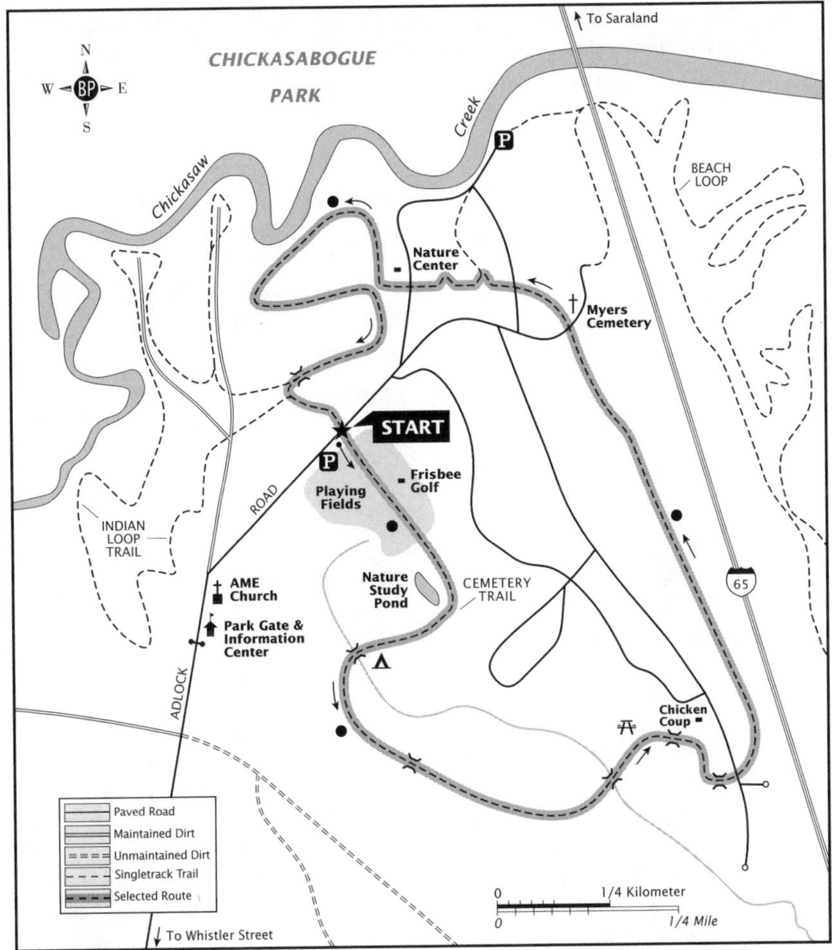

diagonal across the road to the north and continue on the trail.

1.1 Continuing to the north, the trail runs parallel to I-65. A large 130-foot bridge spans a marshy area. Here you'll find marsh marigold growing, as well as cardinal flowers, morning-glory, and wild geranium.

1.4 Come to a Y-intersection. The Cemetery Trail continues on to the northwest on the left fork. Take this. (On the right is the Beach Loop Trail.) Separating the two trails is the cemetery for which the Cemetery Trail is named. The small cemetery of 10 to 15 graves dates back to 1870.

1.5 Cross the paved park road and head back into the woods. The trees thin out here.

1.7 Encounter a sign that reads "SHORT" and points to the northwest. (This is a section of the Beach Loop Trail and leads to the northern most parking lot in the park.) Continue to the west. The trail scampers up a short hill. After weaving around thick brush, the trail once again

MilesDirections (Continued)

intersects the paved park road. To the left, is the playing field. Cross straight across the road to the gravel road on the other side. Continue down the gravel road to the north, passing a Cemetery Trail sign on the left. Continue about 50 feet and the Chickasabogue Nature Center will come into view. A series of informative posters display the wildlife and plantlife in the area. From here, continue north.

1.8 The trail now makes a left turn around some marshy areas until it reaches the banks of Chickasaw Creek. The slow moving muddy waters of the creek provide an excellent and relaxing canoe trip after the hike. Canoes are available at the information center.

2.2 The trail returns to the nature center. Turn to the south.

2.5 One final 60-foot long footbridge crosses a marsh and a small feeder creek of the Chickasaw. Shortly after the crossing, the trail turns to the south. Following the turn, encounter a Y-intersection. To the right, the Indian Loop Trail continues to another meeting with the Chickasaw. Take the left fork.

2.6 The Cemetery Trail intersects with the Indian Loop Trail once again at a T-intersection. Go left.

2.7 Reach a Y-intersection. Either fork will lead back to the parking area.

2.8 The trail ends at Adlock Road directly across from the playing field and the parking area.

Eyes on the Hurricane

The most dreaded words along the Gulf Coast are: "The National Hurricane Center in Miami has issued a hurricane warning."

Hurricanes are among the deadliest forces of nature. According to Frank Lepore of the National Hurricane Center, more people die from flash flooding as a storm moves inland than from the storm where it makes landfall. Storm rainfall in the mountains of Alabama can result in flash floods that sweep people away, including hikers.

Although the technology for tracking storms is considerably better than in the past, hurricanes are still difficult to predict. A storm that seems to be heading up the East Coast can, without warning, make a beeline for the Gulf Coast. Hurricane Elena was a puzzler, traveling back and forth just off the Gulf Coast several times over several days, keeping residents guessing until it finally moved inland over the Florida panhandle.

To avoid being surprised by a major storm, hikers can carry a lightweight battery-powered weather radio. Most of these radios monitor the U.S. Emergency Alert System and activate when an emergency weather situation is imminent.

The good news is that most hurricanes do not make landfall. But the best advice is to stay alert. Check the weather often, and in the meantime, enjoy the normally balmy weather of the South.

to Interstate 65 for a short distance before coming to a small cemetery established in the 1800s. Continuing on, the trail circles around and travels to a small nature center. Here you'll find posters and information about the park and its wildlife and plant life.

At this point, the sports field will again be nearby, offering a good opportunity to cut the trip short and head back to the parking area if you're hiking with small children.

From the nature center, the trail moves into the woods and follows a sandy path that crosses several creeks and marshes on wooden footbridges. Ferns are abundant. The trail travels to the banks of Chickasaw Creek before heading back to the parking area.

Hike Information

Trail Contacts:

Chickasabogue Park, Mobile, AL; (334) 452-8496

Schedule:

Open year round 7 A.M.–dusk. Rangers are on duty 24 hours for campers.

Fees/Permits:

$1 day-use fee for ages 12–59, 50 cents for children 6–11, free for children five and younger and adults 60 and older. Primitive camping is $5 a night, $10 for improved sites. Canoe rentals are $4 an hour or $15 a day.

Local Information:

Saraland Area Chamber of Commerce and Welcome Center, Saraland, AL; (334) 675-4444 or *www.saralandcoc.com*

Local Events/Attractions:

Wildland Expeditions, Chickasaw, AL; (334) 460-8206—*Take a scenic boat tour of south Alabama's wetlands and salt marshes.*

Accommodations:

Best Western, Saraland, AL; (334) 679-7953 • **Comfort Inn**, Saraland, AL; 1-800-228-5150

Restaurants:

Benzi's Pizza, Saraland, AL; (334) 675-9600 • **Kings Seafood**, Saraland, AL; (334) 679-4703 • **Leroy's Real Pit Barbecue**, Saraland, AL; (334) 675-5750 • **Something Special Deli**, Saraland, AL; (334) 675-3023

Local Outdoor Retailers:

Academy Sports, Mobile, AL; (334) 344-0047 • **Ward's Army/Navy Stores**, Mobile, AL; (334) 479-9058

Maps:

USGS maps: Chickasaw, AL • **Cycling and hiking map as well as park information**—*available free at the Chickasabogue Park Information Center, Saraland, AL*

5 CCC Trail

Hike Summary

A wake-up call for those who have hiked the flatter trails of the Gulf Coast region, the CCC Trail leaves the sea level hiking behind and starts to take on some hills. Granted these are not massive mountains, but some of the inclines can get you breathing hard. The trail crosses the beautiful stream that flows from the spillway of the dam at Blacksher Lake, and then rounds the lake and ducks into a thick forest.

Hike Specs

Start: From the southwest end of the main parking area of Claude D. Kelley State Park
Length: 1.5-mile loop
Approximate Hiking Time: 1 hour
Difficulty Rating: Easy to moderate, with a few steep grades; some rocky stretches because of washouts
Trail Surface: Dirt path; some travel on a dirt logging road
Lay of the Land: Dense forest, including slash pine, dogwood, sweet gum, hickory, and live oak
Land Status: State park
Nearest Town: Atmore, AL
Other Trail Users: None
Canine Compatibility: Dog friendly—along the trails; leash required; bring water (sources are seasonal); dogs not permitted at the beach area

Getting There

From Atmore: Take AL 21 north. Go 11 miles past where it crosses with I-65. Turn right onto H. Kyle Road—a sign marking Claude Kelley State Park will be seen on the right. Travel 0.4 miles to the park gatehouse. If the gatehouse is closed, pay at the honor box located on the side of the shack. Continue down H. Kyle Road 0.1 miles to the main parking area on the bank of Little River Lake. Hiking brochures can be picked up at the gatehouse or from the bathhouse at the parking lot. ***DeLorme: Alabama Atlas & Gazetteer:*** Page 57 D6

The folks who drive past Claude D. Kelley State Park and never stop to visit just don't know what they're missing. The park, hidden in the woods about 18 miles north of Atmore, features 960 forested acres and the 25-acre Blacksher Lake. This man-made lake provides swimming and fishing year-round. The CCC Trail affords wonderful views of the lake, plus a bit more of a hiking challenge than many other Gulf Coast hikes.

The Civilian Conservation Corps (CCC) built the trail, and the park itself, in 1938. You can also thank the CCC for the log pavilion and bath-

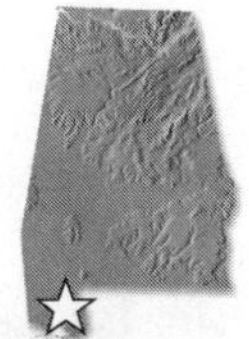

house, as well as the log gazebo perched at the ridge, accessed by the Gazebo Trail (see the following chapter).

The area in which the park lies, Monroe County, was immortalized in Harper Lee's *To Kill a Mockingbird*, the best-selling novel about racial tensions in a small town. The story was set in Maycomb, a fictionalized alias for the nearby town of Monroeville.

This region is home to the Poarch band of the Creek Indians. Following the 1814 battle of Horseshoe Bend, which pitted the Creek's Red Stick band against U.S. soldiers and the Lower Creek tribe, the federal government relocated most of the local tribes to Oklahoma. In appreciation for fighting alongside General Andrew Jackson troops, the Poarch Creek Indians were allowed to establish a reservation here. Each Thanksgiving the tribe invites the public to its annual Thanksgiving PowWow, featuring native foods, rituals, costumes, and dances. The PowWow is held on the Poarch Creek Reservation on Jack Springs Road in Atmore.

The CCC Trail begins by tracing the banks of Blacksher Lake. Early on, you cross the lake's overflow stream. The crossing makes for a scenic spot to rest up or have a bite to eat. At the opposite side of the lake, the trail enters a forest so thick that you can feel the drop in temperature—a blessing during hot and humid summer months. A sign along here says Bell Trail, but don't worry: This is still the CCC Trail.

MilesDirections

0.0 START from the southwest end of the main parking area in Claude D. Kelley State Park. Head to the southwest around the banks of Blacksher Lake, passing the dam that forms the lake.

0.1 The trail comes to a 50-foot long footbridge that spans the spillway stream. A "CCC Trail" sign is here. Cross the bridge heading to the south and once across, turn to the east and head back to the lake. Once you reach the lake, turn right and follow the dirt road along the banks of the lake.

0.2 Pass a "T" fishing pier that extends out into Blacksher Lake. Continue straight until the dirt road ends in a cul-de-sac. To the right is a series of 5 yellow pipes. This is where the loop of the trail rejoins the road on the trip back. A "BELL TRAIL" sign is off to the southeast corner of the cul-de-sac. This is the alternate name for the CCC Trail. Stay left, following the dirt path into the woods to the southeast.

0.3 A short footpath off the main trail leads to the banks of Blacksher Lake for more spectacular views.

0.4 The trail turns to the south and heads away from the lake.

0.5 The trail now starts its climb to the top of the hill and the slash pines become thicker. A few feet up the hill, the dirt path becomes an abandoned dirt road. Due to washouts, the travel becomes rocky in areas.

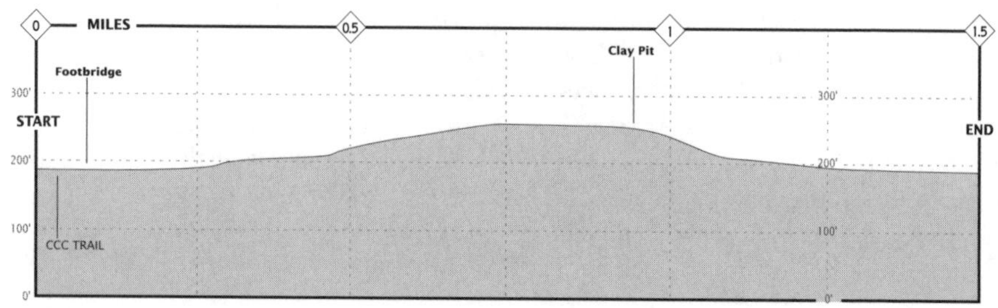

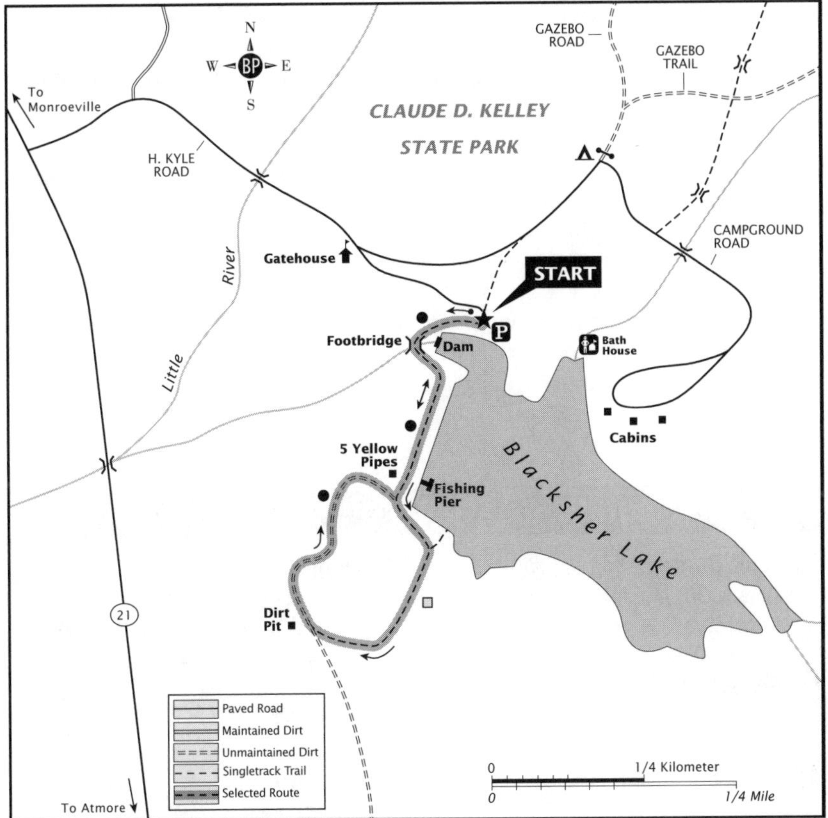

0.9 The road reaches the top of the hill at a clay dirt pit that is about 75–100 feet deep. Be careful of loose footing. A dirt road crosses here from north to south while the road from the lake continues on to the northwest. Turn right and follow the intersecting road. This road is more gravel than sand and begins the descent back down to the lake.

1.2 Continuing downhill, the trail starts heading more to the east. At this point, the downhill walk is on about the same incline as the trip up.

1.3 A jog in the trail is encountered as it starts heading to the north. The trail turns abruptly to the northwest then to the northeast to avoid a 20-foot drop off that looks like it was created by a washout. Continue in this direction. The road runs into the five yellow pipes first encountered at the 0.2-mile point of the trip. Turn left here and follow the dirt road along the west bank of Blacksher Lake.

1.4 Turn left at the dam and head west back to the footbridge over the stream. Cross the bridge and head northeast along the banks of the lake toward the main parking area.

1.5 Return to the parking area.

Slash pines, sweet gum, and hickory fill the forest. In the fall, live oaks provide a sparkling display of color that reflects from the surface of the lake. In early spring the dogwood blooms are particularly beautiful. While hiking, be sure to watch for the many varieties of woodpeckers that live here, including downy, hairy, red-headed, and pileated.

As the trail heads off into the woods, it follows an old dirt and gravel logging road. The grades are a bit steeper here than on other Gulf Coast hikes covered in this guidebook, but the average hiker shouldn't find too much difficulty. The route has many washouts, so watch your footing.

At the top of a ridge, the trail comes to the very edge of the soft clay banks of a large pit. Be careful here: There's a drop-off of 75 to 100 feet. The path eventually loops back down toward the lake to the east, rejoining the main path back to the parking area.

Hike Information

Trail Contacts:
Claude D. Kelley State Park, Atmore, AL; (334) 862–2511

Schedule:
Open year round

Fees/Permits:
Admission to the park is $1 for visitors 12 and older, 50 cents for children 6–11. Tent camping in primitive areas is $6 per day or $10 per day in improved areas with water and electricity at the site. Boats are available for use on the lake at $7.50 per day or pedal-boats at $4 per hour. A freshwater fishing license is required for fishing in the lake.

Local Information:
Atmore Chamber of Commerce, Atmore, AL; (334) 368–3305

Accommodations:
Best Western, Atmore, AL; 1–800–528–1234 or *www.frontier-net.net/~bestwest* • **Days Inn of Atmore**, Atmore, AL; (334) 368–9999

Restaurants:
Buster's Restaurant, Atmore, AL; (334) 368–4931 • **Catfish Junction**, Atmore, AL (334) 368–4422 • **Genie's Bar-B-Que**, Atmore, AL; (334) 446–7534 • **Great Family Restaurant**, Atmore, AL; (334) 368–4422

Local Outdoor Retailers:
Barnett and Associates, Atmore, AL; (334) 368–3571

Maps:
USGS maps: Uriah East • **Hiking map and park brochure**—*available at Claude D. Kelley State Park gatehouse or at the park's beach and bathhouse next to the main parking area.*

The Story of the CCC

The Civilian Conservation Corps was formed in 1933 as the United States was suffering through the Great Depression. The goal of this New Deal program was to provide employment and training for young men and to help conserve the nation's natural resources.

In exchange for a salary of $30 a month plus food and lodging, unmarried and unemployed men spread out across the country to work on reforestation and other conservation programs. They built fire-lookout towers, worked on flood control projects, and helped with soil conservation. They contributed to wildlife protection programs, and they helped develop state parks—including Claude D. Kelley State Park, site of this CCC Trail.

The Corps ceased operation by order of Congress in 1942, but in less than 10 years, this agency provided more than three million jobs and brought countless benefits to all citizens, including hikers and others who love the outdoors.

Local Events/Attractions:

William Station Day, third weekend of October, Atmore, AL; (334) 368–3305 or *www.frontiernet.net/~atmoreal/events.htm*—*"A simpler way of life," that's how the residents of Atmore describe the William Station Day celebration. This is a day to celebrate the town's founding back in 1866. Back then the town was a supply stop called William Station. There are plenty of arts and crafts, music, and stories of the trains that once ruled the area and the legends of the Poarch Creek Indians.*

Poarch Creek Indian Bingo Palace, Atmore, AL; 1–800–826–9121 or *www.frontiernet.net/~cbingo*

Annual Poarch Creek Indian Thanksgiving PowWow, Atmore, AL; (334) 368–3305 or *www.frontiernet.net/~atmoreal/events.htm*—*Each year, the public is invited to celebrate Thanksgiving with the Poarch Creek Indians. The event brings tribal members together and features brilliant displays of authentic dress and exhibition dancing by a variety of tribes. In addition, there are arts and crafts, barbecue, fried chicken, and more.*

Gazebo Trail

Hike Summary

The first sign of any elevation gain in the hikes of the Gulf Coast region of Alabama occurs in Claude D. Kelley State Park. Here the Gazebo Trail travels up the shallow inclines of 300-foot ridges past slash pines towering over pine needle floors. The trail crosses several creeks and streams that feed Blacksher Lake. Along the way, look for small fern forests, as well as Eastern wild turkeys, white-tailed deer, and red-tailed hawks.

Hike Specs

Start: From the north end of the main parking area at Claude D. Kelley State Park
Length: 3.2-mile loop
Approximate Hiking Time: 1½ hours
Difficulty Rating: Easy, on relatively flat trails; moderate during some steep changes in elevation along ridges
Trail Surface: Dirt and sand trails; dirt and gravel road
Lay of the Land: Slash pine, sweet gum, and oak trees; ferns and wildflowers
Land Status: State park
Nearest Town: Atmore, AL
Other Trail Users: Equestrians and motorists on park road
Canine Compatibility: Dog friendly—along the trails; leash required; bring water (sources are seasonal); dogs not permitted at the beach area

Getting There

From Atmore: Take AL 21 north. Go 11 miles past where it crosses with I-65. Turn right onto H. Kyle Road—a sign marking Claude Kelley State Park will be seen on the right. Travel 0.4 miles to the park gatehouse. If the gatehouse is closed, pay at the honor box located on the side of the shack. Continue down H. Kyle Road 0.1 miles to the main parking area on the bank of Little River Lake. Hiking brochures can be picked up at the gatehouse or from the bathhouse at the parking lot. ***DeLorme: Alabama Atlas & Gazetteer:*** Page 57 D6

Tucked away like a little secret off of Alabama 21 is Claude D. Kelley State Park, yet another gift of the Depression-era's Civilian Conservation Corps program. The centerpiece of the 960-acre park is Blacksher Lake. A swimming beach and canoe and paddleboat rentals make the lake easily accessible and a great spot for the family. The 25-acre lake is also good for anglers anxious to reel in a few bass, bream, or catfish—but don't forget your freshwater fishing license.

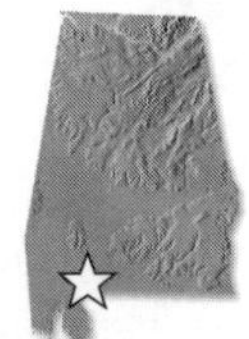

The Gazebo Trail's namesake.

The park is the home of two superb hiking trails: the CCC Trail and the Gazebo Trail (the longer of the two). The CCC Trail, featured in the previous chapter, heads south from the parking area, skirting the lake and forming a lollipop loop. The Gazebo Trail, instead, heads north-to-east of the lot into the rolling ridges above the lake, staying largely on the well-maintained Gazebo Road.

The trail begins at the main parking lot behind the bathhouse next to the lake. You can get park information and a free trail map at the main gate or at the bathhouse. Drinks, snacks, and ice are available for sale.

As you meander down the Gazebo Trail, you'll encounter a variety of plant life. Sweet gums and live oaks provide shade in the hot, humid summers; in the fall, they blaze in colors of red, yellow, and gold. Like most of the Gulf Coast region, the trail courses through an abundance of slash pines.

While gazing up at the pines that tower above the trail, be on the lookout for red-tailed hawks flying high overhead. Back down on the trail, in the right season, you'll see a wide variety of wildflowers lining the way: black-eyed Susans, the yellow-flowered winter honeysuckle, and the lavender flowers of the morning glory.

The trail crosses several creeks on wooden footbridges. From the bridges, you can view the masses of ferns that spring up like miniature forests in the damp surroundings. This is also a place to see white-tailed deer and eastern wild turkeys.

On the way down the trail, you'll notice the boundaries and service roads of Little River State Forest. This forest, maintained by the Alabama Department of Forestry, is used mostly for timber operations.

The Gazebo Trail reaches its farthest point at the top of a ridge, where you'll find a log gazebo with stone fireplace built by the CCC. You can reserve the gazebo for picnics, but reserve it early as it can get a bit crowded here during the summer. Picnickers use the Gazebo Road to ferry their supplies and guests to the gazebo, so watch for vehicles. The trail loops around the gazebo and begins to descend the hill at this point.

As the trail heads back to the parking area, the woods thin out a bit. Watch for woodpeckers in the trees, including red-headed and downy species. Also look for the tracks and burrows of armadillos and gopher tortoises along the sandy shoulders of the road.

MilesDirections

0.0 START from the north end of the main parking area and head north until you reach the dirt and gravel park road. Follow the road to the northeast.

0.1 The dirt road intersects Campground Road. Looking ahead to the north, there will be a closed pipe gate with a sign that reads "Gazebo Road." Turn right and head east on Campground Road.

0.2 Come to a wooden "Gazebo Trail" sign. Take the trail to the left, which leaves the road and heads into the woods. From here out, the trail is only occasionally marked, but the path itself should be easily discernable. Look out for armadillo tracks in the sand.

0.3 The trail crosses several streams and creeks that feed Blacksher Lake. Cross the first creek using a small footbridge. Ferns are plentiful around these crossings.

0.4 Come to the second creek crossing, this one a 40-foot bridge. After the bridge, expect the most difficult climb of the trip. It begins with a 70-foot scramble uphill to the top of a ridge. At the top, the trail levels off for a bit and then sprints up another 75-foot hillside. Once

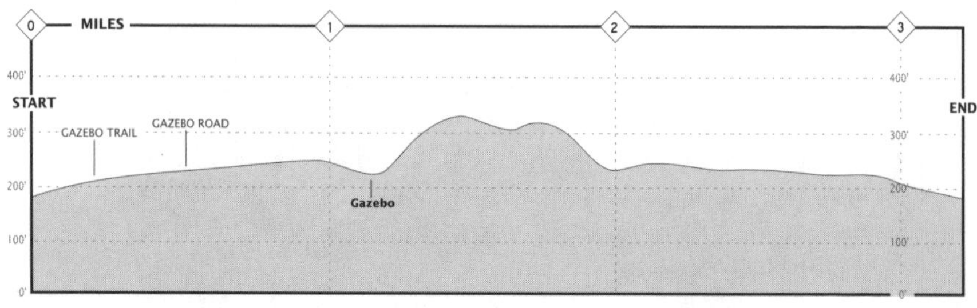

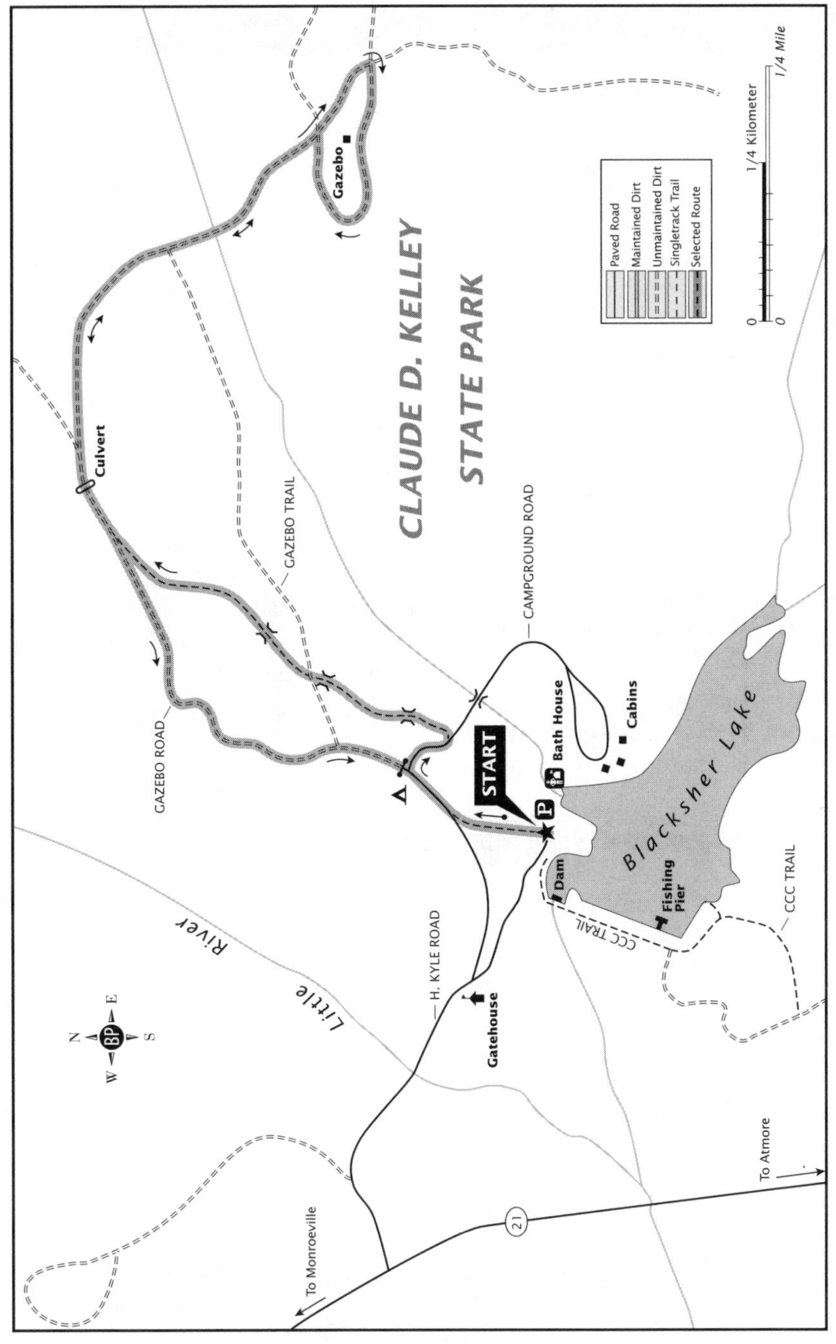

CLAUDE D. KELLEY
STATE PARK
Gazebo
Culvert
GAZEBO TRAIL
CAMPGROUND ROAD
GAZEBO ROAD
START
Bath House
Cabins
Blacksher Lake
Dam
Fishing Pier
CCC TRAIL
CCC TRAIL
H. KYLE ROAD
Gatehouse
Little River
To Monroeville
To Atmore
21
Paved Road
Maintained Dirt
Unmaintained Dirt
Singletrack Trail
Selected Route
0
1/4 Kilometer
0
1/4 Mile
N
E
S
W
BP

MilesDirections (Continued)

reaching the top of this hill, a third footbridge crosses a marshy area.

0.5 Pass a "Gazebo Trail" sign as the trail becomes a dirt and gravel park service road. This road merges with Gazebo Road. Continue east. After about 100-feet, pass a "Horse Trail" sign on the left and a "Gazebo Trail" sign on the right. Along this section, you'll see morning glories and black-eyed Susans, along with stone water culverts built by the CCC.

0.7 A dirt road cuts back off to the right—this is where the loop will return at mile 1.5. To the left is a sign indicating another horse trail. Stay straight.

0.9 Reach the top of the ridge. A "Gazebo Trail" sign points to the west as the trail begins to round the loop.

1.1 Reach the gazebo. This is a nice stopping point for a bite to eat or to watch wildlife. Whitetail deer are common in the area. The gazebo's stone fireplace is good for cooking. Continue on Gazebo Road as it now swings around to the east and back down the hill.

1.5 The loop is completed and you're back to Gazebo Road (mile 0.7). Turn to the left and head downhill.

2.5 Come to a Y-intersection. To the left is the trail you took earlier. Continue straight on Gazebo Road.

2.7 The trail begins a turn to the southwest.

3.1 Gazebo Road runs into the closed pipe gate encountered at the beginning of the trip. Continue down the dirt road to the southwest. You'll see the main parking area to the south.

3.2 Arrive back at the main parking area.

A Favorite of the South: Bread Pudding

1½ cups milk
10 slices white bread
2 tablespoons butter
¼ teaspoon salt
½ teaspoon cinnamon
¼ teaspoon cloves
¼ teaspoon nutmeg
2 egg yolks
⅓ cup sugar
¼ cup sherry
¼ cup white raisins or chopped dates

Heat milk but do not boil. Trim crust off the bread. Slice bread into half-inch cubes. Melt butter in the milk, then add the bread. Soak bread 10 minutes. Stir in remaining ingredients. Pour into oiled skillet and cook over a fire for 30 minutes. Turn and cook 30 more minutes. Best served with jam or honey on top.

Hike Information

Trail Contacts:
Claude D. Kelley State Park, Atmore, AL; (334) 862–2511

Schedule:
Open year round

Fees/Permits:
Admission to the park is $1 for visitors 12 and older, 50 cents for children 6–11. Tent camping in primitive areas is $6 per day or $10 per day in improved areas with water and electricity at the site. Boats are available for use on the lake at $7.50 per day or pedal-boats at $4 per hour. A freshwater fishing license is required for fishing in the lake.

Local Information:
Atmore Chamber of Commerce, Atmore, AL; (334) 368–3305

Local Events/Attractions:
[See Hike 5: CCC Trail]

Accommodations:
[See Hike 5: CCC Trail]

Restaurants:
[See Hike 5: CCC Trail]

Local Outdoor Retailers:
[See Hike 5: CCC Trail]

Maps:
USGS maps: Uriah East • **Hiking map and park brochure**—*available at Claude D. Kelley State Park gatehouse or at the park's beach and bathhouse next to the main parking area.*

Redoubt Trail Loop

Hike Summary

Historic Blakeley State Park looks like a postcard of the archetypal South: long flowing Spanish moss hanging from the trees, shady walkways along the riverbank, and let us not forget Civil War history. Only hours after Lee's surrender to Grant in Virginia, the last major battle of the war occurred here in Blakeley State Park. Today the park is a National Civil War Historic Register Site—in fact, it's the largest site of its kind east of the Mississippi River.

Hike Specs

Start: From the picnic area off of service road at the east end of the park
Length: 6.1-mile loop
Approximate Hiking Time: 3 hours
Difficulty Rating: Easy travel on slightly rolling hills
Trail Surface: Dirt path, some paved and gravel roads, and a boardwalk section
Lay of the Land: Magnolia and slash pine forest with riverside and marsh walks
Land Status: State park
Nearest Town: Spanish Fort, AL
Other Trail Users: Cyclists, motorists, and equestrians
Canine Compatibility: Dog friendly

Getting There

From Montgomery: Take I-65 South to the Stockton exit (AL 225 South). The exit is marked with a brown "Historic Blakeley" sign. Follow the winding highway approximately five miles. The Blakeley State Park entrance sign is on the right.
From Mobile: Take I-10 east to the Spanish Fort exit (AL 225 North). Follow the winding highway approximately five miles. The Blakeley State Park entrance sign is on the left. ***DeLorme: Alabama Atlas & Gazetteer:*** Page 62 C5

The Paleo-Indians first moved into the area around 4,000 years ago—evidence of this is the ancient burial mounds that still dot the park. Over the years the land changed hands numerous times—it would fall under the rule of six different flags—until in 1813 the United States captured the region from Spain. Soon thereafter, a Josiah Blakeley stepped into the picture to buy the land and establish a town in his name.

The town of Blakeley, long since vanished, was chartered in 1814 and became a bustling port city that rose to rival neighboring Mobile. By 1828 a series of yellow fever epidemics, coupled with the greed of land speculators, forced the city of 4,000 into a spiral of decay. By the close of the Civil War, the town was abandoned. Today, all that remains of the old port town are the 400-year-old live oaks that once lined the city streets.

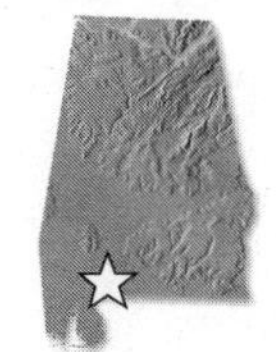

But the biggest thing to hit Blakeley came as the town lay in ruin. On April 8, 1865, 55,000 Union and Confederate soldiers converged in the fields surrounding the old town. The Union army intended to seize Fort Blakeley and then attack and capture the city of Mobile from its eastern shore. The fighting was fierce—216 killed, 955 wounded, and 3,054 captured (3,050 of them Confederates). It was a decisive Union victory. But what made the battle significant had little to do with the casualties. On the second day of this two-day campaign, Confederate General Robert E. Lee surrendered to Union General Ulysses S. Grant at Appomattox Courthouse in Central Virginia—thus making the battle at Blakeley the "Last Major Battle of the Civil War."

Over 100 years later, in 1974, the Alabama Historical Commission placed the site on the National Register of Historic Places, and the effort to preserve the battle site began. Trails were built, breastworks were located, and by 1993, Congress designated the site a "Class A Civil War Site." Three years later, it was added to the National Civil War Trail list.

Within Blakeley State Park's 3,800 acres are a total of 15 miles of nature and historic trails. The trails cross one another so that you can form shorter or longer loops to suit your schedule. All of the trails are well marked with brown signs.

Civil War gravesite at Blakeley State Park.

To access the Redoubt Trail, take the Benjamin Trail from the parking lot for a short hike to a small bridge that crosses a narrow tributary of the Tensaw River. Here, the trail connects with the Randall Trail. Hike the Randall Trail for another quarter of a mile through low lying, swampy areas and over another bridge before circling around to the Redoubt Trail, about half of a mile into the trip.

MilesDirections

0.0 START at the Washington Avenue parking area on the east side of the park along the Tensaw River. The Benjamin Trail begins at the extreme east side of the lot.

0.1 Cross a small wooden walkway over an inlet of the Tensaw River—now on the Randall Trail.

0.3 Cross another small walkway, back over the same inlet from the river.

0.6 The Randall Trail circles around from the inlet to the east approximately 0.2 miles and then heads back to the west for another 0.2 miles. This is the beginning of the Redoubt Trail.

1.1 The Redoubt Trail runs along a small ridgeline dropping down only slightly in places where it crosses streams and creeks, which are usually dry during the summer months. The trail crosses Washington Avenue near the Blakeley Cemetery. While walking, be sure to notice the dugout foxholes used by the Confederate troops.

1.5 The trail takes its largest dip down to Wilkins Hall Pond. This pond, usually dry in the summer, provides excellent wildlife viewing opportunities during the spring and winter. The trail across the pond is a boardwalk. A 100-foot climb up the west bank of the ravine is the most difficult part of the hike.

1.8 The trail meanders to the top of the main Rebel Headquarters. Directly in front is the main fortification, reconstructed to the way it actually looked during the Battle of Blakeley. On the right, is the large grassy field where the Union army charged the Confederate stronghold. Following the fortifications, the trail intersects Battlefield Road, where you'll turn right.

2.2 Follow Battlefield Road for a quarter mile. Come to the Union Line Trail and turn right.

2.5 Follow the Union Line Trail along the opposite side of the battlefield and cross a small wooden walkway over a creek that feeds Wilkins Hall Pond.

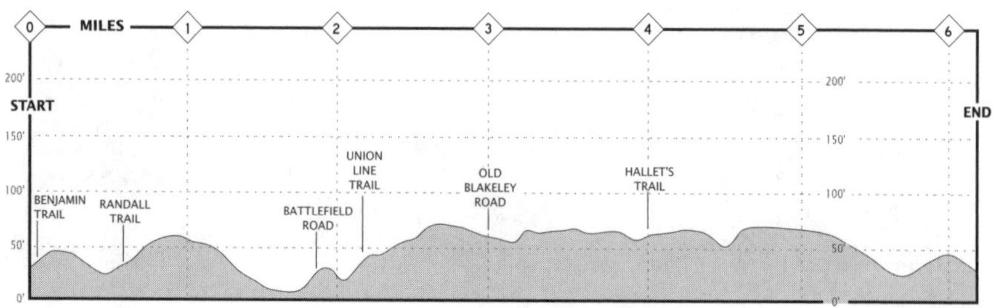

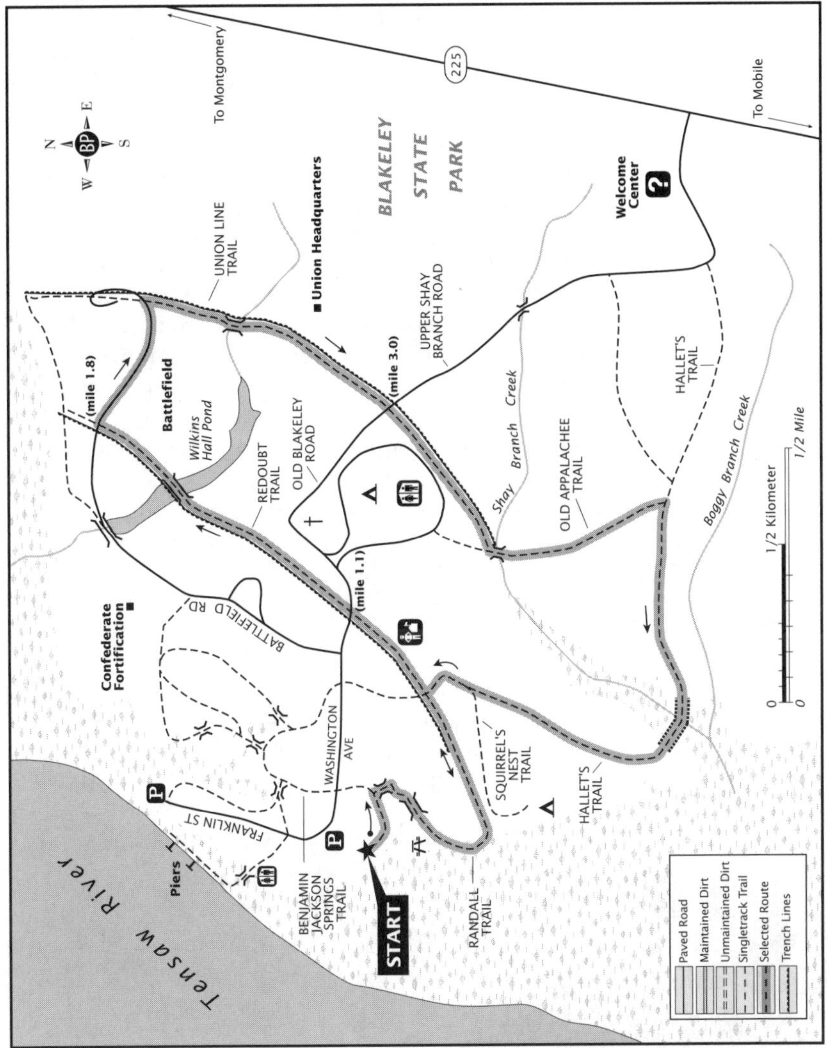

3.0 Cross Old Blakeley Road.

3.5 The Union Line Trail ends at a small wooden bridge that crosses Shay Branch Creek and turns into the Old Appalachee Trail.

4.0 Follow the Old Appalachee Trail through heavily forested areas until it intersects with Hallet's Trail. Turn right on Hallet's Trail.

6.1 Follow Hallet's Trail over a wooden bridge that spans Shay Branch Creek and another inlet of the Tensaw River. The city of Mobile can be seen to the southwest. The trail intersects the Redoubt Trail once again. Take a left onto the Redoubt Trail and retrace the Randall and Benjamin trails back to the parking area.

The Redoubt Trail runs along the top of a small ridgeline. Like all of the trails in the park, the area is heavily forested with magnolia and slash pine trees. Several dugout areas appear along this ridge. These entrenchments were used by Confederate troops "digging in" for the battle to come.

After about a half mile, the trail intersects with the Hallet's Trail. This is a long trail that, if taken, leads you over a number of creeks and swamplands that feed the Tensaw River. Continuing straight on the Redoubt Trail for another 0.6 miles the trail crosses the Washington Avenue service road.

After a total of 1.5 miles of hiking, the trail dips into a ravine and makes its way over Wilkins Hall Pond. Here, brown pelicans and great egrets can be seen, as well as turtles and an occasional alligator. Slash pines and live oaks surround the pond with various marsh grasses waving in the breeze. This part of the trail is along a boardwalk. In the center of the pond area, you'll find a platform with benches.

After passing over the pond on the boardwalk, the most difficult part of the trail is upon you, a 100-foot scramble up the other side of the ravine. Along this incline, there are some wooden stairs, but it's mostly dirt path. Although it is not difficult, those out of shape could feel winded afterward.

After clearing the ravine, the large fortifications of the battlefield come into view. To the right is the actual battlefield where Union troops raced across to take on the Confederates. This is where the Rebel troops were headquartered. The redoubts, now reinforced with wood, have been restored to their original condition.

From here, the trail loops around to the opposite side of the battlefield where the Union troops were headquartered. Still visible are the entrenchments and cannon pits used by the Union army before their charge on the

Looking south toward Mobile along the Tensaw River.

Confederates. Across the flat, grassy battlefield lie the opposing Confederate fortifications.

At this point, the Redoubt Trail converges with the Old Appalachee Trail and follows it for half a mile before merging once again with the Hallet's Trail. Take a right on Hallet's and walk the remaining 2.1 miles back to the parking area, enjoying the spectacular and calming views of the Tensaw River and the wildlife that live along its banks.

Hike Information

Trail Contacts:

Historic Blakeley State Park, Spanish Fort, AL; (334) 580–0005 or *www.siteone.com/tourist/blakeley*

Schedule:

Open year round 9 A.M.–5 P.M.

Fees/Permits:

$2 per person for hiking ($1.50 children 6–12), $4 for biking or horseback riding. Camping is allowed in designated primitive areas but not on the trails.

Local Information:

Eastern Shore Chamber of Commerce, Daphne, AL; (334) 621–8222 or *www.siteone.com/towns/chamber*

Local Events/Attractions:

Annual Blakeley Reenactment, Blakeley State Park, AL; (334) 580–0005—*Hundreds of descendants of the Battle of Blakeley gather and reenact the battle. The event occurs around the weekend of the actual battle date of April 9th.* • **Mardi Gras**, two weeks before Ash Wednesday, Spanish Fort, AL; (334) 621–8222—*The city of Mobile is the birthplace of Mardi Gras in the United States and since it was first introduced, the surrounding area has taken up the Carnival spirit. This is one of the smaller parades, but grows in size every year. Unlike other such celebrations, this one is family oriented.*

Accommodations:

Comfort Suites, Daphne, AL; (334) 626–1113 • **Ramada Inn on the Bay**, Spanish Fort, AL; (334) 626–7200

Restaurants:

Blue Gill Restaurant, Spanish Fort, AL; (334) 625–1998 • **Cheryl's Café and Market**, Spanish Fort, AL; (334) 626–2602 • **David's Catfish House**, Spanish Fort, AL; (334) 626–7903

Local Outdoor Retailers:

Eastern Shore Sporting Goods, Fairhope, AL; (334) 928–8988

Maps:

USGS maps: Bridgehead, AL • **Park brochure and trail map**—*Available for no charge at the park headquarters, Spanish Fort, AL. You can call the park at (334) 580–0005 to have them mailed to you.*

Honorable Mentions

Gulf Coast

There are plenty of great hikes throughout the Gulf Coast region of Alabama that didn't make the A-list. Although many are shorter in length, fantastic scenery and interesting wildlife are still in store. Pay a visit and let us know what you think. Maybe the hike should be upgraded, or maybe you know of a little-known hike that would make a good honorable mention. Let us know.

(A) Black Willow Trail—Meaher State Park

Meaher State Park is interesting in that the park itself occupies only 1,347 acres. But in this small park, a wide variety of flora and fauna can be found, as well as beautiful views of Mobile Bay.

Meaher is known as the "Gateway to the Mobile-Tensaw River Delta," the second largest river delta in the country, second only to the Mississippi. Within the delta are American alligators, wood ducks, blue crabs, brown pelicans, osprey, and great egrets, and the largest black bear population in the state. As for plantlife, pitcher plants and cypress and Tupelo gum trees are in abundance.

The Black Willow Trail is a boardwalk trail that's only 0.5 miles in length, but the views are superb as it hops several islands in the bay. Begin the trip from the west end of the parking area, and travel down a gravel road 100 feet to a small gate. The gate can be opened for handicapped access. Continue 0.1 miles to the start of the boardwalk. From here, the boardwalk travels out into the bay and across several small islands. Be sure to check out the plants and birds, but also look over the railing to see the different varieties of fish and shellfish. The trail loops around and returns to the parking area.

The park is open seven days a week from 7 A.M.–4 P.M. Admission is $1 per person, 50 cents for children 12 and younger and senior citizens. There's a large picnic area on the shores of the bay as well as a fishing pier. Camping is allowed near the picnic areas. Dogs are welcomed but keep an eye on them. A recent visitor nearly lost his dog to an alligator while playing fetch in the bay.

To get to the park from Mobile, go east on U.S. 90 for nine miles. The chain link gate of the park, as well as a brown Meaher State Park sign marks the entrance and the ranger station. Turn right onto the paved park road. Travel 0.4 miles past the gate to the picnic area on the right, where there's ample parking. For more information, contact the park at (334) 626–5529.
DeLorme: Alabama Atlas & Gazetteer: Page 62 D5

(B) Nature Trails of Gulf State Park

Two and a half miles of sugar white beaches, a 500-acre freshwater lake, bicycling trails, and 4.25 miles of nature trails, that's what's in store for visitors to Gulf State Park. Located on the Gulf of Mexico, Gulf State Park is one of Alabama's resort parks featuring lodging in rustic cabins or at the Beachfront Resort Inn. The park is ideal for families.

All of the nature trails within the park loop around the area from the headquarters and are generally 0.3 miles in length. Along the Hurricane Ridge Trail, the hikers see the effects of 1979's Hurricane Frederic, plus live oak trees, palmettos, and sawgrass. Muscadine grapes, commonly used for wine in this region, also grow here and provide food for birds, gray fox, and black bears.

The Bear Creek Trail is handicap accessible. Along its course you'll see aquatic plants such as water lilies, arrowheads, and pickleweeds. The Bobcat Branch Trail intersects Bear Creek Trail and provides glimpses of marsh rabbits. The longest trail in the park is the 1.5-mile Middle Lake Trail. This trail travels alongside 500-acre freshwater Middle Lake, one of three natural spring water lakes in the park, and takes hikers to the park's Nature Center. The trail crosses a small canal that connects Middle Lake with Lake Shelby. Here, small alligators are often seen floating just beneath the surface of the water—remember not to feed them.

Finally, two other trails, the Alligator Marsh Trail and the Holly Trail highlight smaller wildlife found in the park, such as frogs, turtles, lizards, and rabbits.

To get to the park from Gulf Shores, go east on AL 180 from AL 58 for 0.5 miles. The park headquarters is on the left and is open Monday–Friday 8 A.M.–5 P.M., 8 A.M.–4 P.M. weekends and holidays. The headquarters and staff have plenty of information about the park. For park information, contact park headquarters at (334) 948–7275. For information about resort lodging, call 1–800–544–4853. ***DeLorme: Alabama Atlas & Gazetteer:*** Page 64 F3

Ⓒ Beach Loop Trail—Chickasabogue Park

Mobile County owned and operated, Chickasabogue Park is renowned for its mountain bike trails, but it's also known for being a family park with plenty of activities for the old and young. In addition to Cemetery Trail [see Hike 4], you'll also want to check out the Beach Loop Trail. Though it's primarily a mountain bike route, the Beach Loop Trail is just as inviting to hikers. The hike begins at a creek-side pavilion, where swimming is allowed. Of interest along this 3.0-mile trail is "Woodsky's Wallow," a marsh where turtles, frogs, and lizards can be found throughout the day. The trail also travels for approximately 0.3 miles along the banks of Chickasaw Creek.

The trail also intersects a few other smaller trails, such as the Sand Pit Trail, which could make the trip up to five miles long. The only real drawback of this trail is its close proximity to I-65 for the majority of the trip. For more information, contact Chickasabogue Park at (334) 452–8496. *[See Hike 4 for park directions and additional information.]* ***DeLorme: Alabama Atlas & Gazetteer:*** Page 62 B3

(D) Roland Cooper State Park

Along the banks of the Alabama River just south of Selma is the 22,000-acre Dannelly Reservoir. Formed by a dam created by the U.S. Army Corps of Engineers, the reservoir has been a popular recreation area for many years. On the banks of the reservoir is Roland Cooper State Park.

The park consists of 236 acres of pine forests and offers vacation cottages, swimming, fishing, boating, camping, and of course hiking. Hikers can take in breathtaking views of the reservoir along the park's 1.5 miles of nature trails.

After hiking and swimming, there is a nine-hole golf course here that is the site of an annual golf tournament to benefit the American Cancer Society each August. To get to the park, travel south from Selma on AL 41 for 20 miles. To find out more, call (334) 682–4838. ***DeLorme: Alabama Atlas & Gazetteer:*** Page 50 A3

8. Open Pond Trail
9. Five Runs Loop Trail
10. North Loop Trail
11. Conecuh Trail
12. Chattahoochee Trail
13. Wildlife Drive

Southeast

Honorable Mentions

E. Frank Jackson State Park
F. Eufaula Wildlife Refuge Nature Trail

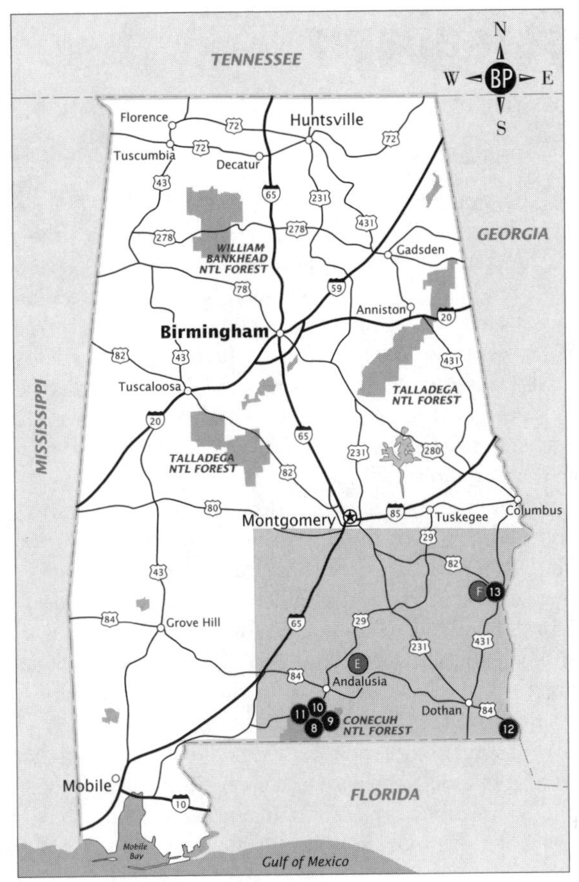
TENNESSEE
N
W
BP
E
S
Florence
Huntsville
Tuscumbia
Decatur
GEORGIA
WILLIAM BANKHEAD NTL FOREST
Gadsden
Anniston
Birmingham
Tuscaloosa
TALLADEGA NTL FOREST
MISSISSIPPI
TALLADEGA NTL FOREST
Montgomery
Tuskegee
Columbus
Grove Hill
Andalusia
Dothan
CONECUH NTL FOREST
Mobile
FLORIDA
Mobile Bay
Gulf of Mexico

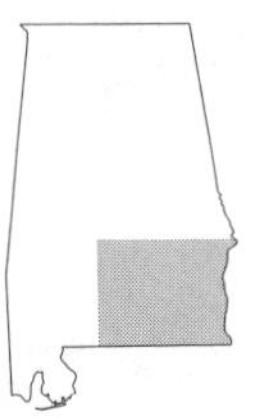

Alabama

Southeast Alabama

The Southeast region of Alabama borders the states of Georgia and Florida. Geographically speaking, this region does not differ greatly from the Gulf Coast region. The hills are a bit higher, at times around 300 feet above sea level, but overall, the region is flat coastal plain.

Two distinct features make this region stand out. The first is the Chattahoochee River, which forms the eastern border between Alabama and Georgia. The river begins in northern Georgia at the convergence of several small streams in the Blue Ridge Mountains and gathers steam before flowing into the Gulf of Mexico.

Hikers will encounter the Chattahoochee twice in this guide: first at the Eufaula Wildlife Refuge. Here, the U.S. Fish and Wildlife Service has established an 11,184-acre wetland by building levees along the banks of the river. Bird watchers are in for a real treat here with over 300 species of birds to be found. In addition, the refuge is home to 40 species of animal life. The second stop along the Chattahoochee is at Chattahoochee State Park, located directly on the southeast corner of Alabama at the Alabama/Georgia/Florida state lines.

The second highlight of the Southeast region is the Conecuh National Forest, renown for its crystal blue spring lakes and its cypress ponds. It is also known for the 20-mile long Conecuh Trail, an easy weekend hike through ponds and lakes and dogwood, holly, longleaf pine, magnolia, and cypress forests.

As with the Gulf Coast region, the weather in the Southeast is sub-tropical, and late summer heat and humidity can make outdoor activities impossible at times. If you're hiking the region during this time, carry plenty of water and of course, insect repellent. Much of the hiking in this region is around swamps and marshes and mosquitoes can be a nuisance. Also like the Gulf Coast region, being in close proximity of the Gulf of Mexico means that the warm moist Gulf air can produce brief but very heavy rainfall unexpectedly.

Although this area is not known for getting the full force of hurricanes, its location near the Gulf still requires hikers to keep an eye on the weather during hurricane season (May through November). A hurricane pushing on shore from the Gulf can mean dangerous tornadoes and flooding to these inland areas.

The hot, humid summer gives way to great hiking weather in the fall and winter, and spring as the temperature moderates from the mid 60s to low 70s. It does get a bit colder in this region than in the Gulf Coast, with temperatures averaging in the 40s in January. Cold snaps of below 30 degrees are more frequent than in the Gulf Coast region.

Open Pond Trail

Hike Summary

The Open Pond Trail, at the southern end of Conecuh National Forest, travels around three ponds—Open Pond, Buck's Pond, and Ditch Pond. The travel is easy, and the scenery is beautiful. The trail begins along the grassy banks of Open Pond, where cypress trees line the banks and an occasional alligator may be seen. As the trail turns into a sandy footpath, it heads into the woods and around Buck's Pond. Finally, it follows a dirt Forest Service road as it rounds Ditch Pond, where herons and egrets abound.

Hike Specs

Start: From the parking lot at Open Pond Recreation Area
Length: 2.1-mile loop
Approximate Hiking Time: 1½ hours
Difficulty Rating: Easy, over low, gentle hillsides
Trail Surface: Dirt roads and sand-covered paths; grassy banks along Open Pond
Lay of the Land: Forests of longleaf and slash pine, magnolia, and dogwood; cypress ponds
Land Status: National forest
Nearest Town: Andalusia, AL
Other Trail Users: Motorists and cyclists
Canine Compatibility: Dog friendly—over easy trails; permit and leash required

Getting There

From Andalusia: Take U.S. 29 south for 9.7 miles. Turn left and head south on AL 137 for five miles. Make a left onto CR 24 east and travel 0.5 miles. Make a right on FS 336A (CR 28) south. The road comes to a fee-station at a Y-intersection. Be sure to pay and place the receipt on your dash. Take the left fork. Travel one tenth of a mile and turn right. The parking area is the dead-end of this road about 50 feet ahead. ***DeLorme: Alabama Atlas & Gazetteer:*** Page 58 F5

Conecuh National Forest, established in 1935, lies on the Alabama-Florida border and consists of just under 83,000 acres. Within its boundaries, the forest provides areas for hunting, timber for local lumber companies, oil and gas wells, and grazing land for cattle. Hikers are treated to easy hiking over small, rolling hillsides and through forested land.

As the Open Pond Trail passes the three separate cypress ponds, you'll encounter a big variety of plant and animal life. Dogwood, holly, longleaf pine, magnolia, and cypress line the trail. Animals that may be seen include white-tailed deer, red foxes, bobcats, river otters, and Eastern wild turkeys.

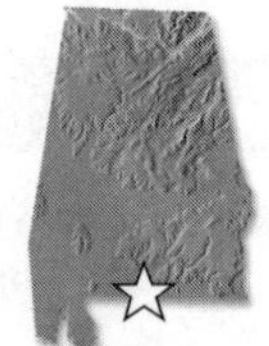

Keep an eye out while traveling around the ponds for a wake in the water, like an invisible boat moving across the surface. Look just below the surface, and you may see an American alligator.

In common with many of the hiking areas of the Gulf Coast and Southeast Alabama, Conecuh National Forest offers bird-watchers a wealth of subjects to feast their eyes upon. Wood ducks are the most prominent birds along the trail. Large herons and egrets soar above the ponds while blue kingfishers, doves, wrens, and goldfinches often dart out of the brush.

The Conecuh Trail and the Open Pond Trail merge here at the Open Pond Campground.

The Open Pond Trail begins by circling its namesake pond, running parallel with a paved service road. At the southern end of the pond, the trail becomes sandy before turning into a dirt footpath as it moves away from the pond. This portion of the trail is carefully designated by white-plastic diamond markers every 20 feet or so. Turns are marked by dark black arrows on the markers, pointing in the direction of travel. The trail passes by the Open Pond Campground, which can be crowded during summer and during hunting season.

Heading away from the campground, the dirt path circles a marsh of Open Pond to the southeast. The trail crosses a footbridge over the marsh and a runoff area. The trail then crosses several feeder creeks until it reaches the second cypress pond on the trip, Buck's Pond. A T-shaped fishing pier juts into Buck's Pond, and many fishermen come here to launch their boats and spend an afternoon on the water.

The trail moves off to the northeast to reach Ditch Pond. This pond is farther from the campground and visited by fewer, so your chances are greater to see wildlife. The pond is home to gray and blue herons and white egrets. Their neighbors include swallows, doves, blackbirds, and kingfishers. Also watch for hawks and woodpeckers.

The trail circles Ditch Pond and heads back to Buck's Pond, where it then turns and travels back to the parking area.

MilesDirections

0.0 START from the northwest end of the parking lot. Here, a cement sidewalk heads to the northwest for 50 feet toward the bathhouse. Continue past the bathhouse over the grass to the banks of Open Pond. At the pond, turn right and head to the northeast.

0.2 The trail starts a turn to the north as it passes the fee station at the entrance to the Open Pond Recreation Area to the right. At this point the trail is still following the grassy banks of the pond, but is running parallel with the paved forest service road. About 20 feet ahead, a boat ramp is passed. In another 20 feet, a parking area will be straight ahead. Turn to the west along the north side of the pond.

0.3 The travel begins to curve around the lake to the southwest. Along these banks, keep an eye out for alligator under the surface. Remember not to feed the alligators. Though they are naturally afraid of man, feeding them changes the rules.

0.5 Pass another parking area on the right.

0.6 Come to a T-intersection. This is a connector to the Conecuh Trail, marked with white diamond markers like the Conecuh. Turn left, heading south. Camping areas are to the right.

1.0 A T-intersection is reached. A spur of the Conecuh Trail heads off to the right to the north. Go left, continuing south. After crossing a short footbridge, come to a sign reading "BUCK'S POND" and "DITCH POND." Head into the woods to the north.

1.2 Come to an intersection. This is where the Open Pond loop closes. Continue to the north 50 feet to the fishing pier at Buck's Pond. The trail turns to the south and heads around the west bank of the pond. The path is once again grass.

1.4 This is a sharp turn to the north. A Conecuh Trail marker points the direction.

1.5 Reach Ditch Pond on the left side of the trail. Shortly, the trail turns to the south and a Conecuh Trail marker with one large arrow points the direction of the turn.

1.6 A side trail intersects the Conecuh Trail to the east. Of the two wooden signs, follow the one to the east that reads "Blue Lake Recreation Area 3 Miles." From here on out, there will be no trail markers. The trail circles around Ditch Pond and comes to a T-intersection with a dirt service road. Turn to the left and head west. This sandy road splits into two "lanes" as it heads around some thick brush. Take the left "lane" which follows the edge of the pond.

1.7 The road passes a picnic area, a dirt boat ramp, and a fishing pier

1.9 The road forks. Stay right. *[**FYI.** The right fork is the dead-end of FS 336A.]*

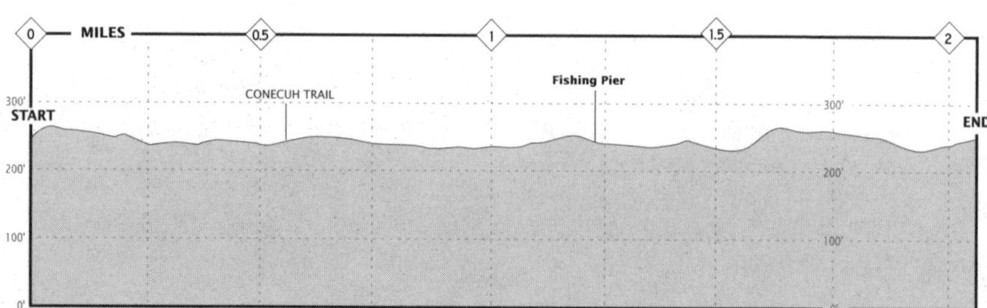

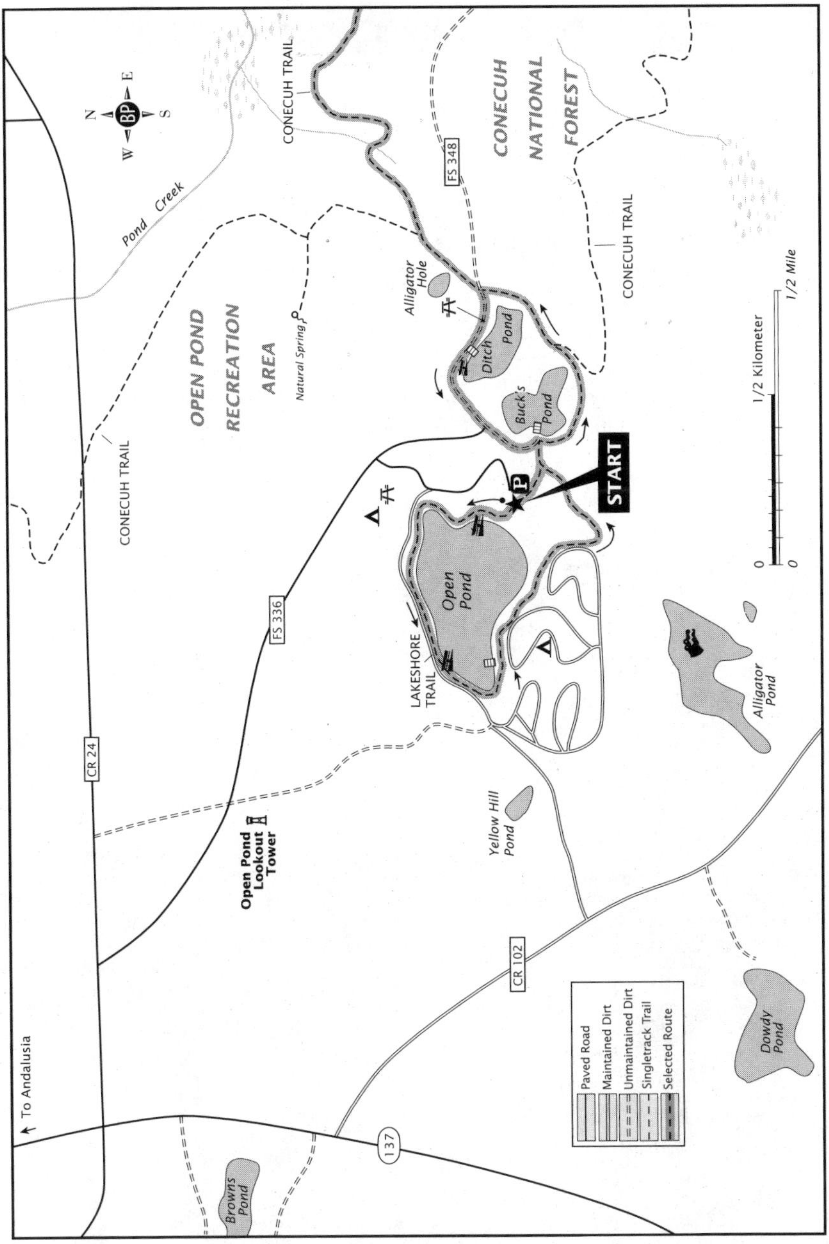

2.0 The road reaches the intersection passed earlier (mile 1.2). Turn right and head to the northwest.

2.1 Come to six wooden poles with yellow paint topping them. This is the end of the trail.

Quick and Too Easy Chicken Almondine

4 cups water
16 oz. canned chicken
4 cups instant rice
½ teaspoon onion salt
½ teaspoon celery salt
2 teaspoons chopped dried onion
1 package sliced almonds (2¾ oz.)
⅔ cup raisins

Place chicken and water in pot and bring to boil. Add remaining ingredients and return to a boil. Remove from heat. Let stand in pot for 10 minutes. Fluff with fork and serve. Makes three servings.

A beautiful fall sky reflects off Open Pond.

Hike Information

Trail Contacts:

Conecuh National Forest, Andalusia, AL; (334) 222-2555 • **Forestry Supervisor**, Montgomery, AL; (334) 832-4470

Schedule:

Open year round. The ranger station is open from 7:00 A.M.–4:30 P.M. Monday–Friday. Camping is allowed in primitive areas and along some sections of the Conecuh Trail. Keep in mind that camping is restricted during hunting season. Check with the forest rangers before making plans.

Fees/Permits:

$2 per person day-use, $1 for children. Camping at primitive sites is $6 per day, $12 at improved sites with electricity and water. State freshwater fishing license is required to fish in the ponds and lakes of the forest. A state hunting license is required for hunting.

Local Information:

Andalusia Chamber of Commerce, Andalusia, AL; (334) 222-2030 or *www.alaweb.com/~chamber/city.html*

Local Events/Attractions:

World Domino Championship, Annually mid-July, Andalusia, AL; (334) 222-5830 • **Three Notch Museum**, Andalusia, AL; (334) 222-2030 or *www.alaweb.com/~chamber/3notch.html—This is a superb museum that is located in the 1899 Central of Georgia Railroad depot and features photographs, railroad memorabilia, authentic log cabins, and a one-room country store.*

Accommodations:

Days Inn, Andalusia, AL; (334) 427-0050 • **Scottish Inn**, Andalusia, AL; (334) 222-7511 • **Winwood Inn**, Andalusia, AL; (334) 222-7511

Restaurants:

Golden Corral, Andalusia, AL; (334) 222-7749 • **Hunan Garden**, Andalusia, AL; (334) 222-3080

Organizations:

Covington County/South Alabama Birding Association (334) 382-2680 or *www.alaweb.com/~kenwood/saba/index.html—This organization provides a tour of the birding areas, bogs, and creeks of Conecuh National Forest in late March.*

Local Outdoor Retailers:

Brightwell's Athletic House, Andalusia, AL; (334) 222-1411

Maps:

USGS maps: Wing, AL • **Trail maps**—*available at the Conecuh National Forest Ranger Station, Andalusia, AL, or by mail for $5 at (334) 832-4470. Two brochures, one entitled "Carnivorous Plants of Conecuh National Forest" and the other called "Camping in Conecuh National Forest," are available at no cost.*

Five Runs Loop Trail

Hike Summary

Although most of this hike along Five Runs Loop is along relatively level Forest Service roads, one hill during the final section of the loop is rather steep. Five Runs Creek and a section of Blue Spring flows near the trail, providing soothing opportunities to sit, relax, and daydream.

Hike Specs

Start: From the parking lot at Open Pond Recreation Area
Length: 3.2-mile loop
Approximate Hiking Time: 2 hours
Difficulty Rating: Easy; moderate in one short stretch due to steepness
Trail Surface: Clay, sand, and dirt roads
Lay of the Land: Forest of longleaf and slash pine, magnolia, and dogwood; marsh and ponds
Land Status: National forest
Nearest Town: Andalusia, AL
Other Trail Users: Equestrians and motorists
Canine Compatibility: Dog friendly—over easy trails; permit and leash required.

Getting There

From Andalusia: Take U.S. 29 south for 9.7 miles. Turn left and head south on AL 137 for five miles. Make a left onto CR 24 east and travel 0.5 miles. Make a right on FS 336A (CR 28) south. The road comes to a fee-station at a Y-intersection. Be sure to pay and place the receipt on your dash. Take the left fork. Travel one tenth of a mile and turn right. The parking area is the dead-end of this road about 50 feet ahead. ***DeLorme: Alabama Atlas & Gazetteer:*** Page 58 F5

Many endangered species call the Conecuh National Forest home, including the flattened musk turtle and the red-cockaded woodpecker. This woodpecker was placed on the endangered species list in the 1970s due to timber cutting that resulted in rapid disappearance of the bird's habitat. The good news is that cooperation among timber companies, government agencies, and private organizations seems to be resulting in survival of both the red-cockaded woodpecker and the lumber industry.

This species differs from other woodpeckers in that it is only about six inches long, does not sport a red head, and resides in live trees instead of dead or dying ones. These woodpeckers prefer to burrow into live pines, taking advantage of the tree sap, which serves as a deterrent to predators and protection from fire.

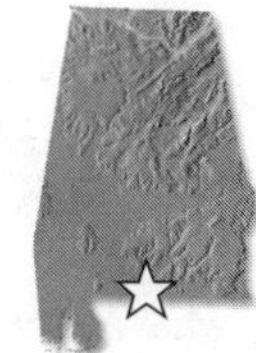

Five Runs Loop Trail passes along the banks of Ditch Pond.

The woodpecker got its name during the Civil War. The Confederate Army distinguished the rank of its officers with a red feather, known as a cockade, on the side of their hats. The male woodpecker of the species has a small red cockade on the side of its head.

While you're in the Conecuh Forest you can expect to see all sorts of wildlife, such as white-tailed deer, bobwhite quail, and wild turkeys, as well as a variety of waterfowl including wood ducks, pied-billed grebes, and belted kingfishers.

From the parking lot at Open Pond Recreation Area, the Five Runs Loop Trail travels along the banks of Buck's Pond, Ditch Pond, and Five Runs Creek. The creek, with an average width of 10 feet, is a feeder stream for the Yellow River that eventually joins the Blackwater River, which then flows to the Gulf of Mexico. One of the best times to visit this area is during the spring, when pitcher plants, orchids, and other wildflowers bloom along the banks of the creek and neighboring bogs.

One especially interesting pond near the trail is called Alligator Hole. This small pond is out of sight, about 50 feet from the trail, at a point only three-tenths of a mile from the start of the hike. Alligators are sometimes sighted here. Heed the posted warnings: Don't feed or molest the alligators. Watch from a safe distance.

Less than half a mile after leaving the trailhead, the loop passes through a wide marsh. The marsh is well worth the time for a visit, especially in the spring, to look for some of the amphibians, reptiles, and marsh plants that live here. On the return trip from Five Runs Creek, the trail ascends somewhat steeply for about two-tenths of a mile.

MilesDirections

0.0 START from the parking lot by heading to the west on the paved road. In 100 feet, turn to the right (south) and notice the sign reading "Hiker's Trail." Follow the footpath to the south into the woods. This is a portion of the Conecuh Trail, identifiable by a white diamond metal marker. (We'll see this numerous times throughout this hike.) In 50 feet, the trail turns to the southeast. A short trail is passed to the to the south. Continue to the southeast heading toward Buck's Pond. In 20 feet, turn left onto FS 348. This is a sandy road that heads around the pond. In another 100 feet, a paved road is passed on the left. Continue on FS 348 to the northeast. After .05 miles, the trail turns to the east and heads around Ditch Pond.

0.2 Come to a T-intersection with an unmarked Forest Service road. Turn to the right and head to the east. In 20 feet, the road crosses the Conecuh Trail.

0.3 Come to a "Road Closed" sign to the east (left) and an abandoned forest service road.

0.5 Pass another abandoned road to the south.

0.6 Cross the Conecuh Trail.

0.7 Pass FS 348 on the right. This is where the road loops back around for the return trip.

0.9 Come to a T-intersection with another sand forest service road. Turn right. Just through the woods to the east, a section of Blue Spring joins with Five Runs Creek. *[**FYI.** Anywhere along this 0.4-mile section is a good place to hike off the trail a short distance and relax by the creek banks.]*

1.0 Cross the Conecuh Trail.

1.4 Reach a T-intersection and turn right, heading to the west on the gravel road.

1.7 At the top of a short hill, come to a house and FS 348 on the right. Turn here and head north.

2.0 The most difficult section of the hike is reached with the trail heading to the north up a rather steep incline for the next 0.2 miles.

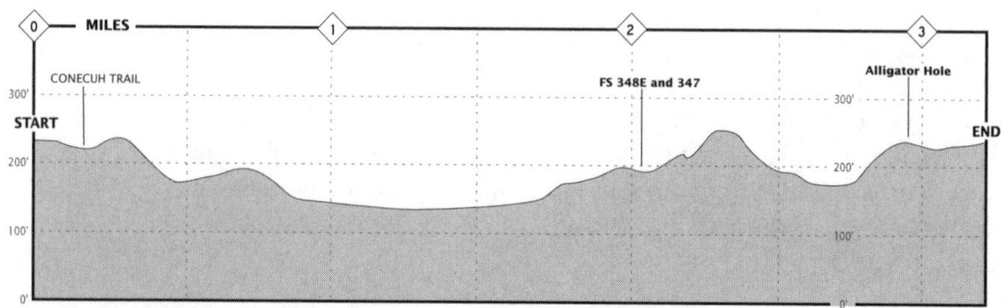

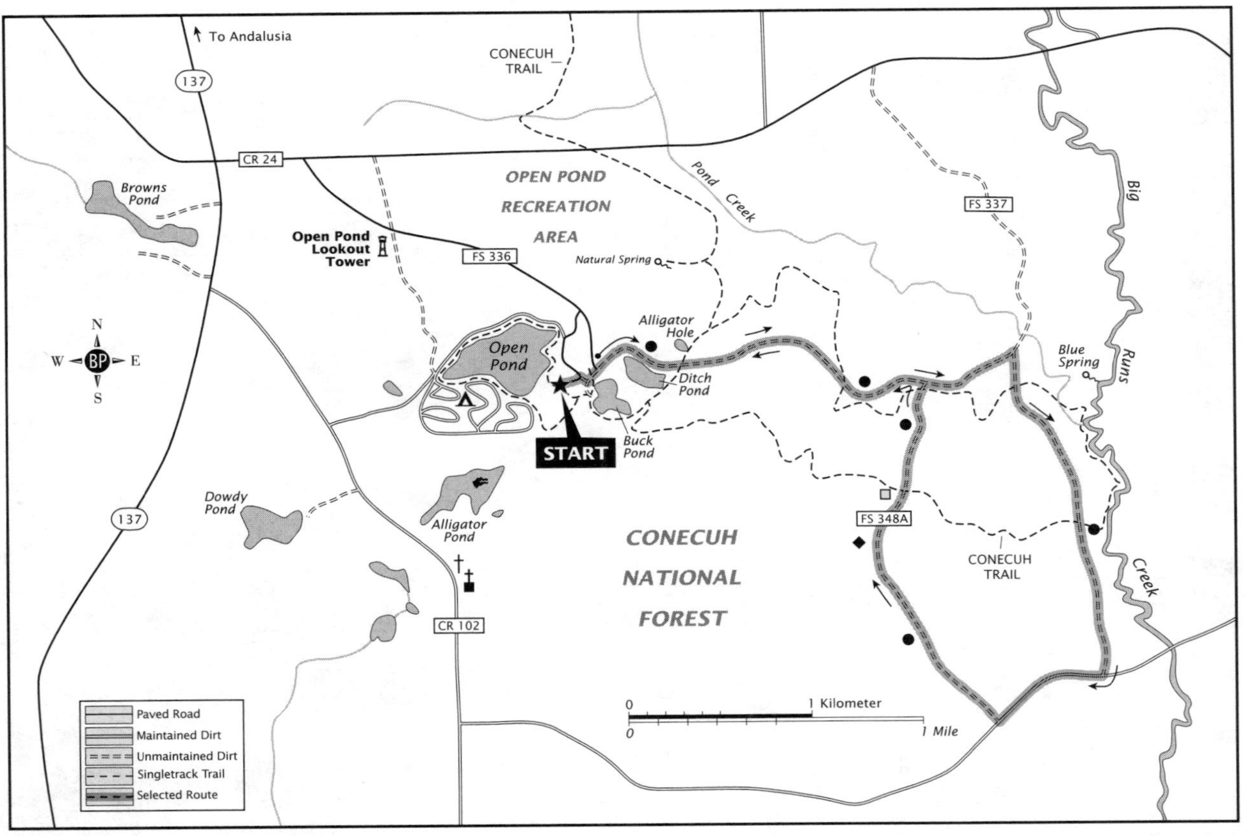
To Andalusia
137
CONECUH TRAIL
CR 24
Browns Pond
OPEN POND
RECREATION
AREA
Pond Creek
FS 337
Big
Open Pond Lookout Tower
FS 336
Natural Spring
N
W
BP
E
S
Alligator Hole
Open Pond
Blue Spring
Runs
Ditch Pond
START
Buck Pond
FS 348A
Dowdy Pond
137
Alligator Pond
CONECUH
NATIONAL
FOREST
CONECUH TRAIL
Creek
CR 102
0
1 Kilometer
0
1 Mile
Paved Road
Maintained Dirt
Unmaintained Dirt
Singletrack Trail
Selected Route

MilesDirections (Continued)

2.1 The road passes FS 348E to the left. In 50 feet, pass FS 347 to right.

2.2 Reach the top of the hill and cross the Conecuh Trail.

2.3 Reach a T-intersection (mile 0.7). This is the end of the loop. Turn left and head back.

2.6 Cross the Conecuh Trail and pass an abandoned road to the south.

2.8 Pass an abandoned road to the right.

2.9 The road now turns to the west and passes FS 322 to the south. In 100 feet, Alligator Hole can be seen to the right.

3.0 Cross the Conecuh Trail again and head west back to Ditch Pond. At the pond, the trail turns to the northwest. Once the southeast bank of the pond is reached, the road forks. Take the left fork and head to the west along the banks of the pond.

3.1 Pass the Ditch Pond fishing pier to the left.

3.2 Cross a short wooden bridge over a feeder creek for Buck's Pond. After crossing the bridge, come to a T-intersection. (To the left is Buck's Pond.) Turn right and head to the west. Shortly, you'll cross the Conecuh Trail one last time. Continue just a few yards farther and come to five metal pipes spaced a few feet apart. This is the west end of the parking lot and the end of the trip.

Just off the trail is Alligator Hole.

Hike Information

Trail Contacts:
Conecuh National Forest, Andalusia, AL; (334) 222–2555 • **Forestry Supervisor**, Montgomery, AL; (334) 832–4470

Schedule:
Open year round. The ranger station is open from 7:00 A.M.–4:30 P.M. Monday–Friday. Camping is allowed in primitive areas and along some sections of the Conecuh Trail. Keep in mind that camping is restricted during hunting season. Check with the forest rangers before making plans.

Fees/Permits:
$2 per person day-use, $1 for children. Camping at primitive sites is $6 per day, $12 at improved sites with electricity and water. A state freshwater fishing license is required to fish in the ponds and lakes of the forest. A state hunting license is required for hunting.

Local Information:
[See Hike 8: Open Pond]

Local Events/Attractions:
[See Hike 8: Open Pond]

Accommodations:
[See Hike 8: Open Pond]

Restaurants:
[See Hike 8: Open Pond]

Organizations:
[See Hike 8: Open Pond]

Local Outdoor Retailers:
Brightwell's Athletic House, Andalusia, AL; (334) 222–1411

Maps:
USGS maps: Wing, AL • **Trail maps**—*available at the Conecuh National Forest Ranger Station, Andalusia, AL, or through their office by mail for $5 at (334) 832-4470. Two brochures, one entitled "Carnivorous Plants of Conecuh National Forest" and the other called "Camping in Conecuh National Forest," are available at no cost.*

North Loop Trail

Hike Summary

This trail is actually the northern loop of the Conecuh Trail *[see Hike 11]*. The loop provides 12 miles of easy walking that can be completed in one day. The path winds in and out of open forests and sections of dense, shady tree cover. You're likely to see plenty of wildlife. Eastern wild turkeys dart from the brush, and hawks sail overhead. Along the loop, away from campgrounds, there's a better chance of seeing an alligator—assuming you want to.

Hike Specs

Start: From the trailhead on AL 137
Length: 12-mile loop
Approximate Hiking Time: 6–7 hours
Difficulty Rating: Easy, over flat to gently rolling hills
Trail Surface: Sandy and grass-covered paths
Lay of the Land: Forest of magnolia, dogwood, holly, and longleaf pine; cypress ponds
Land Status: National forest
Nearest Town: Andalusia, AL
Other Trail Users: Motorists along a portion of dirt road; cyclists along the path
Canine Compatibility: Dog friendly—over easy trails; permit and leash required

Getting There

From Andalusia: Take U.S. 29 south for 9.7 miles. Turn left and head south on AL 137 for four miles. The parking area and trailhead will be on the left. ***DeLorme: Alabama Atlas & Gazetteer:*** Page 58 E5

The Conecuh National Forest provides some interesting hiking along the Conecuh Trail, which runs for about 20 miles. The bulk of the Conecuh consists of this one segment, the North Loop Trail.

There is plenty to take in along this loop. Over its 12-mile length, you will be treated to large cypress ponds and marshes, wide-open spaces, thick forest, sandy trails, and opportunities to see wildlife.

A state highway, Alabama 137, cuts the loop cleanly in half, seeming to create two distinctly different experiences. To the west, towering longleaf pines and grassland are home to woodpeckers and wild turkeys. The eastern side features a thick dogwood and magnolia forest with two large cypress ponds, blue herons, and yes, alligators.

Several species of frogs can be seen, and heard, along the North Loop Trail. These include the dusky gopher frog and the pine barren tree frog. The dusky gopher frog came close to being named the official state amphibian, but eventually lost out to the red hill salamander.

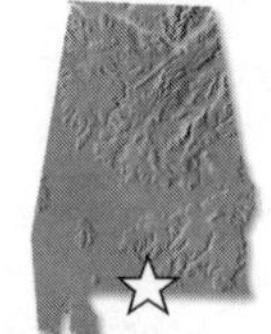

Because the trail is far removed from campgrounds and picnic areas, you may see foxes and will definitely see white-tailed deer. There is also a good chance of hearing a loud splashing sound as you pass the ponds. That's the sound of alligators retreating to safety.

The trail at the trailhead is wide and open.

A variety of plant life grows along the banks of the ponds, including the carnivorous pitcher plant, with its long tubular stem and covered cup at the tip. Water lilies blanket the surface of Gum Pond and Nellie Pond, blooming with large white flowers in the spring. Black-eyed Susans, honeysuckle, and blackberry bushes are also plentiful along the route.

Along the eastern half of the trail, the path crosses through several wooden cattle gates, used to keep cattle on designated grazing lands. Some farm fences are attached to the gates with plastic insulators, normally used for electrified fences. For safety, it's best to assume that all such fences are electrified.

Conecuh is the only national forest in the state to allow livestock grazing on the grasses of the forest—for a fee. Through this area, you'll see several areas that have been intentionally burned in recent years. The prescribed burns help increase the supply of grass for the cattle as well as reduce the chances of range wildfires.

Although the trail can readily be hiked in a day, some folks chose to camp out. The Forest Service permits camping, but asks that tents be pitched far from the trail. Be careful with fire. The best bet is to use a backpacking stove.

During hunting season, camping in Conecuh National Forest requires written permission of the Forest Service (except at Open Pond Recreation Area). Contact the Conecuh ranger office for dates of hunting seasons. If you hike the forest during hunting season, wear hunter orange.

MilesDirections

0.0 START from the AL 137 trailhead by crossing the highway to the west. Here, the first of many "Hiker Trail" signs will be seen. These signs are posted on the opposite side of all road crossings showing where the trail crosses. Here, the trail walks up a series of four wooden steps that go over a barbed wire fence surrounding the forest. A sign here reads "Trail Pond 2½ miles, Mossy Pond 3 miles." After crossing the stairs, the trail turns to the southwest. This first section is very open with towering long leaf pines and open, grassy terrain. Trail markers are white plastic diamonds and can be seen up to a half mile away through this area.

0.5 Cross a bridge.

0.9 Cross a dirt road.

1.4 Cross a bridge.

1.5 Turn to the south.

1.7 Cross a dirt road.

2.3 Cross a bridge.

2.4 Come to a small marsh and pond on the left. This is Trail Pond. Many blue heron call these ponds home.

2.5 The trail forks with a dirt road. Take the right fork and continue northwest.

2.7 Cross a dirt road and follow the trail west.

2.8 Cross another dirt road and head west.

2.9 A dirt road merges with the trail from the northeast. Continue to the west and in 50 feet a sign reads "Road closed March 10–October 18." Mossy Pond is on the right.

3.4 Pass a pond on the left and in 300 feet cross dirt FS 330D.

3.8 Cross a dirt road.

4.0 Cross a dirt road.

4.1 From here to the crossing of AL 137—3.1 mile away—is a controlled-burn area.

4.3 Come to a trail marker with three arrows pointing to the right. Continue east.

4.5 Come to a trail marker with three arrows pointing to the left. Go left and pass a bench on the right. A lush field is on the right behind a barbwire fence.

4.6 Climb the steepest hill on the trip, which isn't that steep. In 100 feet, cross a dirt road.

4.9 Pass a bench on the left and come to a fork. Go right.

5.2 Go right at the trail marker.

5.6 Go right at the trail marker.

6.7 Come to a T-intersection with a dirt road. Turn right and follow the road 100 feet to AL 137. After crossing the highway, another short set of stairs crosses over a barbwire fence.

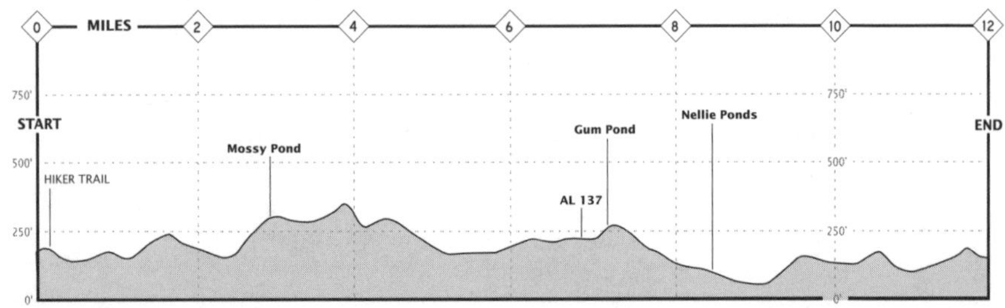

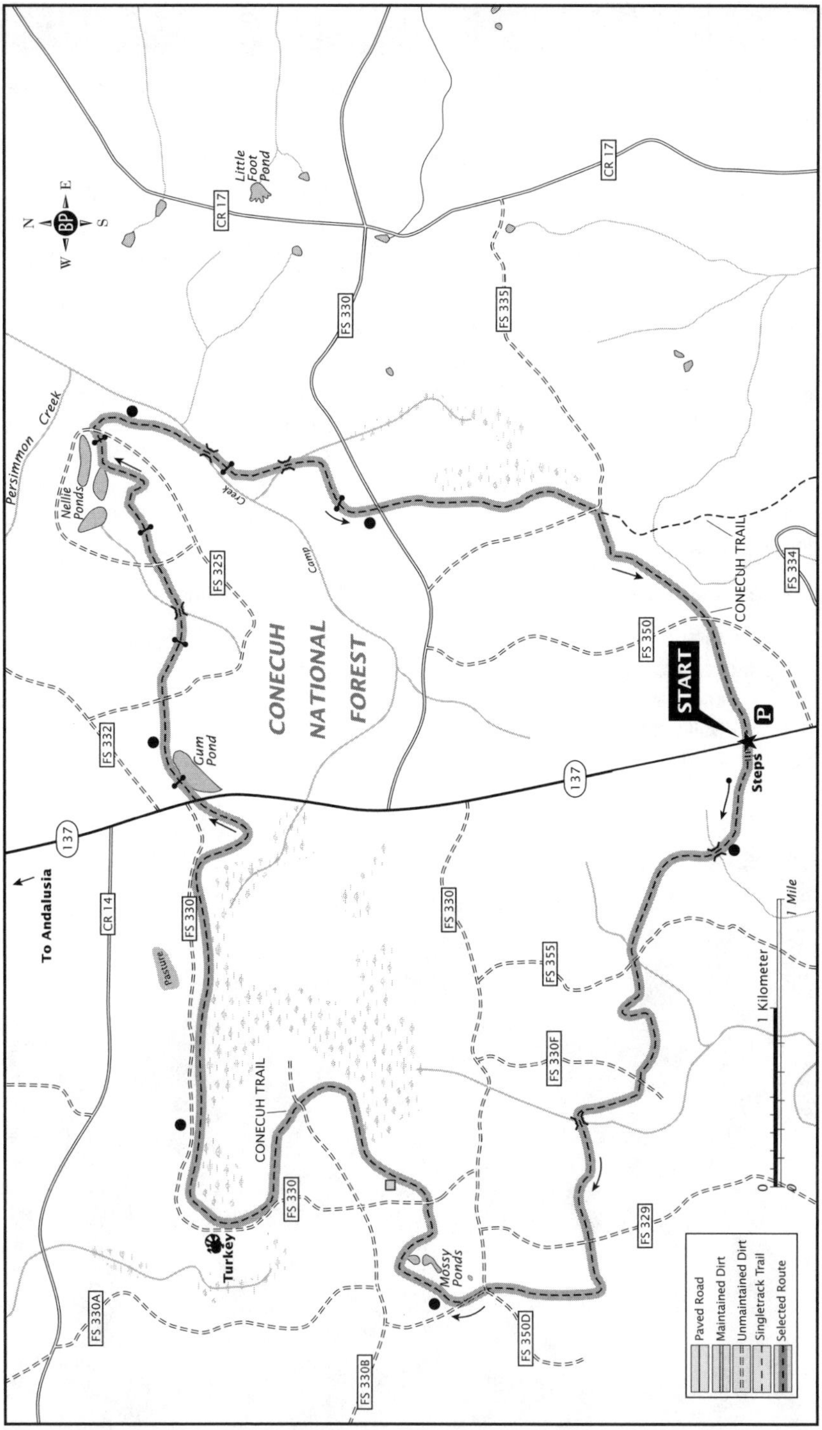

N
E
S
W
Little Foot Pond
CR 17
FS 330
FS 335
Persimmon Creek
Nellie Ponds
Camp Creek
FS 325
CONECUH NATIONAL FOREST
CONECUH TRAIL
FS 334
FS 350
START
Steps
137
FS 332
Gum Pond
To Andalusia
CR 14
Pasture
FS 355
FS 330F
1 Kilometer
1 Mile
0
FS 329
Turkey
Mossy Ponds
FS 350D
FS 330A
FS 330B
Paved Road
Maintained Dirt
Unmaintained Dirt
Singletrack Trail
Selected Route

MilesDirections (Continued)

7.0 Gum Pond is to the right.

7.1 Come to a T-intersection with a dirt road. Turn right. In 100 feet, the trail comes to the edge of the pond. The road turns to the right and dead ends in 50 feet. Turn left and continue to the northeast along the edge of the pond.

7.2 Pass through a cattle gate. The farm fence is attached to the gate with plastic insulators that make it look like it might be electrified.

7.3 Cross a dirt road.

8.3 Cross a dirt road. In 50 feet, pass through a cattle gate.

8.4 Pass the banks of Nellie Pond.

8.6 Pass through another cattle gate and cross a dirt road. A sign here that reads "Nellie Pond" and points back in the direction you just traveled, and "Blue Pond Recreational Area 3 miles."

9.1 Cross a bridge. After crossing, travel 75 feet and cross another bridge over a large marsh.

10.1 Climb a short set of wooden stairs over a barbwire fence and cross a dirt road. A sign here reads "Conecuh Trail."

10.9 Cross a dirt road. *[**FYI.** By turning left and heading down the road 30 feet, the Conecuh Trail continues to the south.]* A sign on the other side reads, "Highway 137 1 mile, Blue Pond Recreational Area ½ mile." Remember, the Conecuh, North Loop, and connectors all use the white diamond markers. Continue into the woods to the southwest.

11.4 Cross a dirt road.

12.0 Arrive at the trailhead.

The trail passes some thick pasture land.

Hike Information

Trail Contacts:
Conecuh National Forest, Andalusia, AL; (334) 222–2555 • **Forestry Supervisor**, Montgomery, AL; (334) 832–4470

Schedule:
Open year round. During hunting season, hunter orange must be worn and camping is restricted to Open Pond Recreational Area. The ranger station is open from 7:00 A.M.–4:30 P.M. Monday–Friday.

Fees/Permits:
Camping is allowed along the trail following National Forest Service guidelines. Camping is restricted to the Open Pond Recreational Area during hunting season. Camping at either Blue Pond or Open Pond Recreation Area is $6 per day at primitive sites is $6 per day, $12 at improved sites with electricity and water. State freshwater fishing license is required to fish in the ponds and lakes of the forest.

Local Information:
[See Hike 8: Open Pond]

Local Events/Attractions:
[See Hike 8: Open Pond]

Accommodations:
[See Hike 8: Open Pond]

Restaurants:
[See Hike 8: Open Pond]

Organizations:
[See Hike 8: Open Pond]

Local Outdoor Retailers:
Brightwell's Athletic House, Andalusia, AL; (334) 222–1411

Maps:
USGS maps: Carolina, AL • **Trail maps**—*available at the Conecuh National Forest Ranger Station, Andalusia, AL, or through their office by mail for $5 at (334) 832–4470. Two brochures, one entitled "Carnivorous Plants of Conecuh National Forest" and the other called "Camping in Conecuh National Forest," are available at no cost.*

Conecuh Trail

Hike Summary

The Conecuh Trail provides the best opportunity for an overnight hike in the Southeast and Gulf Coast regions of Alabama. The trail is just over 20 miles long and travels point-to-point, but connector trails allow for loop trips. The trail passes cypress ponds, and wildlife abounds.

Hike Specs

Start: From the trailhead on AL 137
Length: 19.2-mile point-to-point
Approximate Hiking Time: 10–12 hours
Difficulty Rating: Easy, over Forest Service roads and gentle footpaths
Trail Surface: Sandy and grass-covered paths
Lay of the Land: Forests of hickory, dogwood, magnolia, and longleaf pine; cypress ponds
Land Status: National forest
Nearest Town: Andalusia, AL
Other Trail Users: Cyclists on North Loop
Canine Compatibility: Dog friendly—over easy trails; permit and leash required.

Getting There

From Andalusia: Take U.S. 29 south for 9.7 miles. Turn left and head south on AL 137 for four miles. The parking area and trailhead will be on the left. ***DeLorme: Alabama Atlas & Gazetteer:*** Page 58 E5

Shuttle Point

From Andalusia: Take U.S. 29 south for 9.7 miles. Turn left and head south on AL 137 for five miles. Make a left onto CR 24 east and travel 0.5 miles. Make a right on FS 336A (CR 28) south. The road comes to a fee-station at a Y-intersection. Be sure to pay and place the receipt on your dash. Take the left fork. Travel one tenth of a mile and turn right. The Open Pond parking area is the dead-end of this road about 50 feet ahead. ***DeLorme: Alabama Atlas & Gazetteer:*** Page 58 F5

The North and Central regions of Alabama may have the most challenging hikes in the state, but the Southeast and Gulf Coast weigh in with wild and scenic landscapes. And the wildlife is especially diverse here. The Conecuh Trail, which winds through the Conecuh National Forest, provides an opportunity to take it all in over an easy trail.

Among the wildlife along the Conecuh Trail are white-tailed deer, red foxes, bobcats, and river otters. Eastern wild turkeys are plentiful, often popping out of the brush without warning. And of course, everyone who comes here wants to see an alligator. Well, the American alligator calls the ponds of Conecuh National Forest home. On the North Loop portion of the trail, listen for the loud splashes of alligators getting out of your way. (Although alligators are naturally afraid of humans, don't take chances: Stay a safe distance away.)

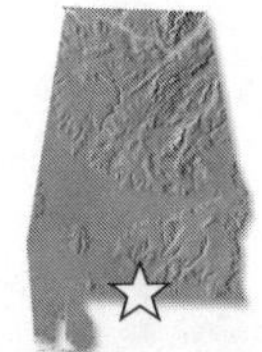

Conecuh wildflowers will be found everywhere along the trail from early spring to early fall.

The vegetation is as varied as the wildlife. Dogwood, holly, longleaf pine, magnolia, and cypress trees line the trail and ponds. Wildflowers such as black-eyed Susans brighten the landscape. At the ponds, look for the carnivorous pitcher plant. Many of the ponds are covered to overcrowding with water lilies.

The bulk of the Conecuh Trail uses the North Loop Trail *[see Hike 10]*. This 14-mile loop takes you far from campgrounds and recreation areas, past remote cypress ponds and marshes over predominantly sandy trails. Here is the best chance to see wild turkeys, herons, and alligators.

The next part of the Conecuh Trail passes by Blue Pond and Open Pond. Blue Pond is popular for fishing, canoeing, and picnicking, and provides a swimming beach. You'll find campsites near Open Pond.

The Conecuh Trail's lower portion, about five miles long, is a smaller version of the Five Runs Loop Trail *[see Hike 9]*. The Five Runs Trail uses Forest Service roads, while the Conecuh takes to the woods. This portion travels past three other ponds: Alligator, Ditch, and Buck's.

The trail also hits the banks of Five Runs Creek, a feeder stream for the Yellow River. A good time to hike here is during spring when wildflowers, pitcher plants, and orchids bloom on the banks of the creek and neighboring bogs. The Conecuh Trail then swings around to end at the bathhouse at Open Pond.

The trail is well blazed with white diamond markers on trees, spaced about 50 feet apart. Keep in mind that some connecting trails that help create loops also use an identical marker, such as the path just to the east of Open Pond *[see Hike 8]*.

MilesDirections

0.0 START from the AL 137 trailhead by crossing the highway to the west. Here, the first of many "Hiker Trail" signs will be seen. These signs are posted on the opposite side of all road crossings showing where the trail crosses. Here, the trail walks up a series of four wooden steps that go over a barbed wire fence surrounding the forest. A sign here reads "Trail Pond 2½ miles, Mossy Pond 3 miles." After crossing the stairs, the trail turns to the southwest. This first section is very open with towering long leaf pines and open, grassy terrain. Trail markers are white plastic diamonds and can be seen up to a half mile away through this area.

0.6 Cross a bridge.

1.1 Cross a dirt road.

1.6 Cross a bridge.

1.7 Turn to the south.

2.0 Cross a dirt road.

2.7 Cross a bridge.

2.8 Come to a small marsh and pond on the left. This is Trail Pond. Many blue heron call these ponds home.

2.9 The trail forks with a dirt road. Take the right fork and continue northwest.

3.1 Cross a dirt road and follow the trail west.

3.2 Cross another dirt road and head west.

3.3 A dirt road merges with the trail from the northeast. Continue to the west and in 50 feet a sign reads "Road closed March 10–October 18." Mossy Pond is on the right.

3.9 Pass a pond on the left and in 300 feet cross dirt FS 330D.

4.4 Cross a dirt road.

4.6 Cross a dirt road.

4.7 From here to the crossing of AL 137—3.1 miles away—is a controlled-burn area.

5.0 Come to a trail marker with three arrows pointing to the right. Continue east.

5.2 Come to a trail marker with three arrows pointing to the left. Go left and pass a bench on the right. A lush field is on the right behind a barbwire fence.

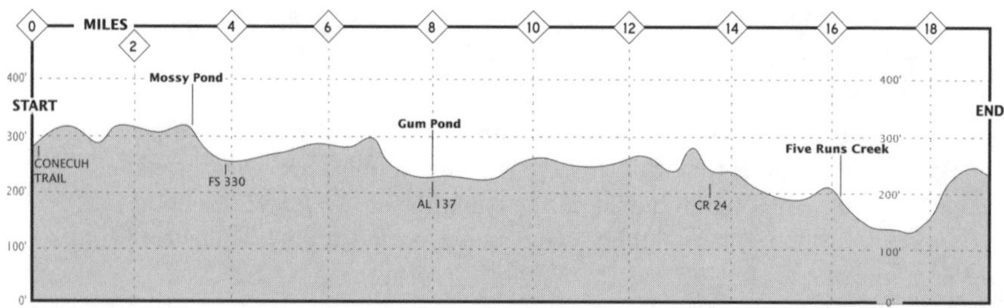

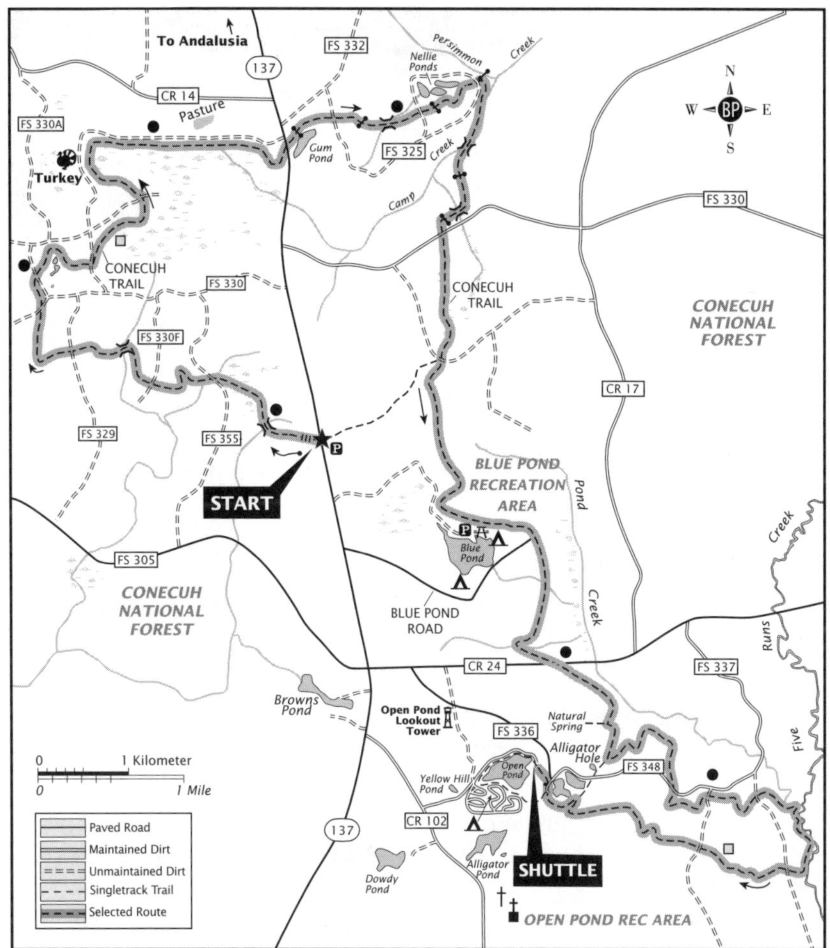

5.3 Climb the steepest hill on the trip, which isn't that steep. In 100 feet, cross a dirt road.

5.7 Pass a bench on the left and come to a fork. Go right.

6.1 Go right at the trail marker.

6.5 Go right at the trail marker.

7.8 Come to a T-intersection with a dirt road. Turn right and follow the road 100 feet to AL 137. After crossing the highway, another short set of stairs crosses over a barbwire fence.

8.0 Gum Pond is to the right.

8.1 Come to a T-intersection with a dirt road. Turn right. In 100 feet, the trail comes to the edge of the pond. The road turns to the right and dead ends in 50 feet. Turn left and continue to the northeast along the edge of the pond.

8.4 Pass through a cattle gate. The farm fence is attached to the gate with plastic insulators that make it look like it might be electrified.

8.5 Cross a dirt road.

MilesDirections (Continued)

8.8 Pass through another cattle gate.

9.0 Cross a bridge.

9.4 Cross a bridge.

9.6 Cross a dirt road. In 50 feet, pass through a cattle gate.

9.7 Pass the banks of Nellie Pond.

9.9 Watch the pond for alligators.

10.0 Pass through another cattle gate and cross a dirt road. A sign here reads "Nellie Pond" and "Blue Pond Recreational Area 3 miles."

10.6 Cross a bridge. After crossing, travel 75 feet and cross another bridge over a large marsh.

11.1 Cross a bridge.

11.8 Climb over a short set of wooden stairs over a barbwire fence and cross a dirt road. A sign here reads "Conecuh Trail."

12.7 Come to a dirt road. *[**FYI.** By crossing the road to the southwest, the trail completes the North Loop in 1.3 miles.]* Turn left here and head down the road 30 feet. A sign reads "Conecuh Trail" where the trail turns right and heads back into the woods. Don't be confused here! The Conecuh Trail, North Loop Trail, and connectors all use the white diamond markers.

13.0 The trail merges with a dirt road for 50 feet and reenters the woods to the southeast. In 200 feet, the brush and trees thicken as you reach a marshy area. Cross a creek.

13.2 Cross another creek.

13.3 Cross a dirt road and head up a short hillside.

13.5 The trail arrives at the Blue Pond Rec. picnic area. In 200 feet, cross the Blue Pond Road.

13.6 Cross a creek.

14.0 The trail bottoms out and crosses a creek.

14.2 Cross CR 24.

14.9 Come to a fork in the trail and go left. *[**FYI.** The right fork is a connector that forms a loop around Open Pond.]*

15.6 Cross a dirt road.

15.7 The trail merges with a dirt road for about 50 feet and then parts.

15.8 Cross a dirt road.

16.2 Cross a dirt road. In 100 feet, the path meets the banks of Five Runs Creek. The trail follows the creek for the next 0.6 miles.

17.3 Cross a dirt road. In 50 feet, cross a creek.

17.6 Cross another creek.

18.2 Reach a T-intersection and turn left toward Buck Pond. *[**FYI.** The right fork is part of the Open Pond Loop Trail.]*

18.9 Come to a fork and go right. *[**FYI.** The left fork is used for the Open Pond Loop.]* In 200 feet, cross a wooden bridge over a creek that feeds Buck Pond. After crossing, make a right turn and head to the north.

19.2 Arrive at the eastern Open Pond parking area and your shuttle car.

Although a fast traveler could easily hike the Conecuh in a single day, the hike is best enjoyed as an overnight trip. You can camp along the way, as long as you keep tents well off the trail itself. Use a backpacking stove in order to help prevent fires. Camping along any trail in Conecuh National Forest during hunting season requires written permission of the Forest Service (except at Open Pond Recreation Area). The Conecuh ranger office can supply the applicable dates. Plan to wear hunter orange if you hike during hunting season.

Hike Information

Trail Contacts:

Conecuh National Forest, Andalusia, AL; (334) 222–2555 • **Forestry Supervisor**, Montgomery, AL; (334) 832–4470

Schedule:

Open year round. During hunting season, hunter orange is required to be worn and camping is restricted to Open Pond Recreational Area. The ranger station is open from 7:00 A.M.–4:30 P.M. Monday–Friday.

Fees/Permits:

Camping is allowed along the trail following National Forest Service guidelines. Camping is restricted to the Open Pond Recreational Area during hunting season. Camping at either Blue Pond or Open Pond Recreation Area is $6 per day at primitive sites, $12 at improved sites with electricity and water. A state freshwater fishing license is required to fish in the ponds and lakes of the forest.

Local Information:

[See Hike 8: Open Pond]

Local Events/Attractions:

[See Hike 8: Open Pond]

Accommodations:

[See Hike 8: Open Pond]

Restaurants:

[See Hike 8: Open Pond]

Organizations:

[See Hike 8: Open Pond]

Local Outdoor Retailers:

Brightwell's Sporting Goods, Andalusia, AL; (334) 222–1411

Maps:

USGS maps: Wing, AL; Carolina, AL • **Trail maps**—*available at the Conecuh National Forest Ranger Station, Andalusia, AL, or through their office by mail for $5 at (334) 832–4470. Two brochures, one entitled "Carnivorous Plants of Conecuh National Forest" and the other called "Camping in Conecuh National Forest," are available at no cost.*

Chattahoochee Trail

Hike Summary

The Chattahoochee Trail provides an enjoyable stroll through the woodlands of the southeastern corner of Alabama. This hike actually combines several trails, providing close-up looks at a variety of plant and animal life. This is excellent flatland hiking for families with small children.

Hike Specs

Start: From the northwest end of the parking lot at Chattahoochee State Park ranger station
Length: 1.5-mile loop
Approximate Hiking Time: 1 hour
Difficulty Rating: Easy, along flat roads
Trail Surface: Clay and sand roads
Lay of the Land: Forest of dogwood, muscadine, oak, and loblolly and slash pine
Land Status: State park
Nearest Town: Dothan, AL
Other Trail Users: Equestrians and motorists
Canine Compatibility: Dog friendly—over a level route; bring water, because it is available only at the lake; leash not required

Getting There

From Dothan: Take U.S. 84 south for 14 miles to AL 95. Turn right and travel nine miles to the Chattahoochee State Park entrance on the left. Turn left between two stonewalls and travel down the dirt road (Upper Road) for 0.3 miles. Come to a fork in the road. Take the right fork (Chattahoochee State Park Road). The ranger station is located just to the right. An honor box for the entrance fee is here. Park and begin the hike here. ***DeLorme: Alabama Atlas & Gazetteer:*** Page 61 G10

The 600-acre Chattahoochee State Park is one of the smaller parks in the state, though it still provides an excellent hiking experience along trails lined with dogwood, muscadine, and oak. The park is situated close to the Chattahoochee River, which forms the mutual boundaries of Alabama, Georgia, and Florida.

The Civilian Conservation Corps built the facilities at Chattahoochee in the late 1930s. Throughout the park are remnants of CCC occupation, including a chimney where the main dining room was located, bunkhouses, and a star-shaped flagpole. Creeks in the park flow into the Chattahoochee River, and eventually into the Gulf of Mexico. The CCC built a stone dam to form a pond on one of these creeks.

The routes that combine to make up the Chattahoochee Trail include the Dogwood Trail (with a dogwood tree marking the start of the path), the

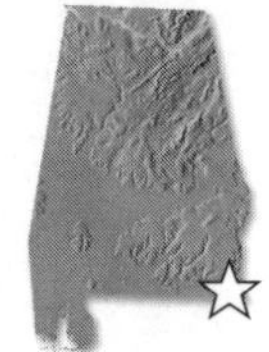

CCC Trail (where many camp remains can be found), and the K.O. Smith Trail, named for a former ranger of the park. The Buck Fever, Tortoise, and Scout trails round out the circuit. Individually each trail is very short, but they can be combined in many ways to provide hiking variety.

Some of the trails use a fire lane that forms the boundary around the park. Areas outside of the lane are privately owned, so visitors should not travel outside the boundary, especially during hunting season. (Hunting is not allowed within the park.)

Many of the trails pass through lightly forested grassy areas. These are excellent places for viewing white-tailed deer and Eastern wild turkeys. Other park inhabitants include opossums, foxes, and coyotes. Of particular interest is the gopher tortoise, which is one of only four species of tortoise in the United States. The gopher tortoise is known for burrowing in the sand. Hikers can examine the burrows—and perhaps a tortoise—firsthand along the Tortoise Trail.

MilesDirections

0.0 START at the parking lot at the ranger station and head to the northwest about 50 feet, crossing the dirt Upper Road. Come to a wooden sign that reads "Dogwood Trail" and the tree that gives the trail its name. Turn left onto the trail and head into the woods. At this point, the trail is an abandoned dirt road. Come to a fork—this is the intersection of the CCC Trail and the Dogwood Trail. Take the right fork onto the CCC Trail. The CCC Trail is marked with orange ribbons tied to trees. Two ribbons together indicate a turn in the trail just like painted blazes. The trail meanders through ruins of the old CCC camp.

0.1 The trail runs into a T-intersection with Upper Road. Turn to the left on the dirt road. Head up the road .05 miles and turn left on the K.O. Smith Trail.

0.3 Come to a split in the trail that reconnects.

0.4 Come to a T-intersection with the Buck Fever Trail and turn right. Small birds such as finches and cardinals dart back and forth along this stretch of the trail through the thickets.

0.5 The trail, still a dirt road, continues south but travels through a marshy area. On damp days, this could make travel rather muddy. Scrub and slash pines become more prevalent.

0.6 Reach a T-intersection with the Tortoise Trail and turn right. Look carefully for the tracks and burrows of the gopher tortoise along this section. In .05 miles, reach a picnic area at the CCC pond. Continue straight to the banks of the pond. A dirt road is here. Turn left and head down the road.

0.7 Come to a T-intersection with another dirt road. Turn left. Travel over the stone dam built by the CCC to form the pond to the north. Head to the sluice at the middle of the dam for excellent views of the pond and the marsh to the north. Turn around here and head back across the dam retracing the previous path.

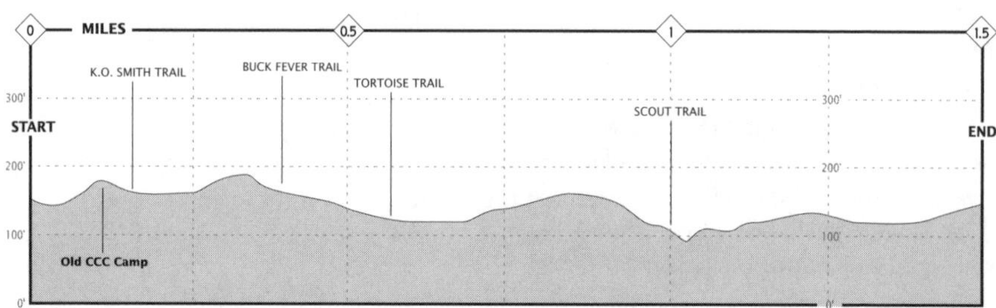

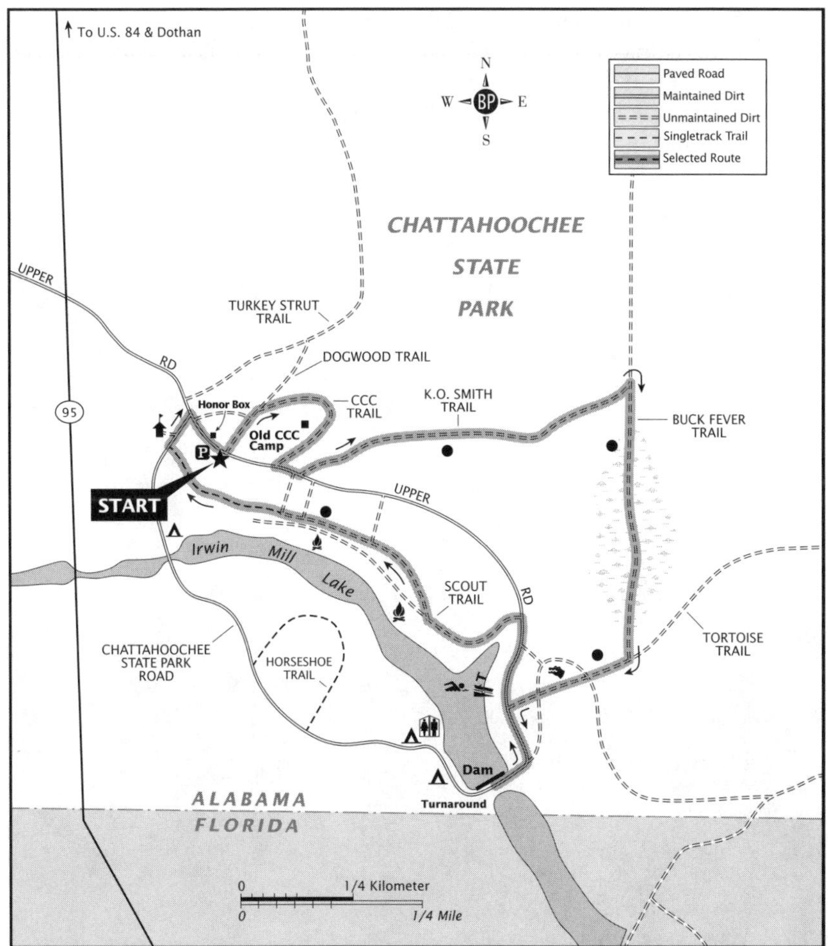

0.8 A few feet after stepping off the dam, the dirt road veers off to the left. Turn left here. In .05 miles, pass the Tortoise Trail on the right.

1.0 Come to a fork. The main dirt road continues to the northeast and a smaller, unused dirt road (the Scout Trail) heads off into the woods to the north. Take the Scout Trail to the left. Fifty feet into the woods, pass the first of three side roads on your right that lead back to the Chattahoochee State Park Road. By the third side road the main Scout Trail is hard to discern. There are no markings. The trail narrows to a small footpath, and the thick leaves make the trail look more like a deer trail.

1.4 Encounter another Scout Trail sign. Reach a T-intersection with the clay Chattahoochee State Park Road. Turn right.

1.5 Reach the parking lot at the ranger station.

The Scout Trail portion of the Chattahoochee Trail takes you to the 25-acre spring-fed pond built by the CCC. There is excellent bass fishing here (a freshwater license and park permit are required). You can also rent a boat. A short walk to the center of the dam provides excellent views of the pond to one side and the marsh and its wildlife on the other.

While in the area, consider visiting the nearby town of Dothan and its revitalized historic district, which includes the Wiregrass Museum of Art, the Dothan Area Botanical Gardens, and the Basketcase Dinner Theater.

The other side of the dam where a marsh is home to many species of wildlife.

Hike Information

Trail Contacts:

Chattahoochee State Park, Gordon, AL; (334) 522-3607

Schedule:

Year round

Fees/Permits:

$1 entrance fee for adults, 50 cents for senior citizens and children 12 and younger. $2 fishing freshwater license. $6.50 camping at primitive sites.

Local Information:

Dothan Area Conventions and Visitor's Bureau, Dothan, AL; 1-888-449-0212 or *www.dothanalcvb.com*

Local Events/Attractions:

National Peanut Festival, early November, Dothan, AL; 1-888-449-0212; *www.dothanalcvb.com/natlpnut.html—Dothan is known as the "Peanut Capital of the World." Each November, the town celebrates with this festival featuring rides, music, plenty of food, and of course, peanuts.* • **Landmark Park and Planetarium**, Dothan, AL (334) 794-3452 or *www.landmarkpark.com*—a unique mixture of an 1890's farmstead, wildlife studies, and planetarium all in a 100-acre park • **Adventureland Theme Park**, Dothan, AL; (334) 793-9100—*a variety of activities for the family including two 18-hole miniature golf courses, bumper boats, arcades, and a go-cart track.*

Restaurants:

Basketcase Dinner Theater, Dothan, AL; (334) 671-1117—*a unique restaurant that four to five times each year features the Opus Nostrum Dinner Theater. Reservations are required.*

Local Outdoor Retailers:

Neil's Sport Shop, Inc., Dothan, AL; (334) 793-0009 • **Southern Outdoor Sports**, Dothan, AL; (334) 793-4590

Maps:

USGS maps: Saffold, AL • **Park brochure**—*available free of charge at one of the honor boxes*

Wildlife Drive

Hike Summary

Wildlife Drive can be driven, but the best viewing is clearly on foot. The waterfowl and wildlife of the area are simply more approachable by foot. The scenery is varied, from areas of hardwood and pine to grasslands and cropland to marshes and the banks of the Chattahoochee River. More than 300 species of birds and 40 species of mammals have been spotted here.

Hike Specs

Start: From the parking lot at the Eufaula National Wildlife Refuge ranger station
Length: 7-mile loop
Approximate Hiking Time: 3½–4 hours
Difficulty Rating: Easy, due to flat walking
Trail Surface: Gravel road
Lay of the Land: Forests of longleaf and slash pine, hickory, and live oak; aquatic plants; farmlands
Land Status: National wildlife refuge
Nearest Town: Eufaula, AL
Other Trail Users: Motorists and cyclists
Canine Compatibility: Not dog friendly—due to the wildlife in the refuge; if you do take a dog, leash required.

Getting There

From Eufaula: Take U.S. 431 north for 7.1 miles. Turn right onto AL 285. Travel 1.9 miles and take a right onto Refuge Road. Travel 0.1 mile to a fork in the road. A sign that lists permitted activities separates the forks. Take the right fork and travel 0.2 miles to the ranger station and parking lot. ***DeLorme: Alabama Atlas & Gazetteer:*** Page 54 B5

Just the Facts... about Alabama

Nickname: *Heart of Dixie*

Motto: *Audemus Jura Nostra Defendere (We Dare Maintain Our Rights)*

Entered the Union: Dec. 14, 1819, as the 22nd state

Capital: *Montgomery*

Population: *4,062,608*

Area: *51,705 square miles, including 938 square miles of water surface*

Highest elevation: *Cheaha Mountain (2407 feet)*

Lowest elevation: *Sea level along the Gulf of Mexico*

Temperature-extreme averages:

Birmingham—January 46°F; July 80°F.
Mobile—January 52.5°F; July 81.3°F

Annual rainfall averages:

Birmingham—51.86 inches.
Mobile—62.23 inches

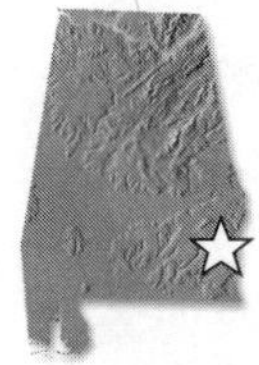

Canadian geese down for the winter.

The 11,184-acre Eufaula National Wildlife Refuge is situated along the banks of the Chattahoochee River, which forms the border between Alabama and Georgia. Maintained by the U.S. Fish and Wildlife Service, Eufaula Wildlife Refuge is a multifaceted preserve. The refuge oversees 2,200 acres of hardwood and pine forest and 1,100 acres of cultivated land. Farmers produce a variety of crops, like corn and short-grass hay, within the refuge, providing both income for the farmers and food for wildlife.

Eufaula Wildlife Refuge also has water, and lots of it: more than 4,000 acres of open water along the Chattahoochee River and its feeder creeks, plus more than 3,000 acres of marshland. Wildlife Drive takes you past all of this.

Although Wildlife Drive is touted as the driving tour of the refuge, the best way to experience the multitude of animal and bird life is on foot. The beauty of this hike is to walk quietly through the refuge and come upon a marsh or pond where ducks or Canadian geese are going about their daily business, or a family of white-tailed deer is foraging for food. Patience and quietness are rewarded with surprising and beautiful encounters.

Short gravel footpaths take you from Wildlife Drive to the two observation platforms within the refuge. Walking along the flat road is easy, and the most difficult part of the trip may be just the distance covered. Most of the areas you'll pass are wetlands, and in summer that could mean mosquitoes—so bring repellent.

The route described here is the summer route. Between November 15 and March 1, however, portions of the route are closed to protect wintering birds and to allow them to rest before heading north in the spring. Wildlife Drive is then shortened to about five miles.

MilesDirections

0.0 START from the parking lot at the ranger station and head to the northeast. Shortly, reach a T-intersection. Take a right. Pass a fenced equipment area with goats keeping the grass in shape. Alongside the road are short-grass hay fields, used not only as hay for cattle and horses but also to provide food for the wildlife that roam the refuge.

0.4 Come to a sign that reads "Wildlife Drive." The road makes a right and heads to the southeast.

0.7 Reach a fork. Turn left. *[**FYI.** To the right and southwest is the Winter Route, open year round to visitors. The left fork to the east is the Summer Route. This route is closed between November 15th and March 1st to allow wintering birds the chance to rest before heading back north.]* Pass the Goose Pen to the north—this is a large marshy area that's home to many migrating birds.

1.4 Pass another pond area. Flocks of Canadian geese, wood ducks, and cranes call this pond home.

1.5 The road intersects Wildlife Drive. Turn left and head to the southeast.

1.7 Come to a fork. Take the left fork and head to the southeast.

2.2 Come to a gravel side-road and turn onto it, heading northeast.

2.3 The road turns into a short gravel path and leads to the Houston Observation Tower a few feet ahead. The tower provides excellent views of a marsh area and the banks of the Chattahoochee River. After viewing, turn back to the southwest on the same path and road just traveled.

2.9 Return to Wildlife Drive and turn to the southeast. Come to a fork a few feet down the road and go left.

3.1 The road makes a turn to the south and heads along the banks of the Chattahoochee River along a levee called the Houston Dike. White tail deer love this area and it is not uncommon to see several walking along the banks.

3.4 Pass a dirt road on the right—this is the Winter Route loop.

4.4 Cross a small dam. On the north side is a pond that is part of the Houston Impoundment Area. On the south side is the Chattahoochee River.

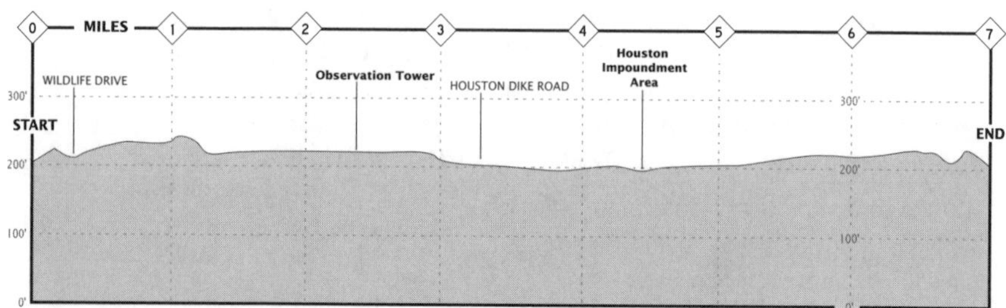

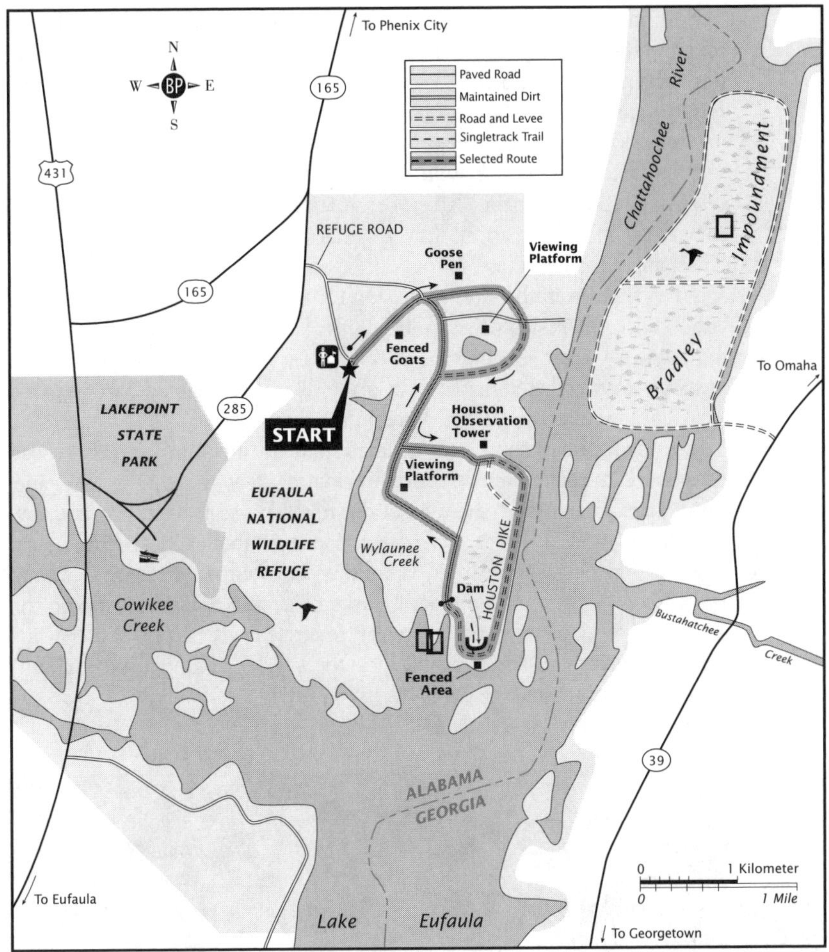

4.8 Pass through a gate that marks where the Winter Route ends.

5.3 Come to a fork in the road. Go left. *[**FYI.** The right fork heads back to the Houston Observation Tower (this is the Winter Route for Wildlife Drive).]*

5.7 Pass a side road. (This is the road taken back at mile 2.2 that leads to the Houston Observation Tower.)

6.2 Pass by the exit road from the Summer Route that was exited at mile 1.7 and continue to the northeast.

6.6 Pass a side road on the right. *[**FYI.** This is a short 0.2-mile out-and-back that travels to the Upland Waterfowl Viewing Platform. This platform (complete with FREE binoculars) overlooks the Upland Impoundment area.]*

6.7 Pass the entrance road of the Summer Route that was taken at mile 0.7.

7.0 Come to a fork and go left, back to the ranger station parking lot.

From the ranger station, the road heads southeast to the Summer Route Road. This road leaves Wildlife Drive and loops around the upland impoundment area and what is called the Goose Pen. These areas are used to grow corn during spring and summer and then are flooded in the fall to provide additional resting areas for wintering waterfowl.

Shortly after rejoining Wildlife Drive, the route turns east and heads toward the Chattahoochee River. Before it gets there, however, you'll reach the Houston Observation Tower. This tower provides views of the Chattahoochee River and surrounding wetlands.

After the tower, the road travels on top of the Houston Dike along the banks of the Chattahoochee. Be on the lookout for white-tailed deer foraging along the river. To the west of the river is the Houston impoundment area, a wetland created by the man-made dike. The wetland harbors wood storks, sand cranes, and other shorebirds.

The road circles the Houston impoundment area and begins to head back north on the return trip. This section features longleaf pine, slash pine, hickory, and live oak to the west of the road. Through here, bobcats, coyotes, and white-tailed deer are among the animals that call the refuge home.

A second observation deck, the Upland Waterfowl Viewing Platform, rounds out the trip and provides a panoramic view of Goose Pen and the upland impoundment wetlands that were circled earlier. The platform is a favorite spot for early-morning bird-watchers. A set of binoculars is mounted at the platform and are available free of charge.

One of many bird observation decks, this one overlooking the Chatahoochee River.

Hike Information

Trail Contacts:
Eufaula National Wildlife Refuge, Eufaula, AL; (334) 687–4065—*Office is open Monday–Friday 7:00 A.M.–4:30 P.M.*

Schedule:
Open year round. The trail is shortened to five miles in the fall and winter to protect wintering birds as they prepare to return to the north. Also, portions of the trail are closed in the fall for hunting. Check with the refuge office for exact dates.

Local Information:
Eufaula-Barbour County Chamber of Commerce, Eufaula, AL; (334) 687–6664; *www.ebcchamber.org/default.htm*

Local Events/Attractions:
Annual Eufaula Pilgrimage, first weekend of April, Eufaula, AL; 1–888–EUFAULA or *www.zebra.net/~pilgrimage—This annual event coincides with the blooming of the azaleas and dogwoods each spring and features tours of historic homes and churches, period costumes from when "Cotton was King," arts and crafts, and an antique show.* • **Blue Springs State Park**, Clio, AL; (334) 397–4875—*The big attraction at Blue Springs is a crystal clear spring water swimming hole. There are also picnic areas, playgrounds, tennis courts, and campgrounds.* • **Tom Mann's Fish World**, Eufaula, AL; (334) 687–3655—*This attraction features what is billed as the world's largest freshwater aquarium. In addition, a large number of Native American artifacts are on display.*

Accommodations:
Kendall Manor Inn, Eufaula, AL; (334) 687–8847 • **Lakepoint State Park Resort**, Eufaula, AL; 1–800–544–5253

Restaurants:
Phil's Bar-B-Que of Eufaula, Eufaula, AL; (334) 687–3337 • **Willy T's Chicken Fingers**, Eufaula, AL; (334) 616–0075

Other Resources:
U.S. Fish and Wildlife Service, Washington, DC at *www.fws.gov*

Local Outdoor Retailers:
Hummingbird Factory Outlet, Eufaula, AL; (334) 687–1930

Maps:
USGS maps: Georgetown, AL; Twin Springs, AL • **Drive map and interpretive brochure**—*available free of charge at the Eufaula National Wildlife Refuge office for free.*

Honorable Mentions

Southeast Alabama

Cypress ponds and crystal blue spring water lakes await the hiker in these little known hikes through Southeast Alabama that didn't make our top list. As with other honorable mention hikes in this book, these treks are typically shorter, but there is plenty of fantastic scenery and interesting wildlife to be seen. Pay a visit and let us know what you think. Maybe a particular hike should be upgraded, or maybe you know of some hidden trip that would make a great honorable mention.

(E) Frank Jackson State Park

The 2,050-acre Frank Jackson State Park is located in Opp, Alabama, 30 miles north of the Conecuh National Forest and only 10 miles east of Andalusia. In the center of the park is a 1,000-acre stream-fed lake. While there is the standard fare of fishing and swimming here, several very nice nature trails provide excellent hiking with one located on a small island in the center of the lake.

To get to the park, go east on U.S. 84 from Andalusia for 10 miles to Opp. Once in Opp, head north on U.S. 331 for about four miles. The park is on the right. For more information, call the park at (334) 493–6988 or 1–800–252–7275. ***DeLorme: Alabama Atlas & Gazetteer:*** Page 59 C8

(F) Eufaula Wildlife Refuge Nature Trail

As mentioned earlier in the Wildlife Drive chapter *[see Hike 13]*, the Eufaula Wildlife Refuge along the banks of the Chattahoochee River is a wonderful spot to view the widest variety of wildlife anywhere in the region. In addition to the hike described earlier, you may want to take in the Nature Trail, an out-and-back totaling about 1.5 miles.

The hike begins at the southwest end of the parking lot at the ranger station and is clearly marked with a wooden sign. The path is a dirt road it's entire length. To the left are open fields used to produce hay for livestock. To the right, slash pine and loblolly pine trees tower above the trail with magnolias and oaks intermingled.

Along the trail, many varieties of birds will be seen darting through the trees. In the fields, be sure to watch for white osprey looking for dinner as they follow the tractors cutting the hay.

For more information, contact (334) 687–4065. *[See Hike 13 for park directions and additional information.]* ***DeLorme: Alabama Atlas & Gazetteer:*** Page 54 B5

14. Bartram National Recreational Trail
15. Horseshoe Bend Trail
16. Tannehill Historic Trail
17. Blue Trail (South Rim Trail)
18. White Trail (Shackleford Point Trail)
19. Yellow Trail (Foothills Trail)
20. Green Trail (Peavine Falls Trail)
21. Lakeshore Trail
22. Chinnabee Silent Trail
23. Skyway Loop Trail
24. Rock Garden Trail
25. Nubbin Creek Trail
26. Cave Creek Trail
27. Odum Scout Trail

Central

Honorable Mentions

G. Talladega National Forest – Oakmulgee Unit
H. Red Trail
I. Treetop Trail
J. Bald Rock Trail
K. Rickwood Cavern State Park

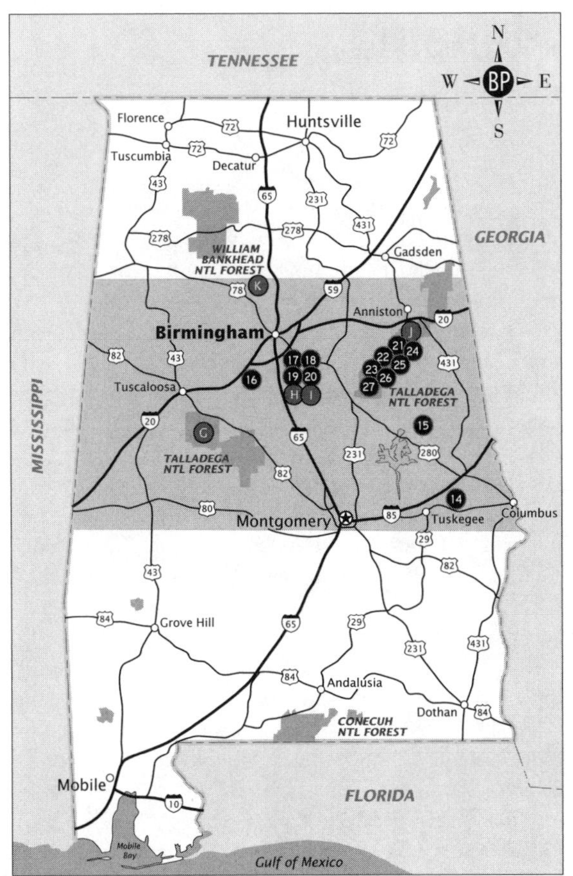
TENNESSEE
N
W
BP
E
S
GEORGIA
MISSISSIPPI
FLORIDA
Gulf of Mexico
Mobile Bay
Florence
Huntsville
Tuscumbia
Decatur
Gadsden
Anniston
Birmingham
Tuscaloosa
Montgomery
Tuskegee
Columbus
Grove Hill
Andalusia
Dothan
Mobile
WILLIAM BANKHEAD NTL FOREST
TALLADEGA NTL FOREST
TALLADEGA NTL FOREST
CONECUH NTL FOREST

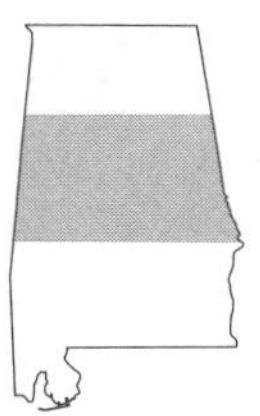

Alabama

Central Alabama

Central Alabama encompasses the area from just south of Birmingham to Montgomery, the state's capital. The southern boundary of this region, just below Montgomery, is known as the fertile Black Belt, the state's most lucrative cotton producing area. Geologically, Central Alabama forms the Piedmont Plateau, an area where the Appalachian Mountain Range terminates. The Central region provides the most challenging and most scenic treks you'll find in the state. It's in this region that you'll find the state's highest mountain, Cheaha Mountain, which stands 2,407 feet above sea level.

At Oak Mountain State Park just south of Birmingham, the hiker is treated to beautiful panoramas from atop Double Oak Mountain. In Cheaha State Park, the views are more spectacular from atop the tower at the summit of Cheaha. The park is surrounded by the enormous Talladega National Forest. Here you'll find the famous Chinnabee Silent Trail. This wonderful trail takes hikers past cascading Cheaha Falls and provides breathtaking views from atop narrow footbridges that traverse gorges leading to the falls. There are several other trails here with equal beauty and challenge such as the Odum Scout Trail, Skyway Loop, and Nubbin Creek Trail.

One of the more famous trails in the state, the Pinhoti Trail, travels the mountain ridges from the Talladega National Forest through Cheaha State Park for over 100 miles. The trail recently gained national attention when the White House placed it on the National Millennium Legacy Trail list, giving the trail full protection by the federal government and also funding for its maintenance. In addition, through the efforts of clubs such as the Alabama Appalachian Trail Club and the Alabama Trails Association, the Pinhoti is currently being touted as a new extension to the Appalachian Trail, linking it with the Appalachian Trail at Springer Mountain, Georgia.

For history buffs, to the east of Montgomery is Horseshoe Bend National Park. One of only two national park areas in the state, Horseshoe Bend provides an historic hike through this famous battlefield, the setting for the decisive 1814 battle between General Andrew Jackson and the local Native Americans. Jackson's victory resulted in the U.S.'s annexation of thousands of acres of land and the tragic displacement of the region's indigenous people along what would become known as the "Trail of Tears."

Bartram National Recreational Trail

Hike Summary

The Bartram National Recreational Trail in Tuskegee National Forest takes you on an easy jaunt through some nicely varied terrain. You'll stroll over gentle hills for the first half. Then, after crossing Alabama 186, the route makes its way through a dense magnolia forest over marshes as it travels toward Choctafaula Creek.

Hike Specs

Start: From the western trailhead on AL 29
Length: 15-mile out-and-back
Approximate Hiking Time: 7–9 hours
Difficulty Rating: Moderate, due solely to length. Easy hike over gently rolling hills and marshes.
Trail Surface: Sand path to the west; dirt path and boardwalks to the east through the marshes
Lay of the Land: Longleaf pines, oaks, and dogwoods through the western section; magnolia forest to the east through the bottomlands
Land Status: National forest
Nearest Town: Tuskegee, AL
Other Trail Users: Cyclists
Canine Compatibility: Dog friendly—over easy trail, but bring water; leash recommended

Getting There

From Tuskegee: Head north on I-85 to Exit 42. Head south on AL 186 for three miles to its intersection with U.S. 29 and turn left. Travel one mile and turn left on a short gravel road. Head down the road only 100 feet to the parking area, information sign, and trailhead. ***DeLorme: Alabama Atlas & Gazetteer:*** Page 46 C5

The Bartram National Recreational Trail was named for William Bartram, the son of famed naturalist John Bartram. Born in Philadelphia in 1739, William spent a great deal of his life under the wing of his famous father. Dubbed Botanist Royal by George III, William's father was far and away the most respected botanist in the colonies. In 1765 father and son embarked on an expedition for the King to locate the source of St. John's River, leading them through Georgia and Florida. Though this would be the elder Bartram's last expedition, it was only the start for William. In 1773, William set out to explore and document the upcountry South, before Europeans would later transform the landscape and disturb the indigenous cultures. The record of this trip, *Travels through North and South Carolina, Georgia, East and West Florida* (1791), is an American classic and became a tremendous inspiration to such naturalists as Henry David Thoreau and John Muir.

This trail runs along a portion of the route historians believe Bartram traveled. Using land features and historic sites from his journal, historians

reconstructed Bartram's path. The western trailhead is believed to be the site of a Native American colony described in his travel log. Benches along the way share quotes from his observations. The full trail is 8.5 miles long, but a portion of it was closed indefinitely because of a bridge washout at Choctafaula Creek at the 7.5-mile marker.

The Bartram National Recreational Trail serves up interesting contrasts for a hiker. For its first half, from the western trailhead to the picnic area at the 3.5-mile mark, the trail travels up and down gently rolling hillsides over a sandy footpath. The forest is tall longleaf pine atop low ridges. Through the ravines, the path is lined with oaks, dogwoods, and muscadine.

After the picnic area, the trail crosses Alabama 186 and begins to travel through large marshes and near Choctafaula Creek. Many varieties of wildflowers adorn the way, filling the air with fragrance during spring and summer. The area becomes thick with magnolia trees as the trail heads west and southwest over boardwalks and dirt paths.

Expect mosquitoes during some periods of spring, especially in and around the marshes. Also, spring rains can put this section of trail deep in mud. Be aware that the trail is popular with mountain bikers. Of all the trails visited in researching this book, the Bartram was the busiest by far.

MilesDirections

0.0 START from the western trailhead/ parking area off of U.S. 29. In 50 feet, come to the first bench. White blazes mark the trail. *[**FYI.** Throughout the hike you will see short strips of rubber mat across the trail. These are used to prevent erosion.]*

0.1 Come to fork and go right.

0.3 Cross a footbridge and come to a fork. Take the left fork. In 50 feet, turn to the southwest where the two trails rejoin.

0.6 Come to a fork and go right

1.3 Come to a dirt road and cross it diagonally—you will see the Bartram National Recreation Trail sign on the other side.

1.4 *[**FYI.** Note the firebreaks alongside the trail.]*

2.1 Come to a fork and go left. *[**FYI.** The right stem leads to a campsite.]*

2.3 Come to the road at its "elbow" and head straight across.

2.8 *[**FYI.** Muscadine can be seen in the trees.]*

3.7 Come to a T-intersection with Ranger Station Road. *[**FYI.** If you turn right, the ranger station is 0.5 miles down the road.]* Turn left onto the road and travel 50-feet. On the right is a gravel road heading back into the woods. Next to the road is a Bicentennial historic marker telling about William Bartram. Turn right here and head into the woods on this gravel road.

4.4 Come to FS 900. Turn left onto the road and walk about 50 feet to AL 186. Cross the highway, to the FS 900 sign. Walk up the dirt road another 50 feet and you'll see the white blazes heading into the woods on your right. Reenter the woods.

4.6 *[**FYI.** Watch for snakes sunning themselves on the boardwalk.]*

6.3 Come to a dirt road. Turn left and follow the road 100 feet—the white blaze can be seen on the right where you'll reenter the woods.

7.5 Come to the edge of Choctafaula Creek and the bridge that used to cross the creek—it's now in the creek. Orange ribbons are tied across the path indicating that this is the end of the road. Turn around and retrace you tracks back to the trailhead.

15.0 Arrive back at your vehicle.

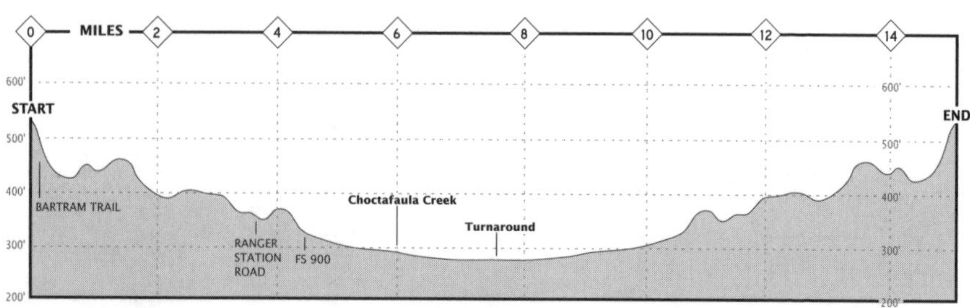

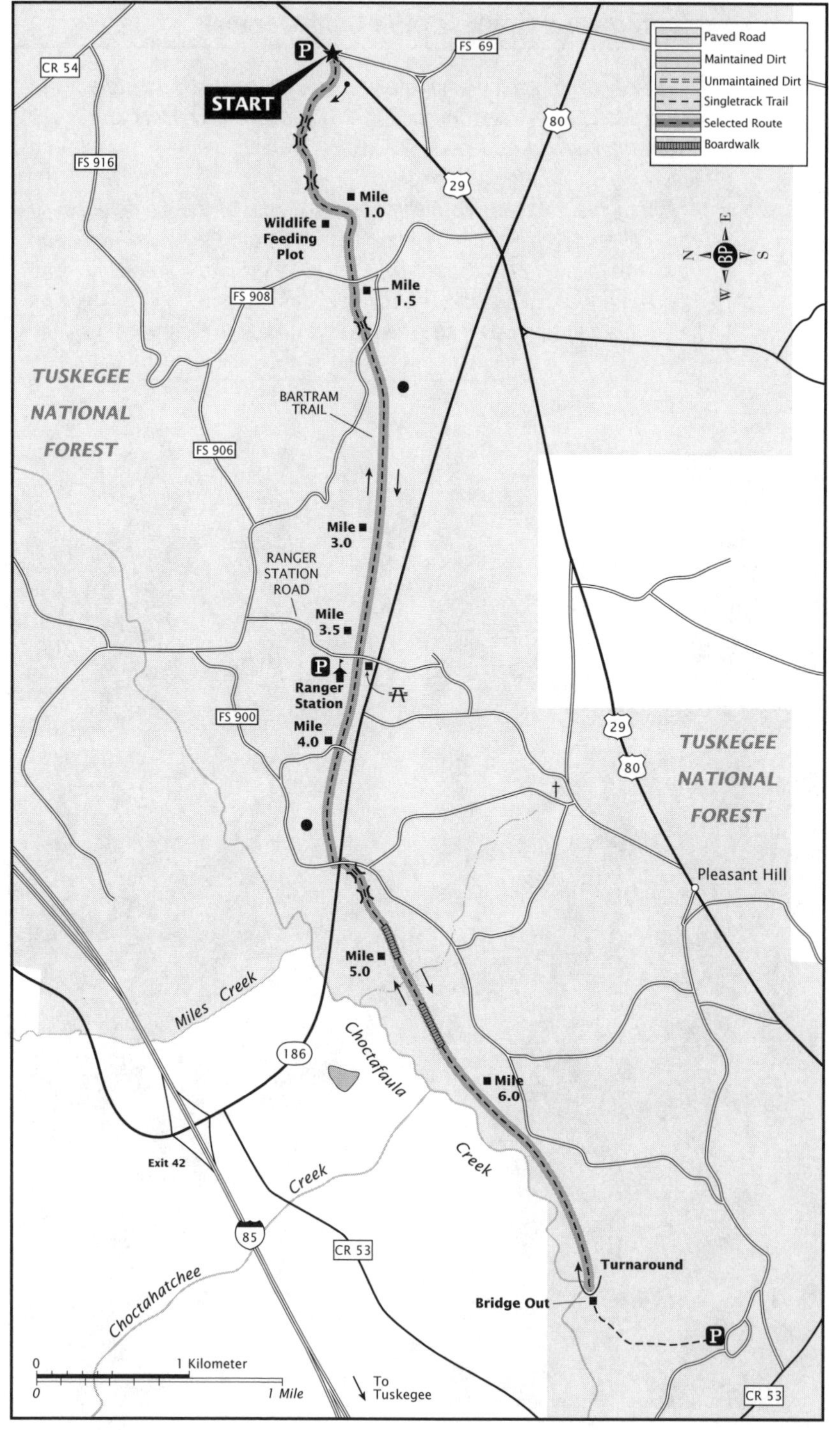
Paved Road
Maintained Dirt
Unmaintained Dirt
Singletrack Trail
Selected Route
Boardwalk
START
CR 54
FS 69
FS 916
FS 908
FS 906
FS 900
80
29
Mile 1.0
Wildlife Feeding Plot
Mile 1.5
TUSKEGEE NATIONAL FOREST
BARTRAM TRAIL
Mile 3.0
RANGER STATION ROAD
Mile 3.5
Ranger Station
Mile 4.0
Pleasant Hill
Mile 5.0
Miles Creek
Choctafaula Creek
186
Mile 6.0
Exit 42
Creek
85
CR 53
Choctahatchee
Turnaround
Bridge Out
0
1 Kilometer
1 Mile
To Tuskegee

Montgomery: Cradle of the Confederacy

The city of Montgomery holds a very special place in the history of the South. Montgomery was founded in 1817 and quickly became a major cotton market and river port. The capital of Alabama was moved from Tuscaloosa to Montgomery in 1847.

Montgomery earned its distinction as Cradle of the Confederacy in 1861 when seven Southern states seceded from the Union. Jefferson Davis was named President of the Confederate States of America, with Montgomery as its capital. The city held this honor for only six months before the decision was made to move the capital to Richmond, Virginia.

The trail is fairly open through the western half, so it's easy to see a cyclist approaching. But keep a careful eye out for them in the eastern half through the dense woods. And as nice as the trail is, there's no avoiding the sounds of nearby Alabama 186 and Wire Road on this half of the route.

The trail is well marked. White paint blazes are spaced between 50 and 100 feet apart. At the road crossings, markers on both sides of the road indicate the trail. Markers show the mileage along the trail every half mile.

Just about any member of the family can hike the Bartram Trail out-and-back in one day, but camping is allowed if you want to make it an overnight trip. Camping is permitted anywhere along the trail within the forest. During hunting season, however, camping is restricted to designated areas and requires a permit. If you plan to hike in fall or winter, contact the ranger office for hunting information and additional guidelines.

While in the Tuskegee National Forest, you may want to check out the Tsinia Wildlife Viewing Area, a 125-acre area set aside for the viewing of animals in their natural habitat. Patience and silence are often rewarded with sightings of white-tailed deer, turkeys, hawks, raccoons, or any of a variety of birds. The viewing area is at the intersection of Interstate 80 and Alabama 83.

Hike Information

Trail Contacts:

Tuskegee National Forest, Tuskegee, AL; (334) 727-2652—*The ranger office is open Monday–Friday, 7:30 A.M.–5 P.M.*

Schedule:

Open year round

Fees/Permits:

No fee to hike the trail. Camping is allowed along the trail using the "dispersal method" and by following standard National Forest Service regulations. Camping is allowed only by permit and in designated areas during hunting season (contact the ranger office for dates).

Local Information:

Tuskegee Area Chamber of Commerce, Tuskegee, AL; (334) 727-6619

Local Events/Attractions:

George Washington Carver Museum, Tuskegee, AL; (334) 727-3200 • **The Oaks**, Tuskegee, AL; (334) 727-3301—*Built in 1899 by the students and staff of Tuskegee University, this was the family home of Booker T. Washington.*

Maps:

USGS maps: Tuskegee, AL; Little Texas, AL • **Brochures** *available free of charge at the ranger office. Maps are available at the ranger station for $5.*

Horseshoe Bend Trail

Hike Summary

This easy trek takes you along gravel paths across forested hillsides. The trail uses interpretive exhibits to trace the Battle of Horseshoe Bend, which ended the Creek Indian War in 1814 and started General Andrew Jackson on the road to fame, and ultimately the White House.

Hike Specs

Start: From the picnic area one-tenth of a mile from the headquarters of Horseshoe Bend National Military Park
Length: 2.8-mile loop
Approximate Hiking Time: 2 hours
Difficulty Rating: Easy, over gently rolling hills
Trail Surface: Gravel
Lay of the Land: Rolling, grassy hills; trees including white oak, hickory, chestnut, and dogwood
Land Status: National military park
Nearest Town: Alexander City, AL
Other Trail Users: None
Canine Compatibility: Dog friendly—over easy trail; bring water; leash required

Getting There

From Alexander City: Take AL 22 north for 13 miles to AL 49. Turn right (south) onto AL 49 and travel one mile. The park entrance is on the left, marked with a National Park Service sign. ***DeLorme: Alabama Atlas & Gazetteer:*** Page 39 D8

Horseshoe Bend National Military Park, just east of Alexander City, is a serene place, far enough out of the way that you'll rarely have to contend with crowds. Operated by the National Park Service, the park is located at a meander, or horseshoe, in the Tallapoosa River. The spit of land within this horseshoe provide the setting for the battle that ended the Creek Indian War (1813–1814).

No sooner than Europeans arrived in the area, they were bartering heavily with the Creek Indians, and this trade forged a bond between the two groups. By the end of the American Revolution, this friendship continued as the Creeks and the Americans signed an agreement guaranteeing the Creeks land.

Throughout the years leading up to the war, many of the tribes in the South trusted U.S. Indian Agent Benjamin Hawkins and his programs for social improvement, especially in agriculture. By 1810, the Creek Nation

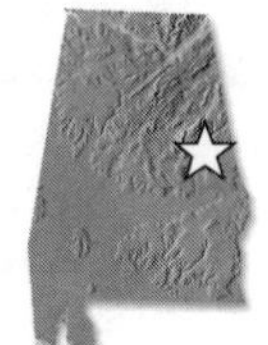

had fractured into two principal camps. The Red Sticks faction was fiercely nationalistic and feared the expansion of white settlements. In 1813 a group of Red Sticks were told erroneously that war had broken out between the United States and the Creek Nation. The Red Sticks attacked and killed several frontier families.

A monument commemorating the Battle of Horseshoe Bend, and a cannon used in the assault.

A Creek tribal council captured and executed those involved in the murders. Red Stick chief Menawa vowed revenge on those connected with the executions and pledged to remove whites from the region. And with that, the Creek War began.

MilesDirections

0.0 START from the picnic area located 0.1 miles from the visitor center. Look for the "hiker" emblem and head into the woods here. The trail is basically a gravel path throughout the entire trip. There are no markers except where the trail crosses roads. The "hiker" emblem will show you where the path reenters the woods.

0.1 The trail tops out and comes to a T-intersection in the woods. (This is where the loop later rejoins itself.) Turn right. In 200 feet, reach another T-intersection. Turn right and engage a rather steep climb. *[**Option.** By turning to the left, you can take a short out-and-back walk to an overlook where Andrew Jackson set his battle line.]*

0.2 *[**FYI.** From "The Overlook," look to your right at the series of white poles across the field. These indicate where the huge Upper Creek barricade once stood.]* Head down the asphalt sidewalk to the parking area 200 feet then turn left and head another 100 feet to reenter the woods on the gravel trail.

0.4 *[**FYI.** Cross Jackson's main line where the Tennessee Militia / 39th U.S. Infantry began the assault.]*

0.5 Come to a fork and go right.

0.6 Reach Exhibit 1, known as the "Island." The view of the Tallapoosa is expansive here, up to 600 feet across. *[**FYI.** Straight ahead is a small 15-acre island in which Lt. Jesse Bean's Tennessee Militia encamped, preventing the Red Sticks from retreating to this position. To the right is the AL 49 Bridge.]* Turn around and retrace the trail back to the fork.

0.7 Return to the fork and turn right.

0.9 Reach Exhibit 2. Head down the sidewalk 100 feet to the parking area. Turn left and in 100 feet cross the park road and reenter the woods on a gravel path.

1.4 Cross the park road.

1.5 *[**FYI.** Topping out on a hill, the trail arrives at the Tohopeka (a Creek word meaning "fort") Village Overlook. Below, the Red Stick's retreated to this grassy field directly in the curve of the "horseshoe" in hopes of the river protecting them from attack; however, Jackson's tribal allies swarmed across the river to attack this position by a surprise attack.]*

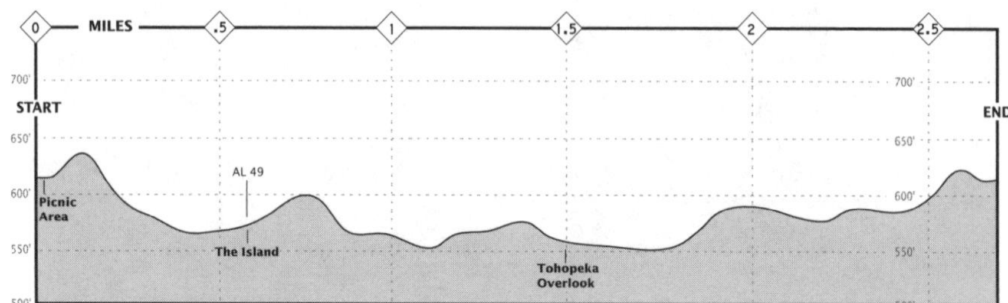

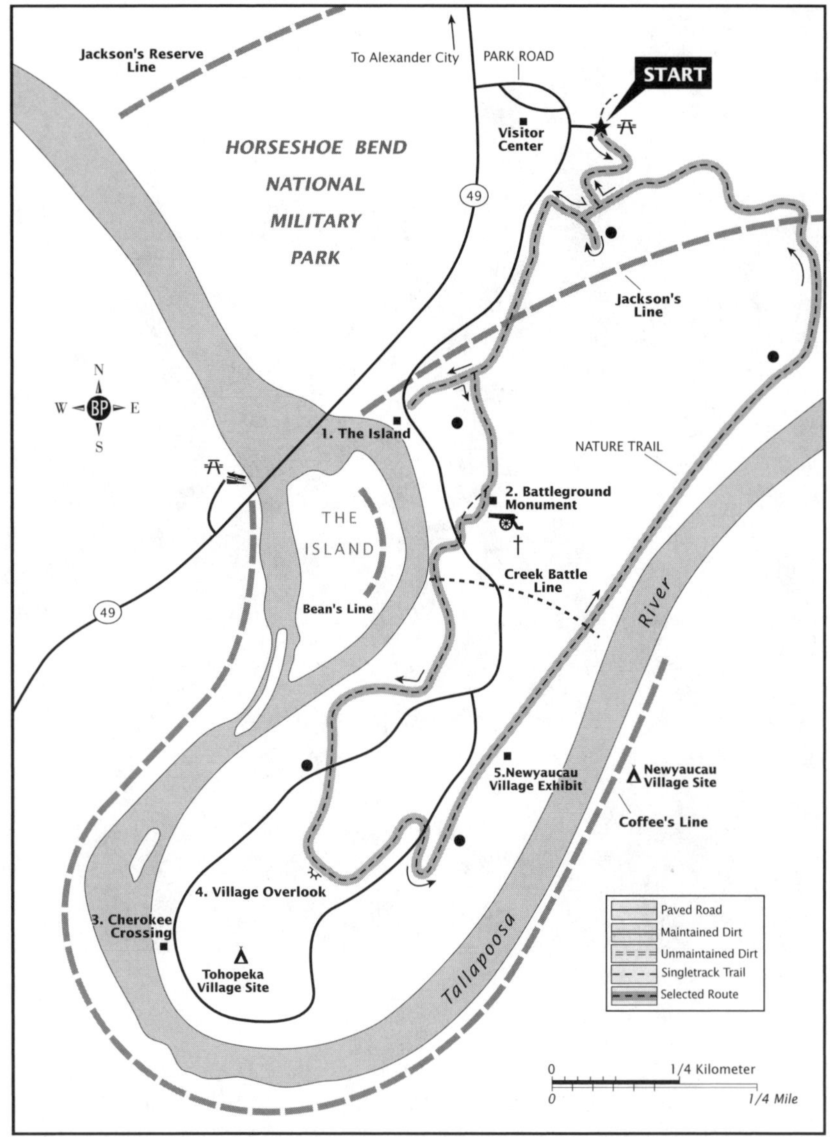

1.6 Reach Exhibit 4. [***FYI.*** *This was the site of an Upper Creek refugee camp for tribal families to relocate after battles elsewhere in the region.]*

1.7 Cross the park road.

1.9 Reach Exhibit 5. [***FYI.*** *Across the river stood the Newyaucau Village. The Georgia militia burned the village and forced its inhabitants to join the other fleeing refuges at Tohopeka.]*

2.7 This is where the loop reconnects with the first section of trail. Turn right.

2.8 Arrive at the picnic area.

A view of the Tallapoosa River.

Andrew Jackson was in charge of U.S. forces. Despite outnumbering the Creeks in every battle, his troops could not bring a decisive end to the war. The situation became worse in July of 1813 when a group of Creeks ambushed a Red Stick ammunition train. The Red Sticks then massacred 250 settlers in Fort Mims, just outside present-day Bay Minette, Alabama.

The war raged for two years, until at last it came to this location—which was called *cholocco litabixee* ("horses flat foot or hoof") by the Creeks, Horseshoe Bend by the United States. On the winning side of the battle were 2,000 men from a Tennessee militia and 600 allied Cherokee and Creek Indians. By the end of the battle, 1,000 Red Sticks lay dead.

The end of the war brought a treaty that turned over 21 million acres of land to the United States and relocated most of the Creeks to Oklahoma along what became known as the Trail of Tears. Those Creeks who fought alongside Jackson were allowed to stay and establish a Poarch Creek Reservation. Formed in 1836, just north of Atmore, the reservation is home to over 2,000 Creeks Indians.

The path at Horseshoe Bend Park passes most of the exhibits that describe the battle. At each exhibit, signs describe what to look for. There are benches for rest, and a roof over the exhibit for shade.

Pick up a free brochure from the visitor center before starting out. The brochure describes the exhibits and the battle in more detail. You can see a 10-minute slide show at the visitor center that gives an overview of the battle and the park. Admission to the park is free, but a donation is requested to help maintain the facility.

Hike Information

Trail Contacts:

Horseshoe Bend National Military Park, Davidson, AL; (256) 234–7111 or *www.nps.gov/hobe—open seven days a week, 8am–5pm, closed December 25*

Schedule:

Open year round

Fees/Permits:

No fee required. A donation to support maintenance is requested.

Local Information:

Alexander City/Lake Martin Chamber of Commerce, Alexander City, AL; (256) 234–3461 or *www.alexandercity.org*

Local Events/Attractions:

Reenactment of the Battle of Horseshoe Bend, last weekend of March, Horseshoe Bend National Military Park, Davidson, AL; (256) 234–7111

Accommodations:

Mistletoe Bough Bed and Breakfast, Anniston, AL; (256) 329–3717 or 1–877–330–3707; *www.bbonline.com/al/mistletoe*

Maps:

USGS maps: Buttston, AL • **Map and brochures**—*available for free at the visitor center*

Tannehill Historic Trail

Hke Summary

The ironworks at Tannehill produced many iron implements used by the Confederate army during the Civil War. The ironworks, which were restored to working condition in 1976, are today the centerpiece of Tannehill Ironworks Historical State Park. The Tannehill Historical Trail travels around the buildings of the ironworks and its furnace. Heading into the woods, the trail encounters the rolling blue-green waters of Roupes Creek and the ruins of the homes of slaves who worked at the ironworks.

Hike Specs

Start: From the visitor center parking lot at Tannehill Ironworks Historical State Park
Length: 4.2-mile loop
Approximate Hiking Time: 2–3 hours
Difficulty Rating: Easy, over wide paths and roads
Trail Surface: Packed clay and dirt
Lay of the Land: Live oak and hickory forest
Land Status: State historical park
Nearest Town: Bessemer, AL
Other Trail Users: Cyclists
Canine Compatibility: Dog friendly—with easy walking; ample water available; leash required

Getting There

From Birmingham: Take I-465 south for 13 miles to Exit 1 (Bessemer/McCalla). Turn left onto Eastern Valley Road and travel 7.3 miles. A sign on the left side of the road indicates the turn to Tannehill Park Road. Turn left onto this road and travel 0.5 miles to the park gate. After paying the fee, continue straight for about 100 feet to the visitor center parking lot. ***DeLorme: Alabama Atlas & Gazetteer:*** Page 30 H3

At one time, Birmingham and its environs rivaled the steel production machine of Pittsburgh and helped keep the Confederate army supplied with weapons. In 1830, Daniel Hillman came to Alabama from Pennsylvania and built a forge along Roupes Creek. Two years after setting up the operation and well before he had a chance to see the fortune that would be produced by the forge, Hillman died. A local farmer, Ninian Tannehill, purchased the forge.

Three tall furnaces were constructed on the site with the use of slave laborers who cut the sandstone bricks by hand. By 1862 the ironworks was in full swing, producing pig iron for the Confederacy. On March 31, 1865, the 8th Iowa Cavalry of the U.S. Army shelled and set fire to the foundry. A few miles up the road, Union troops torched the slave quarters.

A businessman bought the ironworks after the Civil War and tried to rebuild it, but times were bad and the facility was eventually abandoned and soon overgrown.

This brings us to the 1970s, when the state of Alabama and several colleges resurrected the site. Archaeological digs uncovered the old blower house and the main furnace. The furnace was rebuilt and fired up once again. It is now listed on the National Register of Historic Places.

The park encompasses more than 1,500 acres of forest just south of Bessemer. Forty historic structures of the period (from 1830 to 1870) have been brought in and restored for the public to view. Local craftspeople display the making of quilts, furniture, and pottery at the site between March and November of each year.

The Tannehill Historical Trail takes you through the major sites of the park. The trail itself is actually a combination of four separate routes: the Furnace Trail, Slave Quarters Trail, Old Bucksville Stage Road, and Iron Road. Along its route, the trail passes through thick oak and dogwood forests and along several creeks, including Roupes Creek, which helped power the furnace.

Beginning at the visitor center, the path first leads to the Alabama Museum of Iron and Steel, which exhibits many of the artifacts discovered through the years at the site. The trail also passes Plank Road, which features cabins from the mid to late 1800s.

Farther up the trail is the main attraction, the Tannehill furnace. A long wooden walkway leads to the top, and you are invited to stroll around the furnace as well as the blower house next to it.

As the trail moves into the woods away from the campgrounds, it joins the Slave Quarters Trail. You'll pass the foundations of several of the slave

MilesDirections

0.0 START from the visitor center parking lot. Head to the southwest over the paved park road. In 100 feet it becomes gravel. Continue to the southwest toward the Museum of Iron and Steel at the top of a small hill. Travel down the right side of the museum to the north along the gravel road. Behind the museum, turn left and head west down a series of cement stairs.

0.1 Cross a wide cement dam with a creek flowing over it to the north. It's shallow, but requires getting a little wet. Come to a fork and go left—this dirt road is the Furnace Trail.

0.2 Pass a set of cement stairs that leads to Plank Road and the craft cabins next to the trail to the left. Continue to the southeast and the wide white water of Roupes Creek will first be seen to the left.

0.3 Arrive at the furnace and blower house. Continue 300 feet to the southeast until the Snead House is reached (originally built in 1840).

0.4 Cross Folsom Bridge, named after former governor "Big Jim" Folsom. The trail turns into gravel Iron Hill Road. (This is where the loop rejoins itself for the return trip.) In just a few feet, the trail forks. Go straight—this is the Slave Quarters Trail. *[**FYI.** The short trail to the left leads to the creek.]*

0.5 Pass a small amphitheater to the right used for nature and historical lectures.

0.6 The trail is moving between two ridges.

0.8 Come to the "Slave Cabin Sites Circa 1860" sign. Keep an eye out through the next 0.4 miles for the foundations of the cabins.

1.0 A sign on a tree here says, "C.S. Army Quarters Furnace Help." Continue for 100 feet and pass a bench on the left and an old road to the right that leads to a second amphitheater.

1.2 The dirt Old Bucksville Stage Road merges in from the east (the right). Turn right onto this road.

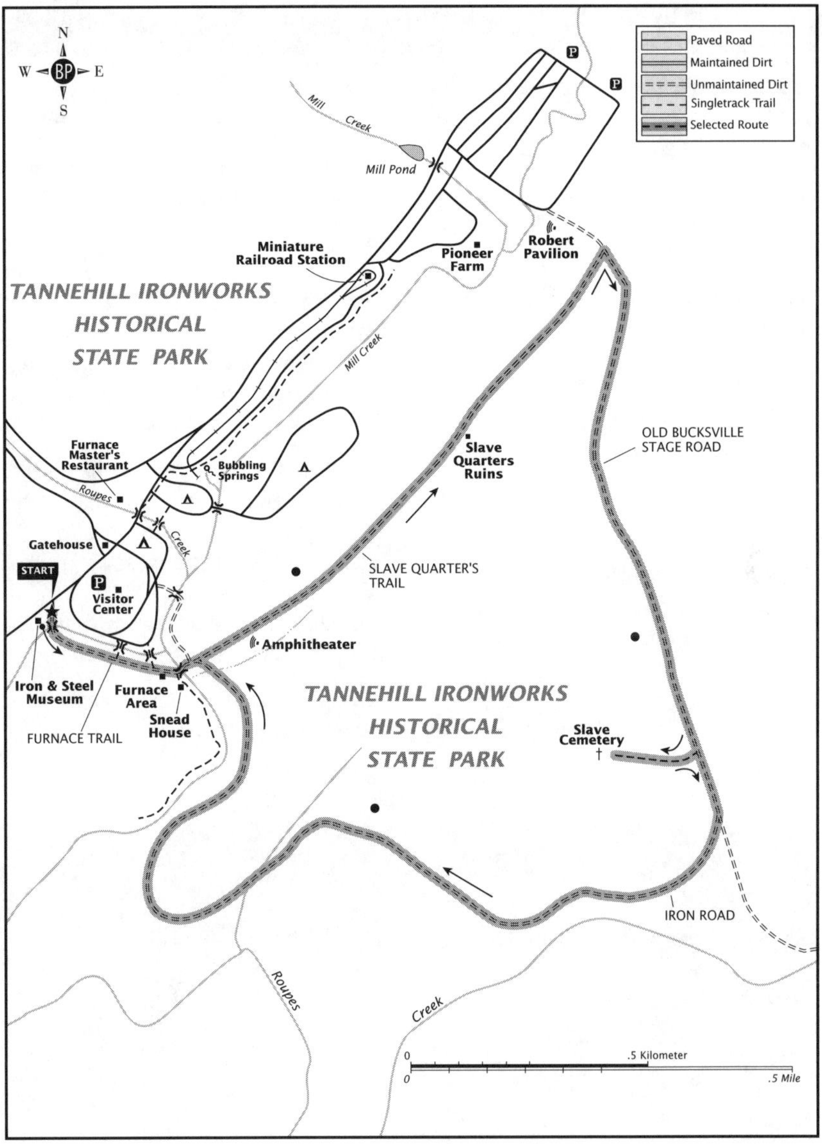

N
S
W
E
BP
Paved Road
Maintained Dirt
Unmaintained Dirt
Singletrack Trail
Selected Route
Mill Creek
Mill Pond
Robert Pavilion
Pioneer Farm
Miniature Railroad Station
TANNEHILL IRONWORKS HISTORICAL STATE PARK
Mill Creek
Furnace Master's Restaurant
Bubbling Springs
Slave Quarters Ruins
OLD BUCKSVILLE STAGE ROAD
Roupes
Creek
Gatehouse
START
Visitor Center
SLAVE QUARTER'S TRAIL
Amphitheater
Iron & Steel Museum
Furnace Area
Snead House
FURNACE TRAIL
TANNEHILL IRONWORKS HISTORICAL STATE PARK
Slave Cemetery
IRON ROAD
Roupes
Creek
0
.5 Kilometer
0
.5 Mile

MILES
0
1
2
3
4
1000'
750'
500'
250'
START
TANNEHILL HISTORIC TRAIL
Slave Cemetery
END

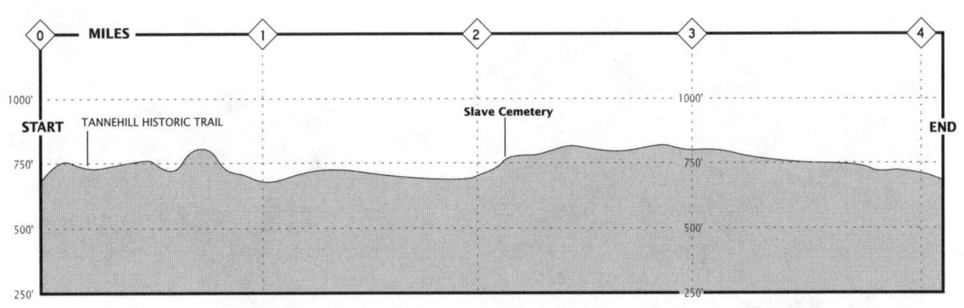

MilesDirections (Continued)

2.0 Come to a fork and go right. This dirt road is a side trail that leads to the slave cemetery. A sign points the way.

2.2 Reach the cemetery. When you're done, turn around and retrace your route back to the fork.

2.4 Turn right onto Old Bucksville Stage Road.

2.5 Come to a fork and go right, onto Iron Road.

2.6 Come to a fork and go right.

2.9 *[**FYI.** The red pebbles that line the trail are iron slag.]*

3.0 *[**Side-trip.** The short 250-foot trail to the left leads to Roupes Creek, a nice place to sit and take in the stream.]*

3.4 Roupes Creek lies straight ahead.

3.5 Come to a fork and go right. *[**FYI.** The left fork is a short grassy trail leading to the creek.]* In 200 feet you'll need to rock-hop across a five-foot wide creek.

3.6 Roupes Creek and the furnace area are in view to the left.

3.8 Come to a T-intersection with the gravel road from the start of the trip. Turn left onto the road. In 100 feet, turn to the right and cross the Folsom Bridge once again. Continue straight to the Snead House. Follow the dirt road between the furnace and blower house.

4.0 Pass the cement steps that lead to Plank Road. In 100 feet, cross the cement dam again. After crossing, head up the stairs again behind the museum (a cotton gin is on the left). Travel 200 feet and on the other side of the museum, turn to the right and head down the gravel road.

4.2 The gravel road turns to asphalt and returns you to the visitor center.

Just prior to the intersection of Iron Road and the Bucksville Stage Road is the slave cemetery. This is the only engraved tombstone.

cabins burned by the Union army during their raid. The trail soon turns onto the Old Bucksville Stage Road, which was the main highway into the area during the mid 1800s.

At the end of the road, a short side trail leads to the slave cemetery. Of the simple, flat rock tombstones that mark the area, only one, that of Josh Stroup, is engraved.

The hike is easy, over well-maintained roads of dirt and clay. After a good rain, however, some of the route can be deep in mud. A $2 entry fee covers admission to the craft houses, museum, and furnace. Artifacts are protected by the state of Alabama and cannot be removed. In other words, don't take home a brick from the furnace.

Hike Information

Trail Contacts:

Tannehill Ironworks Historical State Park, McCalla, AL; (205) 477–5711 or *www.tannehill.org*

Schedule:

Park and trails open year round 7 A.M.–sunset

Fees/Permits:

$2 day-use fee for adults, $1 seniors and children, six–11. Primitive camping is $9 per night for up to four people ($2.50 more for each additional person) or improved campsites with water and electricity are $14 per night.

Local Information:

Bessemer Area Chamber of Commerce, Bessemer, AL; 1–888–4–BESSEMER or *www.bessemerchamber.com*

Local Events/Attractions:

Bessemer Hall of History, Bessemer, AL; (205) 426–1633—*A truly unique museum featuring photos and artifacts from the 1800s, artifacts from the 28th Alabama Infantry from the Civil War, even Adolph Hitler's typewriter. Open Tuesday–Saturday 9 A.M.–4 P.M.* • **Annual Civil War Reenactment**, last weekend of May, Tannehill Historic State Park, McCalla, AL; (205) 477–5711—*Each year Union and Confederate troops gather to reenact the battle for the iron works and to demonstrate life during the 1860s.*

Accommodations:

Masters Economy Inn, Bessemer, AL; 1–800–633–3434

Restaurants:

Audie's Diner, Bessemer, AL; (205) 436–3874

Local Outdoor Retailers:

Wilson Butch Sporting Goods, Bessemer, AL; (205) 428–4642

Maps:

USGS maps: McCalla, AL; Halfmile Shoals, AL • **Brochures and trail maps** *available free of charge from the park office*

Blue Trail (South Rim Trail)

Hike Summary

Although not the most difficult trail at Oak Mountain State Park, the Blue Trail does have some long, constant climbs for the first two miles of the trip up the side of Double Oak Mountain. Once on top, with the help of a little bushwhacking, you will be rewarded with superb views of surrounding mountains and the valley below.

Hike Specs

Start: From the North Trailhead at Oak Mountain State Park
Length: 6.7-mile point-to-point
Approximate Hiking Time: 3–4 hours
Difficulty Rating: Difficult to easy, with steep, rocky inclines at the start, but more level walking the rest of the way
Trail Surface: Dirt path
Lay of the Land: Stands of longleaf pines
Land Status: State park
Nearest Town: Birmingham, AL
Other Trail Users: None
Canine Compatibility: Dog friendly—bring water (sources can be intermittent); leash not required

Getting There

From Birmingham: Take I-65 south for 14 miles to Cahaba Valley Road (Exit 246). Take a right onto Cahaba Valley Road (AL 119) and travel two miles to CR 33 and turn left. Go 2.5 miles to the park gate. Pay the entrance and camping fees and get general information brochures. Trail maps are available at the park office. Travel 6.5 miles straight ahead and the well-marked parking area will be on the left. This lot offers access to the North Trailhead. ***DeLorme: Alabama Atlas & Gazetteer:*** Page 31 G6

Shuttle Point

From Birmingham: Take I-65 south for 14 miles to Cahaba Valley Road (Exit 246). Take a right onto Cahaba Valley Road (AL 119) and travel two miles to CR 33 and turn left. Go 2.5 miles to the park gate. Travel 2.5 miles and turn right onto Terrace Drive. Travel around the lake and up the winding road two miles to the Peavine Falls parking area (the South Trailhead). Be careful driving up the last mile of this dirt road. It winds and there are steep drop-offs. ***DeLorme: Alabama Atlas & Gazetteer:*** Page 31 G6

Alabama is blessed with some beautiful country and the foresight to protect it. While each Alabama state park has something special, none offers more variety than Oak Mountain State Park. Located just 15 minutes south of Birmingham, Oak Mountain's offerings run the gamut from a championship 18-hole golf course to world-class mountain bike trails to vacation cottages. There is a horse stable where trail rides can be organized, and even a demonstration farm. The park is the home of the Alabama Wildlife Rehabilitation Center, which offers shelter and an area of recuperation for injured or orphaned animals.

Oak Mountain's 9,940 acres comprise pine forests and hardwood valleys and mountain ridges that top out at 1,200 feet. This park offers a combination of challenging treks, spectacular views from the top of Double Oak Mountain, and the beauty of Peavine Falls.

Because the park provides such variety and is so close to the state's largest city, it gets a bit crowded in summer—and even more so in the fall when the leaves turn. But the crowding hasn't reached the point where the park has lost any of its appeal to hikers.

The Blue Trail is one of the more popular trails in the park's network because of the views it affords. The trail is 6.7 miles long, from the North Trailhead to the South Trailhead (which is also the Peavine Falls trailhead), but by traveling on connector routes, you can fashion a number of loop trips. The South Trailhead provides access to other trails that would make excellent return routes to the North Trailhead.

Oak Mountain is one of the few state parks to allow overnight camping along trails, and the Blue Trail is the most popular for overnighting. Many backpackers head up to the rocky ridge of Double Oak Mountain—so named because of the dual mountains running parallel to one another—and spend the night overlooking the valley below. Campers must register at the park office before heading out.

A view of the Pelham Valley far below.

The trail is one of the best maintained in the park, due to efforts of the Vulcan Trail Association. The trail is wide and regularly cleared of fallen trees and overgrowth. Berms and washout-prevention steps are replaced frequently. The trail is marked with blue paint blazes about every 50 yards. At the trailhead, a canister invites hikers to make a contribution to help with trail maintenance.

MilesDirections

0.0 START from the North Trailhead. *[**FYI.** Make plans to arrive early as the parking lot tends to fill up quite rapidly since many of the hiking and biking trails begin here.]* Cross John Findley Drive to the southeast and come to a red cattle gate. There is plenty of information here on the trail and other activities. Head through the gate down the gravel road. In a few feet, a wooden sign will be reached that reads "BLUE TRAIL" with an arrow pointing to the left, and "YELLOW TRAIL" with an arrow pointing to the right. Turn left and head to the east slightly uphill.

1.4 Pass the first of two connectors to the Red Trail. (The connector is marked by a red blaze above the Blue Trail blaze.)

1.6 *[**FYI.** To your right (northwest) is Shackleford Point (1260 ft.), the highest point in the park.]*

1.9 Pass through "The Turnstile," two large boulders on either side of the trail.

2.1 *[**Side-trip.** To the right approximately 50 feet away from the trail is a row of rock outcroppings. A short trip over to them provides some nice views of the second mountain forming Double Oak Mountain. This is a popular spot for backpackers to pitch camp for the night as is evidenced by numerous fire rings.]*

2.5 Pass the second Red-Blue connector trail.

3.2 *[**Side-trip.** You can catch some spectacular views of the Pelham Valley by bushwhacking to the rocks outcroppings. Many backpackers choose to hike the rocks, which run parallel to the trail for the next 0.9 miles, instead of the trail. Many hikers also use this area to pitch camp for the night.]*

3.5 The Blue Trail intersects the Orange Trail Connector.

4.7 Pass the White / Blue Connector just past the creek.

5.2 Pass a short side trail to the right. *[**FYI.** It leads down to Peavine Branch and a nice level area, good for camping.]* Shortly thereafter the trail forks. Go right. *[**FYI.** Through the trees to the left is the Peavine Falls Gorge.]*

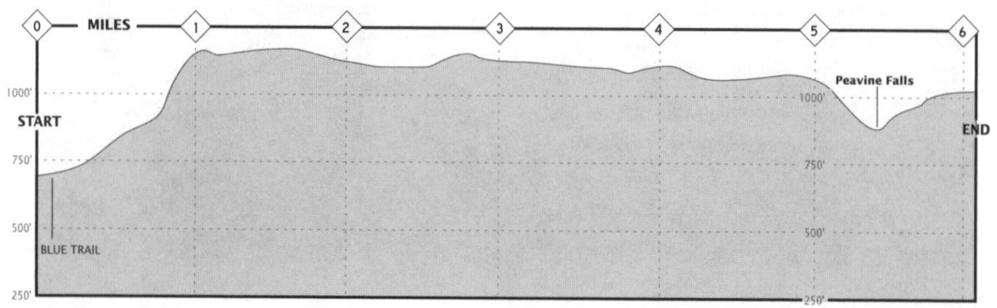

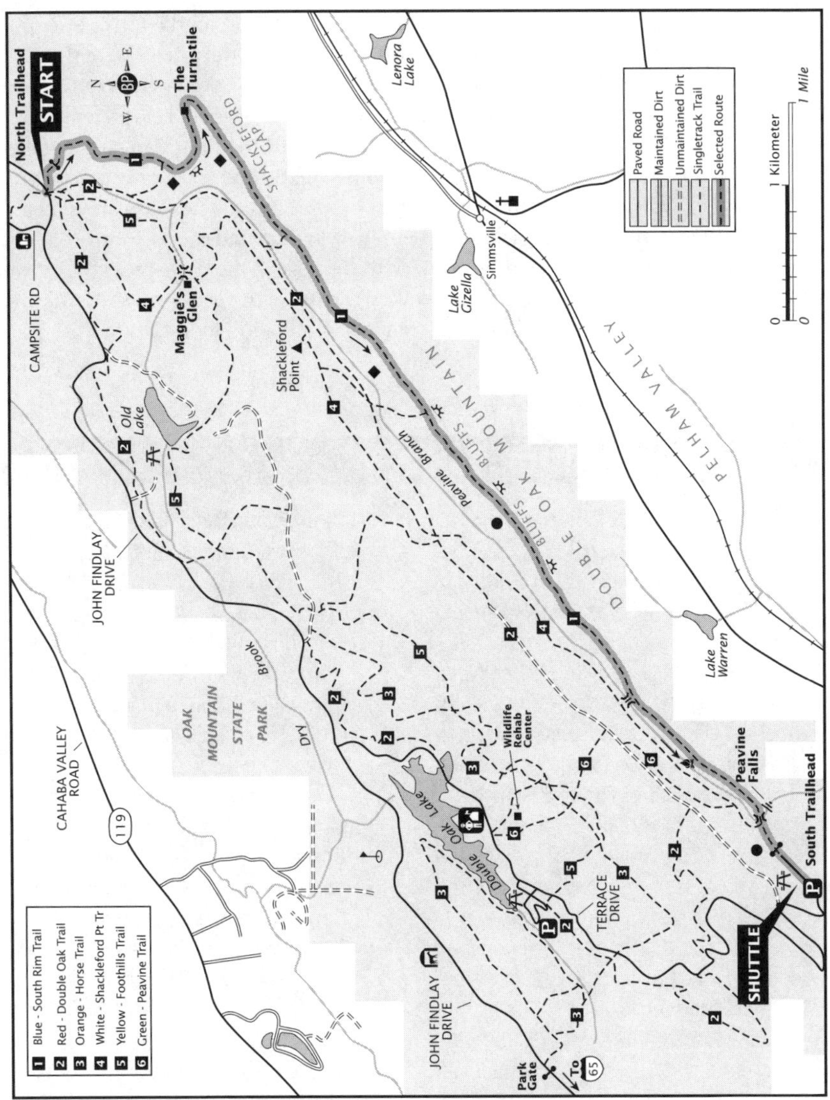

5.3 Come to a "No Camping" sign. A few feet more and a short footpath will split left. Follow this approximately 50 feet to the edge of the gorge where you'll find spectacular views of the gorge and 65-foot Peavine Falls. [***Note:*** *Be VERY cautious here as the rocks are slick and the drop precipitous.*] Along the edge of the gorge is a clay footpath. Turn right and in 40 feet you'll reconnect with the Blue Trail. Continue west on the trail. After crossing Peavine Branch, the White Trail (Shackleford Point Trail) joins the Blue Trail for the remainder of the trip.

6.7 Arrive at the South Trailhead and your shuttle. [***FYI.*** *At the gravel parking area you'll find maps, trail information, a pavilion with picnic tables, and a phone.*]

Since the trail is just slightly lower in elevation than the top of the ridge it follows, you may be wondering what is hiding on the other side of the rock formations to your left. By bushwhacking just a few dozen yards to the outcrops, you can see into the Pelham Valley below. Many hikers prefer to continue bushwhacking along the ridge, which for the most part runs parallel to the Blue Trail. Just remember to tread lightly and leave only footsteps.

The hike culminates in a visit to Peavine Falls. The falls can be heard from a mile away, long before the trail swings around the top of the 65-foot falls and gorge. A short bushwhack to the edge of the gorge provides a spectacular view of the falls, but be very careful as the rocks are slick and the drop is precipitous. Although camping is allowed along the trail, it's prohibited above and below the falls.

Local Events/Attractions:

Alabama Jazz Hall of Fame, Birmingham, AL; (205) 254-2731 —*Jazz legends with ties to Alabama, such as Lionel Hampton and Erskine Hawkins, are enshrined here. The Hall of Fame is opened Tuesday–Saturday 10 A.M.–5 P.M., and Sunday 1 P.M.–5 P.M.. Admission is free.* • **Alabama Sports Hall of Fame**, Birmingham, AL; (205) 323-6665 or *www.techcomm.com/ashof—Through the years, Alabama has provided the sports world with outstanding athletes and they are all enshrined here at the Sports Hall of Fame. Artifacts from such notables as Paul "Bear" Bryant, Hank Aaron, Joe Louis, Joe Namath, Satchel Paige, and many more will be found here. The Hall is open Monday–Saturday 9 A.M.-5 P.M., Sundays 1 P.M.–5 P.M.* **Birmingham Bulls**, Birmingham, AL at *www.birminghambulls.com—The Bulls are a minor league N.H.L./East Coast Hockey League franchise who play at the Birmingham Civic Center.* • **Birmingham Zoo**, Birmingham, AL; (205) 879-0408—*This is the premier zoo in the state with over 900 species of rare and exotic animals all set in natural outdoor settings. Call ahead for their schedule and admission prices.* • **Smith-Harrison Museum**, Columbiana, AL; (205) 669-4545—*This museum has the 2nd largest collection of George and Martha Washington artifacts as well as Robert E. Lee artifacts. The museum is open Monday–Friday 9 A.M.-5 P.M. with free admission.*

Hike Information

Trail Contacts:

Oak Mountain State Park, Pelham, AL; (205) 620–2527 or 1–800–ALA–PARK or *www.bham.net/oakmtn*

Schedule:

Open year round

Fees/Permits:

A day-use permit costs $2 per person. Camping is $8 per night for a primitive site, $13 per night for tent sites with water, $14 with water and electricity.

Local Information:

Birmingham Chamber of Commerce, Birmingham, AL; (205) 323–5461 or *www.birminghamchamber.com* • **Greater Birmingham Convention and Visitor Bureau**, Birmingham, AL; 1–800–458–8085 or *www.bcvb.org* • **North Shelby Chamber of Commerce**, Pelham, AL; (205) 663–4542 or *www.nsoc.com*

Accommodations:

Mountain Brook Inn, Mountain Brook, AL; 1–800–523–7771 • **Oak Mountain State Park**, Pelham, AL; 1–800–ALA–PARK • **Ranchouse Inn**, Birmingham, AL; (205) 322–0691

Restaurants:

The Original Whistle Stop Café (Irondale Café), Birmingham, AL; (205) 956–5258—*Setting for the novel and movie* Fried Green Tomatoes. • **Johnny Ray's Barbecue**, Pelham, AL; (205) 985–7675 • **Cafe Trentuno**, Pelham, AL; (205) 664–7887

Hike Tours:

Vulcan Trail Association, Birmingham, AL; (205) 328–6198 or *www.bham.net/vulcan—The Vulcan Trail Association features a "Second Sunday Walk," when else but the second Sunday of each month at Oak Mountain. The trails they feature are different theme each month and rated easy. Hikes begin at 1 P.M. from the park office.*

Organizations:

Sierra Club Cahaba, Birmingham, AL; (334) 540–7496 or *www.sierraclub.org/chapters/al/cahaba.html* • **Vulcan Trail Association**, Birmingham, AL; (205) 328–6198

Other Resources:

Alabama Trails, Birmingham, AL or *www.alabamatrails.com* • **Bama Environmental News**, Birmingham, AL; (205) 226–7739 or *www.bamanews.com* • **Wild Alabama**,Moulton, AL; (256) 974–7678; *ww.wildalabama.com*

Local Outdoor Retailers:

Alabama Outdoors, Birmingham, AL; 1–800–870–0011

Maps:

USGS maps: Cahaba Heights, AL; Chelsea, AL; Helena, AL • **Brochures and trail maps** *available at the park office. Maps are 50 cents.*

White Trail (Shackleford Pt. Trail)

Hike Summary

A bit more overgrown than other trails at Oak Mountain, the White Trail begins at the park's South Trailhead and passes by Peavine Falls. The trail continues along gently flowing Peavine Branch before gradually heading up to the highest perch in the park, Shackleford Point. Here the trail turns rocky as it follows the ridgeline, with views of mountains to either side. The trek includes a visit to Maggie's Glen, a favorite spot for sitting along the banks of the creek and relaxing.

Hike Specs

Start: From the South Trailhead (Peavine Falls trailhead) at Oak Mountain State Park
Length: 6.3-miles point-to-point
Approximate Hiking Time: 3–4 hours
Difficulty Rating: Easy travel along Peavine Branch and a ridge; moderate climbs up a rocky slope
Trail Surface: Dirt; some rocky areas
Lay of the Land: Forests of longleaf pine, hickory, white oak, and silver maple; boulder-strewn vistas
Land Status: State park
Nearest Town: Birmingham, AL
Other Trail Users: None
Canine Compatibility: Dog friendly—though could be tough on older or out-of-shape dogs on steeper portions; bring water; leash not required

Getting There

From Birmingham: Take I-65 south for 14 miles to Cahaba Valley Road (Exit 246). Take a right onto Cahaba Valley Road (AL 119) and travel two miles to CR 33 and turn left. Go 2.5 miles to the park gate. Travel 2.5 miles and turn right onto Terrace Drive. Travel around the lake and up the winding road two miles to the Peavine Falls parking area (the South Trailhead). Be careful driving up the last mile of this dirt road. It winds and there are steep drop-offs. ***DeLorme: Alabama Atlas & Gazetteer:*** Page 31 G6

Shuttle Point

From Birmingham: Take I-65 south for 14 miles to Cahaba Valley Road (Exit 246). Take a right onto Cahaba Valley Road (AL 119) and travel two miles to CR 33 and turn left. Go 2.5 miles to the park gate. Pay the entrance and camping fees and get general information brochures. Trail maps are available at the park office. Travel 6.5 miles straight ahead and the well-marked parking area will be on the left. This lot offers access to the North Trailhead. ***DeLorme: Alabama Atlas & Gazetteer:*** Page 31 G6

In Oak Mountain State Park, most trails lead to Peavine Falls. The White Trail, also known as the Shackleford Point Trail, is no exception. The trail begins at the South Trailhead and travels north to the park's aptly named North Trailhead. Several trails interconnect through this area, making a variety of loop hikes possible. One of the more popular hikes is to begin at the North Trailhead, hike south on the Blue Trail *[see Hike 17]* to the South Trailhead, and then take the White Trail back to the North Trailhead. This combination makes for a nice overnight backpacking trip. Camping is permitted along the trails, but be sure to register at the park office before heading out. Camping is not allowed just below or above Peavine Falls.

The White Trail follows the northern summit of Oak Mountain, which is not really a single mountain. It is, in fact, two mountains that run parallel to one another, and together are known as Double Oak Mountain. The Blue Trail follows the ridges of the southern summit.

From its beginning at the South Trailhead, the White Trail is narrow as it winds through heavy brush. As it sets out along the banks of Peavine Branch, it runs rocky through white oaks, hickory trees, maples, and dogwoods. After passing by Peavine Falls, the route opens up and enters some fine stands of longleaf pine.

In spring, you're likely to hear the sounds of yellow-billed cuckoos and pine warblers. In summer, thrushes and wrens dart through the brush, and throughout the year, broad wing and red shoulder hawks soar overhead. You also may see wild turkeys.

MilesDirections

0.0 START from the north end of the South Trailhead at Peavine Falls. At first the trail is a combination of the Blue (South Rim) and White trails.

0.2 Come to a fork and go straight (the left fork). *[**Side-trip.** The Blue Trail splits right. It's just a short out-and-back down this trail to the headwaters of Peavine Falls and Peavine Gorge.]* The next tenth of a mile is a combination of the White and Green (Peavine Trail) trails.

0.3 The Green Trail splits and heads back to the park office. Continue straight.

0.4 Pass a popular campsite for backpackers along the Blue Trail, right next to the stream.

1.0 Pass the White-Blue Connector Trail.

1.2 *[**FYI.** A short bushwhack to the rocks on the left and a hike along them will afford excellent views of the mountains to the northeast.]*

1.9 Pass the wide dirt Red Trail, used by mountain bikes. At the top of the hill, pass the Yellow-White Connector Trail, which splits left.

2.6 Come to a T-intersection (with several directional signs) and turn left.

3.3 *[**FYI.** To the right is the parallel mountain that makes up the pair of Double Oak Mountain and where the Blue South Rim Trail can be found.]*

3.9 The White and Yellow trails converge and head northeast.

4.4 Reach Maggie's Glen. *[**FYI.** This is a very nice, flat glen with a wide stream running through it. It is a scenic and popular site among hikers.]* Cross a small footbridge and the Yellow and White trails split. Continue on the White Trail.

6.3 Arrive at the gate of the North Trailhead.

North Trailhead
SHUTTLE
The Turnstile
SHACKLEFORD GAP
CAMPSITE RD
Maggie's Glen
Shackleford Point
Stone Culvert
Old Lake
Lenora Lake
Lake Gizella
Simmsville
Paved Road
Maintained Dirt
Unmaintained Dirt
Singletrack Trail
Selected Route
1 Kilometer
1 Mile
PELHAM VALLEY
DOUBLE OAK MOUNTAIN
BLUFFS
Peavine Branch
JOHN FINDLAY DRIVE
OAK MOUNTAIN STATE PARK
Dry Brook
Lake Warren
Wildlife Rehab Center
Peavine Falls
South Trailhead
START
CAHABA VALLEY ROAD
119
Double Oak Lake
TERRACE DRIVE
Park Gate
To 65
Blue - South Rim Trail
Red - Double Oak Trail
Orange - Horse Trail
White - Shackleford Pt Tr
Yellow - Foothills Trail
Green - Peavine Trail

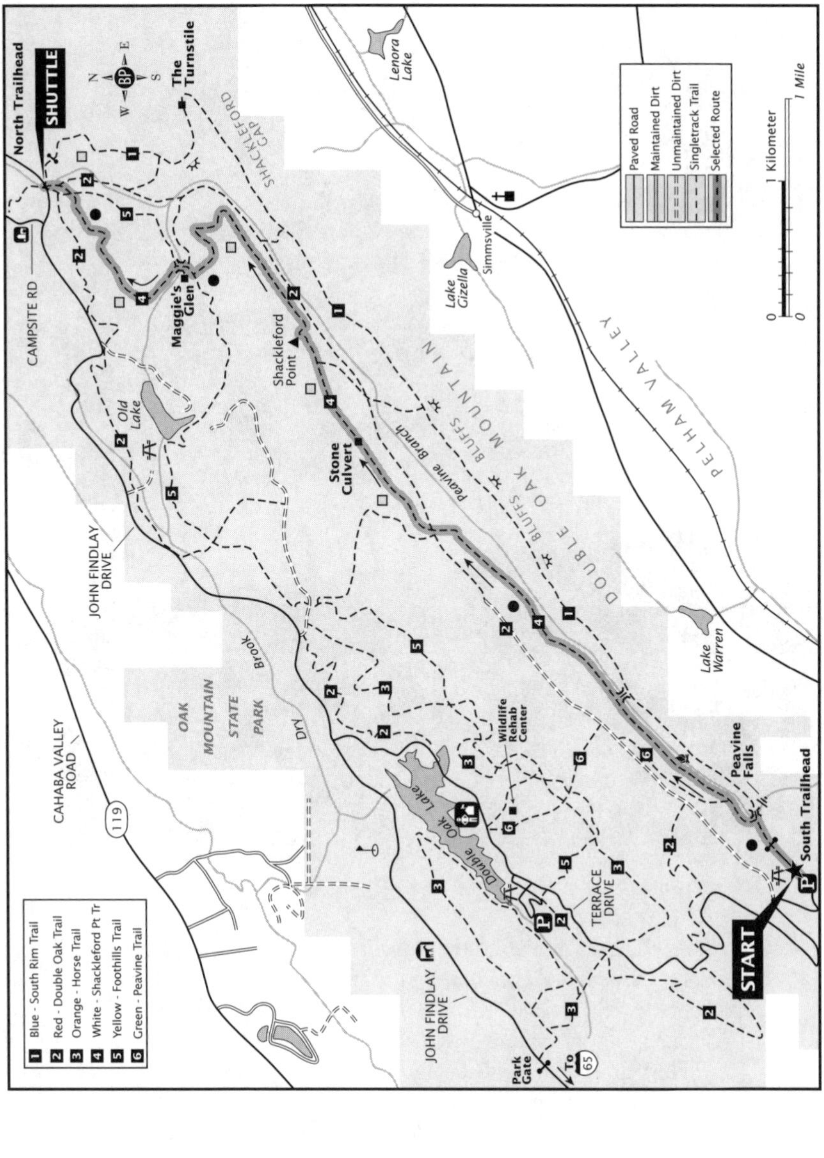

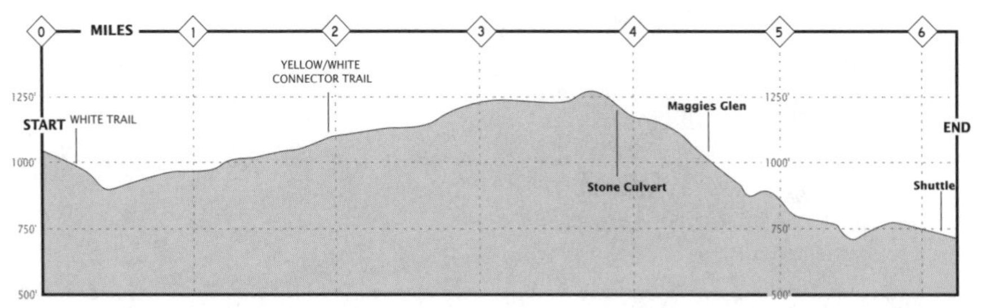

MILES
0
1
2
3
4
5
6
1250'
1000'
750'
500'
START
WHITE TRAIL
YELLOW/WHITE CONNECTOR TRAIL
Stone Culvert
Maggies Glen
END
Shuttle

As the trail moves up the ridgeline, the trail becomes more and more rocky. On top of the mountain, the trail follows just below the rocky outcroppings of the ridge, which block many views. A short bushwhack to the ridge reveals outstanding views of Pelham Valley.

The trail eventually makes its way to the top of some bluffs and outcroppings just before heading back down the mountain. Along this section are some excellent spots to just sit down, kick back, watch the hawks overhead, and take in the views from a rock ledge. Along its route, the White Trail reaches the highest spot in the park, Shackleford Point, at an elevation of 1,260 feet.

A couple of miles before the White Trail nears its end at the North Trailhead, it passes through Maggie's Glen, a flat area situated in a hollow. The glen is grassy, with a wide stream running through it. Spring is a favorite time to visit, when white beeches and dogwoods bloom.

A word of praise has to go out to the men and women of the Vulcan Trail Association. Not only do they provide outdoor training programs to the public, but they also help with trail maintenance. At each trailhead is a metal container for contributions to help with their efforts.

Ride Information

Trail Contacts:

Oak Mountain State Park, Pelham, AL; (205) 620-2527 or 1-800-ALA-PARK or *www.bham.net/oakmtn*

Schedule:

Open year round

Fees/Permits:

A Day-Use permit costs $2 per person. Camping is $8 per night for a primitive site, $13 per night for tent sites with water, $14 with water and electricity.

Local Information:

Birmingham Chamber of Commerce, Birmingham, AL; (205) 323-5461 or *www.birminghamchamber.com* • **Greater Birmingham Convention and Visitor Bureau**, Birmingham, AL; 1-800-458-8085 or *www.bcvb.org* • **North Shelby Chamber of Commerce**, Pelham, AL; (205) 663-4542 or *www.nsoc.com*

Local Events/Attractions:

[See Hike 17: Blue Trail.]

Accommodations:

[See Hike 17: Blue Trail.]

Restaurants:

[See Hike 17: Blue Trail.]

Organizations:

[See Hike 17: Blue Trail.]

Other Resources

[See Hike 17: Blue Trail.]

Local Outdoor Retailers:

Mountain Brook Sporting Goods, Mountain Brook, AL; (205) 870-3257

Maps:

USGS maps: Cahaba Heights, AL; Chelsea, AL; Helena, AL • **Brochures and trail maps**—*available at the park office. Maps are 50 cents.*

Yellow Trail (Foothills Trail)

Hike Summary

The Yellow Trail travels the lower foothills of Oak Mountain State Park through concentrated tree growth that provides a welcoming canopy of shade during hot weather. On the ridges above, longleaf pines tower over the trail. During the hike, watch for large turtles in some of the creeks you'll cross. One of the most popular stopping points along the route is Maggie's Glen.

Hike Specs

Start: From the North Trailhead at Oak Mountain State Park
Length: 8.2-mile point-to-point
Approximate Hiking Time: 5–6 hours
Difficulty Rating: Moderate to difficult due to travel up steep ridges; easy to moderate for the last half of the trip
Trail Surface: Dirt path
Lay of the Land: Thick forest of magnolia, hickory, black walnut, and oak; stands of longleaf pines; many stream crossings

Land Status: State park
Nearest Town: Birmingham, AL
Other Trail Users: None
Canine Compatibility: Dog friendly—but can be tough on the initial steep parts; water available through most of the hike; leash not required

Getting There

From Birmingham: Take I-65 south for 14 miles to Cahaba Valley Road (Exit 246). Take a right onto Cahaba Valley Road (AL 119) and travel two miles to CR 33 and turn left. Go 2.5 miles to the park gate. Pay the entrance and camping fees and get general information brochures. Trail maps are available at the park office. Travel 6.5 miles straight ahead and the well-marked parking area will be on the left. This lot offers access to the North Trailhead. ***DeLorme: Alabama Atlas & Gazetteer:*** Page 31 G6

Shuttle Point

From Birmingham: Take I-65 south for 14 miles to Cahaba Valley Road (Exit 246). Take a right onto Cahaba Valley Road (AL 119) and travel two miles to CR 33 and turn left. Go 2.5 miles to the park gate. Continue on two miles and make a right turn onto Terrace Drive. Head southwest one mile on Terrace Drive, passing the park office. The parking area will be on the right. ***DeLorme: Alabama Atlas & Gazetteer:*** Page 31 G6

Quiet solitude. That's what's in store for you along the Yellow Trail at Oak Mountain State Park. This trail, in the middle of one of the most popular state parks in Alabama, sees little traffic except near its two ends.

The Yellow Trail, also known as the Foothills Trail, travels up and down the northern ridges of Double Oak Mountain. Unlike the higher White and Blue trails, the Yellow Trail reaches a maximum elevation at only 820 feet. The trail commences from the North Trailhead, where several other routes are accessed, including the Red Bike Trail. The parking area isn't that large here, so arrive early to get a parking spot.

To judge by park maps, the trail looks like it should be fairly easy, but the first half of this trip has some difficulty. The trail weaves its way steeply up the foothills of Double Oak Mountain, reaching the 820-foot high point in less than a mile. From there it's a steep descent into Maggie's Glen. Then things level out and the walking becomes easier.

The trail passes through a dense forest of magnolia, oak, hickory, and black walnut. The forest blocks views of the surrounding mountains, but the shade is welcome on hot, humid days. At the points where the Yellow Trail crosses one of the fast-flowing creeks over a wooden footbridge, look in pools at the creek to see if you can spot large turtles.

Of the two areas along the trail that get a fair amount of foot traffic, the first you come to is Maggie's Glen, about a mile from the North Trailhead. Many people come in spring to this grassy area with its lovely stream in order to view the white beeches and dogwoods in bloom. The second popular area is about a mile from the southern end of the trail, where it crosses the Wildlife and Treetop trails. These short interpretive trails make their way down the hillside from the Alabama Wildlife Rehabilitation Center.

MilesDirections

0.0 START from the North Trailhead. *[**FYI.** Make plans to arrive early as the parking lot tends to fill up quite rapidly since many of the hiking and biking trails begin here.]* Cross John Findley Drive to the southeast and come to a red cattle gate. There is plenty of information here on the trail and other activities. Head through the gate down the gravel road. In a few feet, a wooden sign will be reached that reads "BLUE TRAIL" with an arrow pointing to the left, and "YELLOW TRAIL" with an arrow pointing to the right. Turn right and head west on the gravel road leading into the woods.

1.1 Arrive at Maggie's Glen. *[**FYI.** This is a very nice, flat glen with a wide stream running through it. It is a scenic and popular site among hikers.]* Cross a small footbridge and the Yellow and White trails merge for the next 0.1 miles.

1.2 Come to a fork. Take the right fork. (The White Trail forks left fork.)

2.0 *[**FYI.** This a finger of Old Lake, a small lake created by a narrow dam located at mile 2.5.]*

2.5 Pass Picnic Area Number Two. *[**FYI.** This is a quiet, secluded area with picnic tables that makes for a nice place to take a break.]*

3.0 Cross a footbridge.

3.1 Cross a footbridge and them the Red Trail.

4.2 Cross the Red Trail a second time. *[**FYI.** To the left, the ridge of Double Oak Mountain can be seen.]*

4.4 Cross a footbridge. In 100 feet, come to a dirt road. A sign here reads "Main Road." Turn left (to the east) on the road and travel 50 feet. Cross s short bridge and in another 50 feet, a sign will point to the "Yellow Trail." Turn right here and return to the woods. *[**FYI.** Just past this sign on the road about 30 feet farther is another sign pointing the way to the Yellow-White Connector Trail.]*

4.5 Cross a footbridge.

6.0 The Orange (Horseshoe) Trail merges briefly with the Yellow Trail as they head to the southwest.

North Trailhead
START
The Turnstile
SHACKLEFORD GAP
CAMPSITE RD
Maggie's Glen
Old Lake
Shackleford Point
Peavine Branch
BLUFFS
DOUBLE OAK MOUNTAIN
PELHAM VALLEY
Lenora Lake
Lake Gizella
Simmsville
Lake Warren
Peavine Falls
South Trailhead
Wildlife Rehab Center
TERRACE DRIVE
SHUTTLE
JOHN FINDLAY DRIVE
CAHABA VALLEY ROAD
119
OAK MOUNTAIN STATE PARK
Brook
DYJ
Double Oak Lake
Park Gate
To 65
1 Blue - South Rim Trail
2 Red - Double Oak Trail
3 Orange - Horse Trail
4 White - Shackleford Pt Tr
5 Yellow - Foothills Trail
6 Green - Peavine Trail
Paved Road
Maintained Dirt
Unmaintained Dirt
Singletrack Trail
Selected Route
0 1 Kilometer
0 1 Mile

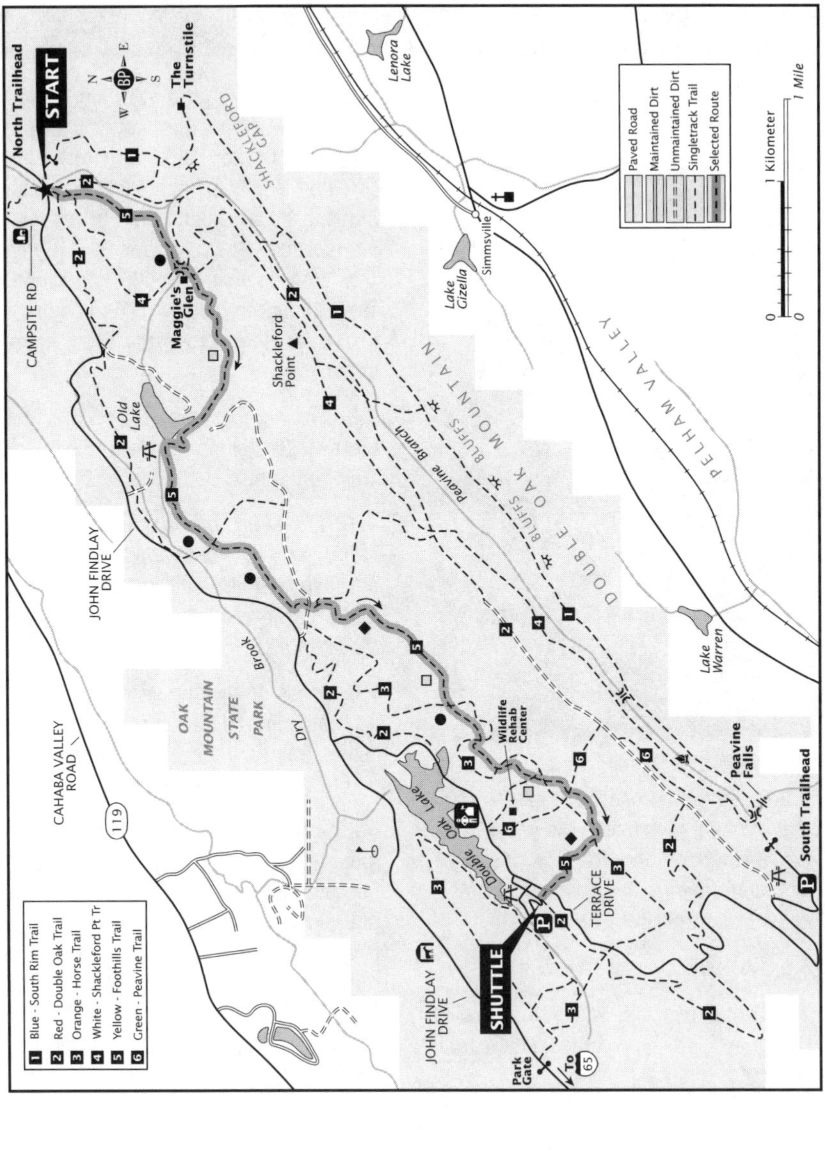

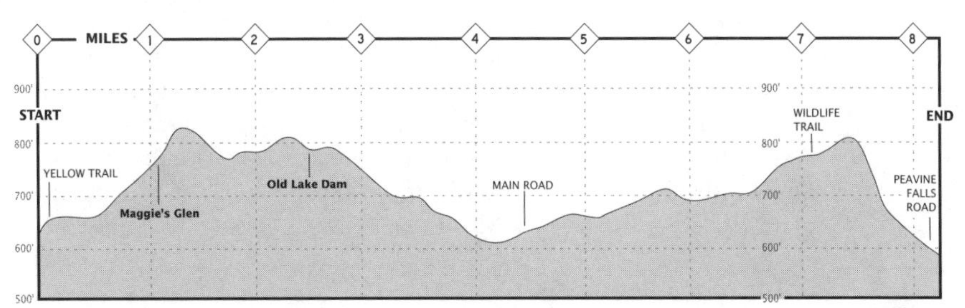

MILES
0
1
2
3
4
5
6
7
8
900'
800'
700'
600'
500'
START
END
YELLOW TRAIL
Maggie's Glen
Old Lake Dam
MAIN ROAD
WILDLIFE TRAIL
PEAVINE FALLS ROAD

MilesDirections (Continued)

6.1 Come to a fork and go right. (The Orange Trail branches left.)

6.7 Cross the Orange Trail again.

The trail here is thick and enclosed.

6.8 Cross the Orange Trail again. In 100 feet, cross a park road—two yellow lines are painted on the road to show the direction. Reenter the woods after crossing a 3-foot wide cement culvert.

6.9 Cross the Orange Trail again.

7.0 Come to a fork where the Wildlife Center Trail merges with the Yellow Trail. Go right.

7.1 Come to a sign that reads, "Yellow Trail" (points back the way you came), "Wildlife Center" (points left), and "Treetop Trail" (points right). Continue straight. In 100 feet, come to a signed intersection. The sign reads, "Wildlife Trail" (points to the south) and "Yellow Trail" (points to the west). Turn south. In just a few feet, cross the Orange Trail again.

7.3 Cross the Green Trail. In 100 feet, the Orange Trail merges with the Yellow Trail for the next 0.4 miles.

7.7 *[**Note.** A line of rocks across the trail indicates that both the Yellow and Horseshoe Trails are turning. There is a path that does continue straight, but make sure to make this turn.]*

7.8 Come to a tree with an Orange (Horseshoe) Trail marker on it. Follow the Yellow Trail as it leaves the Orange Trail and heads into a ravine.

8.2 Come to an intersection with a dirt road. A "Yellow Trail" sign is here. This is Peavine Falls Road. Turn right onto the road. In 100 feet, come to a cattle gate used to shut down the road at night. The road becomes asphalt and is now Terrace Drive. Continue another 100 feet and arrive at the South Trailhead parking lot.

You'll cross several other routes on your hike down the Yellow Trail—including the Orange (Horseshoe), Red, and Green Trails—plus encounter a connector path to the White Trail. These trails can be combined into several loop hikes and some excellent overnight trips. Be forewarned that if you plan to use the White-Yellow connector trail at the 4.5-mile mark, the climb to the White Tail consists of difficult travel straight up the side and over the bluffs of Double Oak Mountain.

Once again we need to mention the work of the Vulcan Trail Association, which helps maintain the trails at Oak Mountain. The Yellow Trail is kept in good shape. Downed trees are cleared away quickly, and trail markers are clear and frequent. The association sponsors excursions in the park on the second Sunday of each month. The public is invited to join these guided hikes, which usually start just after lunch.

Ride Information

Trail Contacts:
Oak Mountain State Park, Pelham, AL; (205) 620-2527 or 1-800-ALA-PARK or *www.bham.net/oakmtn*

Schedule:
Open year round

Fees/Permits:
A day-use permit costs $2 per person. Camping is $8 per night for a primitive site, $13 per night for tent sites with water, $14 with water and electricity.

Local Information:
Birmingham Chamber of Commerce, Birmingham, AL; (205) 323-5461or *www.birminghamchamber.com* • **Greater Birmingham Convention and Visitor Bureau**, Birmingham, AL; 1-800-458-8085 or *www.bcvb.org* • **North Shelby Chamber of Commerce**, Pelham, AL; (205) 663-4542 or *www.nsoc.com*

Local Events/Attractions:
[See Hike 17: Blue Trail.]

Accommodations:
[See Hike 17: Blue Trail.]

Restaurants:
[See Hike 17: Blue Trail.]

Organizations:
[See Hike 17: Blue Trail.]

Other Resources
[See Hike 17: Blue Trail.]

Local Outdoor Retailers:
Homewood Sporting Goods, Homewood, AL; (205) 879-2828

Maps:
USGS maps: Cahaba Heights, AL; Chelsea, AL; Helena, AL • **Brochures**—*General park information available free at the main gate. Trail maps are available for 50 cents at the park office.*

Green Trail (Peavine Falls Trail)

Hike Summary

The Green Trail is the most direct route to the most popular attraction at Oak Mountain State Park, Peavine Falls. The trail travels steeply up and down ridges through a forest lush with vegetation in spring and summer, giving a comfortable enclosed feeling. Although the climbs are steep, the trail may be crowded on weekends because of the popularity of the falls.

Hike Specs

Start: From the South Trailhead (Peavine Falls trailhead) at Oak Mountain State Park
Length: 4.6-mile out-and-back
Approximate Hiking Time: 3–4 hours
Difficulty Rating: Moderate to difficult due to steep grades
Trail Surface: Dirt path
Lay of the Land: Stands of longleaf pine, white oak, and silver maple
Land Status: State park
Nearest Town: Birmingham, AL
Other Trail Users: None
Canine Compatibility: Dog friendly—but bring water (there are no sources until Peavine Branch at the end); leash recommended due to large number of people

Getting There

From Birmingham: Take I-65 south for 14 miles to Cahaba Valley Road (Exit 246). Take a right onto Cahaba Valley Road (AL 119) and travel two miles to CR 33 and turn left. Go 2.5 miles to the park gate. Pay the entrance and camping fees and get general information brochures. Trail maps are available at the park office. Continue on two miles and make a right turn onto Terrace Drive. Head southwest one mile on Terrace Drive. The park office and parking area will be on the right. ***DeLorme: Alabama Atlas & Gazetteer:*** Page 31 G6

Hundreds of people flock to Peavine Falls each weekend—and anytime during the summer months when school is out—to view this 65-foot beauty that cascades down a sheer rock wall into a clear pool. Many visitors take the Green Trail down to the falls because it starts right at the park office and is the most direct route.

The Peavine Falls trailhead is close to some of Oak Mountain's main attractions, including the Alabama Wildlife Rehabilitation Center and the Oak Mountain Demonstration Farm. Far more than just a petting zoo, the Demonstration Farm exhibits life on a farm and the care of livestock. Next door to the farm are the Oak Mountain Stables, with horseback rides available up the mountain or along the Orange (Horseshoe) Trail.

A view looking down into Peavine Falls.

Eighty-five-acre Oak Lake is right next to the park office. Canoes and paddleboats are available for rent, and a swimming beach lies at one end. There is even a bicycle motocross facility just down from the park office. If you like to hit the links while vacationing and while not on the trail, you can take advantage of the 18-hole golf course here. Being in the heart of all this activity, it's no wonder the Green Trail sees so much traffic.

Although the path is a well-maintained dirt route, the climbs up and down the ridges are steep. The trail starts into the woods and then turns sharply uphill, next to the Wildlife Rehabilitation Center. After topping out on the first ridge, it's a steep walk down to the bottom—then back up steeply again to the ridgeline of Double Oak Mountain. The trail finally descends to meet the White Trail and then levels out, making its way to the falls.

As with many of the trails at Oak Mountain State Park, the Green Trail crosses several other trails, including the White, Red, and Orange (Horseshoe) Trails. This makes it easy to create several different loop hikes and some interesting overnight pack trips.

Views along the trail are not as open as those from high atop the twin ridges of Double Oak Mountain on the White and Blue trails. The thick cover of trees on the Green Trail is the scenic highlight on the way to the falls. When you're not concentrating on getting up a hillside, take a look around at the live oaks, silver maples, and dogwoods. At the top of the ridges, the aroma of longleaf pines stands out.

MilesDirections

0.0 START from the park office. Turn right onto Terrace Drive and head to the west 50 feet. The trailhead with a Green Trail sign will be on your left, directly across from the tennis courts. Turn left and head into the woods to the south.

0.6 Cross the Orange (Horseshoe) Trail.

0.7 Cross the Yellow Trail.

1.2 The Green Trail merges with the Red Trail for the next 0.1 miles.

1.3 The Red Trail leaves the Green. Stay on the Green Trail.

2.2 The Green Trail merges with the White Trail for the next 0.1 miles along the banks of Peavine Branch.

2.3 The White Trail leaves the Green. In reality, the Green Trail has officially ended. This short, remaining length of trail is actually the Blue Trail. Continue to the east following blue blazes about 50 feet to the head of Peavine Falls. From here, the trail over looks the gorge for the next 0.1 miles. *[**Note.** Be VERY cautious here. The rocks are slick and the drop precarious. The edge of the gorge is a clay footpath.]* Turn around here for the return trip over the same path described above.

4.6 Arrive back at your vehicle.

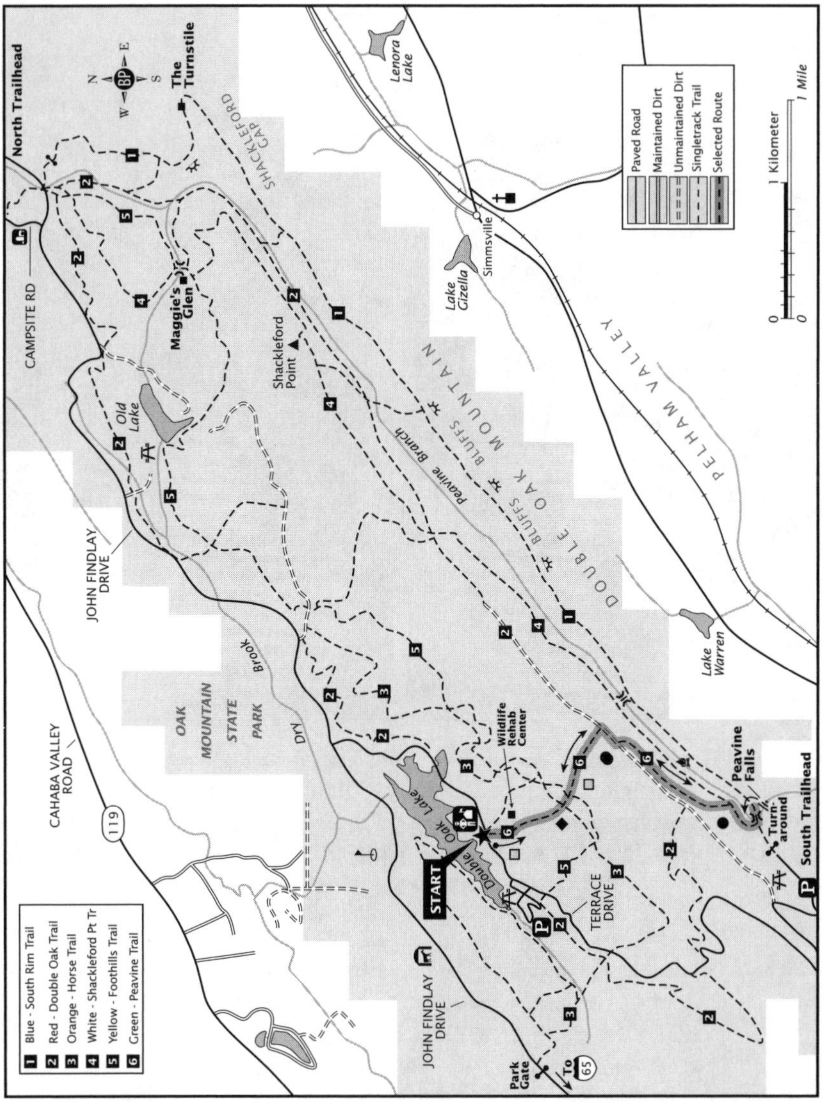

North Trailhead
The Turnstile
CAMPSITE RD
SHACKLEFORD GAP
Maggie's Glen
Shackleford Point
Old Lake
JOHN FINDLAY DRIVE
Peavine Branch
BLUFFS
DOUBLE OAK MOUNTAIN
PELHAM VALLEY
Lenora Lake
Simmsville
Lake Gizella
Lake Warren
OAK MOUNTAIN STATE PARK
Dry Brook
CAHABA VALLEY ROAD
119
Double Oak Lake
START
Wildlife Rehab Center
TERRACE DRIVE
Peavine Falls
Turn-around
South Trailhead
Park Gate
To 65
1 Blue - South Rim Trail
2 Red - Double Oak Trail
3 Orange - Horse Trail
4 White - Shackleford Pt Tr
5 Yellow - Foothills Trail
6 Green - Peavine Trail
Paved Road
Maintained Dirt
Unmaintained Dirt
Singletrack Trail
Selected Route
0
1 Kilometer
1 Mile

MILES
0
1
2
3
4
1250'
1000'
750'
500'
START
END
PEAVINE FALLS TRAIL
Peavine Falls
(Turnaround)

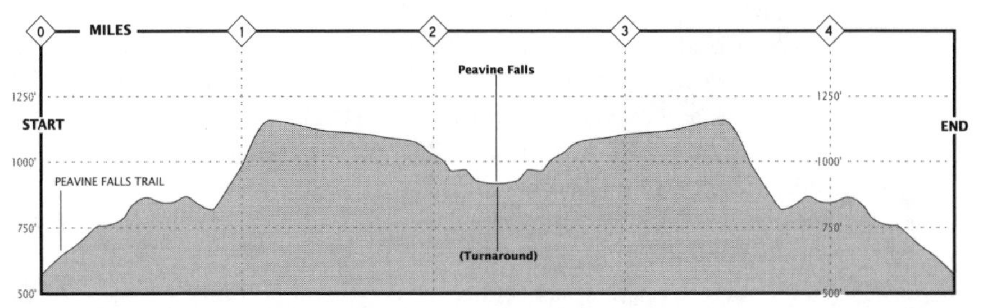

The Alabama Wildlife Rehabilitation Center

The largest environmental organization in the state, the Alabama Wildlife Rehabilitation Center (AWRC) is located in the heart of Oak Mountain State Park. Established in 1977, the center was founded by Anne Miller and a staff of six volunteers.

The AWRC provides both long and short-term care for orphaned and injured animals. A wide variety of animals are brought to the center for care and treatment. Whenever possible, the animals are put into the Release Preparation Facility to get them ready to return to the wild.

At Oak Mountain, the AWRC facility is located 0.5 miles south of the park office on the AWRC Drive. Inside, there are a variety of educational exhibits to demonstrate the role of the center. Don't be surprised to see a few squirrels running in and out of the rafters as you walk through.

The highlight of the facility is the viewing area. Behind a screen, visitors can view the animals as their handlers help them recuperate.

Next to the facility is the Treetop Nature Trail. This is a wide, handicap accessible, elevated boardwalk that takes hikers through the valley. Here you can see red-shoulder and red-tail hawks, horned owls, and turkey vultures. These and many more such animals live in very spacious cages along the trail and receive the best of care. Admission to the facility and the trail is free to the public.

Ride Information

Trail Contacts:
Oak Mountain State Park, Pelham, AL; (205) 620–2527 or 1–800–ALA–PARK or *www.bham.net/oakmtn*

Schedule:
Open year round

Fees/Permits:
A Day-Use permit costs $2 per person. Camping is $8 per night for a primitive site, $13 per night for tent sites with water, $14 with water and electricity.

Local Information:
Birmingham Chamber of Commerce, Birmingham, AL; (205) 323–5461 or *www.birmingham-chamber.com* • **Greater Birmingham Convention and Visitor Bureau**, Birmingham, AL; 1–800–458–8085 or *www.bcvb.org* • **North Shelby Chamber of Commerce**, Pelham, AL; (205) 663–4542 or *www.nsoc.com*

Local Events/Attractions:
[See Hike 17: Blue Trail.]

Accommodations:
[See Hike 17: Blue Trail.]

Restaurants:
[See Hike 17: Blue Trail.]

Organizations:
[See Hike 17: Blue Trail.]

Other Resources
[See Hike 17: Blue Trail.]

Local Outdoor Retailers:
Mountain Brook Sporting Goods, Mountain Brook, AL; (205) 870–3257

Maps:
USGS maps: Cahaba Heights, AL; Chelsea, AL; Helena, AL • **Brochures**—*General park information available free at the main gate. Trail maps are available for 50 cents at the park office.*

The hike culminates in Peavine Falls. The fall is formed by Peavine Branch, a slow meandering flow of water that runs between the two ridges of Double Oak Mountain. Both the Green Trail and the White Trail follow the creek for a portion of their length.

Overnight camping is permitted along the trails in the park, but not in the areas just above and below the falls. Rappelling and climbing are not allowed on the rock walls of the gorge formed by the stream.

Lakeshore Trail

Hike Summary

This easy walk meanders along the banks of Lake Chinnabee, passing through beautiful stands of oak and hickory. Flowering plants are abloom in spring and early summer. At the halfway mark, the trail passes a marsh with lush, green grasses growing on a small island. The Chinnabee Silent Trail and the Skyway Loop Trail both join at the start of this trail.

Hike Specs

Start: From the southeast end of the Lake Chinnabee Recreation Area parking lot
Length: 1.9-mile loop
Approximate Hiking Time: 1–2 hours
Difficulty Rating: Easy travel over gentle hills
Trail Surface: Clay and dirt
Lay of the Land: White oak, hickory, and yellow pine trees, plus mountain laurels, camellias, and rhododendrons
Land Status: National forest
Nearest Town: Anniston, AL
Other Trail Users: None, except for motorists on recreation area road
Canine Compatibility: Dog friendly—leash required

Getting There

From Anniston: Take I-20 east for five miles to Exit 191. Merge into U.S. 431 South. Travel 3.5 miles and turn right onto AL 281. Head south on AL 281 for 16 miles and pass the Cheaha State Park headquarters and lodge on the right. Continue south three miles. Make a sharp right turn onto the Lake/Campground Road and travel 3.5 miles. Turn left onto Lake Chinnabee Road (a national forest sign marks the turn). Head down this road one mile to the parking area. ***DeLorme: Alabama Atlas & Gazetteer:*** Page 32 F5

President Roosevelt created the 377,000-acre Talladega National Forest in 1936. The Lakeshore Loop Trail takes you through only a portion of this large forest reserve, along the banks of Lake Chinnabee. Fishing in the lake is excellent, but don't forget a state freshwater fishing license.

The route is narrow, for the most part, except where it follows the recreation area road to its conclusion. The trek is easy, with only minor climbs up rolling hills that funnel water runoff from the mountainside. If you take small children along for the trip, keep an eye on them because the path along the west-southwest side of the lake has a steep drop-off to the lake bank.

Along the trail in spring, you'll encounter camellias and mountain laurels in bloom. Along with the oak and hickory, you'll see pines, including

The trail crosses just below the dam's spillway.

Southern yellow and longleaf. The region is home to a multitude of reptiles and amphibians. At least 16 varieties of salamanders live here, including the spotted salamander and the red salamander. The salamanders may be hard to find because they change color to blend into their surroundings. But you may hear the sound of rustling leaves as the salamanders dart through the brush. Also be on the lookout for one of the 14 species of frogs. Bullfrogs, Southern leopard frogs,

Just What Is Dixie?

Just before the Civil War, the state of Louisiana issued a note of currency worth $10 called a dix—French for "ten." Eventually the South became known as "dixie." Montgomery, Alabama, was the first capital of the Confederacy, and Alabama is officially known as the Heart of Dixie.

mountain chorus frogs, and barking tree frogs are among those in the neighborhood. Snakes are prevalent in the forest, including ringneck, rat, king, and green snakes. Poisonous snakes include timber and pygmy rattlesnakes and the Eastern cottonmouth, but sightings of these are rare.

The Lake Chinnabee Recreation Area is closed between November 15 and April 15. During this period, the trail is still accessible by parking at the end of the recreation area road and hiking two miles down the road to the trailhead. Deer hunting season generally runs from October 15 to January 31, so wear hunter orange if you're out hiking then.

While at Lake Chinnabee, you might also want to stop by Cheaha State Park [*see Hike 24*], just three miles north on Alabama 281. Cheaha

MilesDirections

0.0 START from the southeast end of the Lake Chinnabee Recreational Area. A metal post blocks the road with a sign that reads "Closed to traffic." Walk down the paved road past the post to the southeast.

0.1 Come to an information board with posted information about various hikes and hiking within the forest. A creek flows next to the trail on the right. The trail is a manmade stone footpath with blue blazes. The blazes are for the Chinnabee Silent Trail, which also begins (or ends) here. In 100 yards, you'll reach a sign that reads "Lakeshore Loop 2 miles" and points to the right. The Chinnabee Silent Trail continues straight ahead to the southeast. Turn right here to the southwest and cross the creek over the rocks. Shortly the white blazes of the loop begin.

0.6 The trail tops out next to the dam.

0.7 Come to a sign that reads, "Lakeshore Trail" and points to the right. Turn right. *[**FYI.** You're going to cross some water soon so make sure those boots are waterproofed.]*

1.6 Come to a sign that reads "Lakeshore Trail—2-mile Loop." Turn right onto the paved road.

1.8 Come to a fork in the road. A sign in the center of the fork reads "Talladega National Forest/Lake Chinnabee Recreational Area." Take the right fork. This is the parking area. Pass a day-use fee box to the right.

1.9 Return to the start of the trail.

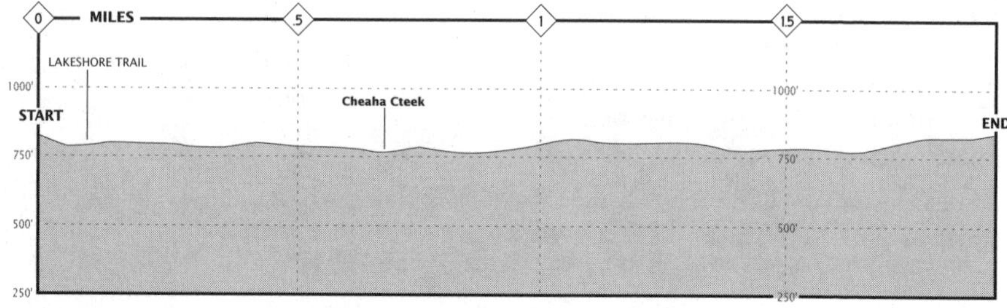

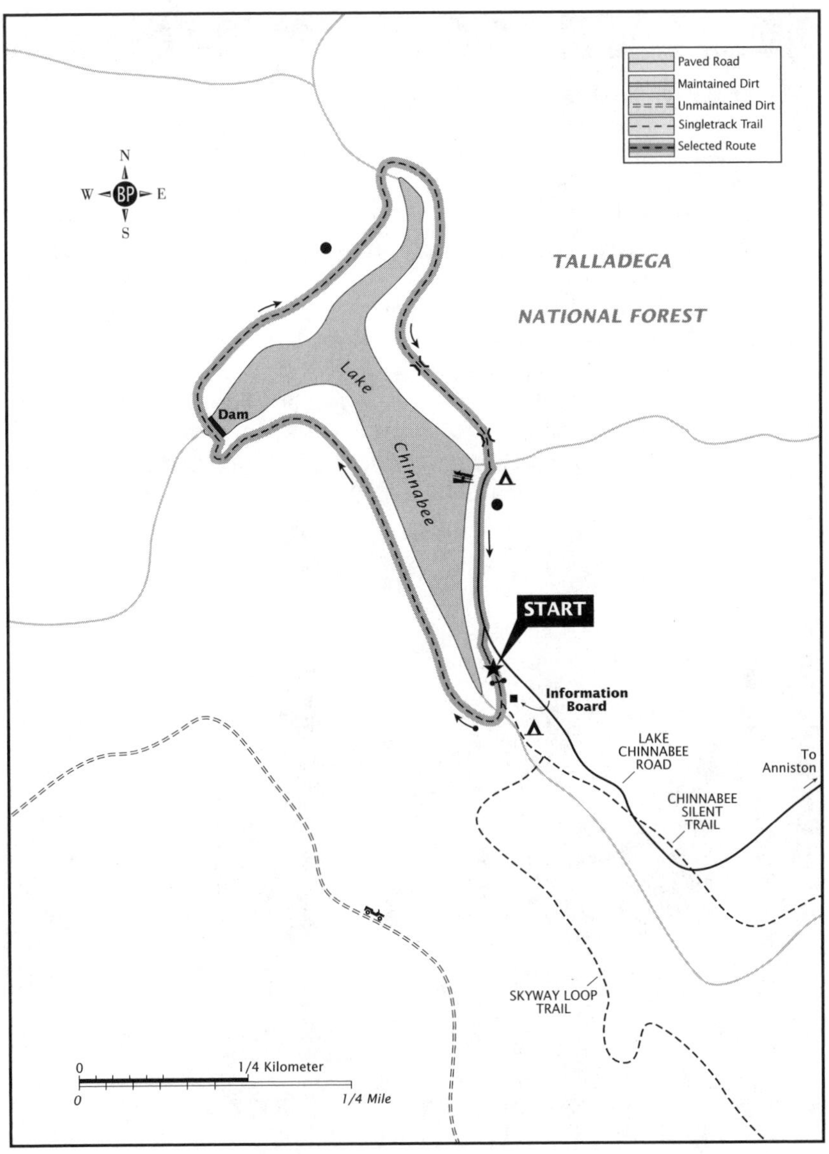

Mountain is the highest point in the state, at an elevation of 2,407 feet. The park offers short trails to some beautiful overlooks, including Pulpit Rock and Bald Rock. In addition, the Civilian Conservation Corps Museum is open daily at the park, without charge. You can see fine examples of the craftsmanship of CCC workers at the Cheaha Observation Tower and Bald Rock Lodge.

Local Events/Attractions:

Church of Saint Michael & All Angels, Anniston, AL; (256) 237–4011 or *www.brasenhill.com/stmikesaa/index.html—This church was built in 1888 by the founding families of the town of Anniston. The church features impressive examples of Norman architecture with Tiffany glass, a 95-foot bell tower and a 12-foot white Carrara marble altar.* • **Anniston Museum of Natural History**, Anniston, AL; (256) 237–6766 or *www.annistonmuseum.org—A museum for the ages, literally, with displays of dinosaurs and fossils, 400 species of birds, authentic Egyptian mummies, and more. Open Tuesday–Friday 9 A.M. –5 P.M., Saturday 10 A.M. –5 P.M., Sunday 1 P.M.–5 P.M.* • **Berman Museum**, Anniston, AL; (256) 237–6261—*The Berman Museum has a very rare collection of art and historic artifacts that run the gambit from bronze sculptures by Remington and Fraser's "The End of the Trail" to rare weapons from around the world, including a sword with 1,295 diamonds embedded in it.*

A view of the lake from the opposite side of the trailhead.

Hike Information

Trail Contacts:

Talladega National Forest, Talladega, AL; (256) 463-2273 or *www.r8web.com/alabama—The office is open Monday–Friday, 7:30 A.M.–5 P.M.*

Schedule:

Trail open year round. Lake Chinnabee Recreation Area is closed from November 15th–April 15th each year due to freeze potential. The trail can still be reached by hiking the two-mile road to the area.

Fees/Permits:

There is a $3 day-use fee at Lake Chinnabee Recreational Area (half price for Golden Age Passport holders).

Local Information:

Anniston / Calhoun County Convention and Visitors Bureau, Anniston, AL; 1-800-489-1087 or *www.calhounchamber.org* • **Greater Talladega Chamber of Commerce**, Talladega, AL; (256) 362-9075 or *www.talladega.com/business/chamber.htm*

Accommodations:

Cheaha State Park Lodge, Delta, AL; 1-800-846-2654—*This hotel is situated atop the states highest mountain. Half of the rooms have panoramic views of the surrounding countryside as does the swimming pool.* • **McClellan Inn**, Anniston, AL; (256) 820-3144

Restaurants:

Cheaha State Park Restaurant, Delta, AL; (256) 488-5115—*From catfish to steaks, the Cheaha Restaurant, located next to the state park's hotel, has wonderful food and a rustic feel. A huge fireplace, and a gigantic window overlooking the valley from the highest point in the state make this a unique dining experience.* • **Backyard Burgers**, Anniston, AL; (256) 236-4544

Organizations:

Alabama Trails Association, Birmingham, AL; *www.alabamatrails.com* • **Sierra Club East Alabama Chapter**, Auburn, AL; (334) 821-9817 • **Appalachian Trail Club of Alabama**, Birmingham, AL *http://sport.al.com/sport/atca*

Other Resources:

Bama Environmental News—Birmingham, AL; (205) 226-7739 or *www.bamanews.com*

Local Outdoor Retailers:

B&S Sporting Goods, Anniston, AL; (256) 237-6986 • **Smith's Sporting Goods**, Anniston, AL (256) 237-2895

Maps:

USGS maps: Cheaha Mountain, AL; Ironaton, AL • **Brochures** *available free of charge at the Cheaha State Park camp store.* • **Park maps**—*Pinhoti Trail Map Section 7 is available for $5.20 at the Cheaha State Park camp store or by mail through the Talladega National Forest ranger office.*

Chinnabee Silent Trail

Hike Summary

The Chinnabee Silent Trail, meandering up a hillside toward Lake Chinnabee, showcases the beauty of Talladega National Forest. Along the way, the wonders of the forest are revealed again and again. Just when you think it can't get any better, it does. In the gorge leading to the lake, the trail clings to rock walls on an elevated wooden platform and provides views of several waterfalls.

Hike Specs

Start: From the trailhead three miles south of the Cheaha State Park office
Length: 7.4-mile out-and-back
Approximate Hiking Time: 4–6 hours
Difficulty Rating: Easy over dirt footpaths and some rock; normally moderate sections made easier by steps
Trail Surface: Dirt path; some travel over rock
Lay of the Land: Mixture of white oak and longleaf pine; plants including rhododendron, flame azalea, and dogwood; waterfalls
Land Status: National forest
Nearest Town: Anniston, AL
Other Trail Users: None
Canine Compatibility: Dog friendly—except for dogs that don't like to climb stairs; ample water available; leash not required

Getting There

From Anniston: Take I-20 east for five miles to Exit 191. Merge into U.S. 431 South. Travel 3.5 miles and turn right onto AL 281. Head south on AL 281 for 16 miles and pass the Cheaha State Park headquarters and lodge on the right. Continue south 4.5 miles. The paved parking area will be on your left. If you pass the Turnipseed Hunting Camp, you've gone to far. ***DeLorme: Alabama Atlas & Gazetteer:*** Page 32 F5

Everyone who visits Cheaha State Park, Cheaha Mountain, and Talladega National Forest seems to return with endless stories about how gorgeous it all is: the overlooks, the waterfalls, the mountain landscapes. Sometimes it seems they exaggerate a bit, but seeing is believing. The area of Cheaha Mountain—at 2,407 feet elevation, the highest in the state—is truly a sight to behold, with massive rock outcroppings, raging streams, and impressive waterfalls. The Chinnabee Silent Trail is rightfully one of the most popular hiking routes in Alabama.

One of the many waterfalls along the trail.

The trail is named for the Creek Indian chief Chinnabee, an ally of Andrew Jackson during the Creek Indian Wars. The designation of "Silent Trail" comes from the trail's builders. Between 1973 and 1976, Boy Scout Troop 29 from the Alabama Institute for the Deaf and Blind, with the help of the U.S. Forest Service, created the trail.

The Chinnabee Silent Trail is actually six miles long, if you start at the Lake Chinnabee Recreation Area and hike all the way to the Pinhoti Trail at Caney Head on the summit of Talladega Mountain. But the most enjoyable way to hike the trail is to start from the trailhead three miles south of the Cheaha State Park office, on Alabama 281, and then travel north to the Lake Chinnabee Recreation Area. The trip is less difficult in this direction and it's two miles shorter. The real plus, however, is that the scenery unfolds at every turn.

MilesDirections

0.0 START from the east end the parking area on AL 281 south. Cross the highway to the north. A sign indicating a hiking trail will be across the highway where the trail enters the woods. The trail is marked with blue blazes.

0.1 At the bottom of the ravine, the trail comes to a small creek. The path looks like it continues straight, but it doesn't. Turn to the left here and cross the creek to the northeast. The trail now starts going up the other side of the ravine.

0.5 Cross a dirt road (a hiker sign will be seen on the other side where it reenters the woods).

1.0 Come to a fork and go right. *[**Side-trip.** It's worth the effort to take the left fork a short one tenth of a mile to the base of Cheaha Falls.]*

1.2 Reach the Cheaha Falls Shelter.

2.5 *[**FYI.** This area was cut in 1998 to prevent the spread of the Southern Pine Beetle through the forest.]*

3.0 *[**FYI.** Below to the left is a popular area for camping, along the banks of the stream. In 200 feet, the trail basically levels out high above the stream and the view of the falls and the canyon are spectacular in this area known as Devil's Den.]*

3.2 At the top of the climb, a 75-foot elevated wooden bridge clings to the rock cliff as it takes the trail to the west.

3.4 Come to a sign that reads "Chinnabee Silent Trail...Devil's Den—0.5 miles, Cheaha Falls Shelter—3 miles, Turnipseed 4 miles, Pinhoti 6 miles." Continue straight. In 50 feet, come to another sign that marks the turn off for the Skyway Loop Trail. Continue straight.

3.5 A stone marker identifies the trail as being built by Boy Scout Troop 29. In 10 feet, another sign marks the turn for the Lakeshore Loop Trail. Continue straight.

3.7 Come to the southeast end of the Lake Chinnabee Recreational Area parking lot and turn around. Retrace your tracks back to the trailhead.

7.4 Arrive back at your vehicle.

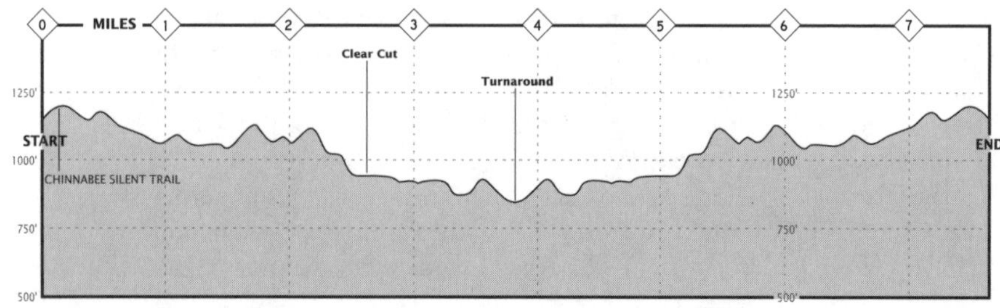

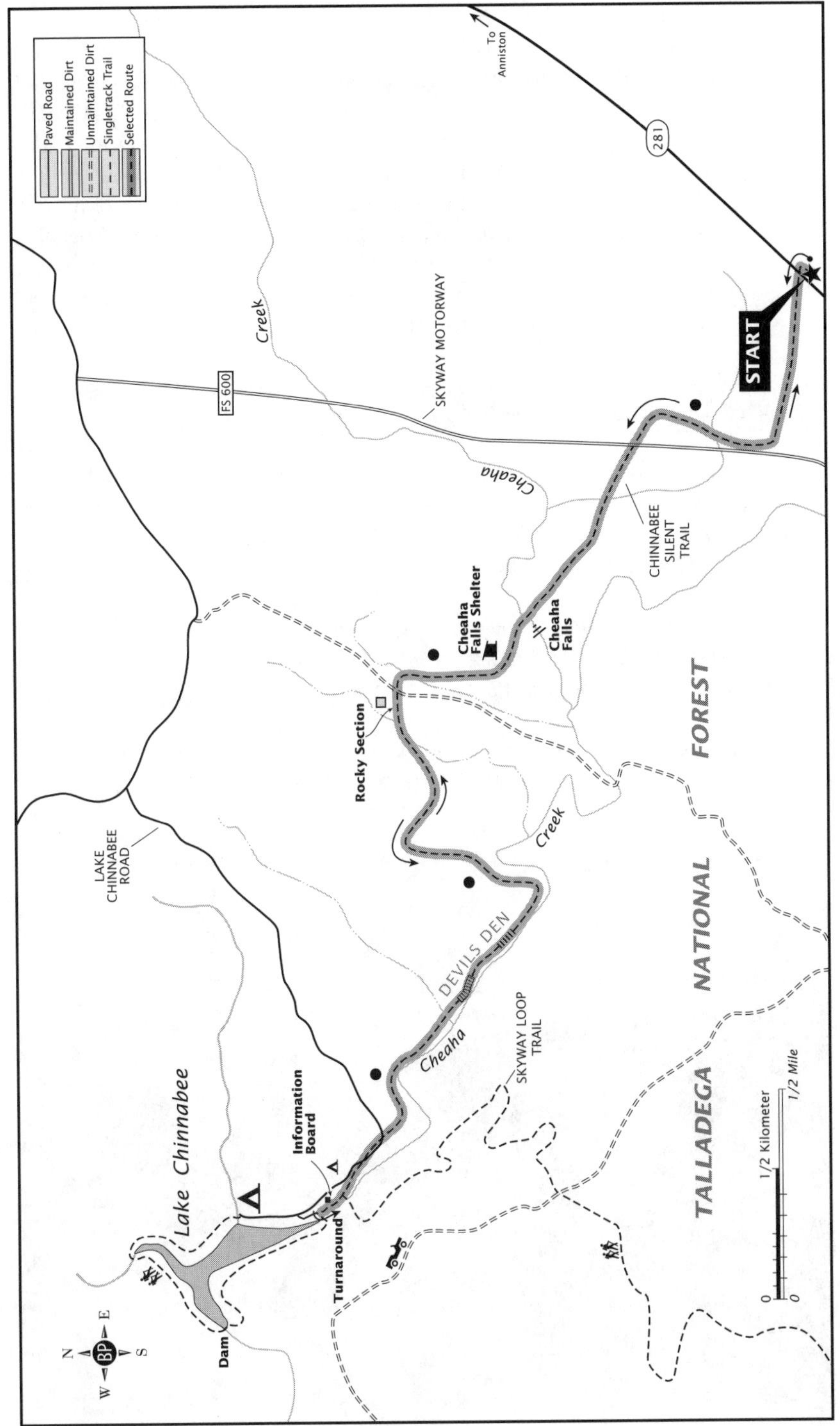
Paved Road
Maintained Dirt
Unmaintained Dirt
Singletrack Trail
Selected Route
To Anniston
281
START
SKYWAY MOTORWAY
FS 600
Creek
Cheaha
CHINNABEE SILENT TRAIL
Cheaha Falls Shelter
Cheaha Falls
Rocky Section
FOREST
NATIONAL
TALLADEGA
Creek
DEVILS DEN
Cheaha
SKYWAY LOOP TRAIL
LAKE CHINNABEE ROAD
Lake Chinnabee
Information Board
Turnaround
Dam
N
E
S
W
BP
0
1/2 Kilometer
1/2 Mile

Starting low and slow from the trailhead, the route winds its way around hillsides until the rushing of water can be heard. You'll soon reach Cheaha Falls—a series of falls with a nice pool at the bottom. A side trail leads for a tenth of a mile to the pool. The Chinnabee Silent Trail crosses Cheaha Creek at the head of the upper fall. A wooden footbridge once crossed here, but Hurricane Opal took care of that in 1995.

Topping the hill from the falls, a fine view unfolds to the left of the surrounding mountains. Here you'll find the spacious Cheaha Falls Shelter, a first-come first-serve facility for overnight backpackers. Farther along the trail—if you're hiking in spring, that is—wildflowers such as spring beauty and downy rattlesnake line the way.

Before Drinking That Water . . .

Alabama is blessed with beautiful mountain streams and lakes. While that clear water may look inviting to drink, even here it's wise to be cautious in order to avoid illness from pollution or disease organisms. Before drinking water along the trail, use one of these three purification methods:

- *Boil the water for three to five minutes before using.*
- *Filter the water with a purifying water bottle or pump.*
- *Put iodine or chlorine tablets into the water.*

If you aren't able to use one of these methods, try to locate a source of water where it first comes out of the ground, because the ground can act as a natural purifier.

View from the Cheaha Falls Shelter.

The trail soon ascends to meet Cheaha Creek again, in the canyon section known as the Devil's Den. Through the canyon, the creek churns white over the rocks. The trail moves progressively higher up the cliffs, eventually crossing the face of the cliffs at one point on an elevated wooden walkway clinging to the rock wall.

The trail ends at the Lake Chinnabee Recreation Area. The Lakeshore Trail begins here and loops for two miles around the lake *[see Hike 21]*. This also serves as a trailhead for the Skyway Loop Trail. A combination of the Chinnabee Silent Trail, Skyway Loop Trail, and Pinhoti Trail creates a 17-mile loop that provides an excellent weekend backpack trip.

All in all, the Chinnabee Silent Trail, with its wildness and its beauty, makes for one of the most enjoyable hikes in the state.

Hike Information

Trail Contacts:
Talladega National Forest, Talladega, AL; (256) 463–2273 or *www.r8web.com/alabama—The office is open Monday–Friday, 7 A.M.–5 P.M.*

Schedule:
Trail open year round. Lake Chinnabee Recreation Area is closed from November 15–April 15 each year due to freeze potential.

Fees/Permits:
No fee to hike the trail. Camping is allowed anywhere in the forest by using the "dispersal" method and following national forest guidelines. Camping at both the Lake Chinnabee Recreation Area and Cheaha State Park is $8 per night (half price for Golden Age Passport holders).

Local Information:
[See Hike 21: Lakeshore Trail]

Local Events/Attractions:
[See Hike 21: Lakeshore Trail]

Accommodations:
[See Hike 21: Lakeshore Trail]

Restaurants:
[See Hike 21: Lakeshore Trail]

Organizations:
[See Hike 21: Lakeshore Trail]

Other Resources:
[See Hike 21: Lakeshore Trail]

Local Outdoor Retailers:
[See Hike 21: Lakeshore Trail]

Maps:
USGS maps: Cheaha Mountain, AL • **Brochures**—*Cheaha and the national forest brochures are available free of charge at the Cheaha State Park camp store.* • **Park maps**—*Pinhoti Trail Map Section 7 is available for $5.20 at the Cheaha State Park camp store or by mail through the Talladega National Forest ranger office. This map also includes the Chinnabee Silent, Odum Scout, Cave Creek, Nubbin, and Skyway Loop trails.*

Skyway Loop Trail

Hike Summary

This hike can be a pretty good overnight trip culminating in a visit to Lake Chinnabee Recreation Area, where you can swim in the pools formed by the falls of Chinnabee Creek. The hike includes views of the surrounding mountains as you travel the ridgelines.

Hike Specs

Start: From Adams Gap trailhead
Length: 14.4-mile out-and-back
Approximate Hiking Time: 8–9 hours
Difficulty Rating: Moderate over rocky ridges; difficult on steep slopes
Trail Surface: Dirt and rock footpath
Lay of the Land: Oaks and longleaf pines; rhododendrons, azaleas, and dogwoods
Land Status: National forest
Nearest Town: Anniston, AL
Other Trail Users: None
Canine Compatibility: Dog friendly—ample water available; no leash required

Getting There

From Anniston: Take I-20 east for five miles to Exit 191. Merge into U.S. 431 South. Travel 3.5 miles and turn right onto AL 281. Head south on AL 281 for 16 miles and pass the Cheaha State Park headquarters and lodge on the right. Continue south 4.5 miles. The road dead-ends at Adams Gap and the trailhead. ***DeLorme: Alabama Atlas & Gazetteer:*** Page 32 F5

The Skyway Trail is a long, winding path around the ridges of Talladega National Forest just to the west of the state's highest peak, Cheaha Mountain. Aptly named, the Skyway Trail travels up and down moderate climbs along the ridges as it makes its way to Lake Chinnabee Recreation Area.

The trail beginning at Adams Gap follows the Pinhoti Trail for the first 0.2 miles. After the trail branches off, watch for families of armadillos rooting through the brush and leaves. Armadillos are determined to stand up to anything they feel endangers them. After walking around a group of armadillos, you may find they are chasing you down the trail. Make a loud noise and they should scatter.

Also along the trail, you may see large numbers of white-tailed deer and wild turkeys (after all, *Pinhoti* means *turkey home*). The trail makes its way through stands of white oaks and Southern longleaf pines. The path is also lined with rhododendrons, flame azaleas, and dogwoods that bloom and brighten the way from spring to fall.

Winding along, the trail crosses several creeks. Two of the largest are Barbaree Creek, near the midpoint of the hike, and Hubbard Creek, near

Chinnabee Creek.

the end. About two miles into the hike, the trail passes through a previously burned area that is very open and affords good views of the neighboring mountains.

The trail eventually begins a steep descent to Chinnabee Creek. The return trip also takes this path, making for a steep uphill climb. Just after the Chinnabee Creek crossing, you have the option of taking a side excursion on the Chinnabee Silent Trail for a half-mile walk to a swimming hole. Here, the creek cascades down a rock wall and forms a deep blue-green pool, just the place for a swim in the cold mountain water. Also there are several nice primitive campsites next to the creek. No fee or permit is required. Camping is also allowed anywhere along the trail except in the Lake Chinnabee Recreation Area.

From Chinnabee Creek, the Skyway Trail leads to Lake Chinnabee and then uses the Lakeshore Loop Trail *[see Hike 21]* for the next two miles to swing around the lake and head back on your original trail for the return to Adams Gap. Lake Chinnabee offers excellent bass fishing—a state freshwater fishing license is required.

If you are looking for a good overnight hiking experience on a loop route, try connecting the Skyway Trail, Chinnabee Silent Trail, and Pinhoti Trail together (leaving out the Lakeshore Loop). This forms a 17-mile circuit beginning at Adams Gap.

MilesDirections

0.0 START from the Adams Gap trailhead. A Pinhoti National Recreational Trail sign marks the entrance. The trail has diamond shaped Pinhoti (turkey) markers on the trees. *[**FYI.** Beware of the armadillos (especially if you have a dog with you).]*

0.2 Come to a fork and go right. (The left fork is the Pinhoti Trail.) Blue triangle blazes soon mark the Skyway Loop Trail.

0.6 Cross an off-road trail to the west. (The marker is hard to see on the other side of the road.)

1.0 Pass a campsite on the left.

2.0 Cross a dirt road.

2.9 Cross an off-road path.

3.0 Cross a dirt road (a hiker sign on the other side shows the path reentering the woods).

3.9 Come to the banks of a Hubbard Creek—a very nice, wide creek. In about 20 feet, cross the creek using stepping stones.

4.0 Come to a fork and go right. (The left fork takes you to a campsite.)

4.5 Cross a dirt road.

4.7 Cross a dirt road.

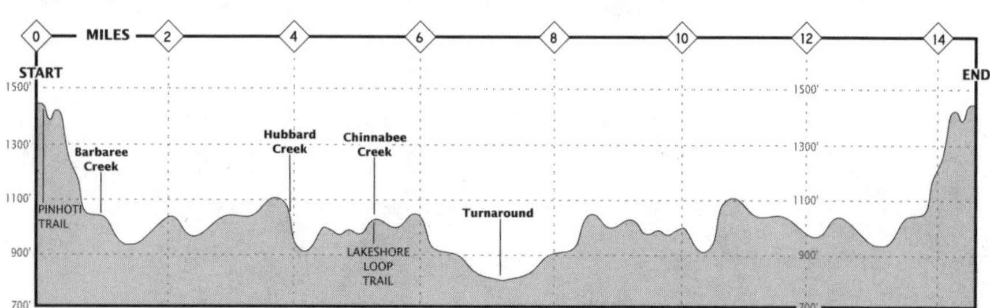

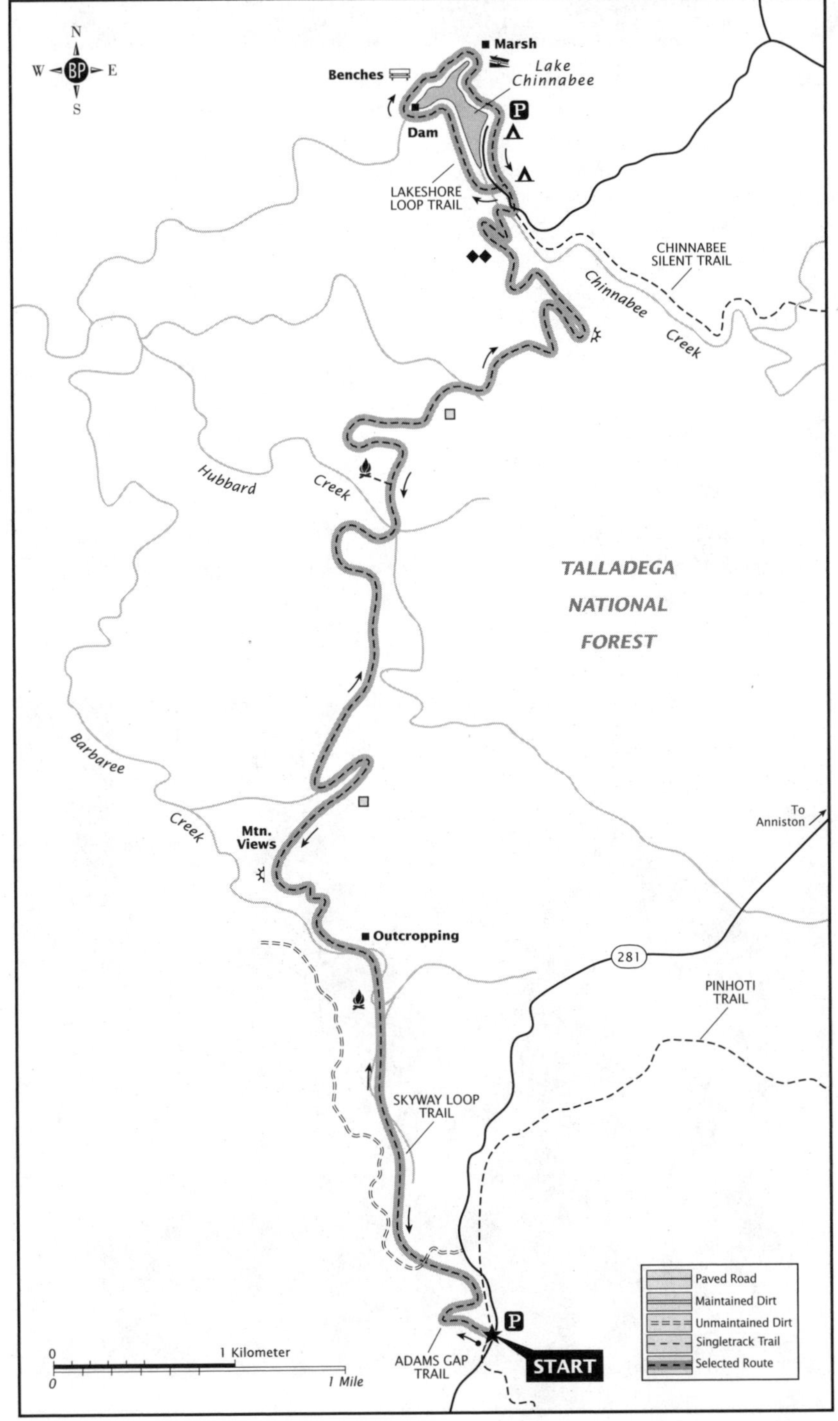
N
W
E
S
BP
Marsh
Benches
Lake Chinnabee
Dam
LAKESHORE LOOP TRAIL
CHINNABEE SILENT TRAIL
Chinnabee Creek
Hubbard Creek
TALLADEGA NATIONAL FOREST
Barbaree Creek
Mtn. Views
To Anniston
Outcropping
281
PINHOTI TRAIL
SKYWAY LOOP TRAIL
ADAMS GAP TRAIL
START
0
1 Kilometer
0
1 Mile
Paved Road
Maintained Dirt
Unmaintained Dirt
Singletrack Trail
Selected Route

MilesDirections (Continued)

5.3 Cross the Chinnabee Creek and come to a T-intersection with the Chinnabee Silent Trail. Turn left here on this wide dirt footpath. Shortly, come to a sign that reads "Lakeshore Loop 2 miles" and points to the left. Turn left here and re-cross the creek over the rocks. On the other side, the trail white blazes of the Lakeshore Loop portion of this hike begin.

6.0 Come to a sign that reads, "Lakeshore Trail" and points to the right. Turn right. *[**FYI.** You're going to cross some water soon so make sure those boots are waterproofed.]*

6.9 Come to a sign that reads "Lakeshore Trail—2-mile Loop." Turn right onto the paved road.

7.1 Come to a fork in the road. A sign in the center of the fork reads "Talladega National Forest/Lake Chinnabee Recreational Area." Take the right fork. This is the parking area. Pass a day-use fee box to the right.

7.2 Come to an information board detailing various hikes within the forest. In 100 yards, come to a sign that reads "Lakeshore Loop 2 miles" and points to the right. Continue straight and a sign that reads "Skyway Loop" and points to the right shows the direction back to the trail. Retrace your steps back to the Adams Gap trailhead.

14.4 Arrive back at the trailhead.

Watch out for the armadillos along the way.

If you plan to hike the Skyway Trail by starting at the Lake Chinnabee Recreation Area and walking to Adams Gap, remember that the recreation area is closed to vehicles between November 15 and April 15. However, the trail is still accessible by parking at the end of the recreation area road and hiking two miles down the road to the trailhead at Lake Chinnabee. Deer hunting season generally runs from October 15 to January 31, so wear hunter orange if you're out hiking then. The Talladega National Forest office has exact dates.

Hike Information

Trail Contacts:
Talladega National Forest, Talladega, AL; (256) 463–2273 or *www.r8web.com/alabama—The office is open Monday–Friday, 7 A.M.–5 P.M..*

Schedule:
Open year round

Fees/Permits:
No fee to hike the trail. Camping is allowed anywhere in the forest by using the "dispersal" method and following national forest guidelines.

Local Information:
[See Hike 21: Lakeshore Trail]

Local Events/Attractions:
[See Hike 21: Lakeshore Trail]

Accommodations:
[See Hike 21: Lakeshore Trail]

Restaurants:
[See Hike 21: Lakeshore Trail]

Organizations:
[See Hike 21: Lakeshore Trail]

Other Resources:
[See Hike 21: Lakeshore Trail]

Local Outdoor Retailers:
[See Hike 21: Lakeshore Trail]

Maps:
USGS maps: Cheaha Mountain, AL • **Brochures**—*available free of charge at the Cheaha State Park camp store* • **Park maps**—*Pinhoti Trail Map Section 7 is available for $5.20 at the Cheaha State Park camp store or by mail through the Talladega National Forest ranger office. This map also includes the Chinnabee Silent, Odum Scout, Cave Creek, Nubbin, and Skyway Loop trails.*

Rock Garden Trail

Hike Summary

The Rock Garden Trail, which happens to be the most challenging hike in this book, begins easy enough from Cheaha Lake but then becomes more strenuous as it climbs sharply up and over boulders and bluffs to a point near the summit of Cheaha Mountain.

Hike Specs

Start: From the Cheaha Lake picnic area
Length: 1.6-mile out-and-back
Approximate Hiking Time: 2–3 hours
Difficulty Rating: Difficult over the towering overlook called the Rock Garden
Trail Surface: Dirt path, turning into a rocky path, then some scrambling up rocks
Lay of the Land: Thick hardwood forest; boulders and bluffs
Land Status: State park
Nearest Town: Anniston, AL
Other Trail Users: None
Canine Compatibility: Not dog friendly—due to steep, difficult climb; if you do take a dog, leash not required

Getting There

From Anniston: Take I-20 east for five miles to Exit 191. Merge onto U.S. 431 South. Travel 3.5 miles and turn right onto AL 281 south. Head south on AL 281 for 19 miles, passing the Cheaha State Park headquarters and lodge. Turn right onto the Lake Road and travel three miles to Cheaha Lake. Turn right and head 0.1 miles to a fork. Take the right fork and travel an additional 0.1 miles. Park at the bathhouse. ***DeLorme: Alabama Atlas & Gazetteer:*** Page 32 E5

This book covers the spectrum of hiking difficulty. The easy, casual walk along the Weeks Bay Nature Trail in the Gulf Coast Region is included to give every member of the family an enjoyable and educational hike. At the opposite end of that spectrum, the Rock Garden Trail described here is included for hikers who like difficulty and steep climbing.

Although this trail in Cheaha State Park is only 1.6 miles, round trip, there's a huge elevation gain on the way up. Beginning at the Cheaha Lake picnic area at an elevation of 1,264 feet, the trail heads straight up Cheaha Mountain to an elevation of about 2,100 feet. That's not far below the 2,407-foot summit of Cheaha, the highest mountain in Alabama.

Not many trails give you a view of the end of the trail from the very start, but this one does. Standing at the trailhead, look up to the north and you'll see the end of the trail at the top of the outcropping known as the Rock Garden, just to the left of the Cheaha Lodge Restaurant.

The starting point, Cheaha Lake—far below.

The Rock Garden Trail begins up a gradual grade, following the banks of a creek up a ravine. But after 0.3 miles, that's where the joyride ends. From there, the trail gets progressively steeper and rockier as it maneuvers around large boulders and outcroppings and courses through a dense forest of white oaks, dappled with rhododendrons, flame azaleas, and dogwoods. At a little over half a mile from the trailhead, the path begins peeking out of the trees at the surrounding views—and they are spectacular.

From this point on, the trail rounds the outcroppings with ever-expanding views of the mountains and valley. Don't be surprised to see rock climbers beginning their ascent of the cliffs or rappelling down. Take a glance skyward and you may even spot a climber high in the air, sliding slowly across on a rope strung from one tall outcropping to another several hundred feet away. Climbers call it "the best view in the house."

The trail finally pops out at the top of two large, flat outcroppings atop the Rock Garden. Here you can relax, take in the view, and watch the activity around the cliffs—and look at your original trailhead far below. Way down at the bottom is Cheaha Lake, waiting for your return.

MilesDirections

0.0 START from the bathhouse at Cheaha Lake. Travel around the paved road until you see a reflective blue trail marker. Head off into the woods on the dirt footpath.

0.5 The hardest part of the trip is upon you.

0.8 The trail levels off considerably and comes to a huge rock outcropping overlooking the valley below. Off to the right is Cheaha Lake, where you started. *[**FYI.** Another 100 feet up the path is a dirt road and the northern trailhead—where you'd park if you drove up.]* Turn around here and head back down.

1.6 Arrive back at the trailhead.

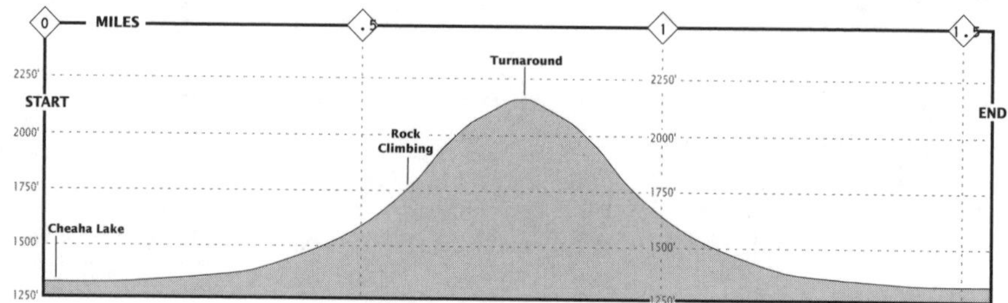

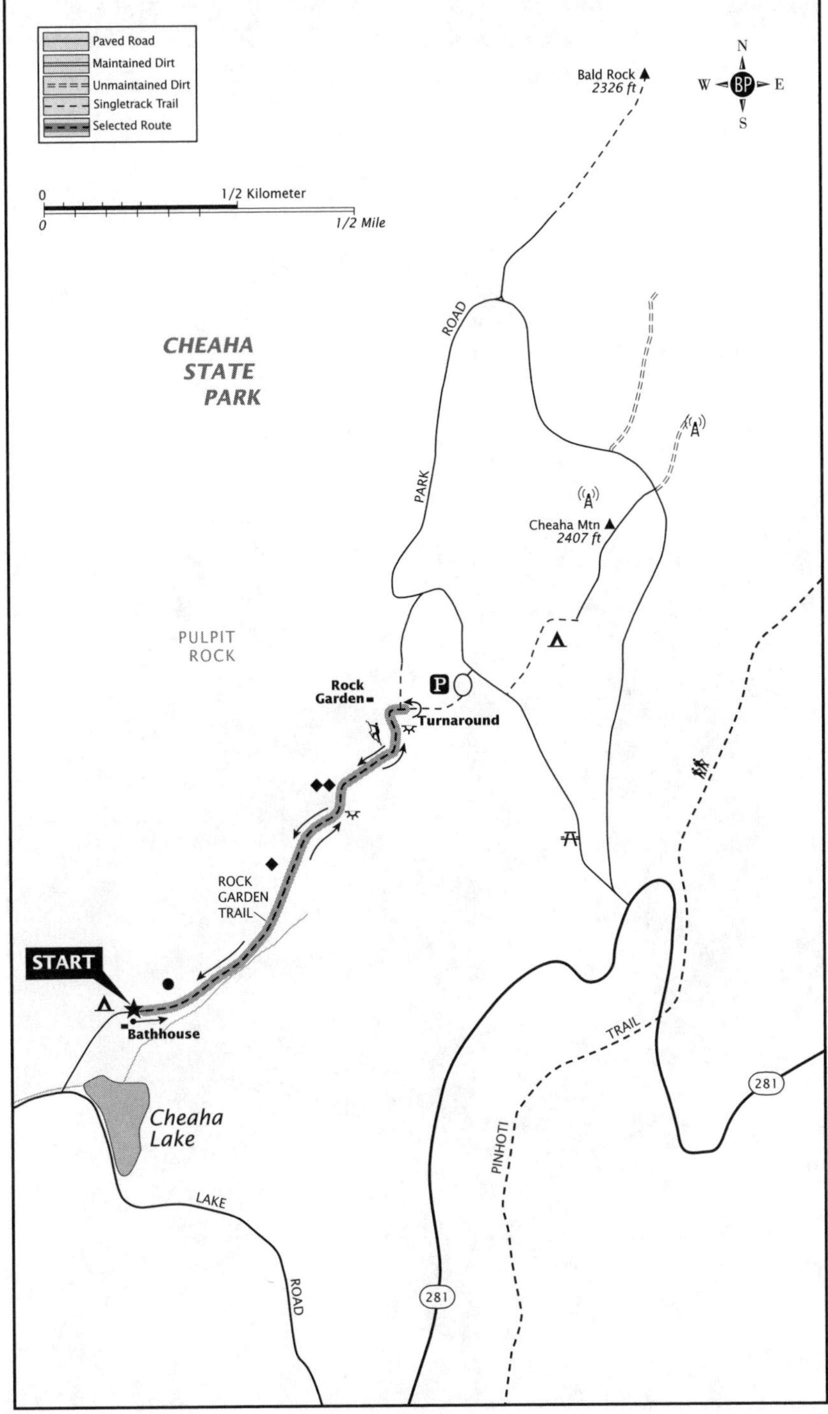
Paved Road
Maintained Dirt
Unmaintained Dirt
Singletrack Trail
Selected Route
0
1/2 Kilometer
0
1/2 Mile
N
W
E
S
BP
Bald Rock
2326 ft
CHEAHA
STATE
PARK
PARK ROAD
Cheaha Mtn
2407 ft
PULPIT
ROCK
Rock
Garden
Turnaround
ROCK
GARDEN
TRAIL
START
Bathhouse
Cheaha
Lake
LAKE
ROAD
281
PINHOTI
TRAIL
281

Local Events/Attractions:

Talladega SuperSpeedway, Talladega, AL; (256) 761–4702 or *www.talladegasuperspeedway.com —NASCAR's most competitive and fastest track. You can make arrangements for a drive around this famous track with an embankment of almost four stories, bus tours available.* • **International Motor Sports Hall of Fame**, Talladega, AL; (256) 362–5002—*Five buildings with cars and memorabilia from 1902 to present. Tributes to sports writers, ARCA Champions and more. Open everyday 9* A.M.*–5* P.M.*, closed Thanksgiving Day, Christmas Day, and Easter Morning.* • *[See Hike 21: Lakeshore Trail]*

The best view in the house.

From the Rock Garden, it's only about a tenth of a mile to the parking area for visitors who choose to drive to the summit of Cheaha Mountain instead of hiking. Many visitors take the easy approach to hiking the Rock Garden Trail, making a one-way trip out of it by starting from the parking area at the summit and then hiking down to Cheaha Lake (where they can be met by a shuttle car).

When you're done with the hike, you can cool down and relax at Cheaha Lake. Swimming is good in the cold mountain lake, and there are diving boards and lifeguards, plus picnic tables, a picnic pavilion, and a bathhouse. There is a $1 day-use fee for parking at the lake or the summit.

Hike Information

Trail Contacts:

Cheaha State Park, Delta, AL; (256) 488-5111 • **Talladega National Forest**, Talladega, AL; (256) 463-2273 or *www.r8web.com/alabama—The office is open Monday–Friday, 7:30 A.M.–5 P.M.*

Schedule:

Open year round

Fees/Permits:

A $1 day-use fee is charged for parking.

Local Information:

Anniston / Calhoun County Convention and Visitors Bureau, Anniston, AL; 1-800-489-1087 or *www.calhounchamber.org* • **Greater Talladega Chamber of Commerce**, Talladega, AL; (256) 362-9075 or *www.talladega.com/business/chamber.htm*

Accommodations:

Anniston Efficiency Motel, Anniston, AL; (256) 238-0060 • **Victoria Inn**, Anniston, AL; (256) 236-0503 • *[See Hike 21: Lakeshore Trail]*

Restaurants:

Old Hickory, Talladega, AL; (256) 362-0677 • **Buena Vista Mexican Restaurant**, Talladega, AL; (256) 362-5754 • **Daily Café**, Anniston, AL; (256) 238-8100 • *[See Hike 21: Lakeshore Trail]*

Organizations:

[See Hike 21: Lakeshore Trail]

Other Resources:

[See Hike 21: Lakeshore Trail]

Local Outdoor Retailers:

[See Hike 21: Lakeshore Trail]

Maps:

USGS maps: Cheaha Mountain, AL • **Brochures**—available free of charge at the Cheaha State Park camp store • **Park maps**—*Pinhoti Trail Map Section 7 is available for $5.20 at the Cheaha State Park camp store or by mail through the Talladega National Forest ranger office. This map also includes the Chinnabee Silent, Odum Scout, Cave Creek, Nubbin, and Skyway Loop trails.*

Nubbin Creek Trail

Hike Summary

Although the full Nubbin Creek Trail is four miles long, the first two miles are the most enjoyable and are described here. The trail meanders gradually up the side of Talladega Mountain, passing three waterfalls and ending with panoramic views. The trail is lined with a variety of wildflowers in spring.

Hike Specs

Start: From the Nubbin Creek trailhead
Length: 3.8-mile out-and-back
Approximate Hiking Time: 2–3 hours
Difficulty Rating: Moderate, due to narrow trail and brush
Trail Surface: Dirt and clay; rock-covered near falls
Lay of the Land: White oak and chestnut forest; longleaf pine forest; rhododendron and mountain laurel; waterfalls
Land Status: National forest
Nearest Town: Anniston, AL
Other Trail Users: None
Canine Compatibility: Dog friendly—though could be tough on older or out-of-shape dogs; ample water available; no leash required

Getting There

From Anniston: Take I-20 east for five miles to Exit 191. Merge onto U.S. 431 South. Travel 3.5 miles and turn right onto AL 281 South. Head south for seven miles and turn left onto AL 49 South. Head south 6.3 miles until the road forks. Take the right fork (this is Nubbin Creek Road). A sign will be seen that says "Nubbin Creek Trailhead 3 miles." In 0.8 miles, the paved road turns into a clay road. Continue an additional 2.2 miles and the Nubbin Creek Trailhead will be to the right. ***DeLorme: Alabama Atlas & Gazetteer:*** Page 32 F5

Waterfalls abound in the Talladega National Forest, and the Nubbin Creek Trail highlights several of them. The main attractions of the trail fall within its first two miles. The final two miles, which aren't covered in this description, are overgrown with vegetation and lack sufficient trail markers. The full 4.0-mile trail ends at its intersection with the Cave Creek Trail *[see Hike 26]*. A round-trip hike to this point could make a good overnight trip, with some nice campsites along the ridge tops.

Even on the first two miles, the Nubbin Creek Trail is dense with rhododendron bushes, covering sections of the route. It's entirely passable, but on a rainy day, a poncho won't be enough to keep your pants dry. A couple sections of the trail are especially narrow, where feeder creeks have washed away parts of the trail, leaving sharp drop-offs. On a day of heavy rain, these spots can be dangerous.

One of many stream crossings along the Nubbin Creek Trail.

With that said, on to the good stuff. Overall, the trail is not difficult. There are some moderate climbs up and around rocky waterfalls. The most picturesque time to hike the trail is in early to mid spring when rains fill the creeks and the waterfalls run full.

From its beginning at the Nubbin Creek Trailhead, the route is narrow, with longleaf pines, white oak, and brush giving the path an enclosed feeling. Details on trail conditions and national forest rules are posted on an information board near the start of the trail. There is also a register here. It's a good idea to fill out the registration card before starting any trip into the wilderness, because you never know when you might want searchers to be able to find you in an emergency.

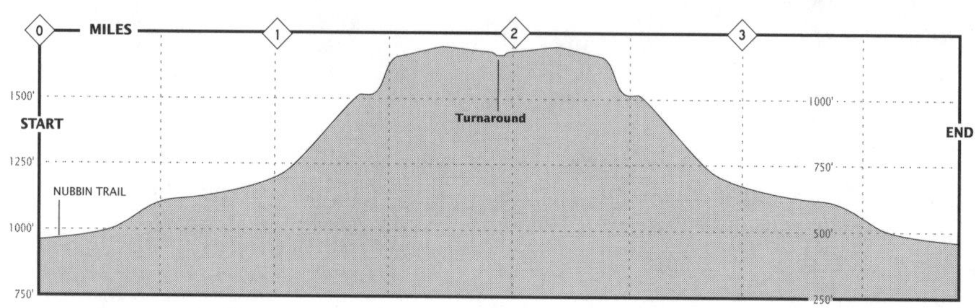

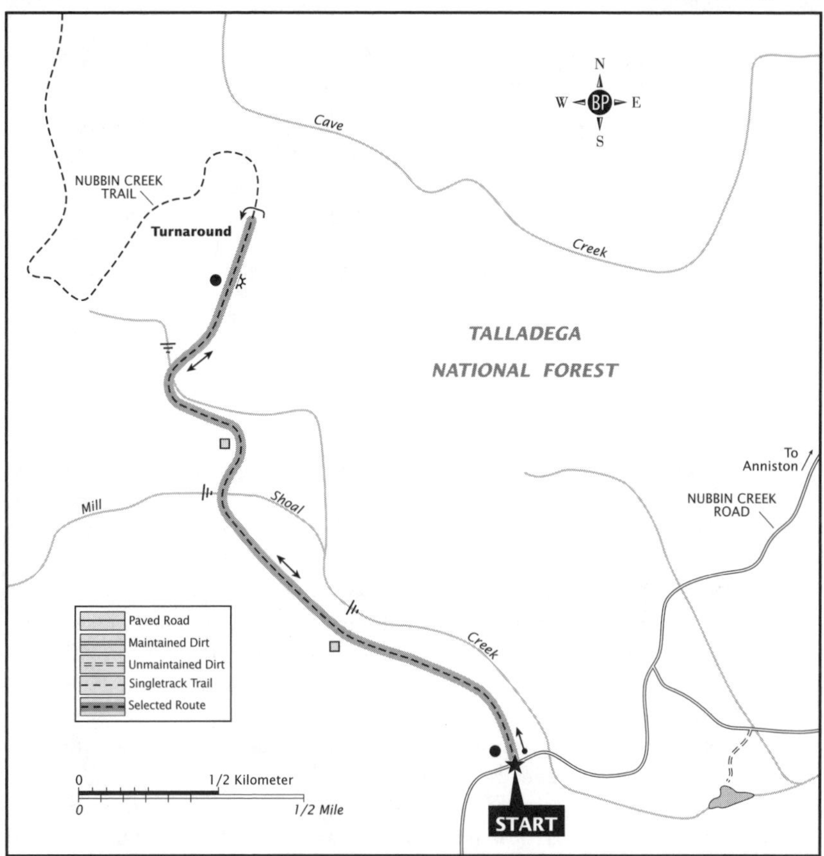

MilesDirections

0.0 START from the Nubbin Creek Trailhead. A hiker sign marks the entrance into the pines. White blazes line the trail.

0.3 Pass a short, unmarked trail to the right. In 100 feet, pass a second side trail. [***Side-trip.*** *This second trail is approximately 100 feet long and rather steep, but leads to a beautiful bluff high above the rushing stream and waterfall.]*

1.4 The trail narrows to a 6-inch rock ledge with a steep drop to the right as it crosses a creek. In 50 feet the trail comes to the base of the falls. Carefully cross the moss covered rocks of the stream.

1.5 The path runs just below the highest elevation of the trip, 1,600 feet.

1.8 The trail markers are all but non-existent through this section.

1.9 The brush thins out as the trail comes to a boulder field. To the right the views of the surrounding mountains open up. Turn around here and retrace your route back to the Nubbin Creek Trailhead. [***Option.*** *You can continue on to the intersection of Cave Creek Trail. The hike from this point on is extremely difficult, not marked, and very overgrown.]*

'Bama Trivia

- *Alabama is the namesake of a Native American tribe, the Alibamu.*
- *Isabella de Soto, wife of explorer Hernando de Soto, planted the first fig tree in the United States, on Dauphin Island, Alabama.*
- *The number of acres of forestland in Alabama ranks third in the nation.*
- *350,000 endangered American gray bats call a waterside cave at Joe Wheeler State Park near Florence, AL, home. Visitors can see them swarm en mass after sunset between April and October.*

The trail winds gradually uphill and you begin to hear Mill Shoals Creek. The first of two short side trails toward the creek comes in from the right. This first side trail goes about 100 yards to the banks of the fast-flowing creek. But the real scenery is on the second side trail, which takes off about 50 feet farther along the trail. This short path takes you to the edge of a bluff that rises more than 100 feet above the creek, which tumbles here over a series of falls. This is definitely the highlight view of the trip.

Back on the Nubbin Creek Trail, you'll hike through an area where white bloodroot and toothwort dot the trail sides in spring. In places where the trees thin out and the surrounding mountains and ridges come into view, look for white dogwoods on the hillsides.

At the 1.4-mile mark—about the time you can spot the next waterfall ahead on the right—the trail makes its way along the side of a ravine and becomes little more than a ledge, less than a foot wide. You'll need to pay close attention to your footing. At one point a feeder creek to the stream far below cuts across the trail. The trail is washed out, and it'll take some careful maneuvering to get safely around this spot.

Shortly after the washout, you'll reach a 70-foot waterfall. The trail crosses the creek at the base of the falls. From here, the trail makes its way into a boulder field for good open views. This is the end point of the hike described here.

Hike Information

Trail Contacts:
Talladega National Forest, Talladega, AL; (256) 463–2273 or *wwwr8web.com/alabama—The office is open Monday–Friday, 7:30 A.M.–5 P.M..*

Schedule:
Open year round

Fees/Permits:
No fee to hike the trail. Camping is allowed anywhere in the forest by using the "dispersal" method and following national forest guidelines.

Local Information:
[See Hike 21: Lakeshore Trail]

Local Events/Attractions:
[See Hike 21: Lakeshore Trail]

Accommodations:
[See Hike 21: Lakeshore Trail]

Restaurants:
[See Hike 21: Lakeshore Trail]

Organizations:
[See Hike 21: Lakeshore Trail]

Other Resources:
[See Hike 21: Lakeshore Trail]

Local Outdoor Retailers:
[See Hike 21: Lakeshore Trail]

Maps:
USGS maps: Cheaha Mountain, AL • **Brochures**—*available free of charge at the Cheaha State Park camp store* • **Park maps**—*Pinhoti Trail Map Section 7 is available for $5.20 at the Cheaha State Park camp store or by mail through the Talladega National Forest ranger office. This map also includes the Chinnabee Silent, Odum Scout, Cave Creek, Nubbin, and Skyway Loop trails.*

Cave Creek Trail

Hike Summary

The Cave Creek Trail travels the side of Hernandez Peak for a trip that takes you through tunnels of rhododendron bushes. You'll also enjoy excellent views of the surrounding mountains. The hiking becomes difficult from the Nubbin Creek Trail junction on Little Caney Head to the end of the trial at the Pinhoti connector on Parker High Point because the trail has become overgrown with thorn bushes and shrubs.

Hike Specs

Start: From the north parking area on AL 281 (Cheaha Trailhead)
Length: 13.8-mile out-and-back
Approximate Hiking Time: 6–7 hours
Difficulty Rating: Easy along the side of Hernandez Peak; moderate climbs over Little Caney Head and Parker High Point; difficult beyond the Nubbin Creek Trail junction due to brush
Trail Surface: Dirt path and rock
Lay of the Land: Rhododendrons and wildflowers, along with longleaf pines, white oaks, and dogwoods
Land Status: State park and national forest
Nearest Town: Anniston, AL
Other Trail Users: None
Canine Compatibility: Dog friendly—bring water, which is scarce after the creeks at the trail beginning; no leash required

Getting There

From Anniston: Take I-20 east for five miles to Exit 191. Merge onto U.S. 431 South. Travel 3.5 miles and turn right onto AL 281 South. Go 13 miles on AL 281 and the Cheaha Trailhead will be plainly marked on the left. ***DeLorme: Alabama Atlas & Gazetteer:*** Page 32 F5

Cave Creek Trail gets its name from a creek at the start of the hike that flows through large rocks to make small "caves." The trail is lined with rhododendron, dogwoods, and white oaks. From spring through fall wildflowers color the mountaintops like a rainbow. Among the wildlife you're likely to see are white-tailed deer, wild turkeys, wild pigs, and foxes. Hawks are often seen soaring around the bluffs.

Once you leave the trailhead, the path is nice and level, though rocky in many places, as it heads south along the side of Hernandez Peak. The trail narrows in several spots, with a steep drop to one side into a hollow. Be careful here, especially over rocky areas.

All along this part of the route, through Cheaha State Park, the trail is lined with rhododendron bushes. The best time to walk this path is in late spring or early summer when the bushes are in full bloom. They are so thick that they form flowering tunnels. Soon the trail leaves the state park and

enters Talladega National Forest. The trail jogs to the west and at this elbow provides a spectacular view of surrounding mountains.

From here the trail follows the side of a ridge and then starts making its way up to just below the top of 2,000-foot-high Little Caney Head. At this point, 4.7 miles into the hike, the Nubbin Creek Trail splits off to the east—and this is where the difficult stuff begins. The park service information will tell you that the Cave Creek Trail is marked with tree blazes, but don't expect to see them. From this point on, to the end of the trail, the brush is so thick that it obscures the trail. It's almost easier to just bushwhack than to try and follow the official route.

MilesDirections

0.0 START from the Cheaha Trailhead off AL 281. The trail leaves the parking area to the west behind a "Pinhoti National Recreational Trail" sign. The trail forks in 200 feet at an information board and registration box. Take the left fork. (The right fork leads to the Pinhoti Trail.)

1.7 Pass the Cheaha Wilderness / Talladega National Forest sign.

2.1 The trail forks. Go right, around the outcropping. (The left fork heads steeply up an outcropping to the south.) Shortly, the two trails rejoin. Continue through a campsite.

2.3 Pass a campsite on the right.

2.5 Pass another campsite on the right.

2.8 *[**Note.** The trail turns rocky and is high above a creek with a steep drop off into a hollow to the left. It's very narrow here, so be careful of your footing as you go around.]*

3.8 Come to a fork where a sign reads "Pinhoti" and points to the north; and "State Park" and points to the northeast. Another sign here reads "Nubbin Creek Road" and points to the southwest. Take the left fork.

4.7 Come to the intersection of the Nubbin Creek Trail and another connector to the Pinhoti (two signs mark the crossing). Continue straight. *[**FYI.** Box turtles can be found here.]*

5.0 Pass a campsite on the right.

5.7 Pass a campsite on the left.

6.3 Come to a fork and go left, continuing up hill.

6.8 The trail is hard to see through the brush as it heads to the west.

6.9 Pass a campsite on the right. The trail is rocky again as it comes to a fork, where a sign marks the intersection with the Odum Scout Trail. Turn around point and retrace your route back to the Cheaha Trailhead. *[**Option.** To make a loop, turn right on to the Odum Trail and take it to its intersection with the Pinhoti Trail, where you'll turn right and follow the Pinhoti back to the Cheaha Trailhead.]*

13.8 Arrive back at the trailhead.

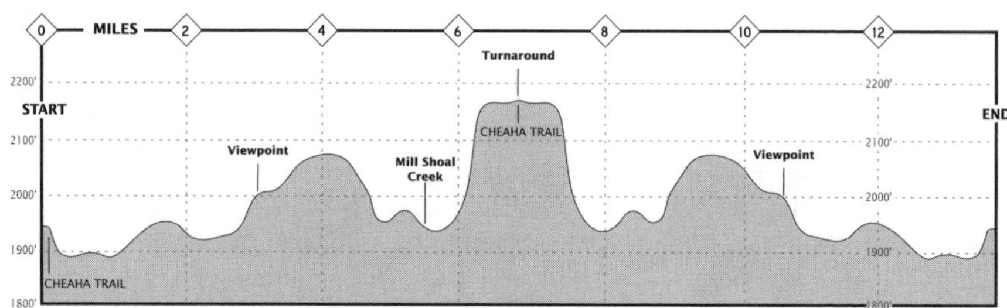

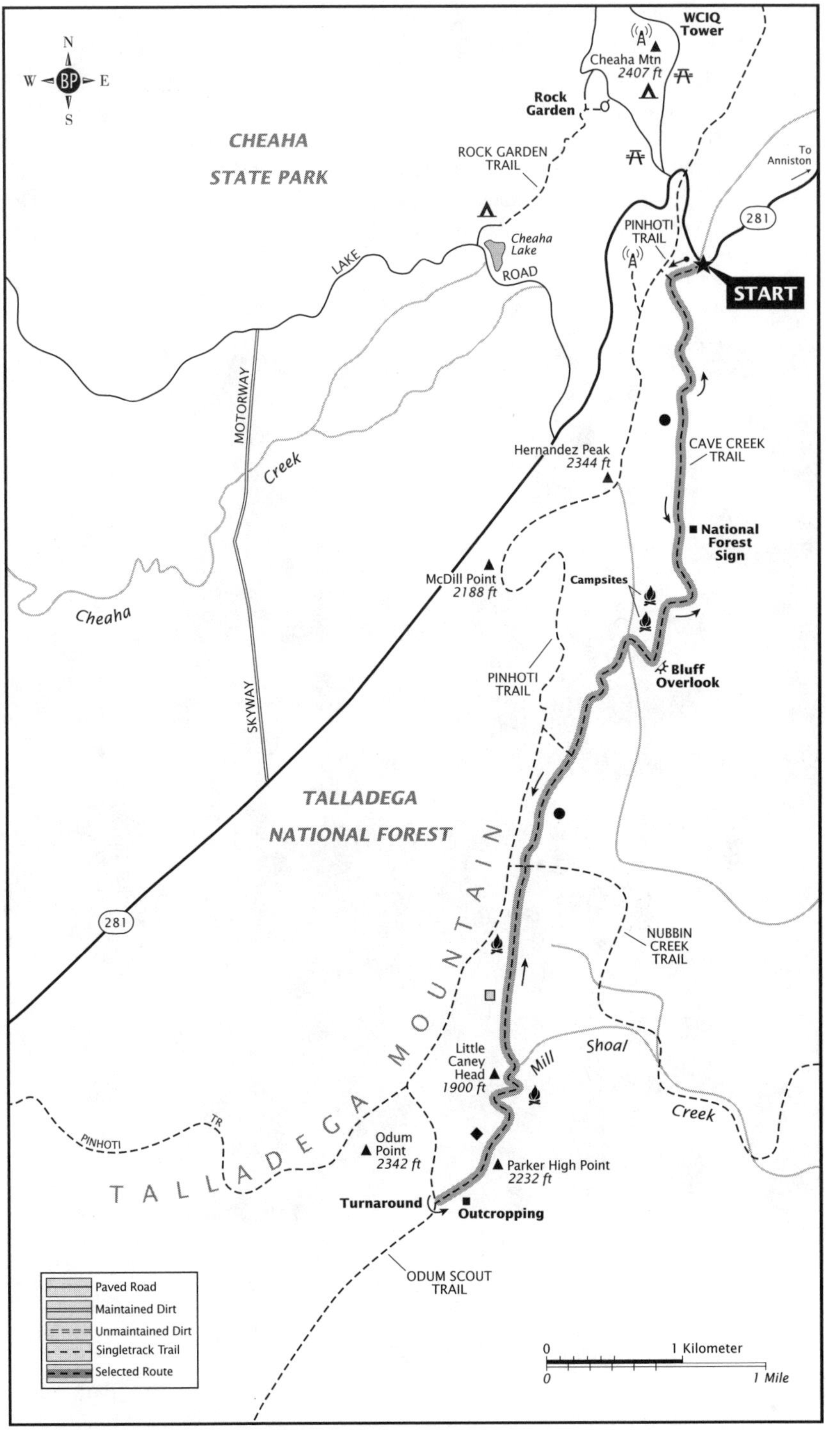

N
W
E
S
BP

WCIQ Tower
Cheaha Mtn
2407 ft
Rock Garden
CHEAHA
STATE PARK
ROCK GARDEN TRAIL
To Anniston
281
Cheaha Lake
LAKE
ROAD
PINHOTI TRAIL
START
MOTORWAY
Creek
Hernandez Peak
2344 ft
CAVE CREEK TRAIL
National Forest Sign
McDill Point
2188 ft
Campsites
Cheaha
Bluff Overlook
PINHOTI TRAIL
SKYWAY
TALLADEGA
NATIONAL FOREST
NUBBIN CREEK TRAIL
281
TALLADEGA MOUNTAIN
Little Caney Head
1900 ft
Mill
Shoal
Creek
PINHOTI TR
Odum Point
2342 ft
Parker High Point
2232 ft
Turnaround
Outcropping
ODUM SCOUT TRAIL

Paved Road
Maintained Dirt
Unmaintained Dirt
Singletrack Trail
Selected Route

0
1 Kilometer
0
1 Mile

The trail reaches its end atop Parker High Point (2,232 feet), where it intersects with the Odum Scout Trail. At this Y-intersection, you have the choice of retracing your outbound route back to the Cheaha Trailhead or following a loop route back to the trailhead. To make the loop, take the right fork at the Y-intersection and head up the Odum Scout Trail until it intersects with the Pinhoti Trail. Turn right and walk the Pinhoti Trail along the ridge of Talladega Mountain. You'll climb over the top of McDill Point (2,188 feet) and Hernandez Peak (2,344 feet) before dropping back to the Cheaha Trailhead.

A box turtle along the trail.

Hike Information

Trail Contacts:
Cheaha State Park, Delta, AL; (256) 488-5111 • **Talladega National Forest**, Talladega, AL; (256) 463-2273 or *www.r8web.com/alabama—The office is open Monday–Friday, 7:30 A.M.–5 P.M.*

Schedule:
Open year round

Fees/Permits:
No fee to hike the trail. Camping is allowed anywhere in the forest by using the "dispersal" method and following national forest guidelines. Primitive camping at Cheaha State Park is $8 per night.

Local Information:
[See Hike 21: Lakeshore Trail]

Local Events/Attractions:
[See Hike 21: Lakeshore Trail]

Accommodations:
[See Hike 21: Lakeshore Trail]

Restaurants:
[See Hike 21: Lakeshore Trail]

Organizations:
[See Hike 21: Lakeshore Trail]

Other Resources:
[See Hike 21: Lakeshore Trail]

Local Outdoor Retailers:
[See Hike 21: Lakeshore Trail]

Maps:
USGS maps: Cheaha Mountain, AL • **Brochures**—*available free of charge at the Cheaha State Park camp store* • **Park maps**—*Pinhoti Trail Map Section 7 is available for $5.20 at the Cheaha State Park camp store or by mail through the Talladega National Forest ranger office. This map also includes the Chinnabee Silent, Odum Scout, Cave Creek, Nubbin, and Skyway Loop trails.*

Pinhoti Trail

The Pinhoti Trail System, located within Talladega National Forest and Cheaha State Park, offers the ultimate backpacking excursion in Alabama. The system connects more than 100 miles of Alabama wilderness and leads through the tallest mountains in the state.

The Pinhoti area received its name from the Native Americans who inhabited the region. Loosely translated, it means turkey home—appropriate because the Eastern wild turkey calls these mountains home.

The Pinhoti Trail System takes off from a trailhead on Alabama 77, north of Ashland, and ends at a spot on U.S. Route 278 just north of Piedmont. Along the hundred-mile hiking route, you'll find comfortable trail shelters and spectacular landscapes. A wide variety of wildflowers bloom from spring through summer, followed later in the year by the beautiful reds and golds of autumn leaves. With 100 miles to cover, a through hike of the Pinhoti System can be quite a challenge. The weather can change without warning, and some creeks run only intermittently in summer.

The Pinhoti System combines several trails in the national forest, such as the Odum Scout Trail, as it makes its way through the southern portion of the Appalachian Mountains. Using a variety of trails, you can devise weekend loop hikes for yourself. In October 1999, the Pinhoti Trail was named a federal Millennium Legacy Trail, making it eligible for federal funding to help maintain and protect it.

The future plans for the Pinhoti Trail are to link it with the 2,167-mile Appalachian Trail that now runs from Mount Katahdin, Maine, to Springer Mountain, Georgia. A hard-working group of volunteers, outdoors organizations, and Forest Service agents are working on bringing the two trails together. This would effectively increase the length of the Appalachian Trail by about another 200 miles.

Construction has already begun on a path to connect the Appalachian Trail with the Benton Mackaye Trail in Northern Georgia. From there, a connector route is to be completed between the Mackaye Trail and Chattahoochee National Forest in Georgia, then from there to the Alabama state line. The Alabama Trails Association recently completed a connector trail between the Georgia state line and the Pinhoti Trail.

Hoping to take the project a step farther, some members of the Florida Trails Association would like to continue the Pinhoti Trail down through the Tuskegee and Conecuh national forests in Alabama and on into Florida, and eventually down to the Everglades using the Florida Trail.

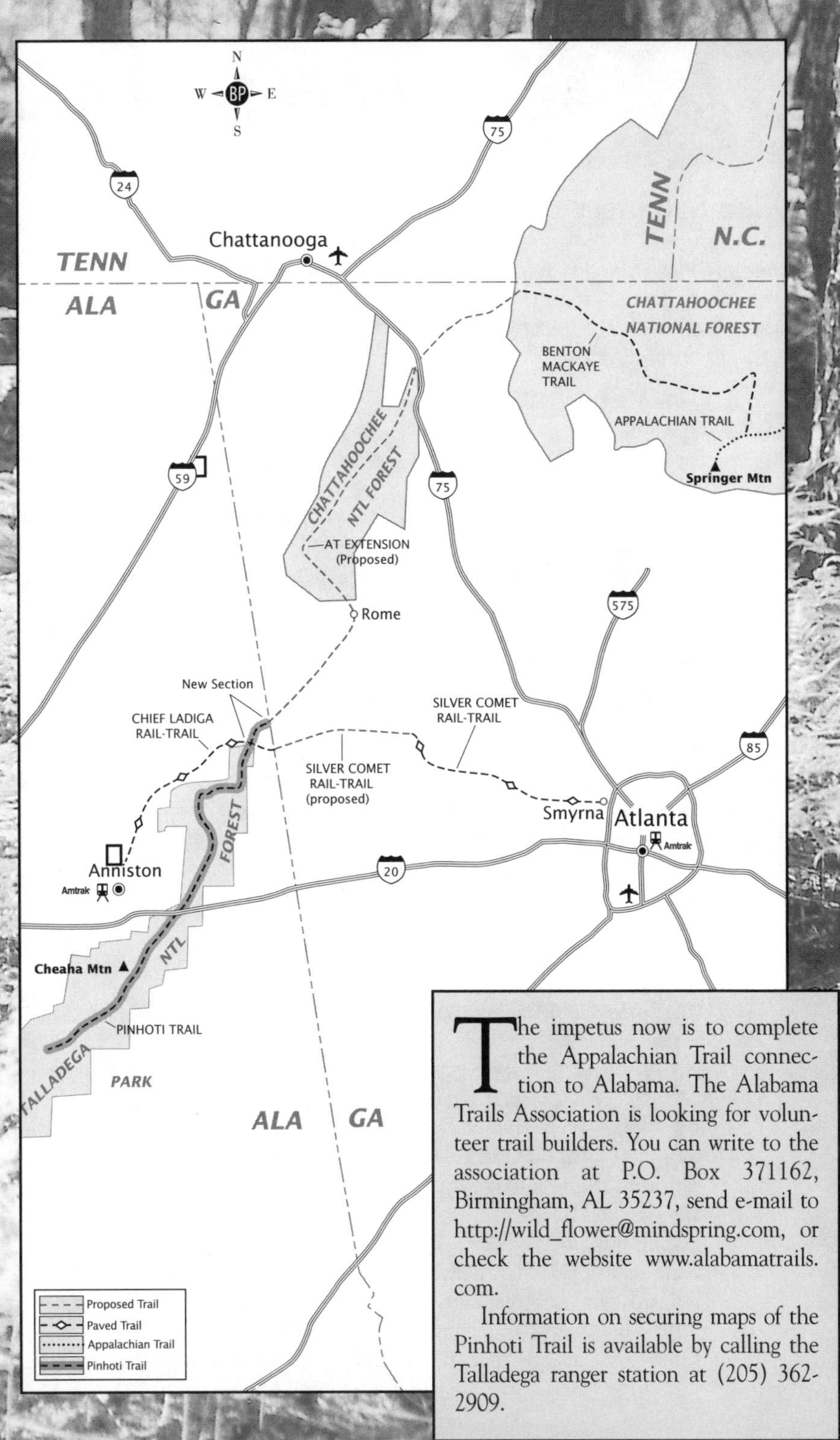

The impetus now is to complete the Appalachian Trail connection to Alabama. The Alabama Trails Association is looking for volunteer trail builders. You can write to the association at P.O. Box 371162, Birmingham, AL 35237, send e-mail to http://wild_flower@mindspring.com, or check the website www.alabamatrails.com.

Information on securing maps of the Pinhoti Trail is available by calling the Talladega ranger station at (205) 362-2909.

Odum Scout Trail

Hike Summary

The scenery and serenity of the Odum Scout Trail makes this one great hike. Right from the start, High Falls adds to the splendor of the scene—and to the difficulty of the hike, as the route ascends stairs to reach the top of the falls. The path then follows the ridgeline of Cheaha Mountain, with wildflowers displaying all imaginable colors and two bluffs providing spectacular views.

Hike Specs

Start: From the High Falls trailhead off CR 31
Length: 9.8-mile out-and-back
Approximate Hiking Time: 4–5 hours
Difficulty Rating: Difficult start, following stairs up rock walls; then easy over the ridge of Cheaha Mountain
Trail Surface: Rock and dirt footpaths
Lay of the Land: High bluffs; wildflowers
Land Status: National forest
Nearest Town: Anniston, AL
Other Trail Users: None
Canine Compatibility: Dog friendly—except for the first half-mile, which is steep and includes stairs; bring water; no leash required

Getting There

From Anniston: Take I-20 east for five miles to Exit 191. Merge onto U.S. 431 south. Turn right in 3.5 miles onto AL 281 South. Go seven miles and turn left onto AL 49 South. Go 10 miles (passing the turn for the Nubbin Creek Trailhead on the right at mile 6.3) and turn right onto CR 31. Travel 1.2 miles and a sign on the right marks the turn for the High Falls Trailhead. Turn right here onto the gravel road and travel 0.3 miles to the trailhead. ***DeLorme: Alabama Atlas & Gazetteer:*** Page 32 F5

Many people believe the Odum Scout Trail is Alabama's most scenic mountain trail. If, after hiking it, you don't agree, you'll have to at least acknowledge that it comes pretty darn close. Situated in the Talladega National Forest, the trail was built by the Cheaha District of the Choccolocco Council of the Boy Scouts, in cooperation with the U.S. Forest Service. Its objective: "to encourage interest in camping and hiking in the great out-of-doors."

The trail, which begins at the High Falls Trailhead, travels the backbone of Cheaha Mountain until it reaches the Pinhoti Trail at Odum Point. Right from the start, nature takes hold of you with breathtaking beauty. Just a tenth of a mile into the hike, the trail reaches High Falls—a three-tiered cascade that leaps from ledge to ledge right next to the trail.

Lower Cascade of High Falls.

The trail heads straight up rock walls to the top of the falls, using steel and wood stairs to make the climb possible. (If you bring the dog, you may end up carrying the animal.)

Farther on, the trail comes to the edge of a bluff on Cedar Mountain, with a panoramic view of the surrounding mountains. Atop the bluff is a flat area that has been used as a campsite, but it's a windy place. It's better to drop down a bit from the outcropping if you plan to spend the night. As

MilesDirections

0.0 START from the High Falls Trailhead. Faded yellow blazes mark the trail. Immediately, come to a fork and go right. (The left fork leads to a series of campsites next to High Falls Branch.)

0.1 Pass the trail registration and information board. In 50 feet the trail crosses High Falls Creek.

0.2 The second cascade of High Falls is straight ahead. Turn left at the falls and in 50 feet come to a set of wooden and steel stairs. At the top of the stairs, the upper cascade is straight ahead.

0.3 Climb two sets of stairs and come to a T-intersection here. Take the left fork. (The right fork leads to the head of the falls.)

0.4 Pass a camp on the left.

0.5 Pass a campsite on the right.

0.7 Pass a campsite on the left. *[**FYI.** Through the trees to the right is Robinson Mountain.]*

2.1 Pass a campsite on the right. Thick brush obscures the trail but you can see it again about 30 feet ahead.

2.4 Pass a decomposer on the right.

2.8 A 50-foot trail breaks left. Continue straight.

3.5 (A short side trail to the left leads to another beautiful view.) Continue straight. The trail is difficult to follow over the rocks here and there are no trail markers; just keep heading northeast.

3.7 Come to a field of rocks. The trail looks like it could go either to the north or northeast. Go to the northeast over the flat rocks (not up the boulders to the left). A faded yellow blaze can be seen on one of the rocks as you walk over it. The path will reappear on the other side.

4.5 Come to a fork with two wooden signs. The right sign reads "Nubbin Creek Trail / Cave Creek Trail 2.0 miles, Nubbin Creek Road 4.0 miles." The left sign reads "Odum Trail.High Falls 3.0 miles." Take the left fork.

4.9 Come to a T-intersection with the Pinhoti Trail (a wooden sign indicates the intersection). Turn around and retrace your tracks back to the High Falls Trailhead.

9.8 Arrive at the trailhead.

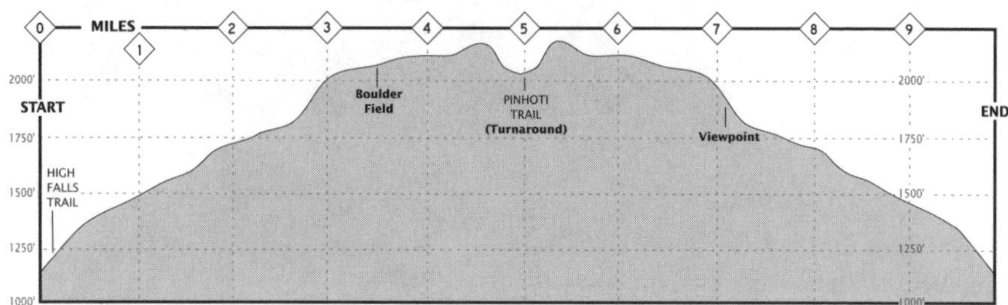

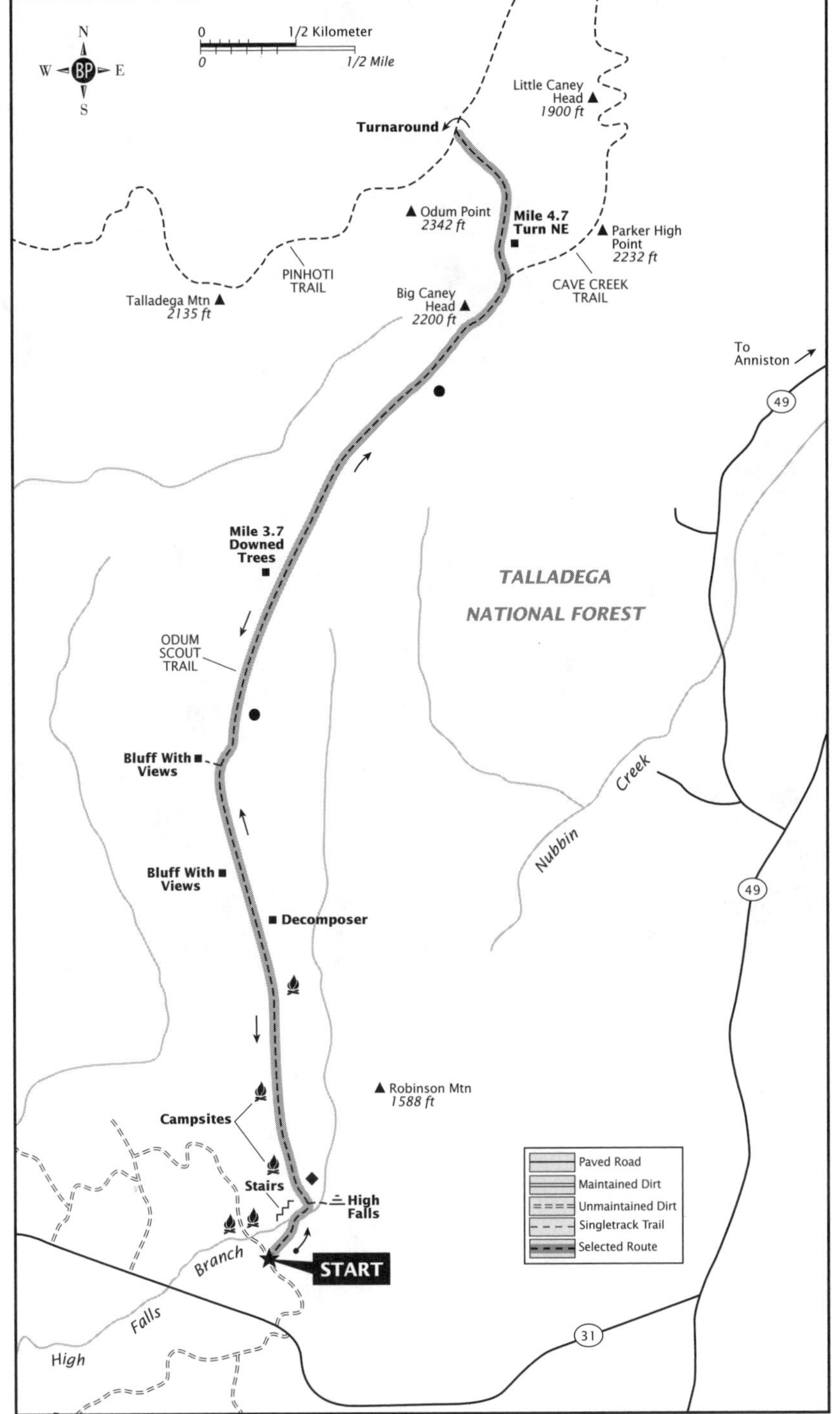
N
S
W
E
BP
0
1/2 Kilometer
0
1/2 Mile
Turnaround
Little Caney Head
1900 ft
Odum Point
2342 ft
Mile 4.7
Turn NE
Parker High Point
2232 ft
PINHOTI TRAIL
CAVE CREEK TRAIL
Talladega Mtn
2135 ft
Big Caney Head
2200 ft
To Anniston
49
Mile 3.7
Downed Trees
TALLADEGA
NATIONAL FOREST
ODUM SCOUT TRAIL
Bluff With Views
Nubbin Creek
Bluff With Views
49
Decomposer
Robinson Mtn
1588 ft
Campsites
Stairs
High Falls
Paved Road
Maintained Dirt
Unmaintained Dirt
Singletrack Trail
Selected Route
Branch
START
Falls
High
31

Rock pile at the trailhead.

the trail heads up Big Caney Head, it reaches the edge of a second bluff, again with a broad view of the mountains.

Among the animals you might cross on your trip are white-tailed deer, wild turkeys, wild pigs, and foxes. Azaleas, dogwoods, and wildflowers line the path—so many wildflowers, in fact, that from spring through fall much of the area is a rainbow of colors. Along the ridge, travel is fairly easy as you walk up and down small grades. With the exception of at the beginning part of the trail, water is pretty scarce, so pack plenty.

The trail is only roughly marked, with faded yellow blazes visible on some trees and rocks. The path is well worn, but brush overgrowing the trail can make it difficult to follow. At places like this, look ahead and you should be able to spot the trail as it continues beyond the brush. In other areas, the trail travels over rocks and disappears completely. Generally if you continue in the same direction of travel, you'll find the path on the other side of the rocks.

Hike Information

Trail Contacts:
Talladega National Forest, Talladega, AL; (256) 463–2273 or *www.r8web.com/alabama—The office is open Monday–Friday, 7:30 A.M.–5 P.M.*

Schedule:
Open year round

Fees/Permits:
No fee to hike the trail. Camping is allowed anywhere in the forest by using the "dispersal" method and following national forest guidelines.

Local Information:
[See Hike 21: Lakeshore Trail]

Local Events/Attractions:
[See Hike 21: Lakeshore Trail]

Accommodations:
[See Hike 21: Lakeshore Trail]

Restaurants:
[See Hike 21: Lakeshore Trail]

Organizations:
[See Hike 21: Lakeshore Trail]

Other Resources:
[See Hike 21: Lakeshore Trail]

Local Outdoor Retailers:
[See Hike 21: Lakeshore Trail]

Maps:
USGS maps: Cheaha Mountain, AL; Lineville West, AL • **Brochures**—*available free of charge at the Cheaha State Park camp store* • **Park maps**—*Pinhoti Trail Map Section 7 is available for $5.20 at the Cheaha State Park camp store or by mail through the Talladega National Forest ranger office. This map also includes the Chinnabee Silent, Odum Scout, Cave Creek, Nubbin, and Skyway Loop trails.*

Honorable Mentions

Central Alabama

As we've seen, Central Alabama offers the hiker much in the way of scenery and challenging treks. The following trails didn't make our A-list, but are well worth mention. Most of these trails are within striking distance of other trails listed in the Central Region section of this book, so stop in, pay a visit, and let us know what you think. Maybe one should be upgraded, or maybe you know of some hidden trip that would make a good honorable mention.

(G) Talladega National Forest – Oakmulgee Unit

The Talladega National Forest is broken into two distinct areas. The first is home to the state's highest mountain, Cheaha. The second is the Oakmulgee Unit, located between Montgomery and Birmingham.

The highlight of the Oakmulgee Unit is the Payne Lake Recreation Area. Here, a variety of activities from swimming to boating to fishing will be found, along with a hiking trail that skirts the banks of the lake. The terrain is not exceptionally difficult and there are ample opportunities to view the wildlife of the region.

As with all national forests in the state, camping is permitted along the trail. Camping at the recreational area with water costs $12 per day. Otherwise, a day use fee of $3 is charged. Remember that hunting is allowed in national forests so camping and hiking become restricted during hunting season. Contact the ranger office Monday–Friday from 7:30 A.M.–5 P.M. at (205) 926–9765 for dates.

To get to the forest, go west from Montgomery on U.S. 82 to AL 5. Turn left on AL 5 and head south for six miles. Turn right onto AL 25. The recreational area will be reached in 15 miles. ***DeLorme: Alabama Atlas & Gazetteer:*** Page 36 E1

(H) Red Trail – Oak Mountain State Park

Oak Mountain State Park is well known for its mountain bike trails and the Red Trail is among its best routes. Totaling 17 miles, this trail follows old dirt roadbeds for the first half of the trip and then a nice footpath around the hillsides for the remainder. Mountain bikers use the trail as a training course and many contests are held here each year.

As with many of the trails in the park, the Red Trail takes the hiker to Peavine Falls and can be accessed either from the Peavine Falls parking lot or the northern parking area near the country store.

The hike is easy to moderate in difficulty. The main drawback is the frequency of bicycles careening down the hillsides. The views are not as spectacular as other trails in the park, but it does travel alongside some streams that make it a pleasant trip. *[See Hike 17 for park directions and additional information.]* Call (205) 620–2527 or 1–800–ALA–PARK for more information or visit *www.bham.net/oakmtn.* ***DeLorme: Alabama Atlas & Gazetteer:*** Page 31 G6

(I) Treetop Trail – Oak Mountain State Park

Just over half a mile in length, the Treetop Trail at Oak Mountain is an elevated walkway through the Oak Mountain forest. What makes the trail interesting is that it's maintained by the Alabama Wildlife Rehabilitation Center. The center provides homes for over 300 species of wildlife that are found injured throughout the state. Here, the animals are protected and cared for until they are well enough to make it on their own in the wild.

The trail travels through the section of the park where the animals recuperate. Here, all manner of wildlife, from cougar to alligators to eagles, can be seen. A.W.R.C. personnel are more than happy to talk with hikers about the wildlife and the rehabilitation program. The trail itself begins at the park ranger office and runs parallel to the Green Trail. *[See Hike 20 for park directions and additional information.]* Call (205) 620–2527 or 1–800–ALA–PARK for more information or visit *www.bham.net/oakmtn.* ***DeLorme: Alabama Atlas & Gazetteer:*** Page 31 G6

(J) Bald Rock Trail – Cheaha State Park

Located on the very top of the highest mountain in the state, the Bald Rock Trail gives you what you would expect from the highest point, spectacular views! This trail is an 1.0-mile loop that is perfect for families with small children and people with disabilities.

The trail begins at the north end of the parking lot, next to the closed Mt. Cheaha Lodge, which is a fine example of CCC craftsmanship. The trail takes two paths here, one to the left and one to the right of a boardwalk that runs down the center of the loop. Either path leads to the same location.

The trail is easy traveling, mostly a dirt footpath with some exposed rock. Half a mile into the trip the trail turns west and comes out right on top of Bald Rock. The view is spectacular and expansive to say the least.

The boardwalk running down the center of the loop is elevated approximately four feet off the ground. It's quite wide, at least six feet, with four-foot high handrails, and it leads directly to the rock. This makes the trip easily accessible for those who are handicapped.

The trail opens at 7 A.M. and closes at sunset. There is a $1 day-use fee to gain entry into the park. *[See Hike 24 for park directions and additional information.]* Call (256) 488–5111 or 1–800–ALA–PARK for more information. ***DeLorme: Alabama Atlas & Gazetteer:*** Page 32 E5

(K) Rickwood Cavern State Park

One of the truly magnificent state park experiences in Alabama is Rickwood Cavern State Park, member of the National Caves Association. The cave is maintained by the state and is the only operational caving park in the state.

Park rangers guide you along the trail through the "Miracle Mile," a solid mile (two-mile round trip) of passages, huge carved rooms, and limestone formations. The cave was formed over 260 million years ago during the geologic Mississippian period. Early fossils of marine life can be seen as well as colorful flowstones and an exhibit of 2,000-year-old artifacts found in the cave.

The park is located about 20 miles north of Birmingham. Take Exit 284 off of I-65. The park is open 10 A.M.–5 P.M. daily on a seasonal schedule, so it's best to call in advance at (205) 647–9692 before heading out. Admission to the cave is $7.50 for adults 12 and older and $3.50 for children six to 11. Admission to the park is $1 for ages six and older. The fee for camping is $12 per night for four people. ***DeLorme: Alabama Atlas & Gazetteer:*** Page 24 H5

28. Bee Branch Trail
29. Trail 200 (Borden Creek Trail)
30. Trail 201 (Magnolia Trail)
31. Trail 209 (Sipsey Fork Trail)
32. South Plateau Loop Trail
33. North Plateau Loop Trail
34. McKay Hollow Trail
35. Stone Cuts Trail
36. Mountain Mist Trail
37. Land Trust Loop
38. Lickskillet Trail
39. Cascade Loop Trail
40. Tom Bevill Interpretive Trail
41. Cutchenmine Trail
42. Camp Road
43. Point Rock Trail
44. Eberhart Trail
45. Rhododendron Trail
46. DeSoto Scout Trail
47. Lost Falls Trail
48. Russell Cave Trail

Northern

Honorable Mentions

- **O.** Dismals Canyon
- **P.** Black Warrior Horse Trails
- **M.** Wheeler National Wildlife Refuge
- **N.** Old Railroad Bed Trail
- **O.** Rainbow Mountain Trail

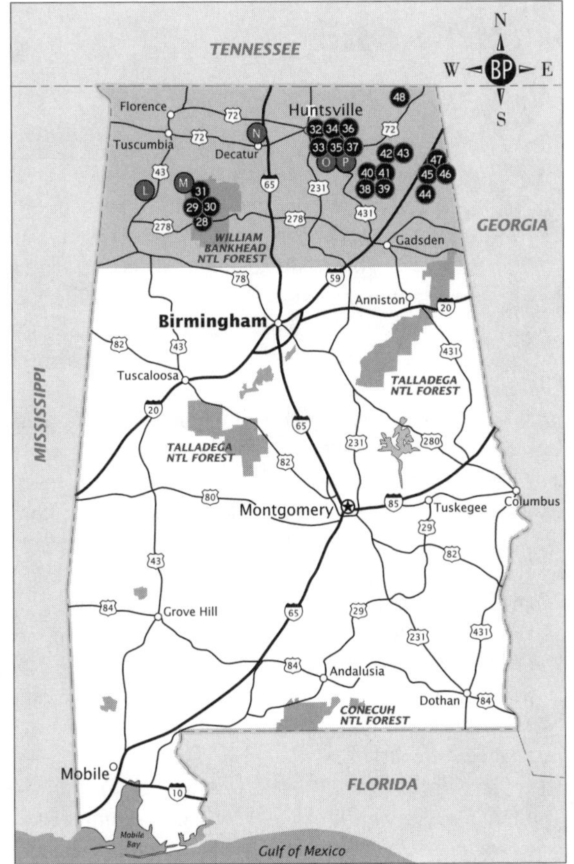

TENNESSEE
N
W
BP
E
S
Florence
Huntsville
Tuscumbia
Decatur
WILLIAM BANKHEAD NTL FOREST
GEORGIA
Gadsden
Anniston
Birmingham
Tuscaloosa
MISSISSIPPI
TALLADEGA NTL FOREST
TALLADEGA NTL FOREST
Montgomery
Tuskegee
Columbus
Grove Hill
Andalusia
Dothan
CONECUH NTL FOREST
Mobile
FLORIDA
Mobile Bay
Gulf of Mexico

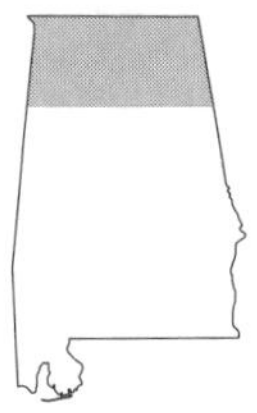

Alabama

Northern Alabama

Northern Alabama stretches from the Tennessee/Alabama border to the state's largest city, Birmingham. This region is known geologically as the Cumberland Plateau. This mountainous region has seen its sandstone heights carved and weathered by the elements and the many waterways that flow through it to create spectacular gorges, cascading waterfalls, and ancient caverns.

Hikers in the region will find plenty of challenge and beauty. Little River Canyon atop Lookout Mountain is one such stop. Carved for thousands of years, the canyon resonates with the thunder of the river, culminating in a spectacular 60-foot waterfall. The views from the canyon rim are something to behold. This is a popular location for whitewater rafters and rock climbers.

The Eberhart Point Trail provides more views of the canyon, but mainly it takes you directly to the raging river for a little rock hopping and views of the canyon from the bottom. DeSoto State Park is also located here with a multitude of trails and sites. In addition to the many panoramic views, several falls are encountered including Lost Falls, Azalea Cascade, and the rapids of the west fork of Little River.

The Russell Cave Trail combines history, hiking, and cave exploration all in one. The trail travels up the side of Montague Mountain and culminates at Russell Cave. Over 8,000 years of Native American history can be found here.

History will probably remember this region most for the Huntsville Space and Rocket Center. This site, along with the nearby Redstone Arsenal, played a key role in sending Americans to the moon. It was here that Werner Von Braun and N.A.S.A. engineers developed the Saturn V rocket that would put Apollo astronauts on the moon. Today, the center is used by N.A.S.A. to test the components of the international space station "Freedom" before delivery to Cape Canaveral for deployment in space by the space shuttle. This is also home to one of N.A.S.A.'s Space Camps for both children and adults. The museum and guided tours are a must see when in the area.

Bee Branch Trail

Hike Summary

The Bee Branch Trail in the Sipsey Wilderness makes for a great overnight trip. The terrain is easy to moderate over dirt and rock trails through a canyon and past several small waterfalls, culminating in the Bee Branch Falls and caves. There is an excellent campsite at the end of the trail, just south of the falls.

Hike Specs

Start: From the Trail 201/202 Trailhead on CR 60
Length: 11.4-mile point-to-point
Approximate Hiking Time: 6–7 hours
Difficulty Rating: Easy, except for moderate through a canyon area
Trail Surface: Dirt path; rocky through canyon
Lay of the Land: Magnolia, holly, hemlock, and oak trees; trillium and pink lady wildflowers
Land Status: Wilderness area
Nearest Town: Double Springs, AL
Other Trail Users: None
Canine Compatibility: Dog friendly—fairly easy walking, with ample water available; no leash required

Getting There

From Cullman: Go west on U.S. 278 for 44 miles to AL 33 in Double Springs. Turn right and head 12 miles north on AL 33 to CR 6. Turn left onto CR 6 and travel 8.6 miles. (CR 6 becomes CR 60 when you enter the Sipsey River Recreational Area.) The trailhead is on the right and is well marked. ***DeLorme: Alabama Atlas & Gazetteer:*** Page 23 B9

The Appalachian Plateau of northwest Alabama bears a close resemblance to the Great Smoky Mountains, with deep canyons and old-growth forest. For thousands of years, the Creek, Cherokee, and Chickasaw Indians hunted and lived here. They used caves along the riverbanks for shelter and hunted a wide variety of game.

Weather and the many rivers and creeks carved out the sandstone canyons, some with walls 300 feet high. Although much of the old-growth oak forest in northwest Alabama is gone, the Sipsey Wilderness preserves much of its original forest.

The wilderness area lies within the William B. Bankhead National Forest, which covers 180,000 acres in two counties, Winston and Lawrence. The forest was set aside as a protected area in 1918 as the Alabama National Forest. In 1942 Congress changed the name to William B. Bankhead National Forest to honor William Bankhead who served in Congress from 1917 to 1940 and was Speaker of the House for those last six years.

In 1975 Congress again looked at the forest and decided that the area in its northwest corner met the criteria to be named an official wilderness area,

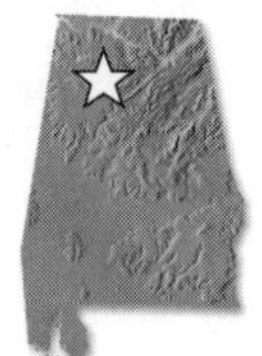

and with that the Sipsey Wilderness was born. Originally the wilderness had 12,726 acres, but this was increased in 1988 to just under 26,000 acres.

This route, despite its popularity, is not an officially numbered trail. The path incorporates Trail 202 (Johnson Cemetery Trail) and Trail 209 (Sipsey Fork Trail) before it branches off and heads up Bee Branch Creek. The Bee Branch Trail is unmarked and, as a matter of fact, if you are hiking up Trail 209, it's quite easy to make a wrong turn and hike the Beach Branch Trail by accident.

The trail starts level, using the gravel road and then the dirt footpath of Trail 202, passing Johnson Cemetery, which was established in the mid to late 1800s. Before reaching Trail 209, the trail comes to the canyon with its high walls, multiple caves and overhangs, and an impressive waterfall.

Soon the path meets the Sipsey River, requiring you to ford the river to reach Trail 209. The Sipsey is a clear, cold, mountain stream. The current here is not that fast, and the river's depth is three feet at the most, depending on rainfall at the time. The bottom is sandy.

Immediately on the other side, Trail 209 heads west, following the river, with nice views of the crystal-clear water, large boulders, and the canyon. In about two miles, the trail comes to what seems like a dead end and makes a

An outcropping on the trail.

right turn. This is where most hikers discover the Bee Branch Trail by accident. To follow Trail 209, you would continue straight across the creek. For the Bee Branch, turn to the right.

If you feel comfortable with map and compass, feel free to head off the trail to explore. Through the trees you'll hear the rush of many waterfalls and realize why the Sipsey Wilderness is called Land of a Thousand Waterfalls. Remember, this is a wilderness area. It's best to register at the trailhead before heading out, in case of emergency, and also to let someone know where you are going and when you expect to be back. Carry plenty of water, matches, some food, a flashlight, and a map and compass.

It's possible to take in the entire trip in one day, but most hikers prefer to do it as an overnight, taking advantage of the campsite just south of the waterfalls and caves at the end of the trail.

MilesDirections

0.0 START from the Trail 201/202 Trailhead off CR 60. Head into the woods behind the information sign—a wooden sign next to the trail reads "201/202."

0.1 Come to a T-intersection with a gravel road that runs northeast/southwest. Turn right.

0.2 Come to a fork and go right. (Trail 201 breaks left.)

0.8 *[**Side-trip.** A short 50-foot side trails heads off to the right to Johnson Cemetery.]*

2.0 A short spur trail (about 10 feet long) leads to the edge of a bluff.

2.3 Come to a large 100-foot waterfall flowing down a cliff.

2.4 Pass a campsite to the right.

2.5 Ford the Sipsey River straight across. *[**FYI.** During normal rain, the river runs up to three feet deep here, but during unusually heavy rainfall, it may be deeper and may not be passable.]* After crossing, a sign points to the direction of Trail 209 (Sipsey Fork). Turn left and follow this. Pass a campsite on the left.

3.3 Come to a fork and continue straight.

3.5 Pass a camp on the left.

3.6 The trail splits around a large uprooted tree and rejoins at the other side at a creek.

3.9 Come to a wooden post that points to Trail 204. Go straight. Pass another campsite. Just after, the trail splits again around some brush and rejoins at the other end.

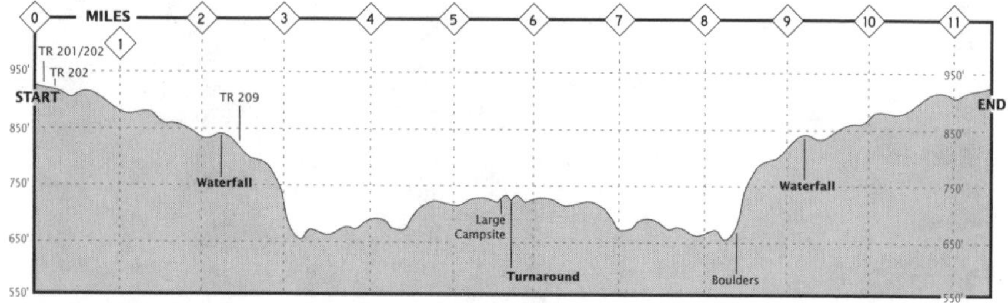

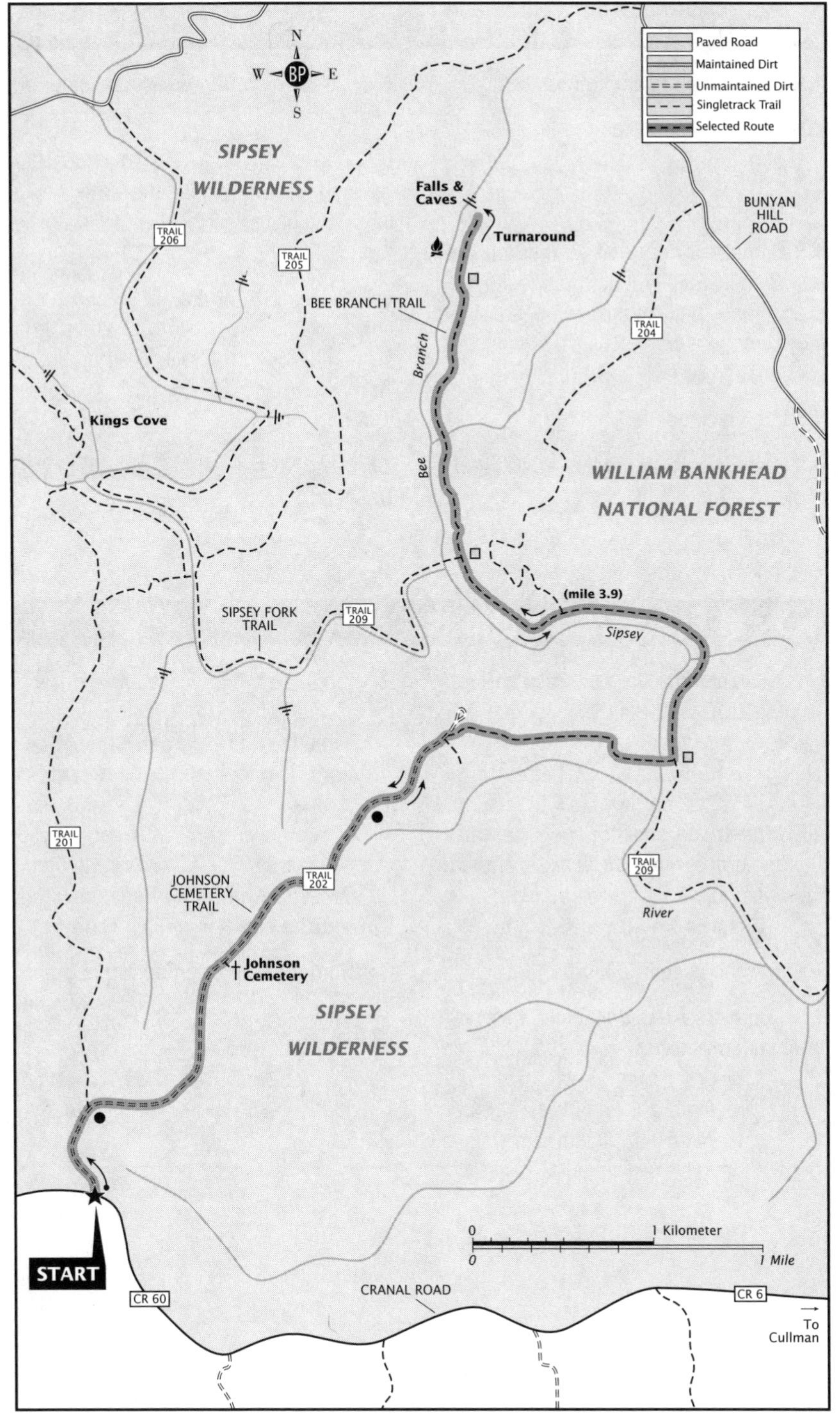
N
S
W
E
BP
Paved Road
Maintained Dirt
Unmaintained Dirt
Singletrack Trail
Selected Route
SIPSEY
WILDERNESS
Falls &
Caves
Turnaround
BUNYAN
HILL
ROAD
TRAIL 206
TRAIL 205
BEE BRANCH TRAIL
TRAIL 204
Branch
Bee
Kings Cove
WILLIAM BANKHEAD
NATIONAL FOREST
(mile 3.9)
Sipsey
SIPSEY FORK
TRAIL
TRAIL 209
TRAIL 201
TRAIL 202
JOHNSON
CEMETERY
TRAIL
Johnson
Cemetery
River
SIPSEY
WILDERNESS
0
1 Kilometer
0
1 Mile
START
CR 60
CRANAL ROAD
CR 6
To
Cullman

MilesDirections (Continued)

4.1 Pass another camp on the right.

4.3 Pass a campsite on the left

4.4 Come to a fork and go right. (The left fork heads to the river.)

4.5 Come to a fork and go right on the Bee Branch Trail. (The left fork looks like a dead-end that drops down a short 8-foot slope to a creek. This is actually the continuation of Trail 209.)

4.8 Pass a campsite.

5.3 Pass a camp on the left. In 200 feet, come to a fork and go right.

5.4 Come to a T-intersection and turn right.

5.6 Come to a fork and go right. Just below, to the left near the creek, is a large campsite, perfect for splitting the trip.

5.7 The end of the trail is reached at a box canyon. Two huge waterfalls and several caves in the rock walls are here. Turn around and retrace your tracks back to the trailhead.

11.4 Arrive at the Trail 201/202 Trailhead.

Local Events/Attractions:

Ave Maria Grotto, Cullman, AL; (256) 734–4110—*In 1934, Brother Joseph began building this site. Covering 3 acres, the Grotto consists of over 125 miniature, hand carved and constructed reproductions of famous churches, shrines, and buildings.* • **Looney's Tavern and Amphitheater**, Double Springs, AL; (205) 489–5000 or *www.bham.net/looneys—Not only does this site feature the famous "Incident at Looney's Tavern" play, but they also feature other major musical productions throughout the year. You'll also find miniature golf, a restaurant, and riverboat rides.* • **Semi-Annual Bluegrass Superjam**, each April and November, Cullman, AL; (256) 747–1650 or *www15.pair.com/festival/ala/cullman.html—featuring Grand Ole Opry style music and pure family entertainment* • **Indian Festival**, Second weekend of June, Cullman, AL; (256) 737–9163 or *www.geocities.com/echota_Cherokee_powwow—This festival features Native American arts and crafts, food, dancing, and more.*

Hike Information

Trail Contacts:

USDA Forest Service William B. Bankhead District, Moulton, AL; (205) 489–5111; *open Monday–Friday 7:30 A.M.–4 P.M.*

Schedule:

Open year round

Fees/Permits:

There is a $3 day-use parking fee at the trailheads. Walk-ins are free.

Local Information:

Alabama Mountain Lakes, Mooresville, AL; 1–800–648–5381 or *www.almtlakes.org* • **Lawrence County Chamber of Commerce**, Moulton, AL; (205) 974–1658 or *www.naiap.com* • **Winston County Chamber of Commerce**, Double Springs, AL; (205) 489–5447 • **Cullman Area Chamber of Commerce**, Cullman, AL; (256) 734–0454 or *www.cullmanchamber.org*

Accommodations:

Moulton Motel, Moulton, AL; (256) 974–0636

Restaurants:

Classical Fruit and Barbeque, Moulton, AL; (256) 974–8813 • **Cardinal Drive-In**, Moulton, AL; (256) 974–9065 • **John's Barbeque**, Moulton, AL; (256) 974–7721 • **Nesmith's Hamburgers**, Moulton, AL; (256) 974–9806 • **Little Kuntry Kitchen**, Moulton, AL; (256) 974–3380

Organizations:

Alabama Trails, Birmingham, AL at *www.alabamatrails.com* • **Sierra Club North Alabama Chapter**, Huntsville, AL at *www.alabama.sierraclub.org/na.html*

Other Resources:

Alabama Environmental Council, Birmingham, AL; (205) 322–3126 or *www.alenvironmentalcouncil.org* • **Alabama Wilderness Alliance**, Mouton, AL; (334) 265 6529 • **Bama Environmental News**, Montgomery, AL; (205) 226–7739 or *www.bamanews.com* • **Hikeweb: Sipsey Wilderness**, *www.montesano.com/hikeweb/sipsey.htm* • **Wild Alabama**, Moulton, AL; (256) 974–6166 or *www.wildalabama.com* • **Wildflowers of Alabama** at *www.duc.auburn.edu/~deancar/index.html* • **Wild Law**, Montgomery, AL; (334) 265–6529 or *www.wildlaw.org*

Maps:

USGS maps: Bee Branch, AL • **Brochures**—*available at the ranger office or by writing*

Trail 200 (Borden Creek Trail)

Hike Summary

This is a great hike for kids and adults alike through the Sipsey Wilderness. Sandstone cliffs tower along the trail, forming a canyon as the route travels along the Sipsey River. The hike gives you a chance to do a little spelunking through a 100-foot cave next to a waterfall.

Hike Specs

Start: From the trailhead on FS 224
Length: 4.8-mile out-and-back
Approximate Hiking Time: 4–6 hours
Difficulty Rating: Easy, over flat footpaths and easy climbs
Trail Surface: Dirt path
Lay of the Land: Hemlock, beech, mountain laurel, and holly forests
Land Status: Wilderness area
Nearest Town: Double Springs, AL
Other Trail Users: None
Canine Compatibility: Dog friendly—with ample water available; no leash required

Getting There

From Cullman: Take U.S. 278 west for 44 miles to AL 33 in Double Springs. Turn right and head 12 miles north on AL 33 to CR 6. Take a left onto CR 6. The road splits. Take the right-hand FS 224 fork and travel 2.5 miles. Pass a sign that reads "Warning – Road Closed," but continue past the sign 0.5 miles. The trailhead is at the end of the road. ***DeLorme: Alabama Atlas & Gazetteer:*** Page 23 B10

Most people don't think of Alabama as a wilderness retreat, but it is. As a matter of fact, the state has three designated wilderness areas. Cheaha Wilderness, with its 7,490 acres, lies in northeast Alabama near Cheaha State Park. The Dugger Mountain Wilderness, near Anniston, has 9,200 acres. And the largest tract is the Sipsey Wilderness, with 26,000 acres—the third largest wilderness area in the United States east of the Mississippi.

The Federal Wilderness Act of 1964 identifies four characteristics for a "wilderness area." First, it's a place where the "earth and its community of life are uncontrolled by man." Second, a wilderness "generally appears to have been affected by the forces of nature, with the imprint of man's work substantially unnoticeable." Third, a wilderness is an area where "man is a visitor who does not remain." Finally, a wilderness provides "outstanding opportunities for solitude or a primitive and unconfined type of recreation."

The Sipsey Wilderness exemplifies these characteristics, with the possible exception of "outstanding opportunities for solitude." Sit at one of the

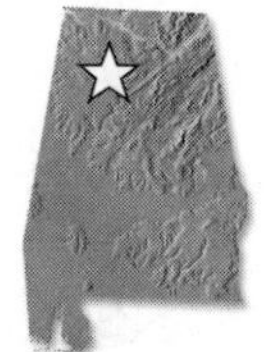

trailheads any weekend and you'll understand. The parking areas are routinely full—so often now that the Forest Service discourages large groups from visiting. But don't let this discourage you. The wilderness is that popular for a reason. Simply call ahead to see when you can hit a slack time, or try to aim for a weekday visit.

Trail 200, better known as the Borden Creek Trail, highlights the best of what makes the Sipsey a true wilderness. Of all of the area's trails, the Borden Creek draws together the wilderness' most attractive elements and does so along a trail that's easy enough for the whole family to enjoy.

From the start, the cold, clear waters of Borden Creek flow alongside the path as it winds its way to meet the Sipsey River. Sandstone cliffs rise above both sides of the trail, some 300 feet high. As you hike, you can hear the sound of feeder creeks continuing the work of erosion, cascading down the walls of the canyon.

MilesDirections

0.0 START from the trailhead behind the information sign. In about 200 feet, pass a campsite to the right next to the river. Continue and cross a feeder creek of the river and another campsite.

0.1 Come to a fork and go left. [***FYI.*** *The trail passes several of these with one fork leading to a campsite. This one is along the right fork.*]

0.2 Pass another campsite.

0.4 Come to a 50-foot waterfall. To the right is a cave, which you'll travel through. [***FYI.*** *The cave is about 100 feet long and gets narrow, and darker, as it goes. By the end, you'll be crawling through it, but it's nothing impassable.*]

1.1 Come to a fork and go right. (The left fork goes to a campsite.)

1.3 Pass a campsite on the right.

1.4 Pass another campsite on the right.

1.7 Pass another campsite on the right.

1.9 Pass a campsite on the left.

2.1 Come to a fork and go right. (The left fork is a short trail to the cliffs.)

2.2 The trail is washed out here along the riverbank, but it's passable. Be careful.

2.3 Come to a fork and go right.

2.4 An engraved stone to the left that dedicates the creation of the wilderness in May 1975. Arrive at the Sipsey River Recreation Area. Turnaround here and retrace your tracks back to the trailhead.

4.8 Arrive back at the trailhead.

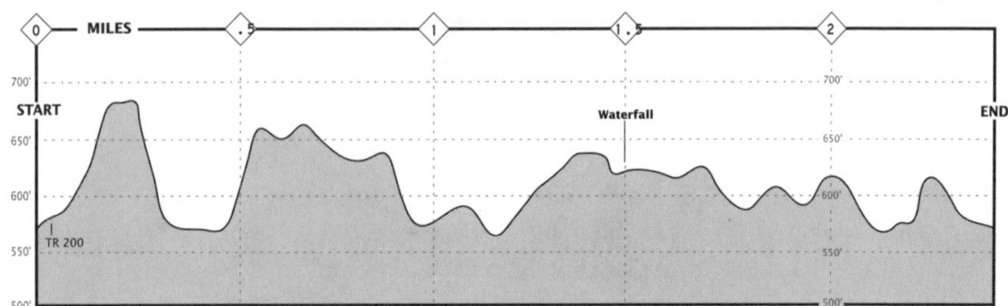

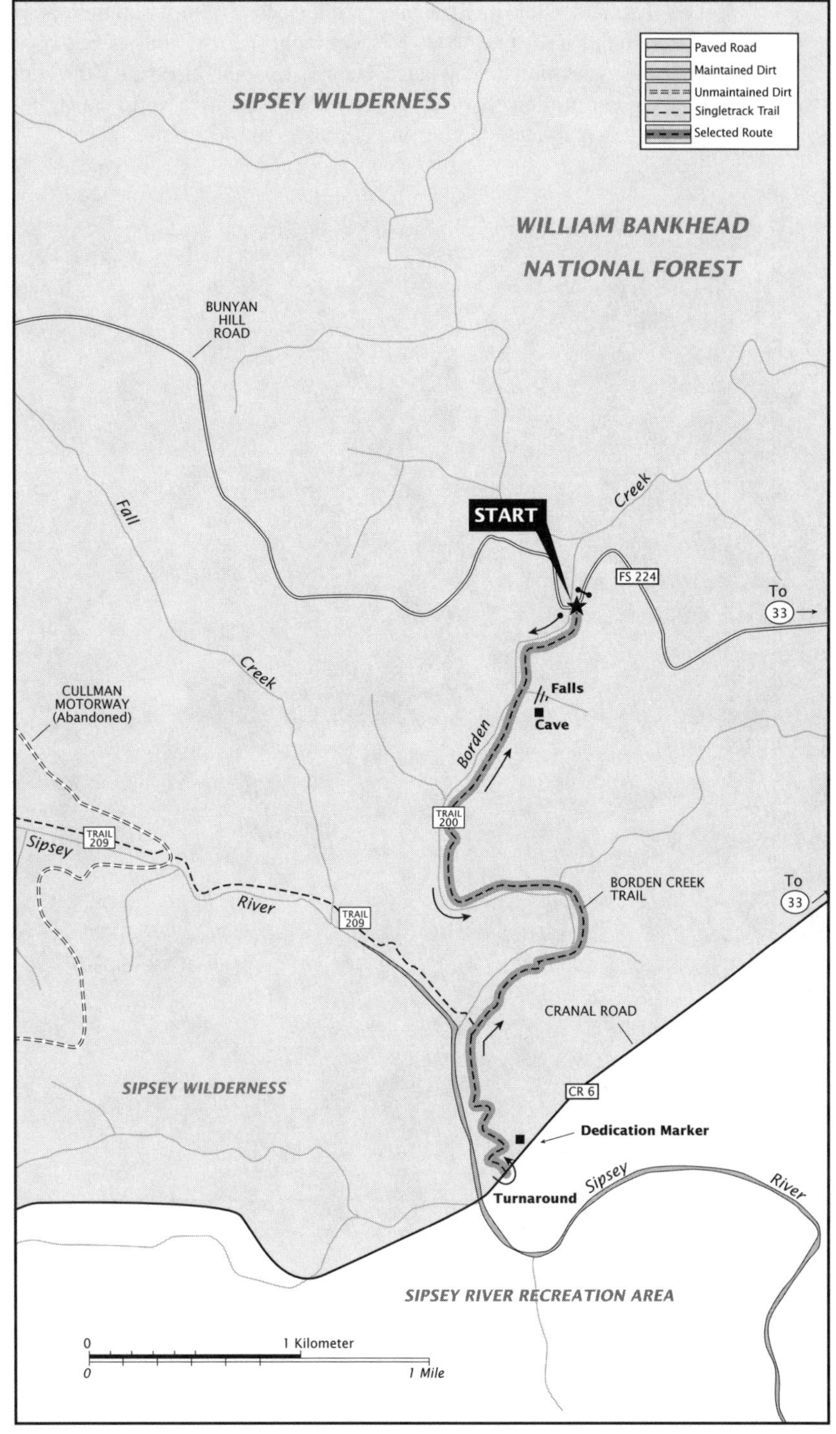
Paved Road
Maintained Dirt
Unmaintained Dirt
Singletrack Trail
Selected Route
SIPSEY WILDERNESS
WILLIAM BANKHEAD
NATIONAL FOREST
BUNYAN
HILL
ROAD
Fall
Creek
START
FS 224
To
33
Falls
Cave
Borden
Creek
CULLMAN
MOTORWAY
(Abandoned)
TRAIL
200
TRAIL
209
Sipsey
River
BORDEN CREEK
TRAIL
CRANAL ROAD
CR 6
Dedication Marker
Turnaround
Sipsey
River
SIPSEY WILDERNESS
SIPSEY RIVER RECREATION AREA
0
1 Kilometer
0
1 Mile

Less than half a mile into the hike, you'll reach a 50-foot waterfall. Next to the waterfall is a cave, about 100 feet long, that the trail travels right through. At first the cave is large enough to walk in comfortably, but toward the end it narrows to the point where you may have to crawl. But the passage isn't difficult, and it simply adds to the adventure.

Borden Creek.

Hike Information

Trail Contacts:
USDA Forest Service William B. Bankhead District, Moulton, AL; (205) 489-5111; *open Monday–Friday 7:30 A.M.–4 P.M.*

Schedule:
Open year round

Fees/Permits:
There is a $3 day-use parking fee at the trailheads. Walk-ins are free.

Local Information:
[See Hike 28: Bee Branch Trail]

Local Events/Attractions:
[See Hike 28: Bee Branch Trail]

Accommodations:
[See Hike 28: Bee Branch Trail]

Restaurants:
[See Hike 28: Bee Branch Trail]

Organizations:
[See Hike 28: Bee Branch Trail]

Other Resources:
[See Hike 28: Bee Branch Trail]

Maps:
USGS maps: Bee Branch, AL • **Brochures**—*available at the ranger office or by writing the ranger office*

As you travel, keep an eye out for other waterfalls on the canyon walls. At the bottom of the cliffs are shallow caves that invite exploration.

Although trails in the wilderness are not marked—except for signs that mark the trailheads and the occasional intersection—keeping on this trail is easy. Unlike Trail 209 (Sipsey Fork Trail), which has several unmarked branch trails that sometimes lure hikers into heading off in the wrong direction, this path is well worn, and the only side trails are short ones leading to campsites.

Trail 201 (Magnolia Trail)

Hike Summary

Trail 201 takes hikers to the Sipsey River at the end of Trail 209 (Sipsey Fork Trail). The hike is level for most of the trip, over dirt footpaths. The trail then descends to follow a small feeder creek down the canyon wall to the Sipsey. The end of the trail is a great place to relax along the river.

Hike Specs

Start: From the Trail 201/202 Trailhead on CR 60
Length: 5.0-mile out-and-back
Approximate Hiking Time: 5–7 hours
Difficulty Rating: Easy along dirt footpaths, with a moderate climb down and then up the canyon wall
Trail Surface: Mostly dirt; rocky at the canyon
Lay of the Land: Old-growth oak forest, along with magnolia, holly, hemlock, and Southern yellow pine; wildflowers such as yellow lady slipper and trillium
Land Status: Wilderness area
Nearest Town: Double Springs, AL
Other Trail Users: None
Canine Compatibility: Dog friendly—along easy path, though the descent to the river is a bit steep; bring water; no leash required

Getting There

From Cullman: Go west on U.S. 278 for 44 miles to AL 33 in Double Springs. Turn right and head 12 miles north on AL 33 to CR 6. Turn left onto CR 6 and travel 8.6 miles. (CR 6 becomes CR 60 when you enter the Sipsey River Recreational Area.) The trailhead is on the right and is well marked. ***DeLorme: Alabama Atlas & Gazetteer:*** Page 23 B9

The Sipsey Wilderness is the only area of old-growth oak forest remaining in the state. Along the trail you'll find magnificent specimens of magnolia, holly, hemlock, and oak. This is also prime wildflower region. Don't be surprised to see a lot of photographers along the trail, capturing images of yellow lady slipper, shooting stars, yellow and white trillium, and other flowers.

There's a good chance you'll spot white-tailed deer, wild turkeys, or foxes. Coyotes have made a comeback in the region, but seeing them is a little unlikely. Bird-watchers love the Sipsey Wilderness, where it's not unusual to see such specimens as Acadian flycatchers, eastern phoebes, and belted kingfishers.

This route is one of the few in the wilderness that doesn't come to a waterfall, but what it lacks in cascading water it more than makes up for with its view of the Sipsey River and surrounding canyon. The route may have a bit of moderate difficulty, but not to the point where hikers of all ages cannot enjoy the trip.

For the first three-quarters of the trail, along Trail 201, the path is a level dirt path. It then intersects with Trail 209 and descends steeply down the canyon to the river. The brush gets thick in some areas, narrowing the trail. The thorny leaves of holly and blackberry vines may leave you with a few scrapes. The real concern is if you are allergic to poison ivy, which also lines the path.

MilesDirections

0.0 START from the Trail 201/202 Trailhead off CR 60. Head into the woods behind the information sign—a wooden sign next to the trail reads "201/202."

0.1 Come to a T-intersection with a gravel road that runs northeast/southwest. Turn right.

0.2 Come to a fork and go left. (Trail 202 breaks right.)

2.0 The gravel trail comes to an intersection. Turn right onto Trail 209 (the Sipsey Fork Trail). (Trail 201 continues to the left.)

2.5 Come to a fork. Go left and head steeply down the canyon wall following a stream to the bottom where the trail ends at the Sipsey River. (The right fork is a short trail that leads to the edge of the canyon with a nice view of the river.) A wooden sign at the bottom indicates the intersection of the two trails. Turn around and retrace your tracks to the trailhead.

5.0 Arrive back at the Trail 201/202 Trailhead.

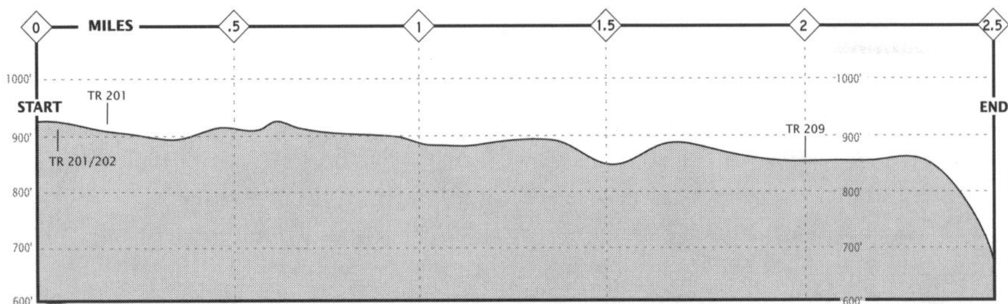

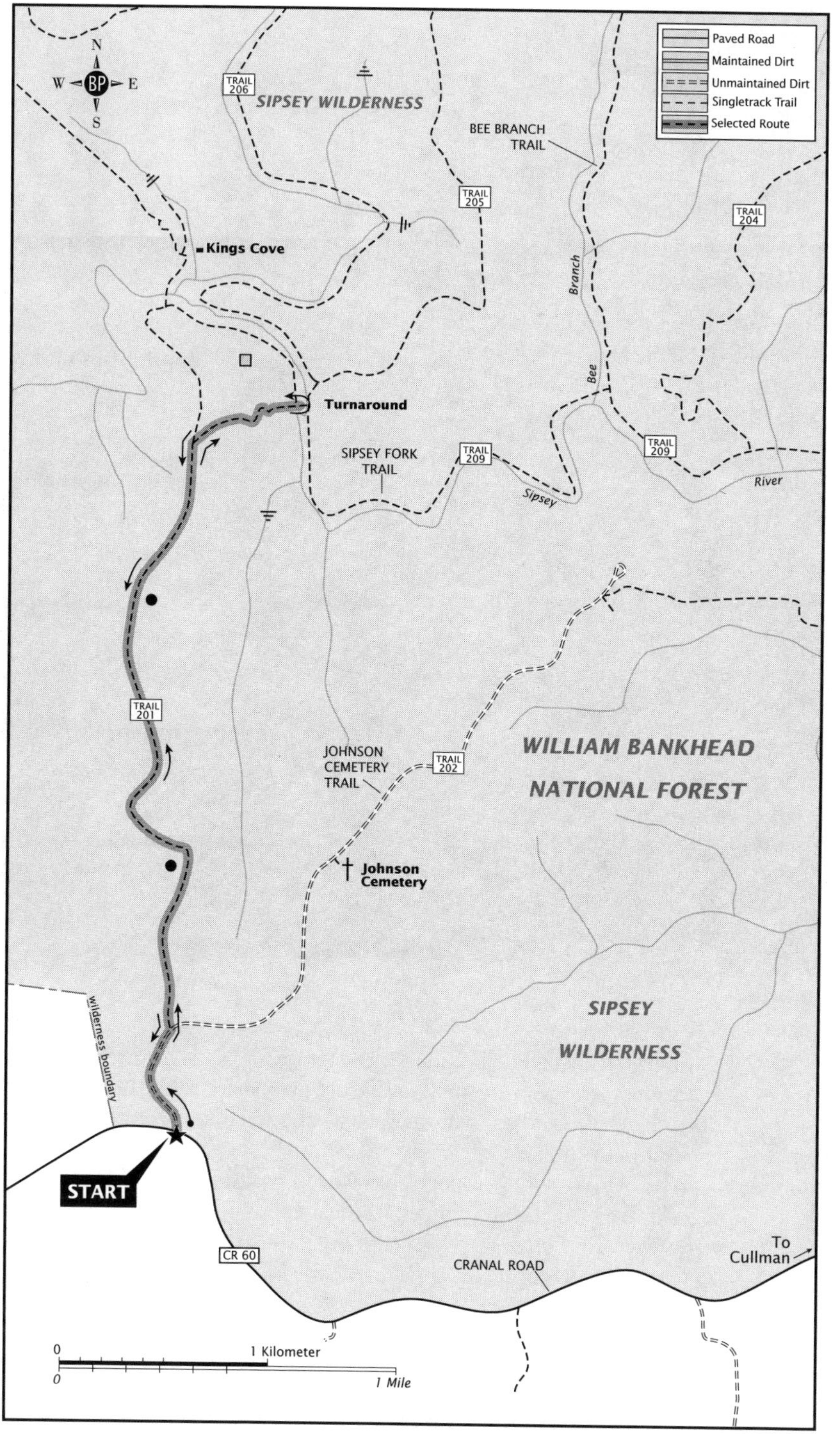

Paved Road
Maintained Dirt
Unmaintained Dirt
Singletrack Trail
Selected Route

N
W BP E
S

TRAIL 206
SIPSEY WILDERNESS
BEE BRANCH TRAIL
TRAIL 205
TRAIL 204
Kings Cove
Bee Branch
Turnaround
SIPSEY FORK TRAIL
TRAIL 209
TRAIL 209
Sipsey River
TRAIL 201
JOHNSON CEMETERY TRAIL
TRAIL 202
Johnson Cemetery
WILLIAM BANKHEAD NATIONAL FOREST
SIPSEY WILDERNESS
wilderness boundary
START
CR 60
CRANAL ROAD
To Cullman

0 1 Kilometer
0 1 Mile

Bushwhacking and off-trailing is encouraged if you are experienced and feel comfortable with orienteering (using map and compass), but be cautious. The area is dotted with high bluffs and waterfalls that can suddenly appear as you come out of dense brush.

Whether off-trailing or not, remember to practice Leave No Trace hiking. As they say, take only pictures; leave only footprints. Carry ample water, even for short hikes. Don't forget that even those lovely waters of the Sipsey and its feeder creeks should be boiled for at least for two minutes, purified, or filtered before drinking. To help prevent fires, use a camp stove instead of a wood fire. If you do use an established fire ring, be sure the coals are completely out before you leave. Hunting is allowed in the wilderness generally between November 15 and March 15. Contact the Forest Service to verify the dates.

If you're looking for a good full-day loop, or even a good overnight, use Trail 201 in conjunction with trails 209 and 202. There are numerous campsites along the banks of the Sipsey.

Hike Information

Trail Contacts:
USDA Forest Service William B. Bankhead District, Moulton, AL; (205) 489–5111; *open Monday–Friday 7:30 A.M.–4 P.M.*

Schedule:
Open year round

Fees/Permits:
There is a $3 day-use parking fee at the trailheads. Walk-ins are free.

Local Information:
[See Hike 28: Bee Branch Trail]

Local Events/Attractions:
[See Hike 28: Bee Branch Trail]

Accommodations:
[See Hike 28: Bee Branch Trail]

Restaurants:
[See Hike 28: Bee Branch Trail]

Organizations:
[See Hike 28: Bee Branch Trail]

Other Resources:
[See Hike 28: Bee Branch Trail]

Maps:
USGS maps: Bee Branch, AL • **Brochures**—*available at the ranger office or by writing the ranger office*

Trail 209 (Sipsey Fork Trail)

Hike Summary

Trail 209 is the longest trail in the Sipsey Wilderness, following the flow of the Sipsey River through most of the canyon, with waterfalls and towering limestone cliffs lining the banks. Among a variety of vegetation along the trail are blackberry bushes and muscadine vines.

Hike Specs

Start: From the Sipsey Wilderness Recreation Area
Length: 17.4-mile out-and-back
Approximate Hiking Time: 12–14 hours
Difficulty Rating: Easy over dirt paths; moderate to difficult at the fording of the Sipsey River near the end of the hike
Trail Surface: Dirt path
Lay of the Land: Magnolia, hemlock, oak, and Southern yellow pine; muscadine vines
Land Status: Wilderness area
Nearest Town: Double Springs, AL
Other Trail Users: None
Canine Compatibility: Dog friendly—with plenty of water available; no leash required

Getting There

From Cullman: Take U.S. 278 west for 44 miles to AL 33 in Double Springs. Turn right and head 12 miles north on AL 33 to CR 6. Take a left onto CR 6 and travel 3.8 miles to the Sipsey Recreational Area. The parking area is on the left and is well marked. ***DeLorme: Alabama Atlas & Gazetteer:*** Page 23 B10

Trail 209 (Sipsey Fork Trail) traces the flow of the Sipsey River for 8.7 miles through the 25,906-acre Sipsey Wilderness. Along the trail, the walls of the canyon rise high, dotted at their base with caves. You'll hear creeks as they cascade down the sandstone walls on their way to the river, and you'll see waterfalls high above the trail. The Sipsey River is an impressive sight to behold. The clear, cold waters run for 61 miles, forming the only nationally designated Wild and Scenic River in Alabama.

Near the end of Trail 209, you get a chance to test your river-fording skills. The crossing is made just before the trail intersects Trail 201. The current is usually not exceptionally strong, but you may want to wear boots or sandals because of the rocky bottom. During heavy rains, the river may be impossible to ford.

Large boulders in the Sipsey River.

As you hike, be on the lookout for white-tailed deer, Eastern wild turkeys, and foxes. If you're into fishing, largemouth bass and bluegill are the main catch—a state freshwater fishing license is required. The trail is lined with magnificent hemlocks, magnolias, and Southern yellow pines. Wildflowers are too numerous to name, but the wildflower photographers who flock to the area in spring and summer will be more than happy to point them out.

The Forest Service encourages experienced hikers to leave the trail and explore the surrounding area. There is plenty to see and discover here. On one excursion I stumbled onto some beautiful waterfalls, with no one around but me and the sounds and sights of the wilderness. The key word here, though, is *experienced.* If you are not familiar with orienteering, (using map and compass), the best thing is to stay on the trail. It's easy to get lost.

MilesDirections

0.0 START from the trailhead at the Sipsey Recreational Area into the woods. In 50 feet, start heading downhill and pass under CR 60.

0.5 Come to a fork where Borden Creek branches off to the northeast from the river and go left. (Trail 200 continues to the right.) Ford the creek and pick up the trail once again on the opposite side.

0.8 *[**FYI.** Keep an eye out for small side trails that lead to the river and nice places to just relax.]*

1.5 The trail merges briefly with a dirt road known as the Cullman Motorway. Shortly, it leaves the road and heads back to the woods to the west.

2.5 Pass a campsite next to the river.

4.5 *[**FYI.** Come to a wooden post with "202" on it, pointing across the river. This is Trail 202 (the Johnson Cemetery Trail). To get to Trail 202 you must ford the river.]* Continue straight and pass a campsite on the left.

5.3 Come to a fork and continue straight.

5.5 Pass a camp on the left.

5.6 A fork in the trail splits around a large uprooted tree and rejoins at the other side at a creek.

5.9 *[**FYI.** Come to a wooden post that points to Trail 204.]* Go straight to the west. In 50 feet, pass another campsite. Just after, the trail splits again around some brush and rejoins at the other end.

6.1 Pass another camp on the right.

6.3 Pass a campsite on the left

6.4 Come to a fork and go right. (The left fork heads to the river.)

6.5 Come to a fork and go left. (The right fork is the Bee Branch Trail and heads uphill following the feeder creek.) The left fork looks like a dead-end that drops down to a creek, but you'll want to take this. Head down the short slope and cross the creek. There will be a campsite on the other side next to the river.

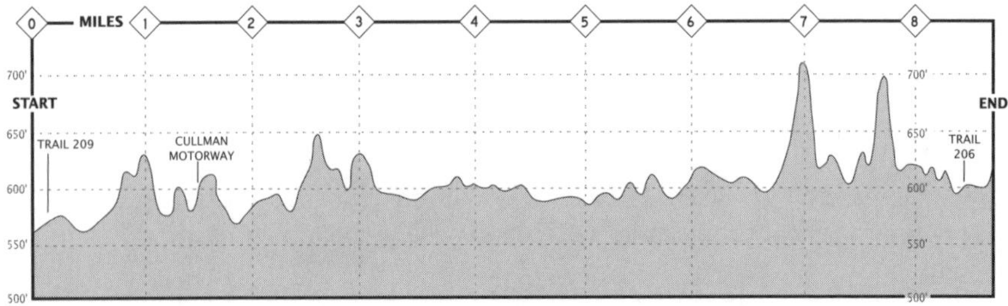

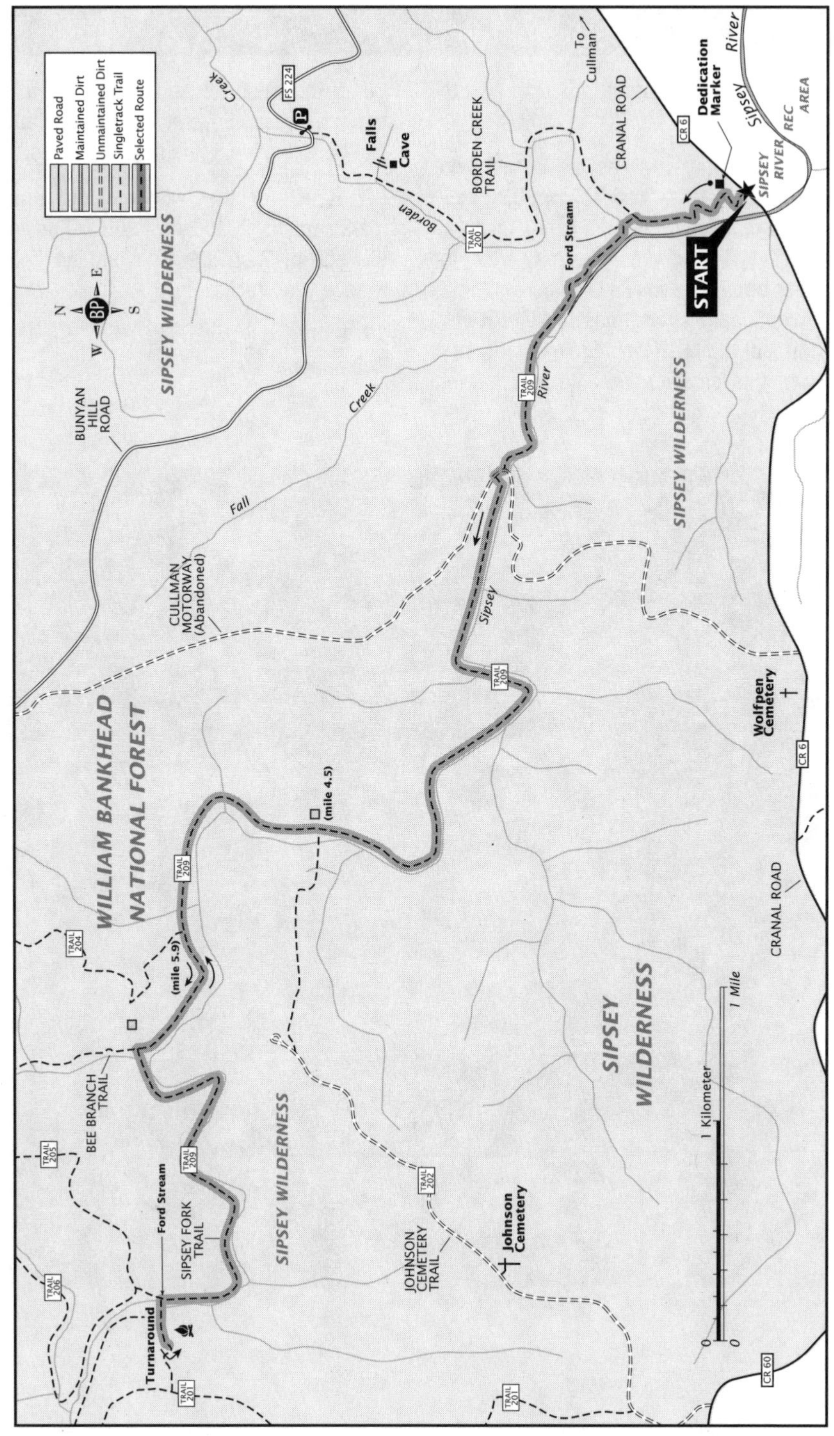
Paved Road
Maintained Dirt
Unmaintained Dirt
Singletrack Trail
Selected Route
SIPSEY WILDERNESS
BUNYAN HILL ROAD
FS 224
Creek
Falls
Cave
Borden
BORDEN CREEK TRAIL
TRAIL 200
To Cullman
CRANAL ROAD
CR 6
Dedication Marker
Sipsey River
SIPSEY RIVER REC AREA
START
Ford Stream
TRAIL 209
River
Fall Creek
CULLMAN MOTORWAY (Abandoned)
Sipsey
Wolfpen Cemetery
WILLIAM BANKHEAD NATIONAL FOREST
(mile 4.5)
(mile 5.9)
TRAIL 204
BEE BRANCH TRAIL
TRAIL 205
TRAIL 206
Turnaround
SIPSEY FORK TRAIL
TRAIL 201
TRAIL 202
JOHNSON CEMETERY TRAIL
Johnson Cemetery
1 Kilometer
1 Mile
CR 60

MilesDirections (Continued)

7.5 Pass a campsite on the right next to the river.

8.4 Come to a trail split. Turn left and cross the river. (A wooden post here indicates that Trail 206 goes right.) The river crossing is rocky so you may want to wear boots or sandals. The current isn't exceptionally strong most days, but you can feel the push. During times of heavy rain, this crossing may be impassible. Climb the opposite bank and pick the trail up again. Several nice campsites can be found along the next 0.3 miles.

8.7 Reach another wooden post that marks trails "201" and "209." This is the end of Trail 209. Turn around and retrace your tracks.

17.4 Arrive back at the Sipsey Recreational Area.

Intersection of Trail #209 and Trail #202 where we cross the river.

Most hikers make the Trail 209 hike into an overnight hike, instead of trying to tackle 17.4 miles in one day. Along the route are plenty of good campsites. To protect the river and the surrounding environment, the Forest Service asks that hikers camp away from rivers, streams, and the trail. But of course, over the years, hikers have made camp at the edge of the river and, in some cases, directly on the trail. Rangers are okay with you using these established campsites because the most damage to an area is when it is first camped on.

Even though the Sipsey River is in a wilderness area, its water should still be treated before you drink it, to kill disease organisms such as those that cause giardiasis, which results in severe diarrhea, nausea, fever, and other symptoms. Boil water for at least two minutes, treat it chemically, or use a filter.

Winter and spring are the best times to enjoy the wilderness. In winter, leaves are gone and there are better views of the canyon. In spring, the wildflowers add color, and the river is running swiftly after spring rain and winter thaw. Summer brings mosquitoes and bugs. The Forest Service allows hunting in the area generally between November 15 and January 31; contact the Forest Service for exact dates.

Hike Information

Trail Contacts:
USDA Forest Service William B. Bankhead District, Moulton, AL; (205) 489–5111; *open Monday–Friday 7:30 A.M.–4 P.M.*

Schedule:
Open year round

Fees/Permits:
There is a $3 day-use parking fee at the trailheads. Walk-ins are free.

Local Information:
[See Hike 28: Bee Branch Trail]

Local Events/Attractions:
[See Hike 28: Bee Branch Trail]

Restaurants:
[See Hike 28: Bee Branch Trail]

Organizations:
[See Hike 28: Bee Branch Trail]

Other Resources:
[See Hike 28: Bee Branch Trail]

Maps:
USGS maps: Bee Branch, AL • **Brochures**—*available at the ranger office or by writing the ranger office*

South Plateau Loop Trail

Hike Summary

This hike travels, as advertised, around the southern plateau of Monte Sano Mountain. The trail is wide and well maintained, and crosses several nice creeks. Highlights of the trip are the short trail spurs that go to rock outcrops for wonderful views of the mountains and valleys of the Huntsville area.

Hike Specs

Start: From the south end of the hiker's trailhead at Monte Sano State Park
Length: 3.1-mile loop
Approximate Hiking Time: 1½–2 hours
Difficulty Rating: Easy, over well-maintained trails
Trail Surface: Dirt path
Lay of the Land: Silver and red maples, sassafras, and pin and live oaks; creeks; rock outcrops
Land Status: State park
Nearest Town: Huntsville, AL
Other Trail Users: None
Canine Compatibility: Dog friendly—over easy path; bring water, because water sources are seasonal; leash recommended

Getting There

From Huntsville: Take U.S. 231 south from I-565 (Exit 19A) for 0.4 miles and merge onto U.S. 431 South—stay in the center lane for this turn. Travel four miles up the side of Monte Sano Mountain and make a sharp left onto Monte Sano Boulevard. Head up the mountain 2.4 miles and make a right onto Nolen Avenue. Continue straight for two miles and Nolen Avenue forks. (To the right is the trailhead.) Take the left fork and travel 0.1 miles to the park office and camp store/campground. Park here. ***DeLorme: Alabama Atlas & Gazetteer:*** Page 19 D8

Madison County is one of the fastest growing counties in the state, yet Monte Sano Mountain and Monte Sano State Park manage to hold on to their wilderness character and maintain some great hiking trails.

Many people say that Monte Sano State Park's proximity to Huntsville makes it seem more like a city park than a state park. Proof of this is that the park is often crowded in spring, summer, and fall with city slickers trying to flee pavement. Even in winter, you're likely to find people walking their dogs, jogging, or just bringing the kids to the playground. The stone amphitheater, large picnic areas, and other development magnify the "city park" image. But this image is largely restricted to the northern plateau of Monte Sano Mountain, and all in all, Monte Sano still presents beauty and challenge to hikers.

Monte Sano Mountain is a limestone formation jutting more than 1,400 feet above sea level. Between 65 million and 150 million years ago, the entire region was under water. When the water receded, much of the marine life was left to fossilize and is visible today in the rock formations along this trail.

Through geologic time, large outcroppings formed around the flat plateau of the summit, forming the rim that marks the route of this hike. The trail leads around the plateau, staying mainly within 30 to 50 feet of the bluffs, affording great views of Round Top and Monte Sano Mountain and of McKay and Mills hollows. Short side trails lead to the bluffs, allowing you to take full advantage of these views. Be particularly observant of signs that read: "Danger, High Bluffs."

Along the route, you may see bobcats, white-tailed deer, opossums, skunks, or woodchucks. The trail passes through forests of red and silver maples and birch trees. From early spring to the beginning of summer, wildflowers such as violets and catchfly will be found blooming.

The trail starts its return trip at the outcropping known as O'Shaughnessy Point, where you can look down into the valley known as Big Cove. The point was named for Colonel James O'Shaughnessy, who came to the region from Dublin, Ireland, to supervise construction of a railroad line from Brunswick, Georgia, to St. Louis, Missouri, that would pass through Huntsville. O'Shaughnessy also helped build the Monte Sano Hotel.

O'Shaughnessy purchased an estate on Monte Sano Mountain to entertain his many guests, but it was destroyed by fire in 1890, not long after he bought it. He soon built another, this one in a spectacular Queen Anne style, with rich wood paneling, ornate fireplaces, and large wraparound porches. A few years after its construction, this home also fell to fire.

MilesDirections

0.0 START from the east end of the hiker's parking lot. A split rail fence surrounds the lot. Head through the fence opening, following the white blazes. *[**FYI.** In 100 feet, pass an old stone C.C.C. water pump.]* Intersect the red-blazed Fire Tower Trail. Continue straight.

0.1 *[**FYI.** Pass the first of several small side trails that lead to the bluffs and views of the Huntsville valley below. Be very careful should you opt to explore these side trails.]*

0.3 Pass a small amphitheater to the left. In 200 feet, come to a fork and go right. This is a short connector trail to the opposite side of the loop.

0.7 The orange-blazed Bog Trail joins the South Plateau Trail.

0.9 The red-blazed Fire Tower Trail merges briefly with the trail.

1.0 The Fire Tower Trail branches off. The South Plateau Trail continues to the left. Another 100 feet ahead, the Bog Trail branches off to the left.

1.2 Pass the first trail shelter on the right.

1.3 The South Plateau Trail merges with the yellow-blazed Mountain Mist Trail. In 200 feet, pass the second, and much better, trail shelter on the right.

1.5 The path begins its loop back to the parking area and comes to a trail split. Turn left. (The Warpath Ridge Trail goes right.) Shortly thereafter the Mountain Mist Trail breaks off to the right. Stay left on the South Plateau Trail.

1.6 Pass a short connector trail to the Mountain Mist Trail on the right. (The Mountain Mist Trail runs below the Southern Plateau Trail and parallel for a time.)

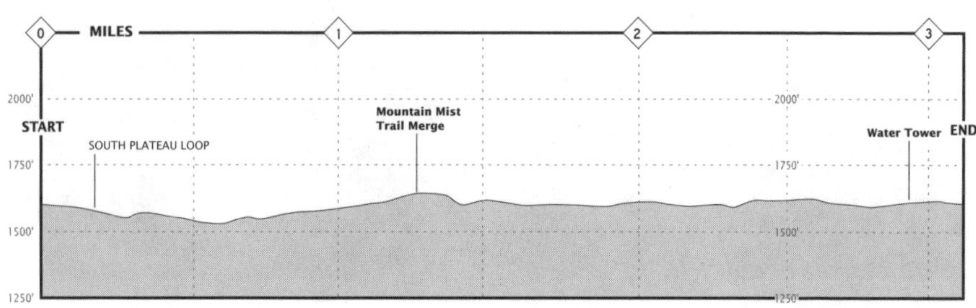

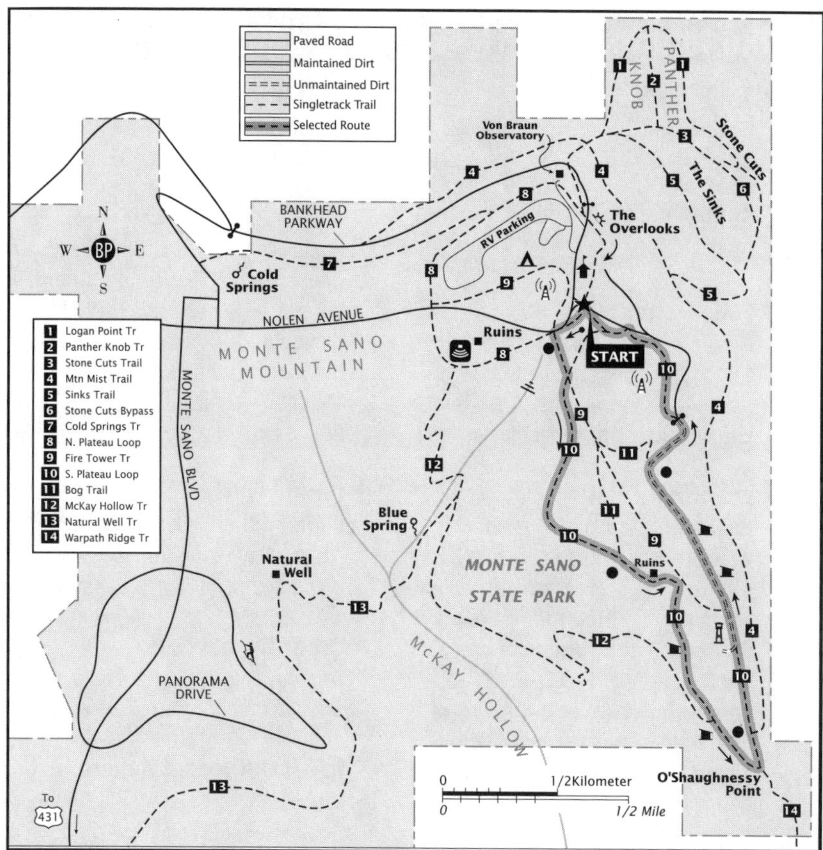

1.9 Pass a third trail shelter on the right. Soon the trail merges with a gravel road. Continue straight.

2.0 Once again the red-blazed Fire Tower Trail intersects the trail. Continue straight.

2.2 Pass the fourth trail shelter.

2.3 The trail intersects the orange Bog Trail. Turn right and follow the South Plateau Trail. In 100 feet, the trail turns off of the road and becomes a clay path heading into the woods.

2.5 The Interpretive Geology Fossil Trail joins the South Plateau Trail. *[**FYI.** Along this section, there are signs giving the hiker an idea of what to look for, including what scientists call today's "Living Fossils:" willows, sassafras, and maple trees, all decedents of trees 63 to 150 million years old.]* Pass the fifth trail shelter.

2.6 Cross a gravel road. The trail swings to the northwest and runs parallel to the park road as it travels over a series of rolling hills.

2.9 Cross a 10-foot bridge and the parking area can be seen ahead to the right.

3.1 The trail intersects with the first section of the trail, as the first section comes out of the parking area. Turn right and head 50 feet to the parking area to end the trip.

Hike Information

Trail Contacts:
Monte Sano State Park, Huntsville, AL; (205) 534–3757

Schedule:
Open year round

Fees/Permits:
No fee to hike. Camping fees are $8 for primitive tent sites, $12 for tent site with water, $14 for tent site with water and electricity.

Local Information:
Huntsville/Madison Chamber of Commerce, Huntsville, AL; (256) 535–2000 or *www.hsvchamber.org* • **Huntsville/Madison County Convention and Visitors Bureau**, Huntsville, AL; 1–800–SPACE–4U or *www.Huntsville.org* • **Alabama Mountain Lakes Association**, Mooresville, AL; 1–800–648–5381 or *www.almtlakes.org*

Accommodations:
Madison Inn, Huntsville, AL; (256) 890–0700 • **Southland Motel**, Huntsville, AL; (256) 539–9391 • **Stamps Inn Bed and Breakfast**, Huntsville, AL; (256) 586–7038 • **Villager Lodge**, Huntsville, AL; (256) 533–0610 • **Wandlers Inn**, Huntsville, AL; (256) 837–6694 • **Charles' Motel**, Meridianville, AL; (256) 828–4801

Restaurants:
Bench Warmer Food and Spirits, Huntsville, AL; (256) 539–6268 • **Bubba's**, Huntsville, AL; (256) 534–3133 • **Café Berlin**, Huntsville, AL; (256) 880–9920 • **Clementine's Field of Greens**, Huntsville, AL; (256) 536–5311 • **Eunice's Country Kitchen**, Huntsville, AL; (256) 534–9550 • **Mr. C's**, Huntsville, AL; (256) 882–1190

Organizations:
Sierra Club North Alabama (Huntsville) Chapter at *www.alabama.sierraclub.org/na.html*

Other Resources:
Tennessee Valley Trails at *www.montesano.com/hikeweb*

Local Outdoor Retailers:
Hibbett Sporting Goods, Huntsville, AL; (256) 533–7515 or (256) 830–5672 • **Parr and Sons**, Huntsville, AL; (256) 882–2236 • **Outdoor Sportsman**, Athens, AL; (256) 233–2277

Maps:
USGS maps: Huntsville, AL; Meridianville, AL • **Park map**—*A brochure with trail map is available at the camp store for 50 cents.*

Local Events/Festivals:

Mountain Dulcimer Festival, 3rd Sunday of September, Huntsville, AL; (256) 536–2882—*Each September at the Burritt Museum on Monte Sano Mountain, the museum plays host to dozens of Mountain Dulcimer players from around the South. The sweet, chiming sounds of the dulcimer are created by using a small "mallet" to tap the strings of the instrument and are indigenous to the South and especially the Appalachians. Admission is free.* • **State Fiddling and Bluegrass Convention**, 3rd weekend of September, Huntsville, AL; (256) 859–4471 • **Polk Salad Festival**, 2nd Friday & Saturday in May, Huntsville, AL; (256) 535–2000—*Polk Salad is a purple, leafy, cabbage like plant indigenous to the South and for two days, becomes the centerpiece for this cooking contest and gathering.* • **Alabama Constitution Village**, Huntsville, AL; 1–800–678–1819—*A living history museum that features tour guides dressed in clothes of the period (1809–1819) who guide visitors through the site where the 1819 Constitutional Convention was held. Admission is charged. Call for dates and prices.* • **Early Works**, Huntsville, AL; (256) 564–8100 or *www.earlyworks.com—This is a hands-on science museum for kids and adults alike.* • **Huntsville-Madison County Botanical Garden**, Huntsville, AL; (256) 830–4447 or *www.hsvbg.org* • **Huntsville Museum of Art**, Huntsville, AL; (256) 535–4350 or *www.hsv.tis.net/hma—Open Tuesday–Saturday 10 A.M.–5 P.M., Sunday 1 P.M.–5 P.M.* • **North Alabama Railroad Museum**, Huntsville, AL; (256) 851–6276 or *www.suncompsvc.com/narm* • **Sci-Quest (North Alabama Science Center)**, Huntsville, AL; (256) 837–0606 or *www.sci-quest.org* • **U.S. Space and Rocket Center**, Huntsville, AL; (256) 827–3400 or *www.ussrc.com—A centerpiece of the U.S. space program, the Space and Rocket Center features a huge museum with the original Apollo 16 capsule, moon rocks from the mission, an Imax theater, and tours of the complex takes visitors to the booster testing facilities and to the actual assembly areas for Space Station Freedom.* • **Von Braun Astronomical Society**, Huntsville, AL; (256) 539–0316 or *www.vbas.org—A wonderful attraction high atop Monte Sano Mountain is the Von Braun Astronomical Society and their observatory/planetarium. Twice a month, the club hosts a show for members and the public. A brief look at the sky in the planetarium is followed by a guest speaker and then, if the skies are clear, a spectacular look at the night sky through their telescopes. Check the website for dates and times of shows.*

North Plateau Loop Trail

Hike Summary

This hike travels around the northern plateau of Monte Sano Mountain. The trail is wide and well maintained and crosses several beautiful creeks. Highlights include a 70-foot waterfall. You'll see an excellent example of the masonry talents of the Civilian Conservation Corps in the remains of the Monte Sano Tavern, built in 1935.

Hike Specs

Start: From the hiker's parking lot next to the Monte Sano State Park office
Length: 1.3-mile loop
Approximate Hiking Time: 1 hour
Difficulty Rating: Easy, over level footpaths
Trail Surface: Clay footpaths
Lay of the Land: Waterfalls and bluffs overlooking the Huntsville valley
Land Status: State park
Nearest Town: Huntsville, AL
Other Trail Users: Cyclists
Canine Compatibility: Dog friendly—over this easy path; ample water available; leash recommended through picnic areas

Getting There

From Huntsville: Take U.S. 231 south from I-565 (Exit 19A) for 0.4 miles and merge onto U.S. 431 South—stay in the center lane for this turn. Travel four miles up the side of Monte Sano Mountain and make a sharp left onto Monte Sano Boulevard. Head up the mountain 2.4 miles and make a right onto Nolen Avenue. Continue straight for two miles and Nolen Avenue forks. (To the right is the trailhead.) Take the left fork and travel 0.1 miles to the park office and camp store/campground. Park here. ***DeLorme: Alabama Atlas & Gazetteer:*** Page 19 D8

While Monte Sano State Park's Southern Plateau Loop Trail focuses more on the geology of the mountains, with broad views from high bluffs, the North Plateau Loop shows more of the history of the area—in addition to views and waterfalls.

The phrase "monte sano" is Latin for *mountain of health.* In the early 1800s, this mountain became a refuge for people with yellow fever, cholera, and malaria who sought out its cool air and clear waters. In 1827, Dr. Thomas Fearn established a colony here for people seeking relief from illness. He built an ornate home for himself and his family, complete with stables and a smokehouse. The colony flourished until Union soldiers destroyed it during the Civil War.

The area was rebuilt after the Civil War and flourished with income from tourists until the Great Depression of the 1930s hit. Members of the Civilian Conservation Corps arrived in 1935, and the rebuilding process began anew: cabins, picnic areas, horse barns, trails, roadways, and even a tavern were constructed. By 1936 Monte Sano State Park was born.

The remains of the Monte Sano Tavern, built in 1935.

The trail begins by following the north plateau to the west. As it moves along a bluff, it passes a small creek and a waterfall. Traveling through a picnic area, the route reveals evidence of the CCC work in the Monte Sano Tavern—built in 1937 but destroyed by fire in 1947. This is one of the largest remains of CCC buildings in the state, and the site offers a fine look at the stone masonry skills of the Corps.

Continuing to the west, you'll see the amphitheater, also constructed by the CCC, which is used for entertainment and educational programs. Just past the amphitheater, a beautiful 70-foot Blue Creek waterfall tumbles down the rocks. As the trail loops around the plateau, you'll enjoy views of the rocky outcroppings that mark the caverns known as The Sinks (where the Stone Cuts Trail travels) and of Mills Hollow.

The trail also leads to Von Braun Observatory. When Dr. Wernher von Braun came to Huntsville to work at the American space program facility, he and his colleagues helped guide the building of this planetarium and observatory, which opened in 1956. The facility is operated by the Von Braun Astronomical Society, which sponsors a public program on the first and second Saturdays of each month. The programs include lectures by astronomers and NASA scientists and, weather permitting, views through the telescopes.

Hike Information

Trail Contacts:
Monte Sano State Park, Huntsville, AL; (205) 534–3757

Schedule:
Open year round

Fees/Permits:
No fee to hike. Camping fees are $8 for primitive tent sites, $12 for tent site with water, $14 for tent site with water and electricity.

Local Information:
[See Hike 32: South Plateau Loop]

Local Events/Attractions:
[See Hike 32: South Plateau Loop]

Accommodations:
[See Hike 32: South Plateau Loop]

Restaurants:
[See Hike 32: South Plateau Loop]

Organizations:
[See Hike 32: South Plateau Loop]

Other Resources:
[See Hike 32: South Plateau Loop]

Local Outdoor Retailers:
[See Hike 32: South Plateau Loop]

Maps:
USGS maps: Huntsville, AL; Meridianville, AL • **Park map**—*A brochure with trail map is available at the camp store for 50 cents.*

MilesDirections

0.0 START from the west end of the hiker's parking lot. Follow the blue blazes along a gravel footpath. Shortly you'll cross the red Fire Tower Trail. Continue straight.

0.1 *[**Side-trip.** Come to a short 30-foot side trail to the left. This short path is worth the time as it heads to the head of a waterfall.]*

0.2 *[**FYI.** Pass the ruins of the Monte Sano Tavern, built by the C.C.C. in 1937. The tavern was destroyed by fire in 1947.]*

0.4 *[**FYI.** Pass a picnic pavilion. Behind the pavilion is the best waterfall of the trip. Many artists come here to paint and draw the falls and surrounding rock formations.]*

0.6 Cross the park road just below another picnic area. Soon thereafter, the red Fire Tower Trail merges and then departs from the trail. In another 200 feet, pass primitive campgrounds. *[**FYI.** The winds pick up significantly here during the winter months as it makes its way to the north side of the mountain.]*

0.8 Pass another picnic area on the right.

0.9 *[**FYI.** The red blazed Sinks Trail that leads to the Stone Cuts can be seen to the left down below. The Von Braun*

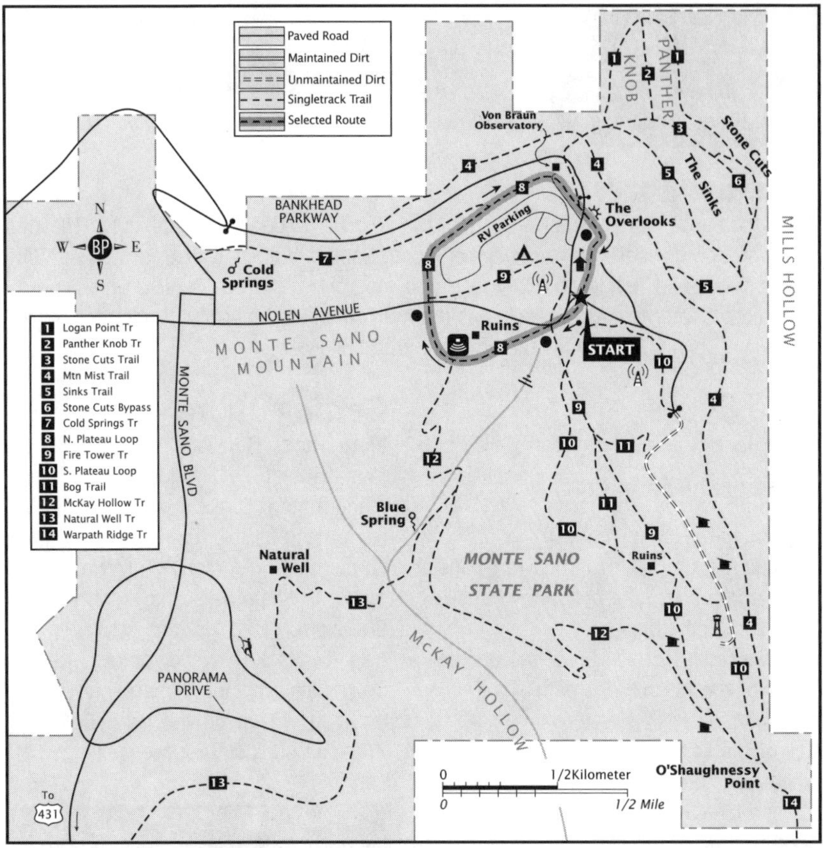

Observatory will be passed shortly on the right.]

1.1 Come to the Overlooks, a paved cul-de-sac that gives the park's most spectacular view of the Huntsville valley. Make a right here and cut across the paved road. The trail reenters the woods.

1.2 Come to the park's cabin road and turn right. Pick up the trail again on the other side of the road as it dips back into the woods.

1.3 Come to the park road. Head straight across the road to the south and arrive back at the hiker's parking area.

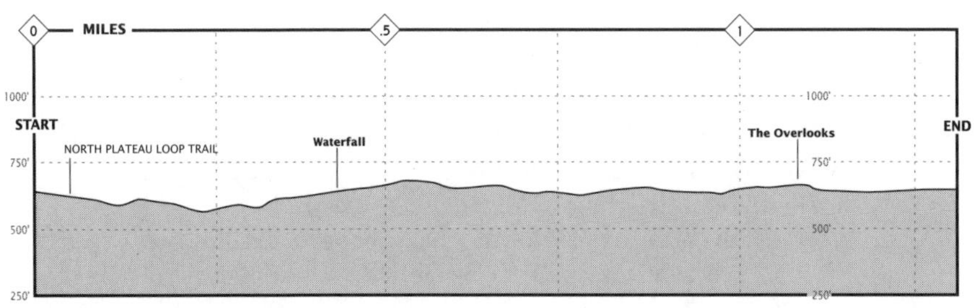

McKay Hollow Trail

Hike Summary

Plenty of people love to tackle the McKay Hollow Trail despite its difficulty. The trail drops steeply down the western ridge of Monte Sano Mountain, with great views of Blue Spring Falls, and heads down through imposing cliffs and boulders. O'Shaughnessy Point comes into view as the trail goes down and then up the hollow. The route also follows Blue Spring Creek along the bottom of the hollow.

Hike Specs

Start: From the southern picnic area at Monte Sano State Park
Length: 5-mile out-and-back
Approximate Hiking Time: 3–4 hours
Difficulty Rating: Difficult due to climbs down and then up the hollow, over rocky ledges and outcroppings
Trail Surface: Rock-covered trail on the sides of the hollow; dirt path along the creek
Lay of the Land: Sassafras, maple, and white oak forest; wildflowers, including iris and larkspur
Land Status: State park
Nearest Town: Huntsville, AL
Other Trail Users: None
Canine Compatibility: Not dog friendly—due to steep, rocky terrain; if you do take dog, no leash required

Getting There

From Huntsville: Take U.S. 231 south from I-565 (Exit 19A) for 0.4 miles and merge onto U.S. 431 South—stay in the center lane for this turn. Travel four miles up the side of Monte Sano Mountain and make a sharp left onto Monte Sano Boulevard. Head up the mountain 2.4 miles and make a right onto Nolen Avenue. Continue straight for 1.4 miles and the picnic area will be on the right. ***DeLorme: Alabama Atlas & Gazetteer:*** Page 19 D8

Hiking trails are only one of the lures of Monte Sano State Park. Visitors also can walk through one of several gardens on display at the park. The Japanese Garden, near the camp store, shows off delicate flowers, a rock garden, red bridges, and a teahouse.

The McKay Hollow Trail travels down and then back up the limestone cliffs and outcroppings that line each side of McKay Hollow. The trail connects the western ridge of Monte Sano Mountain to just north of O'Shaughnessy Point on the eastern side.

One of the high points of the trip, Blue Spring Waterfall, arrives just after the trail begins at the southern picnic area. This 100-foot-tall waterfall

View of the Huntsville Valley.

attracts visitors from all over, and it's not uncommon to find artists all season long sketching or painting the scene. A short side trail leads directly to the falls, where it's possible to duck into the small cave behind the falling water.

From here the path follows a narrow, rocky ledge down the side of an impressive limestone cliff. It may be tempting to explore the rock formations on the cliff sides, but it's best to heed the words of the park rangers and stay on the marked trail, safe from the loose rock of the cliff. Also be wary of where you rest. Snakes live in the rocks and might not enjoy the company and could let you know about it.

On the way down, you can enjoy views of O'Shaughnessy Point and the mountains of Huntsville trailing off into the distance. Watch for the yellow blazes marking the trail as it weaves its way downward. In several areas, hikers have cut paths to shorten the trip, and many deer trails cross through here; it's only too easy to get off trail.

At the bottom of the cozy hollow, with its dense hardwood forest, the trail follows along the banks of Blue Spring Creek. Wildflowers bloom en masse in the brush. Lizards dart in and out along the path as it meanders along the creek. This is the easiest part of the trip as the trail follows the tiny creek for about 0.6 miles before beginning to climb again.

The trail up the other side of the hollow provides a steep hike up limestone cliffs and around large boulders. The McKay Hollow Trail ends at its intersection with the South Plateau Trail. If you don't relish the idea of retracing your tracks along the McKay Hollow Trail, then use the South and North Plateau trails as an easy exit back to the parking area.

Hike Information

Trail Contacts:
Monte Sano State Park, Huntsville, AL; (205) 534–3757

Schedule:
Open year round

Fees/Permits:
No fee to hike. Camping fees are $8 for primitive tent sites, $12 for tent site with water, $14 for tent site with water and electricity.

Local Information:
[See Hike 32: South Plateau Loop]

Local Events/Attractions:
[See Hike 32: South Plateau Loop]

Accommodations:
[See Hike 32: South Plateau Loop]

Restaurants:
[See Hike 32: South Plateau Loop]

Organizations:
[See Hike 32: South Plateau Loop]

Other Resources:
[See Hike 32: South Plateau Loop]

Local Outdoor Retailers:
[See Hike 32: South Plateau Loop]

Maps:
USGS maps: Huntsville, AL; Meridianville, AL • **Park map**—*A brochure with trail map is available at the camp store for 50 cents.*

MilesDirections

0.0 START from the southeast end of the picnic area parking. There is a chain blocking a gravel road to the south. The creosote poles that hold the chain have yellow blazes on them. Cross the chain and head southwest on the gravel road. Yellow blazes are on the trees.

0.1 Cross the North Plateau Loop Trail (blue blazes). Come to a shelter. *[**Sidetrip.** In a short while a side trail leads to 70-foot waterfall which can be seen from the trail.]*

0.2 Come to a fork and go right.

0.3 Walking below some tall bluffs to the right, the trail comes to what looks like a fork. *[**FYI.** There are a series of these forks heading down the mountain. Some are deer trails, others are shortcuts created by hikers. The best bet is to stay on the main trail.]* Take the right fork and head over large boulders. In 50 feet, come to another fork and go right.

0.4 Come to another fork and go right. In 80 feet, come to another fork and go right.

1.0 Come to a T-intersection with a deer trail. Turn left. The trail will loop back to the southeast. It's very steep through here. Shortly, pass a small deer trail to the southeast and continue to the east.

1.1 The trail splits around some brush and rejoins in 30 feet.

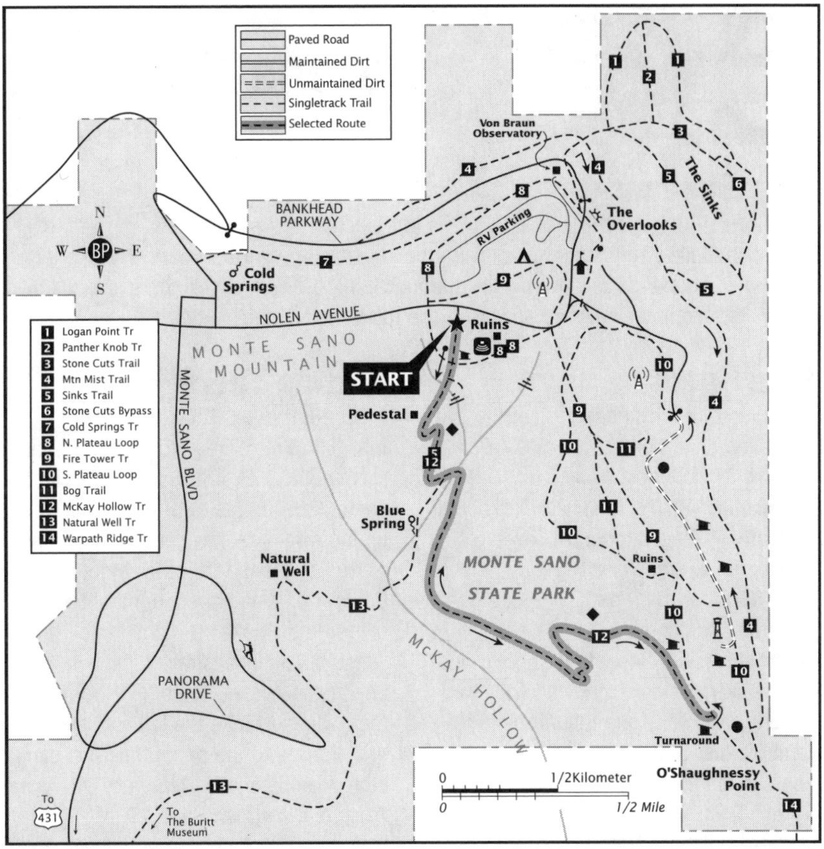

1.2 Come to an intersection with the Natural Well Trail and go left. *[**FYI.** The Natural Well Trail is an easy 2.5-mile path that will take you almost to the doorstep of the Burritt Museum.]*

2.5 The trail makes a final steep grade and intersects the South Plateau Trail. Turn around here and retrace your tracks. *[**Option.** To form a loop and an easier exit, take a left on the South Plateau Trail and then a left on the North Plateau Trail and then a right on the McKay Hollow trail it back to your car.]*

5.0 Arrive back at the picnic area parking lot.

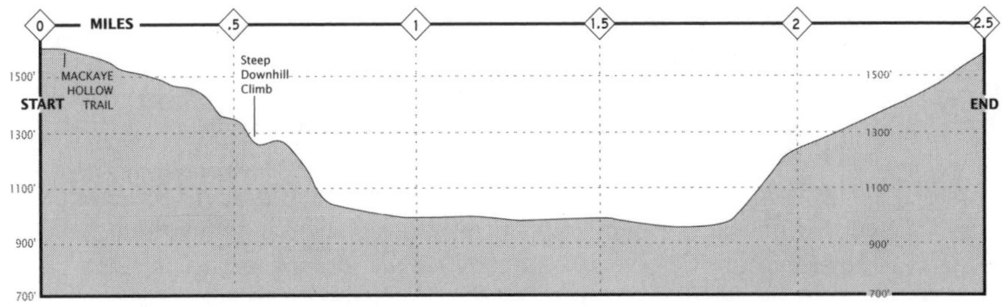

Stone Cuts Trail

Hike Summary

The Stone Cuts are deep erosional clefts in a section of limestone and form the highlight of this hike. The Stone Cuts Trail runs straight through the heart of these large, high-walled cuts. Kids will love climbing around in here. Mountain climbers love the high cliff walls, and small cavelike spaces in the rocks attract spelunkers.

Hike Specs

Start: From the northeast end of the hiking trailhead at Monte Sano State Park
Length: 3-mile loop
Approximate Hiking Time: 2.5–3.5 hours
Difficulty Rating: Moderate, over rocky terrain; some steep trail
Trail Surface: Dirt path studded with rocks and boulders
Lay of the Land: Sassafras, maple, and white oak forest; iris and larkspur wildflowers; rock walls and tunnels
Land Status: State park
Nearest Town: Huntsville, AL
Other Trail Users: Cyclists on the Mountain Mist section
Canine Compatibility: Dog friendly—but may be difficult for some dogs due to large boulders; bring water; leash not required

Getting There

From Huntsville: Take U.S. 231 south from I-565 (Exit 19A) for 0.4 miles and merge onto U.S. 431 South—stay in the center lane for this turn. Travel four miles up the side of Monte Sano Mountain and make a sharp left onto Monte Sano Boulevard. Head up the mountain 2.4 miles and make a right onto Nolen Avenue. Continue straight for two miles and Nolen Avenue forks. (To the right is the trailhead.) Take the left fork and travel 0.1 miles to the park office and camp store/campground. ***DeLorme: Alabama Atlas & Gazetteer:*** Page 19 D8

Monte Sano State Park's Stone Cuts Trail puts you in personal touch with the geological processes of the Highland Rim region as it passes through spectacular rock formations and tunnels, all of which was once covered with a shallow ocean. As the land began to emerge from the waters, shell banks and coral reefs were left high and dry. Their remains formed the limestone bedrock that makes up the mountains in this region. Throughout this hike, check the exposed rock and boulders for the fossils of ancient sea creatures.

Limestone is an extremely soft rock, and over time erosional forces have created numerous sinkholes, caverns, outcroppings, and cuts throughout the region. The Stone Cuts section is just one example of this process.

The trail is only moderate in difficulty, but be aware that the return hike can be rather steep, especially for hikers not physically ready for it. To begin this trip, the trail travels through an area called the Overlooks—a parking area with a 180-degree view of Mills Hollow and Panther Knob. After following a closed park road, the trail heads back into the woods and heads steeply down Monte Sano Mountain to the bottom of Mills Hollow. Watch for the cyclists in the hollow who use the yellow-blazed Mountain Mist Trail.

MilesDirections

0.0 START from the northeast end of the hiker's parking area. Head across the park road. A blue-blazed gravel path is on the opposite side. This section of the loop follows the North Plateau Loop Trail.

0.1 Come to the dead end of the park's cabin road. Cross the road and walk between the openings of a split rail fence.

0.2 Come to the Overlooks. *[**FYI.** This paved cul-de-sac offers up the most spectacular view of the Huntsville valley in the park.]* Cut across the paved parking area to where a closed park road is. The red blazes of the Sinks Trail begin here.

0.4 The trail makes a sharp turn into the woods. *[**Note.** The trail is deep dirt and after a rain is very slick and muddy.]*

0.6 Cross the yellow-blazed Mountain Mist Trail.

0.7 The trail merges with the orange-blazed Logan Point Trail. At the bottom of the hill, stay straight on the white-blazed Stone Cuts Trail. (The red Sinks Trail turns to the right.)

0.8 Come to a T-intersection and turn right on the white-blazed Stone Cuts Trail. (The orange-blazed Logan Point Trail splits left.)

0.9 A double white blaze will be seen as the blue Panther Knob Trail branches off to the left. Continue on the Stone Cuts Trail to the right. *[**FYI.** Behind you are the observatory and the cliffs of the Overlooks. Along this section, notice the layering of the rock formations from erosion.]*

1.0 *[**FYI.** This area is known as the Sinks. There are some huge cliffs and boulders here to explore but be very careful.]*

1.3 Reach the Stone Cuts.

1.4 *[**FYI.** From here, the trail traverses through the actual stone cuts with its 100-foot high walls dripping with water and dark cavern passageways.]*

1.6 Come to a fork. The blue Stone Cuts Bypass Trail breaks right from the Stone Cuts Trail and will eventually rejoin. Go right.

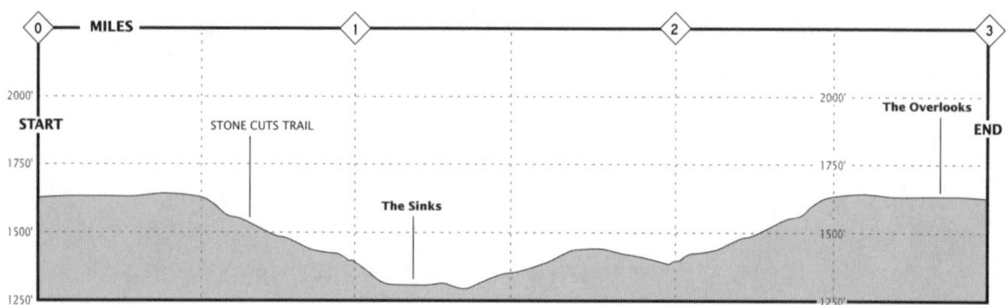

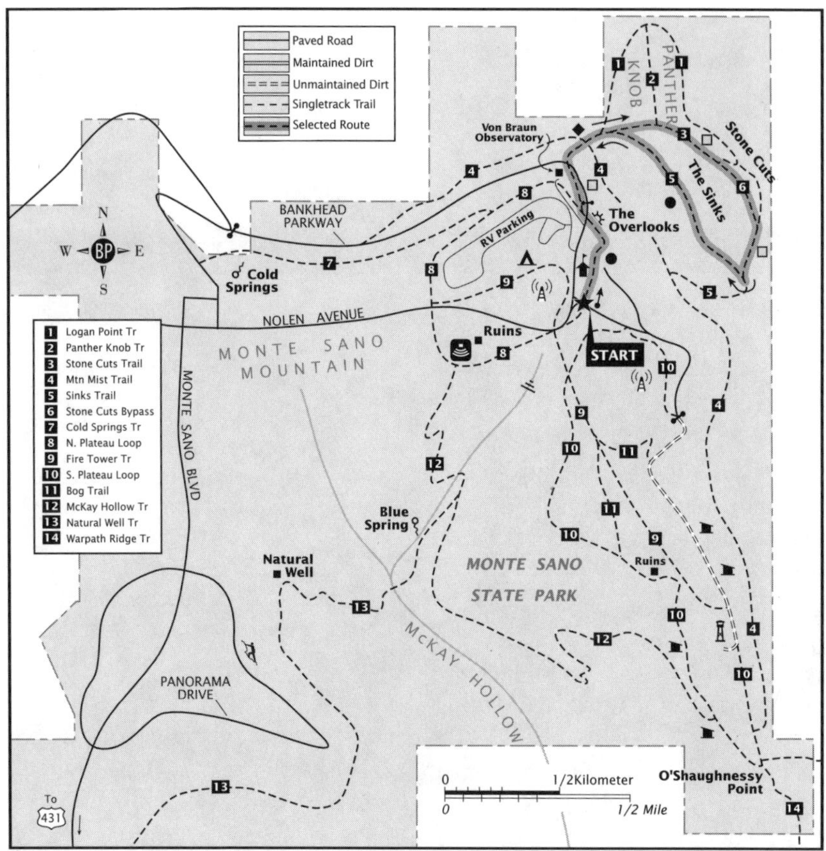

1.7 The trail merges with the Sinks Trail. The blazes are now red.

1.8 Come to a fork, with a nature trail splitting off. Turn right.

2.0 The Sinks Trail intersects the yellow Mountain Mist Trail. Turn right and head north on the Mountain Mist Trail. *[**Note.** Cyclists also use this trail so be on the lookout for them.]*

2.4 Come to a T-intersection with the Sinks Trail. Turn to the left onto the Sinks Trail. (The Mountain Mist Trail continues to the north.) Begin making a steep zigzag trip back up the hill, retracing the trip down. *[**Note.** This is the most difficult stretch of the trail.]*

2.6 Reach the closed park road behind the observatory. Turn left onto the road. *[**FYI.** The Stone Cuts can be seen to the left.]*

2.7 Walk through the gate that closes the road to traffic. Head across the Overlooks and the blue blazes of the North Plateau Loop will be seen. Reenter the woods at this point.

2.8 Come to the park's cabin road and turn right. Pick up the trail again on the other side of the road as it dips back into the woods.

2.9 Cross the park road.

3.0 Arrive back at the hiker's parking area.

The Stone Cuts Trail then heads up the side of Panther Knob At the top of the knob, you'll reach a group of rocks called The Sinks—a series of outcroppings exposed over the years to the elements. The path follows a route just to the right of The Sinks, but an easy hike on one of the tiny side trails takes you over to them. Huge boulders and crawl spaces invite exploration. But be careful. Water seeping through cracks in the rocks makes hiking slippery, and the bluffs here are both high and dangerous.

The trail then continues to the Stone Cuts, and actually travels through the cuts. Rock walls tower 100 to 200 feet above trail. Rappellers and rock climbers appreciate this area for obvious reasons. And just as it seems the scenery can't get any better, turn a corner and it does.

In several areas, the trail travels into the rock through short, dark tunnels. Water trickles down into the cuts, letting us know that this is a work in progress. Again, footing can be tricky over the wet surfaces. Throughout the entire trip through the Stone Cuts, the white paint blazes are easy to find. Even through the tunnels there should be no problem navigating this unique trail.

Wildlife that may be found along the trail include bobcats, white-tailed deer, opossums, skunks, and woodchucks. The hardwoods of the hollow and mountainsides include silver and red maples, sassafras, and pin and live oaks. Wildflowers include larkspur (its blue and white flowers bloom in late summer), yellow lady slipper, and purple dwarf iris.

Hike Information

Trail Contacts:
Monte Sano State Park, Huntsville, AL; (205) 534–3757

Schedule:
Open year round

Fees/Permits:
No fee to hike. Camping fees are $8 for primitive tent sites, $12 for tent site with water, $14 for tent site with water and electricity.

Local Information:
[See Hike 32: South Plateau Loop]

Local Events/Attractions:
[See Hike 32: South Plateau Loop]

Accommodations:
[See Hike 32: South Plateau Loop]

Restaurants:
[See Hike 32: South Plateau Loop]

Organizations:
[See Hike 32: South Plateau Loop]

Other Resources:
[See Hike 32: South Plateau Loop]

Local Outdoor Retailers:
[See Hike 32: South Plateau Loop]

Maps:
USGS maps: Huntsville, AL; Meridianville, AL • **Park map**—*A brochure with trail map is available at the camp store for 50 cents.*

Mountain Mist Trail

Hike Summary

The Mountain Mist Trail gives you a good opportunity to explore the region known as the Highland Rim. The trail travels through the hollow just below the area known as the Overlooks. It's a pleasant walk through hardwood forest. This loop was created by combining several routes: the North and South Plateau trails, the Stone Cuts Trail, and the Mountain Mist Trail.

Hike Specs

Start: From the hiker's parking lot next to the Monte Sano State Park office
Length: 3.7-mile loop
Approximate Hiking Time: 2–3 hours
Difficulty Rating: Easy hiking just below the plateau of Monte Sano Mountain; moderate climb up to intersection with the South Plateau Trail
Trail Surface: Dirt path
Lay of the Land: Sassafras, maple, and white oak forest; wildflowers, including iris and larkspur
Land Status: State park
Nearest Town: Huntsville, AL
Other Trail Users: Cyclists
Canine Compatibility: Dog friendly—with only a moderate rocky climb at the southern end; bring water; leash recommended

Getting There

From Huntsville: Take U.S. 231 south from I-565 (Exit 19A) for 0.4 miles and merge onto U.S. 431 South—stay in the center lane for this turn. Travel four miles up the side of Monte Sano Mountain and make a sharp left onto Monte Sano Boulevard. Head up the mountain 2.4 miles and make a right onto Nolen Avenue. Continue straight for two miles and Nolen Avenue forks. (To the right is the trailhead.) Take the left fork and travel 0.1 miles to the park office and camp store/campground. ***DeLorme: Alabama Atlas & Gazetteer:*** Page 19 D8

Monte Sano State Park's Mountain Mist Trail, when combined with the Stone Cuts Trail and the North and South Plateau trails, makes for a great loop hike that just about everyone in the family can enjoy. The virtues of the loop are easier trailhead access and scenery that incorporates the beauty of four different trails.

The trail begins on the North Plateau Trail by following a closed park road, quickly reaching the area called the Overlooks, a parking area with a full 180-degree panorama of Mills Hollow and Panther Knob. The trail soon heads into the woods directly behind Von Braun Observatory and drops steeply down Monte Sano Mountain to near the bottom of Mills Hollow using the Stone Cuts Trail.

Here the trail turns south and travels just below the Monte Sano plateau over fairly level terrain. The peaceful walk through the hollow allows you to put a little distance between yourself and weekend visitors to the park.

Dense forest provides a cozy enclosed feeling as the trail winds through silver and red maples, sassafras, and oaks. At creek crossings, wildflowers bloom. Larkspur, yellow lady slipper, purple dwarf iris, and violets bloom from early spring to midsummer. Be aware that some sections of the trail can get pretty muddy after a good rain. Also, be conscious of the fact that cyclists share the Mountain Mist Trail with hikers.

The trail eventually makes a moderate climb up a rocky slope, the toughest of the trip, to its intersection with the South Plateau Trail. The easy South Plateau route follows the southern rim of the plateau at the top of Monte Sano Mountain.

MilesDirections

0.0 START from the northeast end of the hiker's parking area. Head across the park road. A blue-blazed gravel path is on the opposite side. This section of the loop follows the North Plateau Loop Trail.

0.1 Come to the dead end of the park's cabin road. Cross the road and walk between the openings of a split rail fence.

0.2 Come to the Overlooks. *[**FYI.** This paved cul-de-sac offers up the most spectacular view of the Huntsville valley in the park.]* Cut across the paved parking area to where a closed park road is. The red blazes of the Sinks Trail begin here.

0.4 The trail makes a sharp turn into the woods. *[**Note.** The trail is deep dirt and after a rain is very slick and muddy.]*

0.6 Come to the yellow-blazed Mountain Mist Trail and turn right. *[**Note.** Cyclists also use this trail so be on the lookout for them. The travel is very easy through here but can be very muddy during rainy weather.]*

0.9 Pass the Sinks Trail spur.

2.2 The Mountain Mist Trail intersects with the South Plateau Trail. Turn right up the South Plateau Trail, following the white blazes.

2.3 Pass a short connector trail to the Mountain Mist Trail on the right with a sign pointing the direction to the trail.

2.6 Pass a trail shelter on the right. Shortly, the trail merges with a gravel road.

2.7 Pass the red-blazed Fire Tower Trail on the left. Continue straight.

2.9 A second trail shelter is passed.

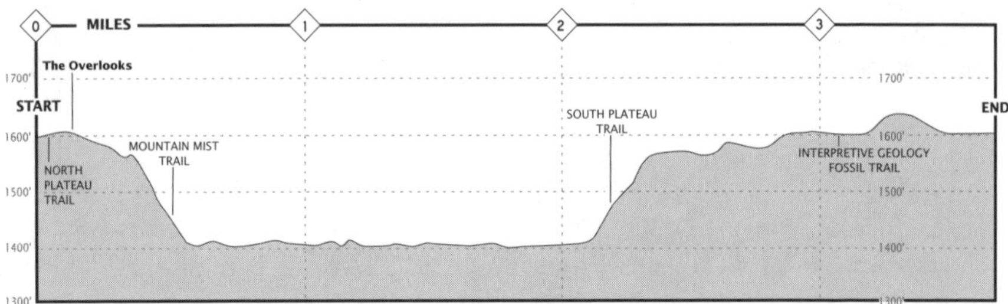

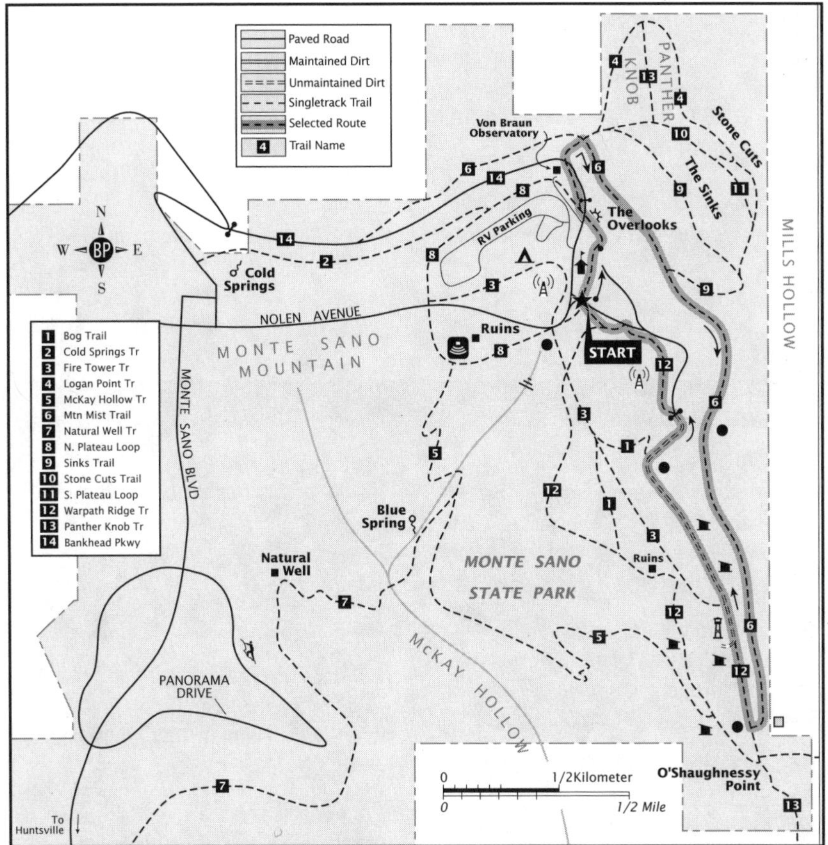

3.0 The trail intersects the orange Bog Trail. Turn right and follow the South Plateau Trail. In 100 feet, the trail turns off of the road and becomes a clay path heading into the woods.

3.1 The Interpretive Geology Fossil Trail joins the South Plateau Trail. *[**FYI.** Along this section, there are signs giving the hiker an idea of what to look for, including what scientists call today's "Living Fossils:" willows, sassafras, and maple trees, all decedents of trees 63 to 150 million years old.]* Pass the third trail shelter.

3.2 Cross a gravel road. The trail swings to the northwest and runs parallel to the park road as it travels over a series of rolling hills.

3.5 Cross a 10-foot bridge and the parking area can be seen ahead to the right.

3.7 The South Plateau Trail rejoins itself. Turn right and head 50 feet to the parking area to end the trip.

Panther Knob.

'Bama Firsts

- *The first ice-making machine was created in Mobile.*
- *The first national Veterans Day was celebrated in Birmingham in 1947.*
- *The gigantic meteor shower of 1833 was the basis for the title of Jimmy Buffett's song, "Stars Fell on Alabama."*
- *Orville and Wilbur Wright started the world's first flight school, in 1910 in Montgomery, Alabama.*
- *The world's first electric trolley system was introduced in Montgomery in 1886.*

The trail passes within 30 feet of high bluffs, from which you'll find great views of McKay and Mills Hollows, Round Top, and Monte Sano Mountain. Short side trails lead to overlooks, but be sure to heed the signs: "Danger, High Bluffs."

The trail offers good opportunities for amateur geologists, and their children. Fossils of sea life from ancient ocean reefs can be found almost anywhere along the way if you look closely.

Hike Information

Trail Contacts:
Monte Sano State Park, Huntsville, AL; (205) 534–3757

Schedule:
Open year round

Fees/Permits:
No fee to hike. Camping fees are $8 for primitive tent sites, $12 for tent site with water, $14 for tent site with water and electricity.

Local Information:
[See Hike 32: South Plateau Loop]

Local Events/Attractions:
[See Hike 32: South Plateau Loop]

Accommodations:
[See Hike 32: South Plateau Loop]

Restaurants:
[See Hike 32: South Plateau Loop]

Organizations:
[See Hike 32: South Plateau Loop]

Other Resources:
[See Hike 32: South Plateau Loop]

Local Outdoor Retailers:
[See Hike 32: South Plateau Loop]

Maps:
USGS maps: Huntsville, AL; Meridianville, AL • **Park map**—*A brochure with trail map is available at the camp store for 50 cents.*

Land Trust Loop

Hike Summary

The hike travels through a preserve created by volunteers and donors on the west side of Monte Sano Mountain in Northern Alabama. The Land Trust Loop Trail is rugged and can be a challenge. Along the route are waterfalls and the huge Three Caves Quarry. Climbs down (or up) the upper Bluffline Trail and the Waterfall Trail are steep.

Hike Specs

Start: From the southeast end of the Land Trust parking lot on Bankhead Parkway
Length: 4.7-mile loop
Approximate Hiking Time: 2½–3½ hours
Difficulty Rating: Difficult hiking on a section of steep, rocky paths
Trail Surface: Part dirt path; part boulders and rocks
Lay of the Land: Black walnut, hickory, and live oak trees and muscadine vines; waterfalls and rock quarry
Land Status: State park
Nearest Town: Huntsville, AL
Other Trail Users: Cyclists
Canine Compatibility: Dog friendly—though some areas may be difficult for some dogs; ample water available; no leash required

Getting There

From Huntsville: Take Exit 19C off of I-565. Turn left off the ramp onto Washington Street, and at the first light, make a right onto Pratt Avenue. (Pratt Avenue eventually becomes Bankhead Parkway.) Go 2.6 miles and the next right is the Land Trust parking lot. ***DeLorme: Alabama Atlas & Gazetteer:*** Page 19 D8

Through the years, the mountain area around Huntsville has seen its share of business and residential development, posing a threat to forests along Round Top and Monte Sano Mountain. For a time, Monte Sano State Park was the only oasis of preservation. All that changed when a group of volunteers formed the Land Trust of Huntsville. Their objective: to "preserve nature in Madison County." Through contributions and land donations, several preserves were established and more are on the way.

Among the nature sanctuaries created by the Land Trust are Wade Mountain Preserve and Rainbow Mountain. Wade Mountain Preserve features broad views along the ridge of the mountain. Rainbow Mountain offers a 2.5-mile trail to Balance Rock, a giant boulder that resembles a spinning top and that stands on its point.

Huge, worn cliffs along the Waterfall Trail. There are normally falls here.

The largest of the sanctuaries is Monte Sano Preserve, where we find this hike. With the acquisition of 567 acres, most of the forested hillside of Monte Sano Mountain received protection from further development. The Land Trust has done an excellent job of creating trails that show off the preserve's rugged beauty.

The Land Trust Loop traces the west side of Monte Sano Mountain. The area where the trail begins was once a Huntsville landfill, but the Land Trust has turned the property around. The first section of the route, known as the Bluffline Trail, travels just below massive limestone bluffs. The trail crosses several creeks, passes two waterfalls, and goes by a section where bluffs came crashing down in a 1998 landslide.

The path then turns down the Waterline Trail, where sections of a water main used during the 1950s are exposed. Suddenly the trail becomes steep and difficult, both up and down, along a streambed. A waterfall comes into view about halfway along this section, the rocks forming a huge horseshoe.

MilesDirections

0.0 START from the southeast end of the Land Trust parking lot and head down the paved road. Pass the Alms House Trail on the right. (This is where the loop returns.) The pavement ends and turns to gravel. *[**FYI.** Monte Sano Mountain can be seen ahead to the right.]* Come to a T-intersection with a wide gravel road. A sign here reads "Railroad Trail Bed/Bluffline Trail." Turn right. The trail is marked with silver diamond blazes reading "HLT-Bluffline Trail." *[**FYI.** Notice the glass on the road here. This short section was once a dumpsite for the city of Huntsville.]*

0.1 Continue through an intersection. (A sign here reads "Railroad Bed" and points to the south, "Bluffline," pointing northeast to southwest, and "Fagen Springs," pointing to the south.)

0.2 Pass an unnamed trail to the right.

1.0 *[**FYI.** This is the site of the 1998 Landslide.]*

1.2 The Wagon Trail merges from the northwest (a sign here marks the intersection).

1.3 Come to a fork and go left onto Bluffline Trail, a sign marks the intersection.

1.9 The High Trail merges from the northeast (a sign indicates the trail). For the next 0.1 miles, there are two markers on the tree, one for the High Trail, the other for the Bluffline Trail.

2.0 Come to a fork and go right onto the Waterline Trail. (The Bluffline Trail continues to the left.) The trail is marked with diamond markers that read "Waterline Trail."

2.2 *[**FYI.** The trails namesake, the old waterline from the 1950s, is visible.]*

2.3 *[**FYI.** To the right is a huge seasonal waterfall. Even without water, the rock formation is spectacular, forming a 75-foot tall cirque.]*

3.0 Come to a fork and go left. (The Alms House Trail turns to the right.) In another 10 feet come to another fork and stay left.

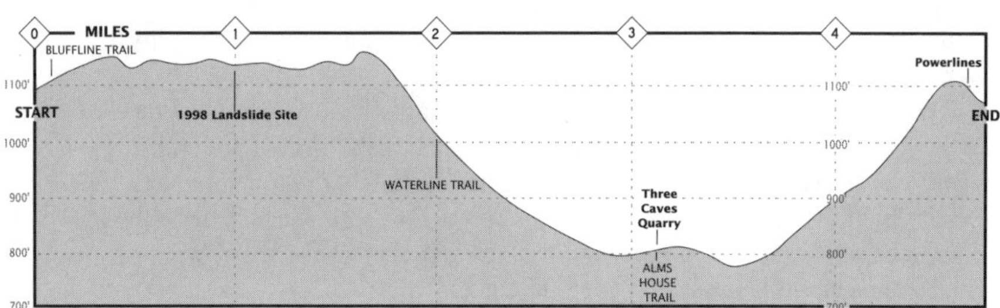

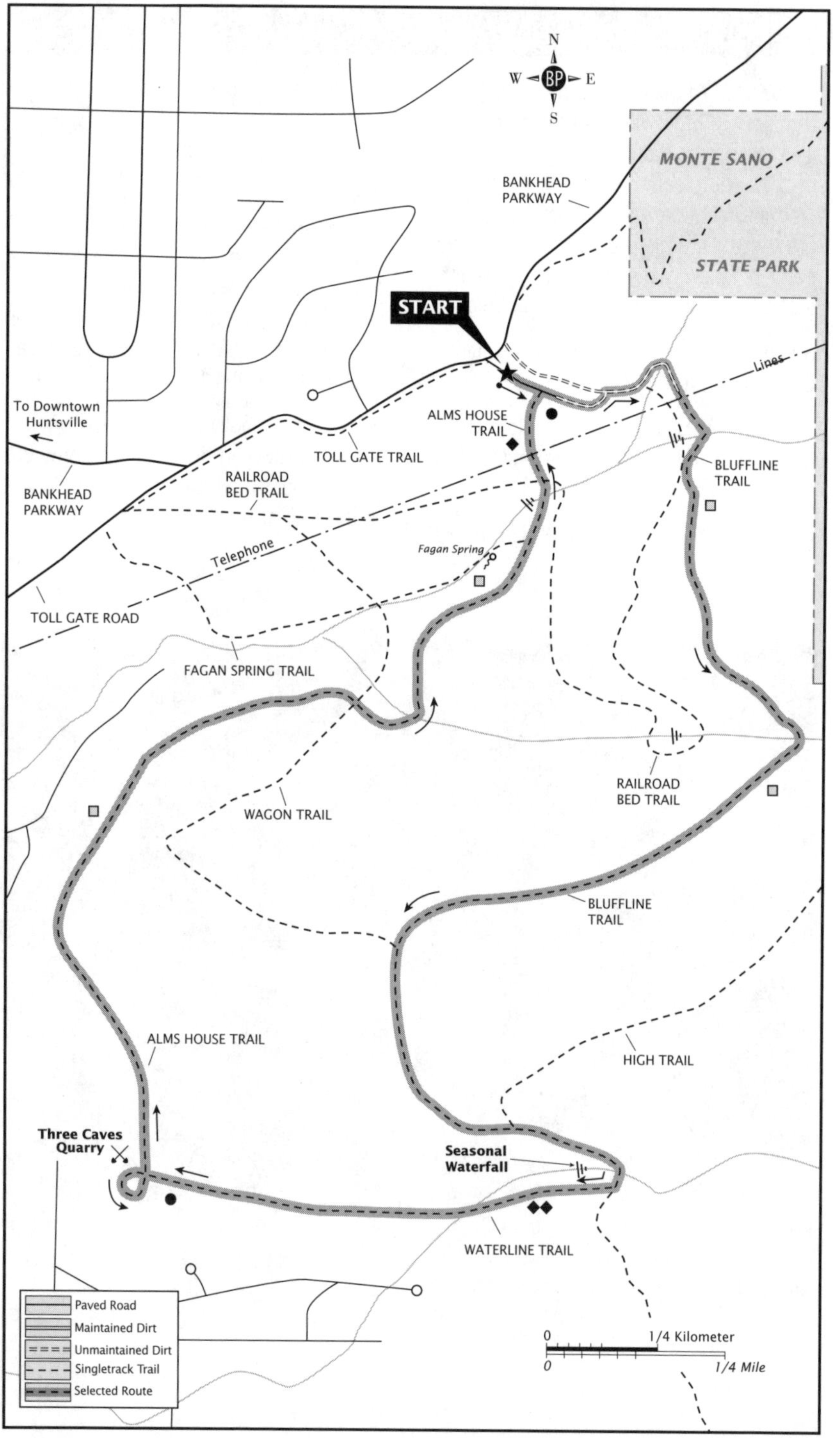

N
W
BP
E
S
MONTE SANO
STATE PARK
BANKHEAD PARKWAY
START
Lines
To Downtown Huntsville
ALMS HOUSE TRAIL
TOLL GATE TRAIL
BLUFFLINE TRAIL
BANKHEAD PARKWAY
RAILROAD BED TRAIL
Telephone
Fagan Spring
TOLL GATE ROAD
FAGAN SPRING TRAIL
RAILROAD BED TRAIL
WAGON TRAIL
BLUFFLINE TRAIL
ALMS HOUSE TRAIL
HIGH TRAIL
Three Caves Quarry
Seasonal Waterfall
WATERLINE TRAIL
Paved Road
Maintained Dirt
Unmaintained Dirt
Singletrack Trail
Selected Route
0
1/4 Kilometer
0
1/4 Mile

MilesDirections (Continued)

3.1 *[**Note.** The trail leads to the edge of the Quarry. Be VERY careful here.]* The trail rejoins the Waterline Trail. Turn right. In 150 feet, come to the Alms House Trail intersection and turn left. (Not only are there diamond markers, but also red paint blazes on the tree identifying the trail as it heads to the north/northeast.)

3.6 Pass the Wagon Trail (on the right). Continue on the Alms House Trail.

3.8 Comes to a very big hole, which marks a T-intersection. Turn right. (An unmarked trail breaks left.)

4.0 Cross the Wagon Trail (a sign marks the path).

4.4 Come to a fork and go right. (The left fork heads to a small area with log benches used for lectures.)

4.5 Pass the Fagen Springs Trail, which intersects to the right. *[**FYI.** The Fagen Springs Trail is a short 0.6-mile path that leads to a nice spring.]* Continue on until you come to a fork. Go right, staying on the Alms House Trail. (The Railroad Bed Trail takes the left fork.)

4.7 The trail finally starts to level off and turns to gravel. In 50 feet it emerges out of the woods and back to the beginning of the trail at the parking lot.

View of Three Caves Quarry.

At the intersection of the Waterline Trail and the Alms House Trail is Three Caves Quarry. At the bottom of the quarry's tall walls are three caves cut into the mountainside. The trail comes up to the edge of the quarry, which is no longer in use. The quarry is a dangerous place. Landslides are possible, the drop is steep, and entry is allowed only by permission of the Trust.

The Alms House Trail levels things out for a bit through gently rolling hills and over several creeks. On the final stretch to the parking lot, however, you'll be hiking steeply uphill one last time.

Hike Information

Trail Contacts:
The Land Trust of Huntsville and North Alabama, Huntsville, AL; (256) 534–5263 or *www.landtrust-hsv.org*

Schedule:
Open year round

Fees/Permits:
No fee to hike

Local Information:
[See Hike 32: South Plateau Loop]

Local Events/Attractions:
[See Hike 32: South Plateau Loop]

Accomodations:
[See Hike 32: South Plateau Loop]

Restaurants:
[See Hike 32: South Plateau Loop]

Organizations:
[See Hike 32: South Plateau Loop]

Other Resources:
[See Hike 32: South Plateau Loop]

Local Outdoor Retailers:
[See Hike 32: South Plateau Loop]

Maps:
USGS maps: Madison, AL; Meridianville, AL • **Brochure**—*A brochure on the Railroad Bed Trail is available at any Alabama Welcome Center or online*

Lickskillet Trail

Hike Summary

A pleasant walk through the woods and some of the best views of Town Creek and Lake Guntersville are in store along this trail. The route provides a moderate hike for the first half of the trip over a long and often rocky climb up Bailey Ridge. Then the trail joins the easier Seales and Meredith trails to complete the loop.

Hike Specs

Start: From the camp store on Audrey J. Carr Road
Length: 5-mile loop
Approximate Hiking Time: 2½–3½ hours
Difficulty Rating: Easy to moderate over wide, leaf- and needle-covered paths, with some rocky portions and steep drop-offs.
Trail Surface: Dirt path
Lay of the Land: Mixed forest, with hickory, maple, chestnut, upland willow oak, and pine
Land Status: State park
Nearest Town: Guntersville, AL
Other Trail Users: None
Canine Compatibility: Dog friendly—over dirt footpaths; bring water; leash required

Getting There

From Guntersville: Take AL 227 north to the park office. From the park office, continue on AL 227 for two miles. Turn left onto a short connecting road and travel 0.2 miles. Come to a T-intersection and make a left turn. Travel one mile. Make a left turn onto Audrey J Carr Road. The camp store and parking area will be on the left. ***DeLorme: Alabama Atlas & Gazetteer:*** Page 26 A2

Lake Guntersville State Park is a favorite with tourists and residents year-round, and this is not surprising. Water-related activities on the 66,470-acre lake are almost endless: swimming, boating, water skiing, and of course, great fishing. The park also has an 18-hole golf course and pro shop, tennis courts, picnic areas, and campgrounds.

The park has 31 miles of trails around the peaks, lake, and rivers. Among the trails is a half-mile nature walk, behind the park lodge, which serves up an overview of the local geology and natural life. Trails within the park are well maintained and clear of downed trees, limbs, and brush. Hikes are easy to moderate in difficulty.

The Lickskillet Trail, combined with the Seales and Meredith trails, makes for a nice hike around Bailey Ridge and the banks of Town Creek. Much of the trail travels through tall members of the beech family, includ-

As the trip follows the Meredith Trail, we get a glimpse of Town Creek and Stubblefield Mountain.

ing chestnuts and upland willow oaks. The chestnuts provide food for squirrels, woodchucks, and other animals. Keep your eyes open as it's not uncommon to see groups of deer wandering through these woods, unfazed by the intrusion of hikers.

Wildflowers often line the path. The lavender-leafed liatris blooms in early fall. The smooth foxglove grows on the side of willow oak trees, bearing yellow flowers from June through October. Also showing off seasonally is the purple penstemon, with leafy clusters of 50 or so lavender flowers.

The orange-blazed Lickskillet Trail heads uphill from its start at the camp store to just below the summit of Bailey Ridge. The moderate hiking eases in a hollow of Bailey Ridge as the Lickskillet reaches its junction with the red-blazed Meredith Trail. The Meredith offers an easy, rolling trip around one of the points of the ridge. As it moves to the northeast, views open up of Stubblefield Mountain and of Hurricane Branch, a feeder stream of Town Creek.

Soon the trail runs headlong into the banks of Town Creek at the Seales Trail. This trail, with its blue blazes, was named for Rick and Ruth Seale, who led the building of the park's 31 miles of trail. They continue to be active in maintaining the trails, and it is only fitting that the prettiest trail in the park bears their name. Maple, hickory, oak, and other trees along the trail provide spectacular colors in the fall, and a thick, leafy path to walk on.

MilesDirections

0.0 START from the parking lot of the camp store. Follow the Audrey J Carr Road to the east 500 feet. The trailhead with a wooden sign reading "Lick Skillet Trail" will be seen across the road. Enter the woods here. The trail is well marked with orange paint blazes.

0.2 Pass a short connector that branches off to the right and heads up the hill to the Lake Guntersville Lodge. Continue straight. *[**FYI.** On park maps, connecting trails are marked with black dots. In reality, the trails have white blazes.]*

0.6 Cross a paved park road.

1.2 Cross a gravel power line road.

1.7 A white blazed connector trail crosses the path here. Continue straight.

2.0 Intersect the red-blazed Meredith Trail and turn left. (Lick Skillet continues straight.)

2.3 At the bottom of the hill, 20 feet of the banks of Town Creek, the Meredith Trail comes to a T-intersection with the Seales Trail. Turn to the left onto the blue-blazed Seale Trail.

2.9 Come to a fork and go right. (To the left are blue blazes with a sign reading "High Water Bridges.") *[**Note.** Don't be confused by the two different blazes, just take the right fork.]*

3.0 Cross the gravel power line road and reenter the woods.

3.3 *[**FYI.** The trail opens up to nice views of Stubblefield Mountain to the right.]*

4.3 Pass a white-blazed connector trail on the left.

4.4 Come to the gravel Campground Road and turn left. The road turns into a paved road and heads through the campground.

4.6 Pass the park's tennis court on the left.

4.7 Pass a road that leads to the park's nature center on the left.

5.0 Arrive back at the camp store parking area.

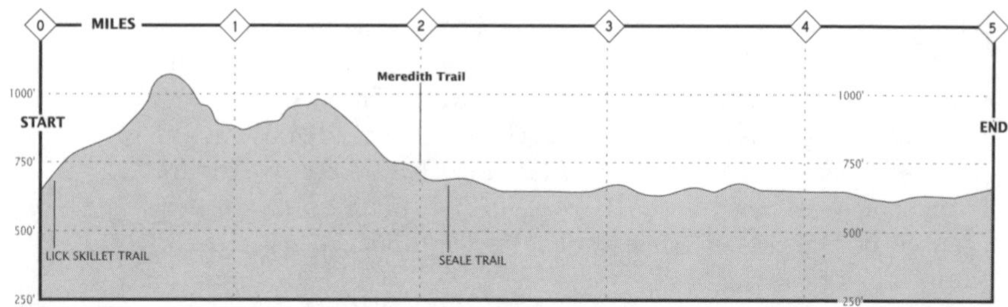

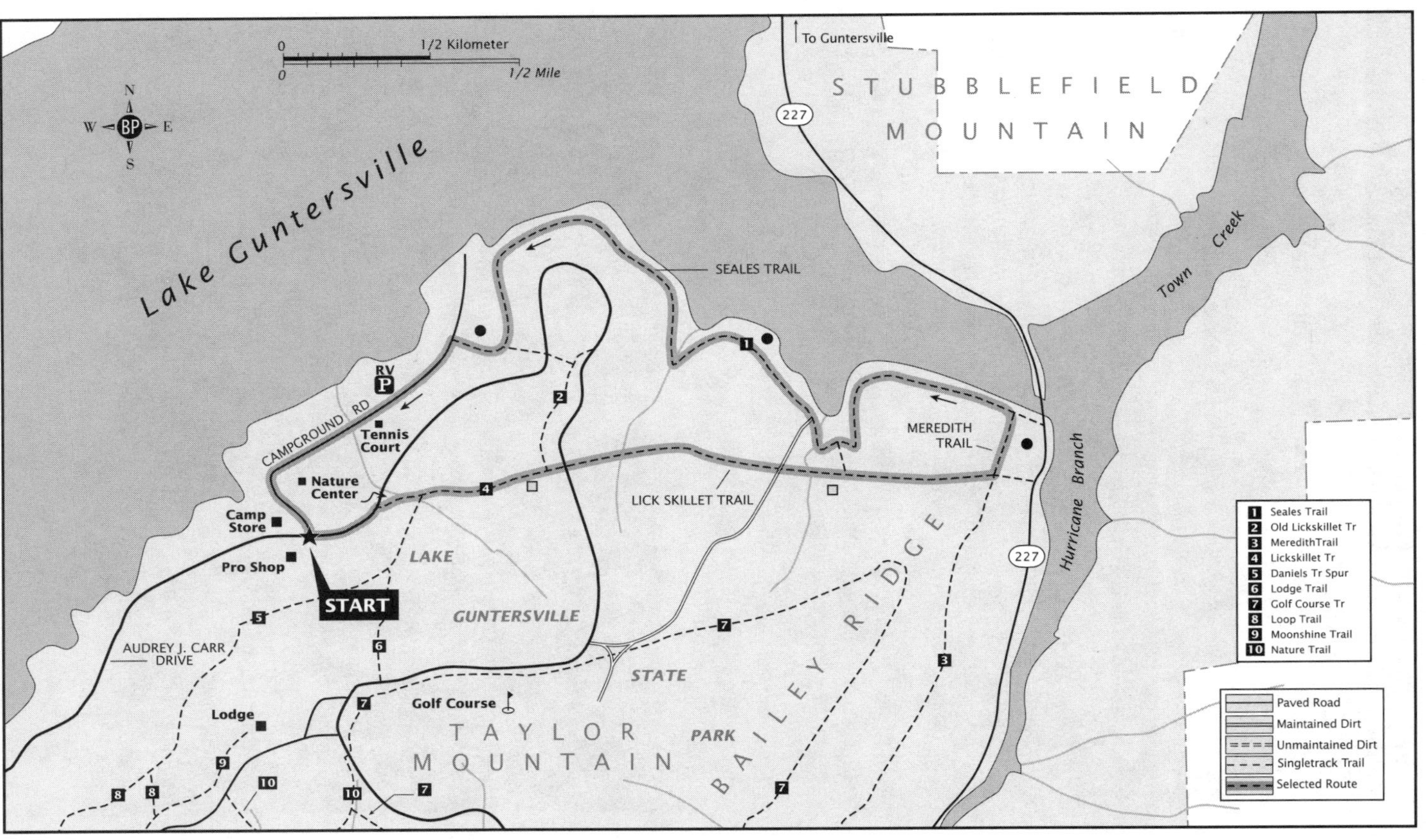
0 1/2 Kilometer
0 1/2 Mile
N E S W
BP
Lake Guntersville
To Guntersville
227
STUBBLEFIELD
MOUNTAIN
Town Creek
SEALES TRAIL
RV P
CAMPGROUND RD
Tennis Court
Nature Center
Camp Store
Pro Shop
START
MEREDITH TRAIL
LICK SKILLET TRAIL
Hurricane Branch
227
LAKE
GUNTERSVILLE
STATE
PARK
AUDREY J. CARR DRIVE
Golf Course
Lodge
TAYLOR
MOUNTAIN
BAILEY RIDGE
1 Seales Trail
2 Old Lickskillet Tr
3 MeredithTrail
4 Lickskillet Tr
5 Daniels Tr Spur
6 Lodge Trail
7 Golf Course Tr
8 Loop Trail
9 Moonshine Trail
10 Nature Trail
Paved Road
Maintained Dirt
Unmaintained Dirt
Singletrack Trail
Selected Route

Local Events/Attractions:

Eagle Awareness, weekends in January, Guntersville, AL; (256) 571-5440—*American Bald Eagles have made a huge comeback in Alabama and each January, hundreds come to Guntersville State Park to view the birds. There is a special 5 A.M. watch as the eagles leave their nests and a 4 P.M. return-to-roost watch.* • **Summerfest**, 2nd weekend of August, Guntersville, AL; (256) 582-3612—*A weekend filled with music, arts and crafts, and food, held at the Civitan Park.* • **The Whole Backstage Theatre**, Guntersville, AL; (256) 582-SHOW or *www.wholebackstage.com—Marshall County's well-known community theater, which features four shows every season including a summer musical in July.* • **Noccalula Falls Park**, Gadsden, AL; (256) 549-4663—*A 90-foot waterfall and canyon. Legend has it that an Indian princess, faced with the choice of being married to someone she didn't love, jumped to her death at these falls, and so they were named for her. On a happier note, the beautiful park has nature trails, a botanical garden with more than 25,000 azaleas, pioneer village, war memorial, gift shop, children's playground, and campground.*

A rock outcropping along the banks of Town Creek.

The most striking views on the trail are of Town Creek and Lake Guntersville. The trail mostly follows a narrow ledge along the banks of the creek and lake, with a sharp drop-off of about 50 feet. A cable is strung in some sections between trees for use as a handrail.

Just before the meandering trail returns to the campground, it opens up into a stand of pines. A small, grassy finger of land juts out into the lake, making a great place to just sit and relax.

Hike Information

Trail Contacts:

Lake Guntersville State Park, Guntersville, AL; (256) 571-5444 or 1-800-LGVILLE

Schedule:

Open year round

Fees/Permits:

No fee charged for hiking. Camping is $8 per night for a primitive site, $13 per night for tent sites with water, $14 with water and electricity.

Local Information:

Lake Guntersville Chamber, Guntersville, AL 1-800-869-LAKE or *www.lakeguntersville.org*

Accommodations:

Lakeview Inn, Guntersville, AL; (256) 582-3104 • **Overlook Mountain Inn**, Guntersville, AL; (256) 582-3256 • **Covenant Cove**, Guntersville, AL; (256) 582-1000 • **Lake Guntersville State Park Lodge**, Guntersville, AL; 1-800-548-4553

Restaurants:

Bluffside Coffee Shop, Guntersville, AL; 1-800-LGVILLE—*Perched along the banks of Guntersville Reservoir in the park, this coffee shop is open for breakfast and lunch.* • **State Lodge Restaurant**, Guntersville, AL; (256) 582-3666

Other Resources:

Alabama Mountain Lakes (North Alabama information), Mooresville, AL; 1-800-648-5381 or *www.almtlakes.org* • **Bama Environmental News** (205) 226-7739 or *www.bamanews.com* • **Wildflowers of Alabama** at *www.duc.auburn.edu/~deancar/index.html*

Local Outdoor Retailers:

Canyon Outdoors, Fort Payne, AL; (256) 845-0777 or *www.canyonoutdoors.com*

Maps:

USGS maps: Columbus City, AL • **Brochures**—*Trail and park brochures and trail maps are available free of charge at the park office.*

Cascade Loop Trail

Hike Summary

During times of decent rainfall, the Cascade Loop is an especially wonderful hike. You'll pass numerous creeks and cascades as the trail leads to a 200-foot-high rock wall. Here the trail travels a narrow ledge around the cliff and past a shallow cave. As it loops around and returns, the trail passes the remains of an old moonshine still.

Hike Specs

Start: At the Terrill Trail trailhead on Audrey J. Carr Drive
Length: 2.3-mile loop
Approximate Hiking Time: 2–3 hours
Difficulty Rating: Moderate, with some steep sections up a rock wall and along a rocky creek
Trail Surface: Rocky at the start; then dirt.
Lay of the Land: A mixture of oak, hickory, maple, and pine trees; lichen-covered boulders and fern-lined pathways; 200-foot cliffs
Land Status: State park
Nearest Town: Guntersville, AL
Other Trail Users: None
Canine Compatibility: Dog friendly—with ample water available; leash recommended near the halfway point due to the number of people on the intersecting nature trail

Getting There

From Guntersville: Take AL 227 north. Make a left turn into the park across from the Pure gas station. Head up this short entrance road 0.1 mile and make a right onto Audrey J Carr Road. Travel 0.6 miles. The Terrell Trail parking area, a grassy shoulder with a Terrell Trail sign, will be on the left. ***DeLorme: Alabama Atlas & Gazetteer:*** Page 26 A1

The Cascade Loop Trail at Lake Guntersville State Park is just a fun trail. That's all, plain and simple. After a brief start along the Terrell Trail, the loop trail starts a moderate climb over large rocks along a stream. The stream is seasonal, but after some rain, views of the cascade make the hike even better.

The hike gets even more interesting as it approaches tall rock walls. The trail makes an abrupt turn and heads up the cliff to a point about 50 feet above its base, and then travels around the cliff on a two-foot-wide rock ledge. In the middle of this "mountaineering," you'll pass a 60-foot-deep cave to the left that was carved into the rocks by wind and weather over the years.

At the top of the cliff, the trail briefly joins the Nature Trail that visitors to Lake Guntersville Lodge use for morning exercise. It then turns south onto the Waterfall Trail. The trail follows another streambed downhill. Once again, the stream is seasonal, but after a good rain, you'll discover a waterfall here.

Just before you reach the intersection with the Cascade Trail that completes the loop for the return trip, the trail goes east to reach the site of an old moonshine still. Here is a collection of parts and equipment used to make moonshine liquor during Prohibition. Take a walk around the site and note the deep ax cuts in the metal parts. It may not have been Elliot Ness, but the revenuers made an appearance here and shut this operation down with axes.

As with all paths at the park, these hiking trails are in excellent condition. All are well maintained and virtually clear of downed trees, limbs, and brush. Trail markers consist of paint blazes on the trees. On this hike, the colors include orange for the first tenth of a mile, where the Terrell Trail begins the trip; white for the connecting trail that links the Terrell Trail with the Cascade Trail; blue on the Cascade Trail; orange again on the Waterfall Trail; and finally red on the part of the route to the old still.

MilesDirections

0.0 START from the Terrell Trail parking area off of Audrey J Carr Drive. Cross the road to the north and pick up the yellow-blazed Terrell Trail as it enters the woods.

0.1 Come to a T-intersection and turn right, following white blazes. A sign here says "Cascade Trail" and points to the east and "Waterfall Trail" and points to the west. White blazes now line the trail. This is a connector between the Terrell and the Cascade Trails. The trail runs parallel to the road.

0.3 The path comes within 50 feet of Audrey J Carr Drive. Next to the road, a sign marking the Cascade Trail will be seen. Turn left here, away from the road, to the northeast. This is now the Cascade Trail with blue blazes.

0.7 Come to a fork and go right. (The left fork, marked by a sign, is the Old Still Path Trail that we'll use on the return trip.)

0.8 Pass a 60 to 70-foot deep cave in the cliff to the left.

0.9 Come to a fork and go left. (A sign indicates that Town Creek and Meredith Trail go right. The other sign here says "Cascade / Lodge" and point to the northwest.) Shortly, pass the white connector trail.

1.0 An unmarked white connector trail heads off to the north. Continue straight.

1.1 Turn left onto the yellow-blazed Waterfall Trail. (A Nature Trail travels down to this intersection from the lodge and continues straight ahead to the west.)

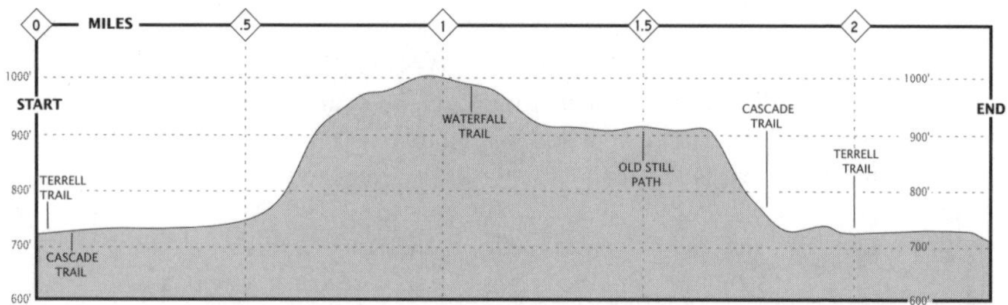

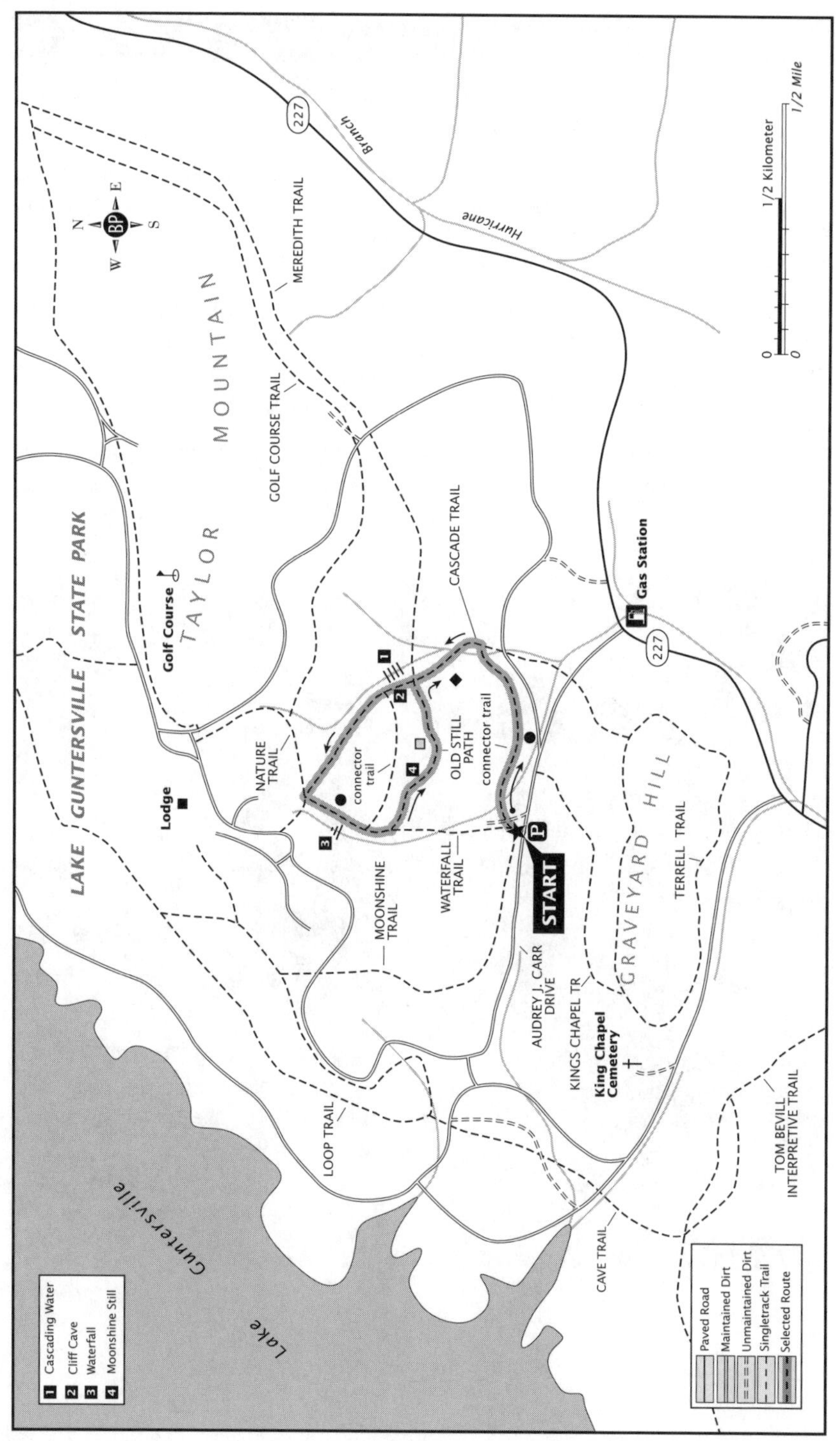
1 Cascading Water
2 Cliff Cave
3 Waterfall
4 Moonshine Still
Paved Road
Maintained Dirt
Unmaintained Dirt
Singletrack Trail
Selected Route
1/2 Kilometer
1/2 Mile
0
0
N
E
S
W
BP
LAKE GUNTERSVILLE STATE PARK
TAYLOR MOUNTAIN
GRAVEYARD HILL
Lake Guntersville
Hurricane
Branch
227
227
MEREDITH TRAIL
GOLF COURSE TRAIL
CASCADE TRAIL
Golf Course
Gas Station
Lodge
NATURE TRAIL
connector trail
OLD STILL PATH
connector trail
MOONSHINE TRAIL
WATERFALL TRAIL
START
P
AUDREY J. CARR DRIVE
KINGS CHAPEL TR.
King Chapel Cemetery
TERRELL TRAIL
LOOP TRAIL
CAVE TRAIL
TOM BEVILL INTERPRETIVE TRAIL

MilesDirections (Continued)

1.3 Pass the white connector trail that leads back to the Cascade Trail to the left.

1.5 The Old Still Path intersects the Waterfall Trail from the southeast. Turn left here and head on the orange blazed trail to the southeast.

1.6 *[**FYI.** Arrive at the "Old Still Site." This was a moonshine still used in the 20s and was destroyed by the Feds. Notice the axe marks in the metal.]*

1.8 Come to a T-intersection with the Cascade Trail and turn right, following the blue blazes back downhill retracing our previous path.

2.0 Come to the edge of Audrey J Carr Drive and make a sharp right turn. Follow the white-blazed connector trail back toward the Terrell Trail.

2.2 Return to the intersection of the Terrell Trail with the white connector trail. Turn left here and follow the Terrell back to the parking area.

2.3 Arrive at the Terrell Trail parking area.

Yep. You're in Appalachia. This is the remains of a moonshine still.

The trail travels through mixed forest that includes tall members of the beech tree family, like chestnut and upland willow oaks. Squirrels and woodchucks are abundant here, feeding off the chestnuts. White-tailed deer are seen here in large numbers, and ring-necked pheasants may surprise you from the brush as you round the mountainside.

From early spring through fall, wildflowers line the trail. These include the lavender-leafed liatris, which blooms in early fall. You'll also find penstemon, with leafy clusters of 50 or so lavender flowers. The smooth foxglove grows on the side of white oak trees, bearing yellow flowers from June through October.

If it's a hot day, complete the Cascade Loop and then head in the car up Audrey J. Carr Drive for about another mile. On the left is a day-use area with a great beach for swimming in Lake Guntersville. There is also a picnic area and a nice little country store for snacks and some of the extra supplies you may need.

Hike Information

Trail Contacts:
Lake Guntersville State Park, Guntersville, AL; (256) 571–5444 or 1–800–LGVILLE

Schedule:
Open year round

Fees/Permits:
No fee charged for hiking. Camping is $8 per night for a primitive site, $13 per night for tent sites with water, $14 with water and electricity.

Local Information:
[See Hike 38: Lickskillet Trail]

Local Events/Attractions:
[See Hike 38: Lickskillet Trail]

Accommodations:
[See Hike 38: Lickskillet Trail]

Restaurants:
[See Hike 38: Lickskillet Trail]

Other Resources:
[See Hike 38: Lickskillet Trail]

Local Outdoor Retailers:
[See Hike 38: Lickskillet Trail]

Maps:
USGS maps: Columbus City, AL • **Brochures**—*Trail and park brochures and trail maps are available free of charge at the park office.*

Tom Bevill Interpretive Trail

Hike Summary

The Tom Bevill Interpretive Trail circles around the summit of Ellenburg Mountain. The hike is highlighted by numbered stops that provide a look at the geology and plant life of the mountain. You'll spot old farmhouse ruins along the way.

Hike Specs

Start: From the parking lot at the Lake Guntersville State Park office
Length: 3.8-mile loop
Approximate Hiking Time: 2–3 hours
Difficulty Rating: Easy walking on dirt footpaths, except for a moderate tenth-of-a-mile rocky section at the start
Trail Surface: Dirt path; short rocky stretch
Lay of the Land: Mixture of oak, hickory, maple, and pine trees; lichen-covered boulders and fern-lined pathways
Land Status: State park
Nearest Town: Guntersville, AL
Other Trail Users: None
Canine Compatibility: Dog friendly—over easy trail; bring water; no leash required.

Getting There

From Guntersville: Take AL 227 north to the park office. The trailhead is directly across AL 227 from the park office. ***DeLorme: Alabama Atlas & Gazetteer:*** Page 26 A2

This path is a nature trail, pure and simple, but the high route around Ellenburg Mountain and the variety of wildlife and vegetation that can be seen make it a special hike for people of all ages.

To hike the trail most enjoyably, pick up a copy of the brochure "A 3 Mile Walk With Nature," available free at the Lake Guntersville State Park office across from the trailhead. Throughout the hike, numbered markers on trees point out historical and natural sites that correspond with a description in the brochure. (The office is open Monday through Friday from 7:30 A.M. to 5:00 P.M. and on Saturday and Sunday from 8:00 A.M. to 5:00 P.M.)

Up until 1980, the trail was a simple footpath around Ellenburg Mountain. In that year, members of the Youth Conservation Corps of the Tennessee Valley Authority took it upon themselves to make the trail something more. The Youth Conservation Corps is a nationwide group of

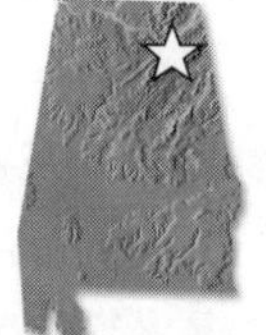

Lake Guntersville.

teenagers who earn school credit and learn about the environment while working to protect and enhance it.

In a short time, the youngsters cleared and improved the trail and rerouted it to highlight unique features of the mountain. They also prepared the brochure and marked the corresponding sites along the route.

The trail takes you through a variety of plant life. Hardwoods such as sweet gum, yellow poplar, white oak, and maple line the trail. Of course, no walk in the Southern woods would be complete without pine trees. Along the Tom Bevill Trail, named for a U.S. congressman from Alabama, you'll find loblolly, Virginia, and shortleaf pines. Flowers to be seen include pink azaleas, which serves up a deep fragrance as they bloom in spring, and oak leaf hydrangea, which blooms in late June.

On the west side of Ellenburg Mountain, watch for royal ferns. On the east side, look for Christmas ferns. On the northwest side, muscadine vines grow entangled in the trees. The grapelike fruit of the muscadine has been

MilesDirections

0.0 START from the park office and cross AL 227. A trail sign marks the entrance. Head into the woods along the orange-blazed trail.

0.1 Come to a T-intersection with the Tom Bevill Trail and take a left. (This is where the trail loops back onto itself for the return trip.)

0.4 Pass marker #4 and the "Decomposer" tree.

0.8 Pass marker #5 and the Century Tree.

1.9 Come to marker #9 and the intersection of the Cave Trail (to the left). Turn right onto the Spring Trail. (Straight will take The Tom Bevill Trail merges with the Cave Trail here and blue and orange blazes will be seen. The Cave Trail heads to Cemetery Hill and to the King's Chapel Cemetery where many of the early settlers who lived here are buried.

2.2 Come to a deep ravine. The blaze on the tree here is blue-orange-blue-orange. At the bottom, the Tom Bevill splits from the Cave Trail. Turn to the south. It will only be orange blazes from here.

2.3 *[**FYI.** To the right is an old stone chimney and a stone foundation. At one time, this was a one-room cabin that was used for cooking by area settlers. Heading straight 100 feet, the trail runs into an old sandstone foundation. This was an old farmhouse and root cellar.]*

2.7 *[**FYI.** There is a nice view of Graveyard Hill and King Hollow to the left.]*

3.0 Pass marker #14.

3.6 Turn left onto the side trail to the park office. (A sign marks the turn.)

3.8 Arrive at the parking lot.

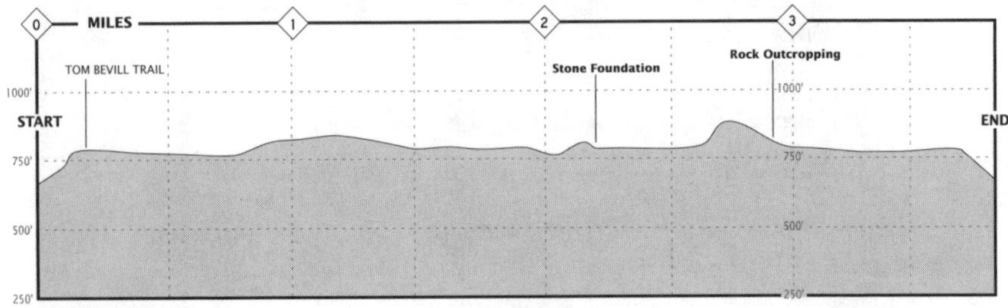

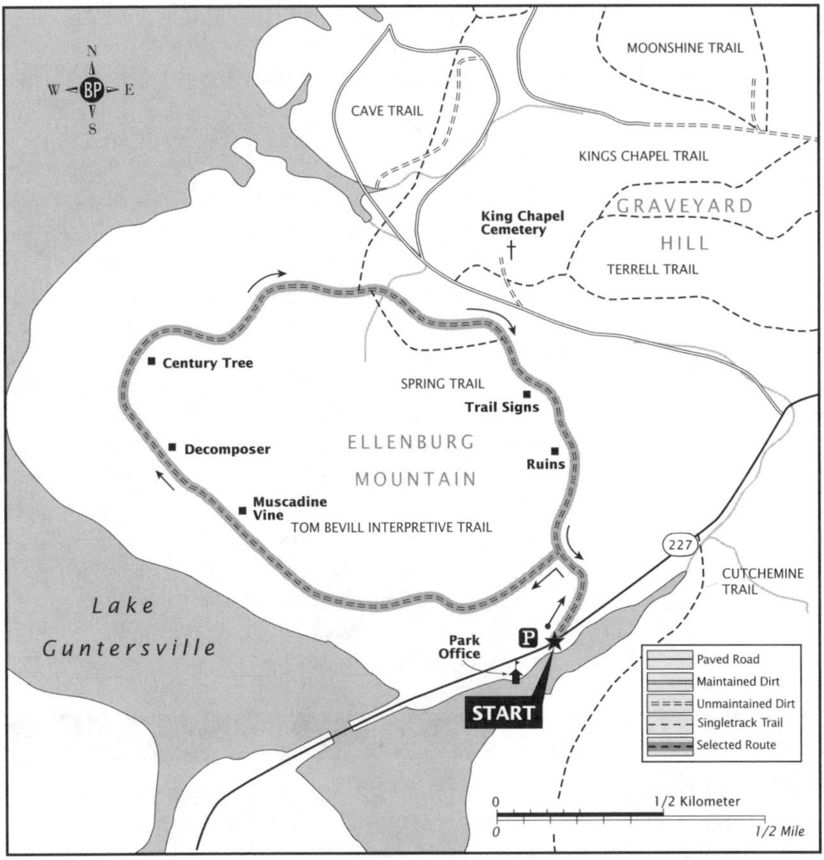

Ruins of an old farmhouse.

used for jelly, and muscadine wine has been called the original American wine. Muscadine is also a source of food for wildlife.

With patience and quiet walking, you can see the wildlife of the Tom Bevill Trail. From the rocky top of the mountain, the screeching of red-tailed hawks may be heard. On the ground, raccoons, foxes, wild turkeys, and white-tailed deer are the most common animals.

The area has a fare share of human history. Families such as the Kings, the Terrells, and the Newmans—you'll encounter their names on various landmarks—moved to this region to farm. The ruins of a large farmhouse with its root cellar sits near the trail, along with a one-room cabin that was used for cooking. Note how the settlers fashioned sandstone into bricks and made them fit together to build these structures.

A few nice views grace the trail. Near the start of the hike, to the left, the waters of Lake Guntersville glint through the trees. As the trail swings around to the northeast, views open up to Graveyard Hill, where many of the early settlers to the area are buried. A short side trail leads to the cemetery.

The Tom Bevill Interpretive Trail offers an opportunity to learn more about the environment and how humans interact with it. It's an excellent hike for children, providing a way to get outdoors and involved in something educational—probably without them even knowing it. If you're with young children, give them a helping hand during the first tenth-of-a-mile, where the trail is moderately steep.

Hike Information

Trail Contacts:
Lake Guntersville State Park, Guntersville, AL; (256) 571–5444 or 1–800–LGVILLE

Schedule:
Open year round

Fees/Permits:
No fee charged for hiking. Camping is $8 per night for a primitive site, $13 per night for tent sites with water, $14 with water and electricity.

Local Information:
[See Hike 38: Lickskillet Trail]

Local Events/Attractions:
[See Hike 38: Lickskillet Trail]

Accommodations:
[See Hike 38: Lickskillet Trail]

Restaurants:
[See Hike 38: Lickskillet Trail]

Other Resources:
[See Hike 38: Lickskillet Trail]

Local Outdoor Retailers:
[See Hike 38: Lickskillet Trail]

Maps:
USGS maps: Columbus City, AL • **Brochures**—*Trail and park brochures and trail maps are available free of charge at the park office.*

A State of Perpetual Motion

In Addition

The hiking trails of Alabama provide a variety of challenges and scenery for everyone. But there are plenty of other outdoor activities in the state to keep people on the move outdoors.

Probably the fastest growing outdoor activity is mountain biking. Trails are popping up all over. And, of course, hikers and cyclists are battling it out in many areas over the question of how to coexist and protect the environment at the same time.

The State of Alabama is going out of its way to provide areas for both in some of the prettiest of places. The Red Trail (a.k.a. the Bump Trail) at Oak Mountain State Park is a world-class track that has served as a training course for Olympic mountain bikers. The park also boasts a huge bicycle motocross facility. Cheaha State Park offers a bike trail that takes cyclists around Cheaha Mountain, the highest point in the state. The Mountain Mist Trail at Monte Sano State Park is the site of regular competitions. Even the smaller city parks are joining in. Near Mobile, Chickasabogue Park has the multi-use Cemetery Trail, which has cyclists traveling in one direction and hikers in the opposite direction.

The waters of Alabama provide a lot of rafting, canoeing, and kayaking options. On the Gulf of Mexico, sea kayaking is popular at places like Orange Beach, Gulf Shores, and Dauphin Island. In Northeast Alabama, the rapids of the Little River were used for training by Olympic kayakers. In the Sipsey Wilderness, canoeists float down the Sipsey River through some of the most pristine forests and canyons in the country.

For those who love horses, equestrian trails are scattered throughout the state. Most state parks have trails set aside just for horseback riding. Many parks are near stables where horses can be rented. And some parks, like Oak Mountain State Park, have stables right on site and offer guided rides.

People in Alabama also find adventure on the rocks. Little River Canyon National Preserve, Point Rock at Buck's Pocket State Park, and the Rock Garden at Cheaha State Park are favorite sites for rock climbers.

Cutchenmine Trail

Hike Summary

The Cutchenmine Trail, once a mining road, follows the banks of Lake Guntersville, going through a dense forest of hickory, maple, and beech trees. The highlight of this trip in Lake Guntersville State Park is the wildlife, which include herons and ducks. The trail is a prime location for spotting eagles.

Hike Specs

Start: From the Cutchenmine trailhead on AL 227
Length: 4.2-mile out-and-back
Approximate Hiking Time: 2–3 hours
Difficulty Rating: Easy walk around the base of Berry Point and along the banks of Lake Guntersville
Trail Surface: Dirt footpath
Lay of the Land: Mixture of hickory, maple, and large beech trees, with some loblolly pines
Land Status: State park
Nearest Town: Guntersville, AL
Other Trail Users: None
Canine Compatibility: Dog friendly—along a level dirt footpath; bring water; leash not required

Getting There

From Guntersville: Take AL 227 north to the park office. Continue past the office a short 0.6 miles. The trailhead parking area is a shoulder along the right side of the highway. A sign marks the location. ***DeLorme: Alabama Atlas & Gazetteer:*** Page 26 A2

Mining in Alabama goes back to the mid 1800s, when large deposits of coal and iron were discovered throughout what became known as the state's "black belt." A miner by the name of Cutchen, looking to transport his loads of coal to buyers, built the original roadway along Berry Point and the banks of Lake Guntersville. Today that roadway is the scenic Cutchenmine Trail.

The real beauty of this trip is not so much the history of the area as it is the wildlife to be seen, especially birds. Large blue herons soar off the pond and marsh area at the beginning of the walk. Mallards and wood ducks float along the shores of the lake as red-tailed hawks circle overhead.

The big excitement at the lake comes each January for a winter round of eagle watching. Each weekend throughout the month, crowds of birdwatchers descend on the area bearing binoculars, cameras, lots of snacks, and hot chocolate. In the cold, crisp air just before dawn, the raptor watchers plod the trail and get a vantage point to watch bald eagles take to the skies.

After catching the morning show, the watchers return to the lodge at the park to hear speakers lecture on the subject of eagles. This month of activ-

Lake Guntersville.

ity, known as Eagle Awareness, has become the most popular and anticipated birding event in the state.

Once at serious risk, the bald eagle has made a remarkable comeback and now makes Lake Guntersville one of its nesting areas. The eagle population in the state had dropped to just a few during the 1960s and 1970s, but a program established in the mid 1980s began to bring them back. Although January has been set aside for the Eagle Awareness program, bald eagles can be seen just about any time of the year at the lake.

The Cutchenmine Trail is a level dirt route that winds around the base of Berry Point just east of a finger of Lake Guntersville. The lake is in sight through most of the trip, just 50 to 60 feet from the trail. Be prepared for a bit of disappointment if you decide to walk down to the lake itself. Debris such as milk cartons and soda bottles often washes up here. During late spring and summer when the heat starts to rise, so do the number of mosquitoes, so bring bug spray.

The trail goes to the southern end of Lake Guntersville State Park, where it ends at the CCC Trail, a trail built by the Depression-era Civilian Conservation Corps. This is a short, white-blazed connector trail that leads to the westernmost boundary of the park.

Hike Information

Trail Contacts:
Lake Guntersville State Park, Guntersville, AL; (256) 571–5444 or 1–800–LGVILLE

Schedule:
Open year round

Fees/Permits:
No fee charged for hiking. Camping is $8 per night for a primitive site, $13 per night for tent sites with water, $14 with water and electricity.

Local Information:
[See Hike 38: Lickskillet Trail]

Local Events/Attractions:
[See Hike 38: Lickskillet Trail]

Accommodations:
[See Hike 38: Lickskillet Trail]

Restaurants:
[See Hike 38: Lickskillet Trail]

Other Resources:
[See Hike 38: Lickskillet Trail]

Local Outdoor Retailers:
[See Hike 38: Lickskillet Trail]

Maps:
USGS maps: Columbus City, AL; Albertville, AL • **Brochures**—*Trail and park brochures and trail maps are available free of charge at the park office.*

MilesDirections

0.0 START from the orange-blazed Cutchenmine trailhead on AL 227.

0.1 *[**FYI.** Ellenburg Mountain, the home of the Tom Bevill Trail, can be seen to the right.]*

0.5 *[**FYI.** On the right is the lake and ahead to the northwest is a nice view of Bald Knob across the lake.]*

2.1 The trail reaches a creek bed and the trail dead-ends into the white-blazed CCC Trail. Turn around here and retrace the path back to the parking area.

4.2 Arrive back at the parking area.

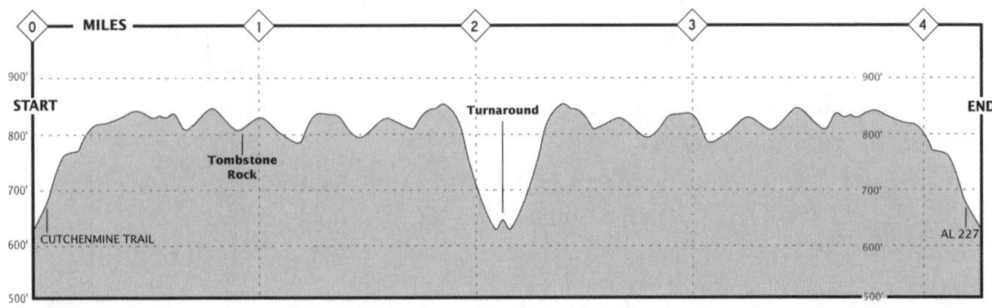

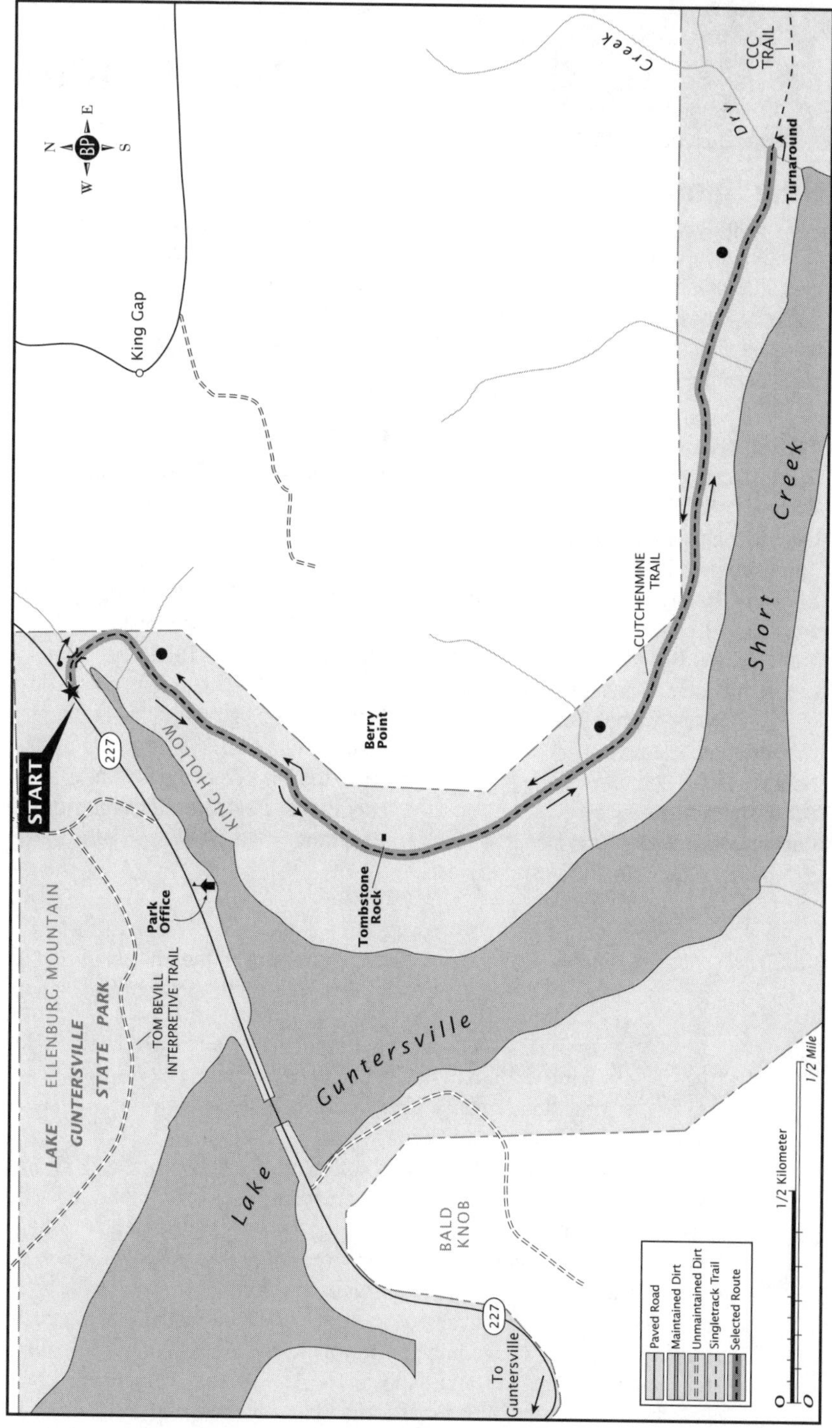
START
227
KING HOLLOW
Berry Point
Tombstone Rock
Park Office
CUTCHENMINE TRAIL
Short Creek
Dry Creek
CCC TRAIL
Turnaround
King Gap
LAKE GUNTERSVILLE STATE PARK
ELLENBURG MOUNTAIN
TOM BEVILL INTERPRETIVE TRAIL
Guntersville
Lake
BALD KNOB
227
To Guntersville
Paved Road
Maintained Dirt
Unmaintained Dirt
Singletrack Trail
Selected Route
0
1/2 Kilometer
0
1/2 Mile
N
E
S
W
BP

Camp Road

Hike Summary

The Camp Road Trail at Buck's Pocket State Park is an easy hike along the dirt camp road that follows the flow of South Sauty Creek. The Sauty is lined with sandstone boulders that create active rapids. During periods of low rainfall, you can hike along the banks of the river, which runs parallel to the trail—though you may find some of the boulders difficult to get around. The views of the sandstone cliffs along Hilley Point are quite beautiful.

Hike Specs

Start: From the parking area of the Buck's Pocket State Park office
Length: 2.6-mile out-and-back
Approximate Hiking Time: 1½–2½ hours
Difficulty Rating: Easy, over dirt road and footpath
Trail Surface: Dirt road
Lay of the Land: Sandstone cliffs; blue beech and white walnut trees
Land Status: State park
Nearest Town: Guntersville, AL
Other Trail Users: None
Canine Compatibility: Dog friendly—level dirt roads, ample water; no leash required

Getting There

From Guntersville: Follow AL 227 north through Guntersville State Park. Just after crossing the bridge over Town Creek and Lake Guntersville, come to an intersection. AL 227 turns right here. Continue 2.8 miles and make a left onto CR 19. In 1.6 miles CR 19 becomes CR 152. In 0.6 miles, the road comes to a fork. Take the right fork (this is the park road) and travel 0.3 miles to the parking lot on the left side of the road next to the park office. ***DeLorme: Alabama Atlas & Gazetteer:*** Page 20 H3

Located just a few miles from Guntersville, Buck's Pocket State Park is another jewel in the Alabama park system, offering waterways, sandstone bluffs, rare plants, and high overlooks for taking it all in. The 2000-acre park cradles the ruggedly beautiful South Sauty Creek, which is responsible for the park's stunning canyon scenery.

The Camp Road Trail follows the flow of South Sauty Creek to just above Morgan's Cove. The trail has no markers, but is easily followed. The walk travels along the banks of the creek for a short distance until huge boulders force the route onto the campground road. It's possible to hike the entire trail along the riverbank, but this can be difficult as some of the boulders make formidable obstacles—some boulders are more than 20 feet high. And in spring after heavy rains or snowmelt, the area is prone to flooding and the stream runs fast and dangerously. The beautiful blue-green creek averages 30 to 50 feet in width as it tumbles over the rocks.

South Sauty Creek.

The route affords not only great views of the creek and its rapids, but also of Hilley Point to the northwest, with its high bluffs, cliffs, and overlooks. Keep an eye on the cliffs for the rock climbers who congregate here. Hilley Point was formed at a time in the geological past when a vast ocean covered the region. Eventually the area was thrust upward and the sea receded, leaving the action of the stream to shape the canyon.

The route displays some interesting plant life as it runs along the base of Sand Mountain. A rare species of trillium, the wake robin trillium, with its elliptical cluster of flowers, blooms here in May and June. This species is found in Buck's Pocket and nowhere else in the world. The white yellow-centered flowers of the bloodroot also bloom along the trail. The flower got its name from the red fluid inside the plant, which was used by Native Americans for paint.

Rhododendrons, with their broad, waxy leaves and lavender or white flowers, favor this area. You may also see foamflowers—wildflowers with leaves that resemble those of the maple. The flowers, white with a touch of orange, cluster on the stem. Along the route are several varieties of fern, including Christmas, broad beech, and rattlesnake ferns.

You'll also be walking in the company of trees like the white walnut, blackjack oak, and smooth-barked blue beech. Also seen are painted buckeyes, small trees that display yellow-green leaves and are usually found as underbrush. Sassafras, whose bark can be used to brew sassafras tea, also grow here, but since all vegetation in Alabama state parks is protected, you can't remove the bark.

To add a bit more distance, continue down the trail on the dirt road another mile to Morgan's Cove. The route makes a turn south and ascends steeply one-third of the way up Bethune Point before heading down to the cove, which is on 66,470-acre Lake Guntersville. The cove offers picnic areas, swimming, and fishing; an Alabama freshwater fishing license is required.

If you've brought the kids along and are looking for an easy stroll, follow the white-blazed South Sauty Creek Trail, which you'll use at times on this route. The South Sauty Trail crosses the creek at the dam and leads to fine views of the river and its many rapids.

MilesDirections

0.0 START from the parking lot at the park office. Walk behind the park office and come to the banks of South Sauty Creek. (The water will be to the right throughout the entire hike .) At the creek, turn left and walk along the bank. *[**Note.** There are no markings for this hike.]*

0.6 Intersect a road that runs over the top of the dam. Cross the road and continue following the creek. In 200-yards, the trail scrambles over some boulders. But wait! After 100 feet the boulders are HUGE! It is advised to take the short 50-foot side trail uphill to the left and take the dirt camp road for the next two-tenths-of-a-mile.

1.4 The road comes to a feeder stream flowing down from the mountain. Turn around here and follow the road all the way back to the park office. *[**Option.** If the water level permits, you can hike back to the office along the creek.]*

1.8 The road splits around some brush and a few trees and then reconnects in 30 feet. Continue 100 feet and come to a locked gate. Walk around the gate and continue on the road.

2.1 Come to a closed metal gate. Walk around the gate and the road is now paved. Follow the road until it comes to a fork and go right. (To the left is the dam road under which the South Sauty flows.

2.2 Come to a fork and go left. A sign here reads "Office/Camping." *[**FYI.** Point Rock can be seen ahead to the right through the trees.]*

2.6 Arrive back at the parking lot.

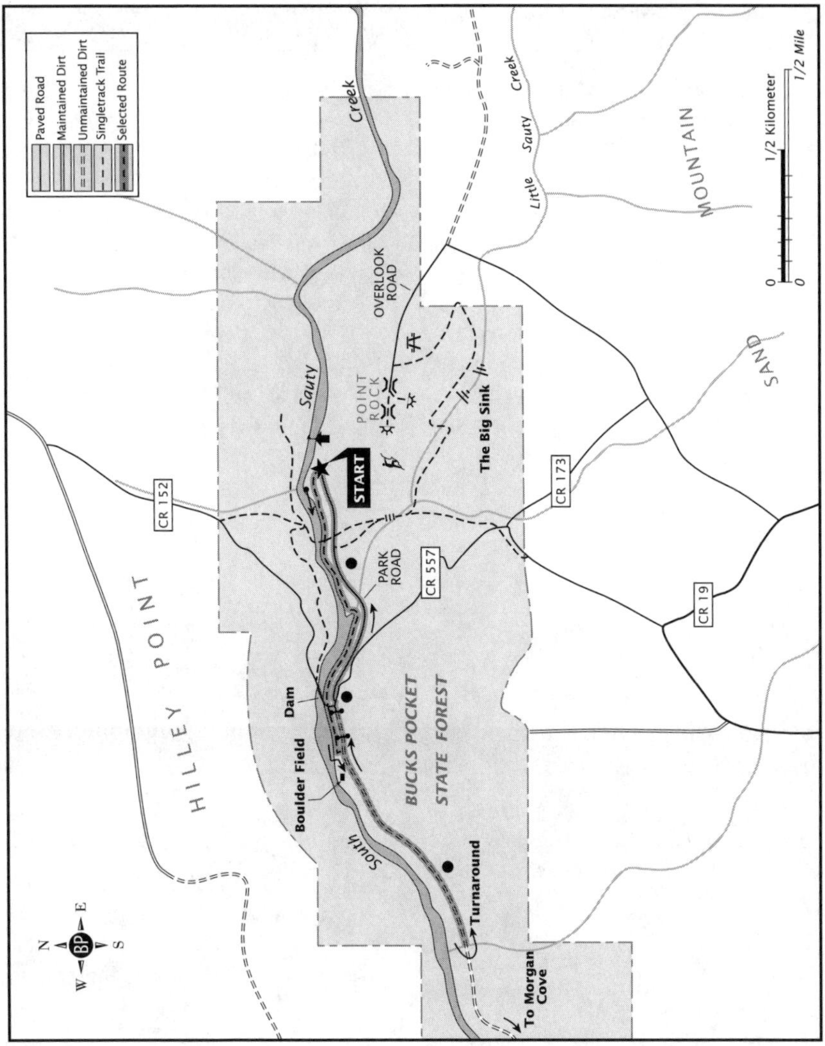

Paved Road
Maintained Dirt
Unmaintained Dirt
Singletrack Trail
Selected Route
Sauty Creek
Little Sauty Creek
MOUNTAIN
SAND
1/2 Kilometer
1/2 Mile
OVERLOOK ROAD
POINT ROCK
START
The Big Sink
CR 152
CR 173
CR 557
PARK ROAD
CR 19
HILLEY POINT
Dam
Boulder Field
BUCKS POCKET STATE FOREST
South Sauty
Turnaround
To Morgan Cove
N
E
S
W

MILES
0
.5
1
1.5
2
2.5
800'
750'
700'
650'
600'
START
END
CAMP ROAD TRAIL
CAMP ROAD
CAMP ROAD TRAIL
Turnaround
Locked Gate

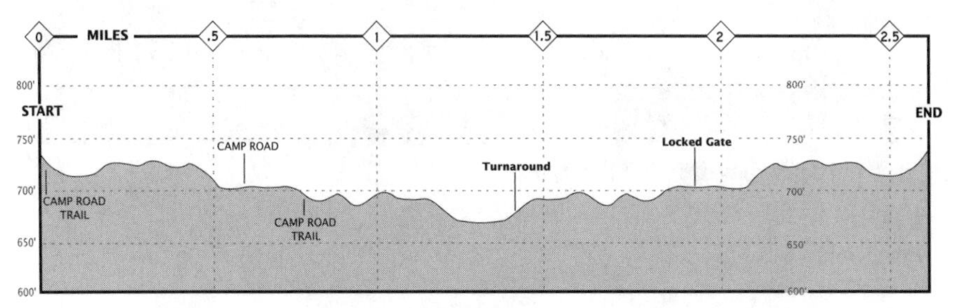

Local Events/Attractions:

Guntersville Museum and Cultural Center, Guntersville, AL (256) 571–7597—*In addition to displays of Native American artifacts, steamboat exhibit, and a local art collection, this museum also has special exhibits throughout the year. Admission is free. Closed on Mondays.* • **Pre-Civil War Cemetery**, Albertville, AL; 1-800-878-3821—*Stroll through this cemetery where the inscriptions on the stones tell unique and fascinating stories of the region. Admission is free.* • **Unclaimed Baggage Center**, Scottsboro, AL; (256) 259–1525 or *www.unclaimedbaggage.com—Oprah Winfrey called this the best-kept shopping secret. The center is the largest purchaser of lost and unclaimed luggage in the country and in turn, "sells them direct to you!" Closed on Sundays.* • *[See Hike 38: Lickskillet Trail]*

It is possible to hike the riverbank when the water is low—but did I mention it's a bit rocky?

Hike Information

Trail Contacts:
Buck's Pocket State Park, Grove Oak, AL; (256) 659–2000—*The park office is open from 7:30 A.M.–5 P.M. Monday–Friday, 8 A.M.–5 P.M., Saturday and Sunday.*

Schedule:
Open year round

Fees/Permits:
No fee for hiking. Camping is $8 for primitive tent sites, $14 for improved with water.

Local Information:
Marshall County Tourism Commission, Guntersville, AL; 1–800–582–3682 • **Lake Guntersville Chamber**, Guntersville, AL; 1–800–869–LAKE or *www.lakeguntersville.org*

Accommodations:
Covenant Cove, Guntersville, AL; (256) 582–1000 • **Lake Guntersville Bed and Breakfast**, Guntersville, AL (256) 505–0133 • **Lakeview Inn**, Guntersville, AL; (256) 582–3104 • **Overlook Mountain Inn**, Guntersville, AL; (256) 582–3256

Restaurants:
Bluffside Coffee Shop, Guntersville, AL; 1–800–LGVILLE —*Perched along the banks of Guntersville Reservoir in the park, this coffee shop is open for breakfast and lunch.* • **State Lodge Restaurant**, Guntersville, AL; (256) 582–3666

Other Resources:
Alabama Mountain Lakes (North Alabama information), Mooresville, AL; 1–800–648–5381 or *www.almtlakes.org* • **Bama Environmental News** (205) 226–7739 or *www.bamanews.com* • **Wildflowers of Alabama** at *www.duc.auburn.edu/~deancar/index.html*

Local Outdoor Retailers:
Canyon Outdoors, Fort Payne, AL; (256) 845–0777 or *www.canyonoutdoors.com*

Maps:
USGS maps: Grove Oak, AL • **Brochures**—*available free of charge at the park office*

Point Rock Trail

Hike Summary

The high point of Buck's Pocket State Park is this hike to Point Rock. The trail starts out around a boulder-strewn runoff area that, during periods of rainfall, can have a wild tropical look to it, with heavy moss. Before the trail ascends to Point Rock, a 70-foot waterfall pops out of the boulders and drops into the underground caverns known as the Big Sink. From the top of the point are expansive views of the sandstone cliffs lining surrounding mountains.

Hike Specs

Start: From the parking area of the Buck's Pocket State Park office
Length: 3.5-mile out-and-back
Approximate Hiking Time: 2–3 hours
Difficulty Rating: Moderate, due to large boulders and ascent to Point Rock
Trail Surface: Dirt path; some rocky trail
Lay of the Land: Butternut and blue beech trees; wildflowers, including Jack-in-the-pulpit and trout lily
Land Status: State park
Nearest Town: Guntersville, AL
Other Trail Users: None
Canine Compatibility: Not dog friendly—due to large boulders; no leash required

Getting There

From Guntersville: Follow AL 227 through Guntersville State Park. Just after crossing the bridge over Town Creek and Lake Guntersville, come to an intersection. AL 227 turns right here. Continue 2.8 miles and make a left onto CR 19. In 1.6 miles CR 19 becomes CR 152. In 0.6 miles, the road comes to a fork. Take the right fork (this is the park road) and travel 0.3 miles to the parking lot on the left side of the road next to the park office. ***DeLorme: Alabama Atlas & Gazetteer:*** Page 20 H3

Situated within a deep canyon, Buck's Pocket State Park encompasses more than 2,000 acres of forest and canyon. The canyon was formed by erosion from the turbulent action of South Sauty Creek. The result is a park with such features as Point Rock, standing 900 feet above sea level, and the boulder-strewn Big Sink ravine.

The first inhabitants of the area were Native Americans, mainly Cherokee, who used the canyon overhangs as protection from the weather. The park derives its name from a story about a Native American hunter who cornered a buck atop one of the high bluffs above the creek. Rather than be taken, the buck decided to jump to its death in the "pocket" of the canyon.

The blue-green waters of South Sauty Creek cascade over the boulders of the canyon floor, putting on a splashy show as the creek heads to Morgan's Cove and into Lake Guntersville. The best times to see the creek are in the

winter and spring, when rain is more frequent. The creek often dries up in summer.

The Point Rock Trail begins at the park office and heads into the woods at the bottom of a ravine, where it climbs over huge boulders. Just before the trail turns to ascend the mountain, a 70-foot waterfall on Little Sauty Creek pops out from deep within the rocks and then drops back underground as it travels to meet South Sauty Creek.

A sign next to the park office reads, "A Haven for Defeated Politicians." The park got this nickname when former governor "Big" Jim Folsom, conceding defeat in an election bid for the U.S. Senate, said he was going to Buck's Pocket to gather his thoughts and lick his wounds.

The trail makes its way to the top of Point Rock, a 285-foot-tall sandstone bluff whose top is at an elevation of just over 900 feet. An outcropping popular with rock climbers drops off steeply here. The trail makes its way to the very edge of Point Rock, offering panoramic views of the canyon and its sandstone walls.

From February until late June, wildflowers bloom by the trail. Among them are Jack-in-the-pulpit (also known as Indian turnip) and bright yellow-flowered trout lilies. Among the trees along the Point Rock Trail is blue beech, an extremely hard wood—also known as ironwood—that was once used to make tool handles. Also on the trail are butternut, or white walnut, trees with an ash gray trunk. The walnuts are good to eat, but tough to crack.

The park has an ample supply of tent campsites, both primitive or with drinking water. The best part about camping at Buck's Pocket is the natural air conditioning: A cool breeze blows through the canyon most of the year, even in the dead of summer when the rest of the state is sweltering.

MilesDirections

0.0 START from the park office, head down the paved park road. South Sauty Creek runs parallel to the right.

0.2 Come to a sign that reads "Hiking Trail to Point Rock." Turn left here and onto the trail into the woods. Shortly you'll begin to see red blazes.

0.8 *[**FYI.** Point Rock can be seen through the trees to the left.]*

1.0 *[**FYI.** A stream will be seen to the right tumbling through the rocks of the ravine and disappearing underground. This is an area known as "The Big Sink."]*

1.1 *[**Side-trip.** Come to a short 30-foot side trail that leads to the falls seen to the right. There you'll find nice spots to sit and lunch.]*

1.6 Cross the paved overlook road and come to the edge of the cliffs. *[**FYI.** This is a popular area for rock climbers and repelers.]* At the edge, a sign reads "Lynn Overlook Area." Turn left and head down a gravel footpath. The trail turns into a wooden footbridge that travels over Point Rock. Continue on the footbridge as it circles the outcropping. The bridge ends and turns into another gravel footpath.

1.7 A short 50-foot-long footbridge heads to an overlook. Turn to the left and come to the main bluff. This is the end of the hike. Retrace the trail back down to the parking area. *[**Note.** The blazes are less noticeable on the downhill trip, so keep an eye out for them.]*

3.5 Arrive back at the parking lot.

Hike Information

Trail Contacts:

Buck's Pocket State Park, Grove Oak, AL; (256) 659-2000—*The park office is open from 7:30 A.M.–5 P.M. Monday–Friday, 8 A.M.–5 P.M., Saturday and Sunday.*

Schedule:

Open year round

Fees/Permits:

No fee for hiking. Camping is $8 for primitive tent sites, $14 for improved with water.

Local Information:

[See Hike 42: Camp Road]

Local Events/Attractions:

[See Hike 42: Camp Road]

Accommodations:

[See Hike 42: Camp Road]

Other Resources:

[See Hike 42: Camp Road]

Local Outdoor Retailers:

[See Hike 42: Camp Road]

Maps:

USGS maps: Grove Oak, AL
Brochures—*available free of charge at the park office*

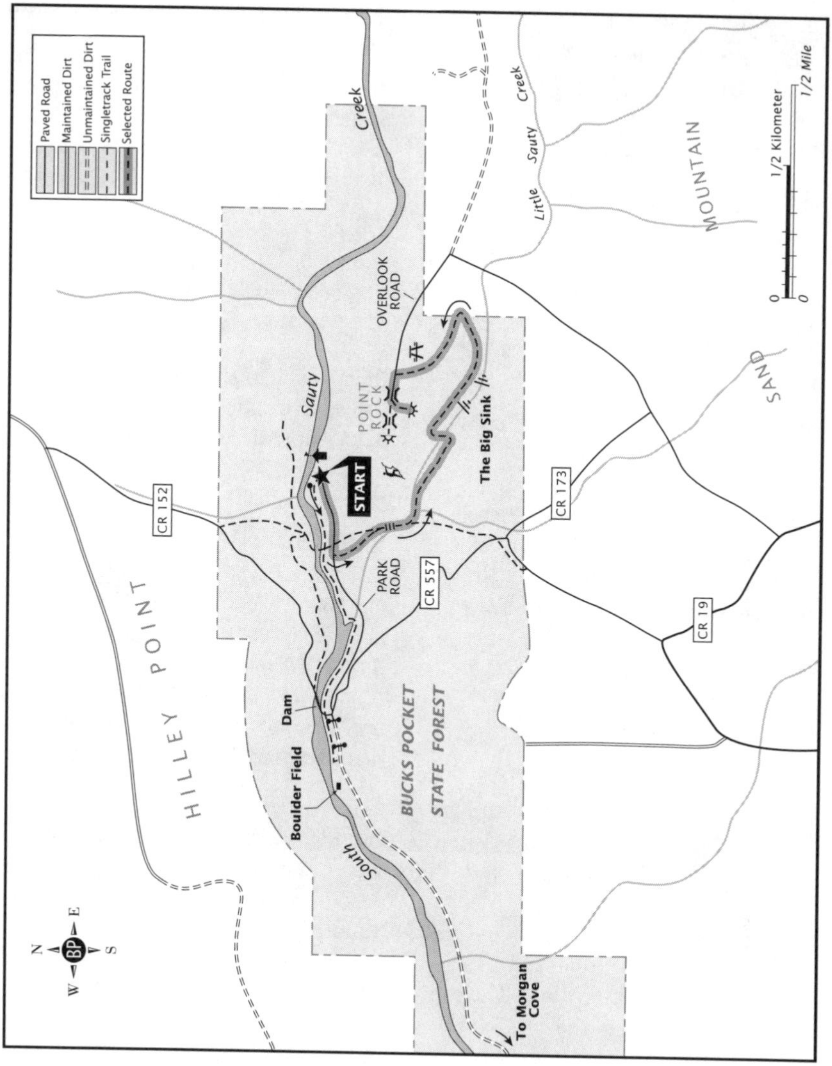

Paved Road
Maintained Dirt
Unmaintained Dirt
Singletrack Trail
Selected Route
Sauty Creek
Little Sauty Creek
MOUNTAIN
SAND
HILLEY POINT
OVERLOOK ROAD
POINT ROCK
START
The Big Sink
CR 152
CR 173
CR 557
CR 19
PARK ROAD
Dam
Boulder Field
BUCKS POCKET STATE FOREST
South
To Morgan Cove
1/2 Kilometer
1/2 Mile
0
0
N
E
S
W
BP

MILES
0
1
2
3
Point Rock
The Big Sink
START
POINT ROCK TRAIL
END
Turnaround Point
1000'
750'
500'
250'

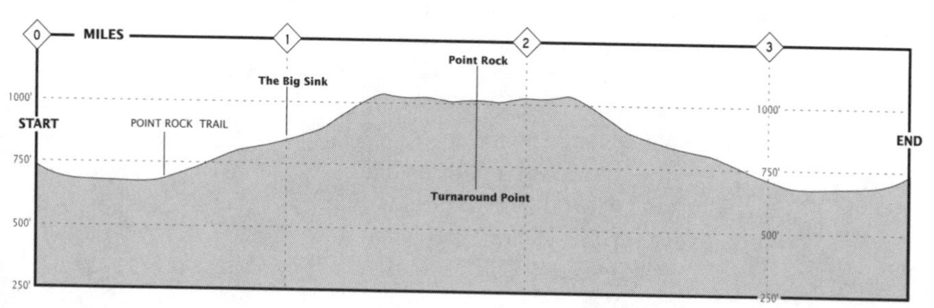

Eberhart Trail

Hike Summary

Here's a fine hike to the bottom of a major canyon. It's a steep climb down a wide, nicely graded and grass-covered path to the rocky banks of Little River. The canyon walls rise high above as you trek down toward the blue-green waters of the river, all as waterfalls continue to work their magic shaping the soft sandstone.

Hike Specs

Start: From the Eberhart Point parking area on AL 179
Length: 1.8-mile out-and-back
Approximate Hiking Time: 1½–2½-hours
Difficulty Rating: Difficult due to steep hiking into and out of Little River Canyon
Trail Surface: Grass path on the way down; rocky along the river
Lay of the Land: Sandstone cliffs; thick rhododendron
Land Status: National preserve
Nearest Town: Fort Payne, AL
Other Trail Users: None
Canine Compatibility: Not dog friendly—due to steep incline; no leash required

Getting There

From Fort Payne: Take AL 35 East and make a right turn onto AL 176 West. (A sign clearly marks "Little River Canyon.") Drive 11.4 miles to a sign that reads "Canyon Mouth Park." The parking area and trailhead is to the right. ***DeLorme: Alabama Atlas & Gazetteer:*** Page 27 A7

Little River gets its start high atop Lookout Mountain in Georgia and flows along the mountain into Alabama through Alabama's DeSoto State Park and the adjacent Little River Canyon National Preserve—a preserve of more than 14,000 acres that was added to the national park system in 1992. The canyon through which it courses was formed by the action of the river on the soft sandstone over thousands of years, creating the deepest and largest canyon east of the Mississippi. The National Park Service considers the river to be one of the cleanest in the South, and one of the wildest—thanks to prohibitions on dam construction and other development.

Eberhart Trail is a short out-and-back route that makes for a tough hike, but it's worth the effort. Although the trail is wide—about 10 to 15 feet—it winds sharply down the canyon wall to the river. A saving grace is that the path is sod-covered, making it comfortable for walking. Benches are strategically placed for resting.

Views on the way down are obscured a bit by the trees. Watch for the overlook halfway down the trail, behind one of the benches. Thick rhododendron lines the path. The real payoff is at the bottom. The first thing you see is a 600-foot sandstone wall across the river, towering above the rocky

Little River and a view of the canyon walls to the south.

beach. Turning to the left and heading upriver, the trail becomes rough, with rocks six to 12 inches wide covering the route. Here, the river races through narrow, boulder-strewn channels.

Keep safety in mind during this hike. While Eberhart Trail is a hike and not a rock climb, several places—including the overlook along the way—hang out over the canyon. Don't bushwhack off the paths. There could be hidden drop-offs.

The auto route at the preserve, Canyon Rim Parkway, offers views as spectacular as those on Eberhart Trail. Along the drive down the canyon, several overlooks afford an opportunity to park and take in the vistas. At the Hawk's Glide Overlook, you may see rock climbers at play. Grace Falls Overlook shows off the pencil-thin, 600-foot waterfall plunging down the canyon wall. Also along the way is Needle Rock, where the forces of wind and water have created crawl spaces and overhangs that the kids, and adults, love. At the bottom of Canyon Rim Parkway is Canyon Mouth Park, a day-use facility with a nature trail and picnic area.

Don't let this picture fool you. The grade is extremely steep.

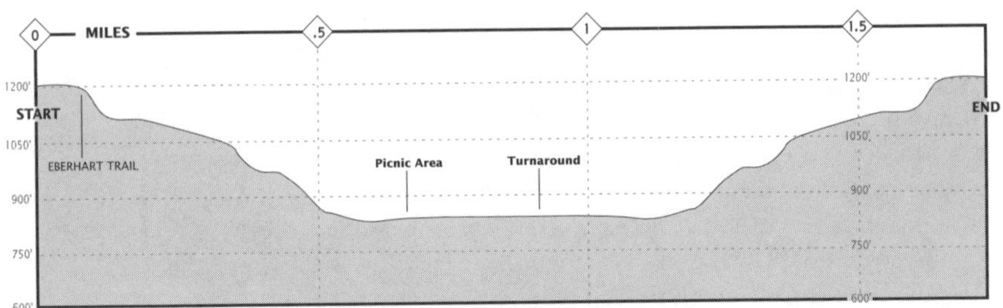

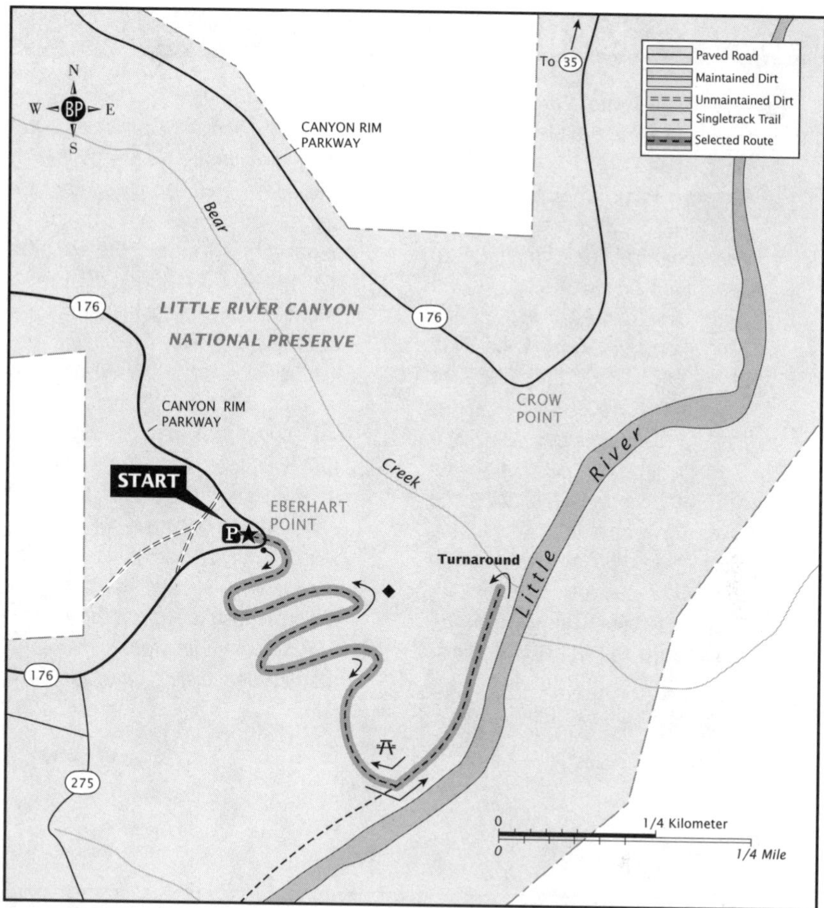

MilesDirections

0.0 START from the Canyonland parking lot and cross Canyon Rim Parkway to an information board on the other side. Head into the woods beyond the sign. Come to a T-intersection and turn left.

0.3 Behind the bench here is a short 20-foot side trail that comes out on top of a ledge that overhangs the canyon wall. *[**Note.** Be VERY careful here.]*

0.6 The trail turns into solid rocks as it comes out at the banks of Little River. Straight ahead across the river is an impressive 600-foot canyon wall. Turn to the left and meander up the river for the next 0.3 miles. *[**Note.** The path is very rocky, so watch your footing. Remember the currents in the river are swift, so be careful along the rapids as well.]*

0.9 Turn around and retrace your tracks back to the parking area.

1.8 Arrive back at the parking area.

Local Events/Attractions:

Arts and Crafts Festival, third weekend in May, Mentone, AL; (256) 845-3957 • **DeSoto Caverns Park**, Childersburg, AL; 1-800-933-2283 or *www.cavern.com/desoto/index.html—Large cathedral type caves featuring the Great Onyx Cathedral and a laser light show.* • **DeSoto Falls**, Fort Payne, AL; (256) 845-5380 or *www.mentone.com/desoto—DeSoto Falls plunges 104 feet from the end of DeSoto Lake as the waters form the raging Little River. The area is touted as having the largest crop of wildflowers in the world outside of China.* • **Shady Grove Dude Ranch/Cloudmont Ski & Golf Resort**, Mentone, AL; (256) 634-4344—*Bringing "Montana to Mentone," this resort features snow skiing in the winter and a "dude" ranch with trail rides through the mountains to DeSoto and Veil Falls. And of course, golf! Open year round.* • **Sequoyah Caverns**, Fort Payne, AL; (256) 635-0024 or *www.sequoyahcaverns.com—Sequoyah Cavern is a quarter-mile deep cave in the side of Sand Mountain. Inside, there are a series of rooms with pools of mineral water, 120-foot high ceilings, and Native American artifacts. The cavern is so named because Cherokee Chief Sequoyah and his tribe used the cave for shelter. A column in the cave has etched in it the words "1830–Sam Houston." Houston married Sequoyah's daughter.*

And the Winner Is . . .

It's official. Add to the list of state birds, songs, trees, and whatever else, Alabama's official amphibian.

In April 2000, students from Fairhope Elementary School presented a bill to the state legislature to make the red hill salamander the official state amphibian. The debate on the floor was intense. One House member was upset because his earlier effort in favor of the dusky gopher frog had failed. Another member wondered whether the red hill salamander would make good fishing bait.

When the dust cleared, the salamander was voted in, 95-0.

Hike Information

Trail Contacts:
Little River Canyon National Preserve, Fort Payne, AL; (256) 845–9605 or *www.nps.gov/liri*

Schedule:
Open year round

Fees/Permits:
No fee charged for hiking. Hunting is allowed in the preserve at specified times of the year. Contact the National Park Service for dates.

Local Information:
Alabama Mountain Lakes Association, Mooresville, AL; 1–800–648–5381 • **DeKalb County Tourist Association**, Fort Payne, AL (256) 845–3957 or *www.mentone.com/tourist* • **Fort Payne** at *www.fortpayne.net/Default.htm—including information on DeSoto State Park, Little River Canyon, and Lookout Mountain*

Accommodations:
DeSoto State Park Cottage and Motel, Fort Payne, AL; (256) 845–5380 • **Mentone Inn**, Mentone, AL; 1–800–455–7470 • **Mountain View Motel**, Fort Payne, AL; (256) 845–2303 • **Shady Grove Dude Ranch**, Mentone, AL; (256) 634–4344

Restaurants:
Blue Moon Café, Fort Payne, AL; (256) 997–9908 • **DeSoto State Park Lodge**, Fort Payne, AL; 1–800–568–8840 • **Jack's Char-Co Broiled Hamburgers**, Fort Payne, AL; (256) 845–3565

Other Resources:
Tennessee Valley Trails at *www.montesano.com/hikeweb*

Local Outdoor Retailers:
DeSoto Athletic, Fort Payne, AL; (256) 845–3626

Maps:
USGS maps: Little River, AL • **Brochures**—*available free of charge by writing the preserve*

Rhododendron Trail

Hike Summary

The Rhododendron Trail provides an easy-to-moderate walk through DeSoto State Park. The western section follows gentle rolling hills; the eastern section has the added challenge of large rocks and possibly downed trees. The trail is lined with rhododendron bushes that bloom in late spring. The path takes you past Indian and Lodge Falls.

Hike Specs

Start: From the country store parking lot
Length: 1.3-mile loop
Approximate Hiking Time: 2 hours
Difficulty Rating: Easy, over gentle rolling hills; moderate, over rocks and some downed trees
Trail Surface: Primarily dirt path
Lay of the Land: Rhododendron bushes, plus live oak and longleaf pine forest
Land Status: State park
Nearest Town: Fort Payne, AL
Other Trail Users: Cyclists along sections near the campgrounds
Canine Compatibility: Dog friendly—on the western part of the trail, which has ample water and easy terrain; not dog friendly along the eastern section due to large rocks along the river; leash is recommended

Getting There

From Fort Payne: Go east on AL 35 for about a mile, and turn left onto DeSoto Parkway. Travel 5.1 miles (DeSoto Parkway turns into CR 89) to the park entrance. Continue straight for 2.1 miles and park at the country store on the left. ***DeLorme: Alabama Atlas & Gazetteer:*** Page 21 G7

Situated at an elevation of about 1,750 feet on top of Lookout Mountain, DeSoto State Park includes the beginnings of Little River Canyon. The park is near Fort Payne, home of the superstar country group Alabama. Walking the trails here and seeing the river and canyon, you can picture Alabama singing a line from one of their songs: "From high on Lookout Mountain I look down with pride and say that my home's in Alabama."

The Rhododendron Trail gets its name, quite obviously, from the dense collection of rhododendron bushes that line the way, particularly along the banks of the west fork of the Little River. The off-white blossoms and their sweet fragrance fill the air in late spring, usually peaking by the third week of May.

The most beautiful part of this trail is the section between DeSoto State Park Lodge and the river. The trail winds around the canyon wall as it travels to the river. Along the way you'll pass Lodge Falls, just below the lodge, and Indian Falls, where a new park recreation building was just constructed above the head of the falls. And of course there is the Little

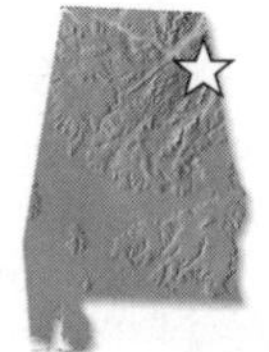

Another view of the Little River.

River itself, its blue-green waters rushing through narrow sections of rapids and around huge boulders.

Along the river and canyon, the trail can be a bit difficult. The hike up and down the canyon wall is moderately steep in some areas. And along the river where the trail joins and follows the DeSoto Scout Trail, you'll have to climb over large boulders from time to time.

The runoff from rainfall has gouged out routes that look in some places like trails. Many hikers end up on these runoff paths and soon find themselves bushwhacking as they look for the main trail. Keep in mind that hiking to the top of the canyon should lead you to the lodge or cabin area, while hiking down to the river should take you to the section where the Rhododendron and DeSoto Scout trails join together along the riverbank.

As you hike the Rhododendron Trail, don't be surprised if you have to scramble around some downed trees. A severe ice storm in 1999 dropped many trees, and park managers expect cleanup to be a long-term job.

The full Rhododendron Trail extends farther to the western section of DeSoto State Park, near the wilderness campground, but the greatest beauty of the hike lies along the 1.3-mile loop described here.

MilesDirections

0.0 START from the parking lot at the country store. Cross CR 89 to the park picnic area and fee station. Head down the paved picnic area road and continue to the opposite end of the parking lot.

0.1 Head past a picnic pavilion built by the CCC in the 30s. A short pole with a hiker emblem on it will be seen here. Although not marked, the worn dirt trail should be fairly easily seen heading down an easy hill. In 100 feet, the trail ducks into the woods and shortly comes to a T-intersection. Turn right. *[**Side-trip.** In 20 feet, a short 30-foot path leads to an overlook to the left for a good view of Indian Falls.]* Continue to a wooden bridge that spans Indian Falls. (There is an area of very heavy downed trees at the far end of the bridge and requires that you get off the bridge into the shallow creek and bushwhack around the debris.) After the bridge, come to a fork and go right. Follow the white blazes of the Rhododendron Trail.

0.2 *[**FYI.** Lodge Falls can be seen through the trees.]*

0.3 The Rhododendron Trail merges with the DeSoto Scout Trail as it heads along the banks of the Little River. (The blazes are now the yellow markers of the DeSoto Scout Trail.)

0.5 Come to a T-intersection and turn right on the hard dirt path. (To the left, an unmarked trail leads up hill to the park's swimming pool.)

0.6 The white-blazed Rhododendron Trail returns and makes a sharp turn to the left (the DeSoto Scout Trail continues to the straight). Follow the Rhododendron Trail.

0.8 *[**FYI.** Through the trees to the left, the DeSoto State Park swimming pool building can be seen.]*

0.9 Comes to a fork and go left.

1.0 Exit the woods, pass the tennis courts, and come to CR 89. Cross the highway and head back into the woods.

1.1 A short, unmarked trail merges into the Rhododendron Trail from the southeast. Make a sharp left turn and head down this trail to the southeast.

1.3 Come to the campground road and turn left. Follow the road to the parking lot at the country store.

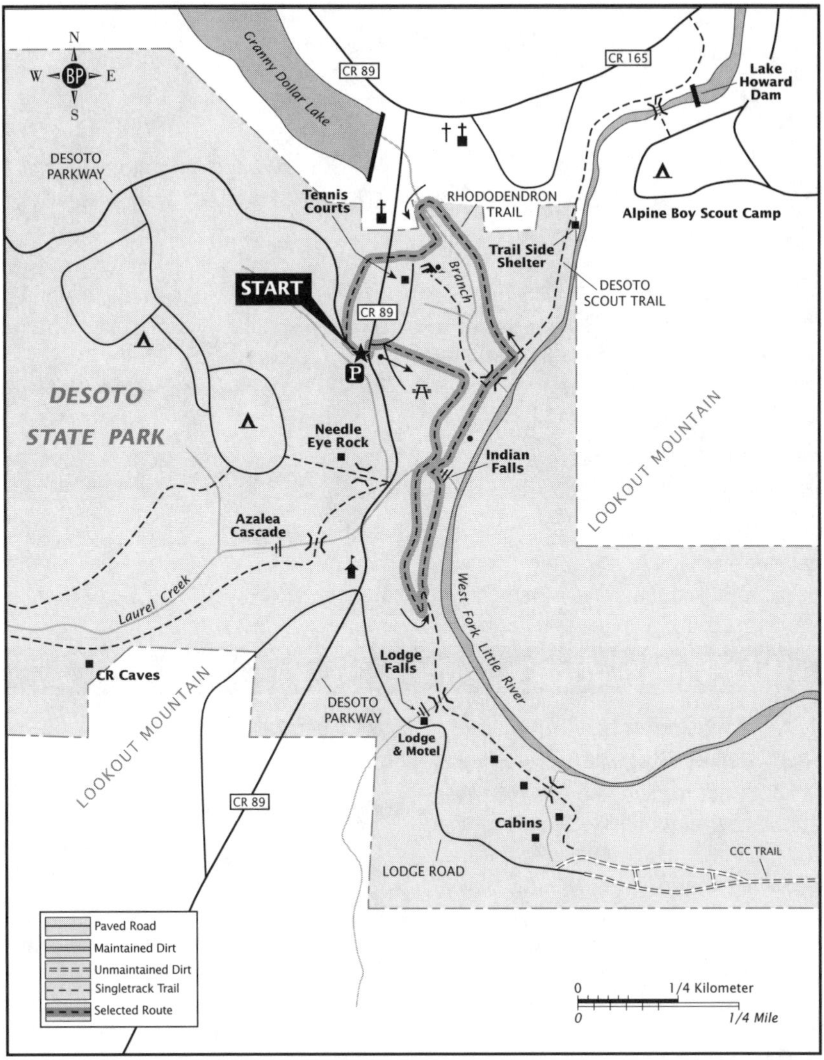

N
W
E
S
BP
Granny Dollar Lake
CR 89
CR 165
Lake
Howard
Dam
DESOTO
PARKWAY
Tennis
Courts
RHODODENDRON
TRAIL
Alpine Boy Scout Camp
Trail Side
Shelter
Branch
DESOTO
SCOUT TRAIL
START
CR 89
P
DESOTO
STATE PARK
Needle
Eye Rock
Indian
Falls
LOOKOUT MOUNTAIN
Azalea
Cascade
Laurel Creek
West Fork Little River
CR Caves
Lodge
Falls
DESOTO
PARKWAY
Lodge
& Motel
LOOKOUT MOUNTAIN
CR 89
Cabins
CCC TRAIL
LODGE ROAD
Paved Road
Maintained Dirt
Unmaintained Dirt
Singletrack Trail
Selected Route
0
1/4 Kilometer
0
1/4 Mile

0
MILES
0.5
1
RHODODENDRON TRAIL
CAMPGROUND
ROAD
START
END
DE SOTO TRAIL
CR 89
Indian Falls
1600'
1500'
1400'
1300'
1200'

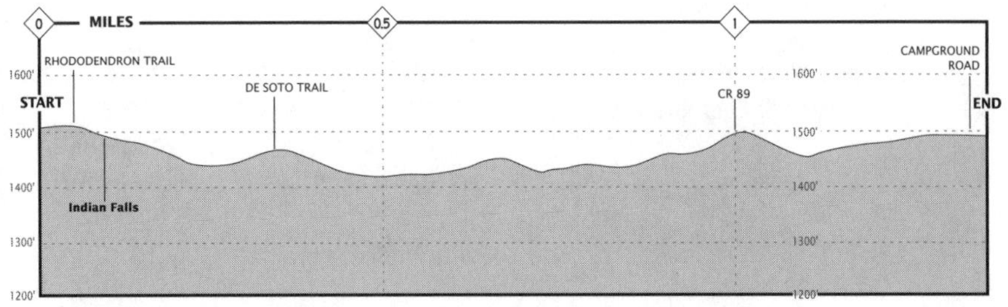

Indian Falls.

Hike Information

Trail Contacts:
DeSoto State Park, Fort Payne, AL; (256) 845–0051 or *www.mentone.com/desoto*

Schedule:
Open year round

Fees/Permits:
No fee charged for hiking

Local Information:
[See Hike 44: Eberhart Trail]

Local Events/Attractions:
[See Hike 44: Eberhart Trail]

Accommodations:
[See Hike 44: Eberhart Trail]

Restaurants:
[See Hike 44: Eberhart Trail]

Other Resources:
[See Hike 44: Eberhart Trail]

Hike Tours:
Adams Outdoors, Fort Payne, AL; (256) 845–2988—*Whether it's rafting, rappelling, or horseback riding, Adams Outdoors provides guided tours for it.*

Local Outdoor Retailers:
[See Hike 44: Eberhart Trail]

Maps:
USGS maps: Valley Head, AL-GA; Jamestown, AL-GA • **Brochures**—*available free of charge at the camp store*

Is Kudzu King?

When kudzu was introduced to Americans at the 1876 Centennial Exposition in Philadelphia, it was to a warm reception. The Japanese government had honored the United States' 100th birthday by constructing a garden exhibit of their native plants. American gardeners were quick to fall in love with the oversized leaves and the sweet, grape-smelling blooms.

It wasn't until the 1920s that the soon-to-be-a-pest plant found a more legitimate function. Those looking to point fingers should look to Chipley, Florida, where Charles and Lillie Pleas made the unfortunate discovery that livestock took a shine to the tasty foliage. In no time kudzu plants were flying out of their door and through the mail.

To make matters worse, the Depression-era Soil Conservation Service found another use for the plant, as a ground-stabilizing agent. They government's army of out-of-work bachelors, the Civilian Conservation Corps, were enlisted to spread the plant. By the 1940s farmers were being paid upwards of $8 an acre to further distribute this "miracle vine."

In the South kudzu had found its perfect host. Not only was the weather ideal, but Southerners seemed to encourage its spread. In short order it had worn out its welcome. By 1953 the government ceased promoting the plant. And in 1973 the USDA delivered the heaviest blow. The former darling of the Centennial Exposition was officially a "weed."

Why all the fuss? Well, in the summer months kudzu can grow as much as a foot a day—60 feet a year under optimum conditions. And as it blankets all that doesn't move, it robs precious sunlight from competing vegetation, effectively suffocating most everything beneath it. Today kudzu covers over seven million acres of the Deep South and reaches as far north as Pennsylvania. And though we can put a man on the moon, researchers still haven't found an effective means to rid the South of this insidious vine.

Though many consider it a scourge on the South, kudzu does, in all fairness, have its well-wishers. Not only are resourceful Southerners coming up with recipes for kudzu jelly and soup, but some are erecting websites in homage to the adopted creeper.

Love it or hate it, kudzu may be here a while. Might as well learn to make tea with it.

DeSoto Scout Trail

Hike Summary

The DeSoto Scout Trail follows the rapids of the west fork of Little River as the stream twists its way through the mountains. Overall, the narrow trail is relatively easy, but the necessity of clambering over large boulders and the occasional downed tree makes the trip moderately difficult.

Hike Specs

Start: From the south trailhead at the end of the road that leads to the DeSoto State Park lodge and cabins
Length: 4.6-mile out-and-back
Approximate Hiking Time: 4–6 hours
Difficulty Rating: Moderate, due to rocky areas; may be some downed trees on the trail
Trail Surface: Rocky footpath
Lay of the Land: Thick rhododendron and pine
Land Status: State park
Nearest Town: Fort Payne, AL
Other Trail Users: None
Canine Compatibility: Not dog friendly—because of the rocky path and possible downed trees; leash is recommended

Getting There

From Fort Payne: Go east on AL 35 for about a mile and turn left onto DeSoto Parkway. Travel 5.1 miles (DeSoto Parkway turns into CR 89) to the park entrance. Continue straight 2.1 miles to the intersection of Lodge Road (located at the park office) and make a right turn. Travel 0.9 miles. A sign reads "Trailhead parking." Make a left turn here and in 100 feet, an immediate right into a grassy parking area. ***DeLorme: Alabama Atlas & Gazetteer:*** Page 21 G7

Over time, the Little River of Northern Alabama has cut through soft sandstone to form the deepest and largest canyon east of the Mississippi—23 miles long, with an average depth of 600 feet. The region is wild and beautiful, but fragile. Recognizing this, the state of Alabama and the federal government teamed up to help protect the region.

In the mid 1930s the Civilian Conservation Corps, under guidance of the National Park Service, created DeSoto State Park, which encompasses the northern portion of the river, including the west fork that flows into Little River Canyon. The National Park Service then established Little River Canyon National Preserve, a narrow stretch of land that protects the canyon itself, from where it begins at Little River Falls.

The DeSoto Scout Trail offers great vantage points for viewing the river. The full trail begins farther north, at the Comer Boy Scout

Overlooking Little River from the trail shelter.

Reservation, but the section described here falls within the boundaries of DeSoto State Park.

This route begins on top of the ridge that runs high above the river. Descending at an ever-increasing grade from the park's cabins, the trail eventually reaches the west fork of Little River. As the trail travels along the cold, blue-green waters of the river, you'll see pools and eddies that harbor bass and trout. Large, flat boulders in the river provide popular spots for sunbathers.

Moving away from the river, the trail heads up a short hill to the north and soon reveals spectacular views of the cliffs overlooking the river. Some of the best views are from a trail shelter along this part of the hike.

Much of this hike is over a rocky path along the banks of the river—including some clambering over large boulders. You may also encounter downed trees on the trail, victims of storms. An especially severe ice storm in 1999 left the trail littered with trees and handed park managers a huge cleanup job.

MilesDirections

0.0 START from the trailhead parking lot and head into the woods. Come to a T-intersection and turn left. (A bike trail goes right.) Follow the white paint blazes.

0.2 Come to a fork and go right. (The left fork leads to a cabin.) Pass another cabin on the left with a trail that branches off to that cabin.

0.3 Come to a fork in the trail and go right. (The white-blazed trail goes left.)

0.4 Come to a T-intersection with the DeSoto Scout Trail along the banks of the Little River. Turn left and follow the flow of the river.

0.7 Pass an unmarked trail to the left. (This path leads straight up the hillside to the lodge.) Continue along the river.

0.8 *[**Note.** This is a very heavy area of downed trees and will require some bushwhacking. Just remember to keep heading along the riverbank and you'll come out of it.]*

0.9 Pass a side trail on the left. (A yellow sign reads "D.S.T.")

1.1 Cross a 10-foot wooden bridge over Lodge Falls Creek.

1.2 Come to a fork. The white Rhododendron Trail turns uphill and heads to the lodge, continue straight ahead to the northeast. The trail will once again reach the banks of the river in just a few feet.

1.4 Come to a T-intersection and turn right. (An unmarked trail goes left and leads up hill to the park's swimming pool.)

1.5 The white-blazed Rhododendron Trail turns back to the northwest. The Desoto Scout Trail levels off.

1.8 Come to a fork and go left. (The right fork is a short trail to the edge of the bluffs and is very dangerous! Be careful if you go there.) In 100 feet, the two forks rejoin.

2.3 Pass a short bridge to the right, which leads over the river to the Alpine Boy Scout Camp. Continue straight. The trail ends at CR 165. Turn around here and retrace your route back to the parking area.

4.6 Arrive back at the parking area.

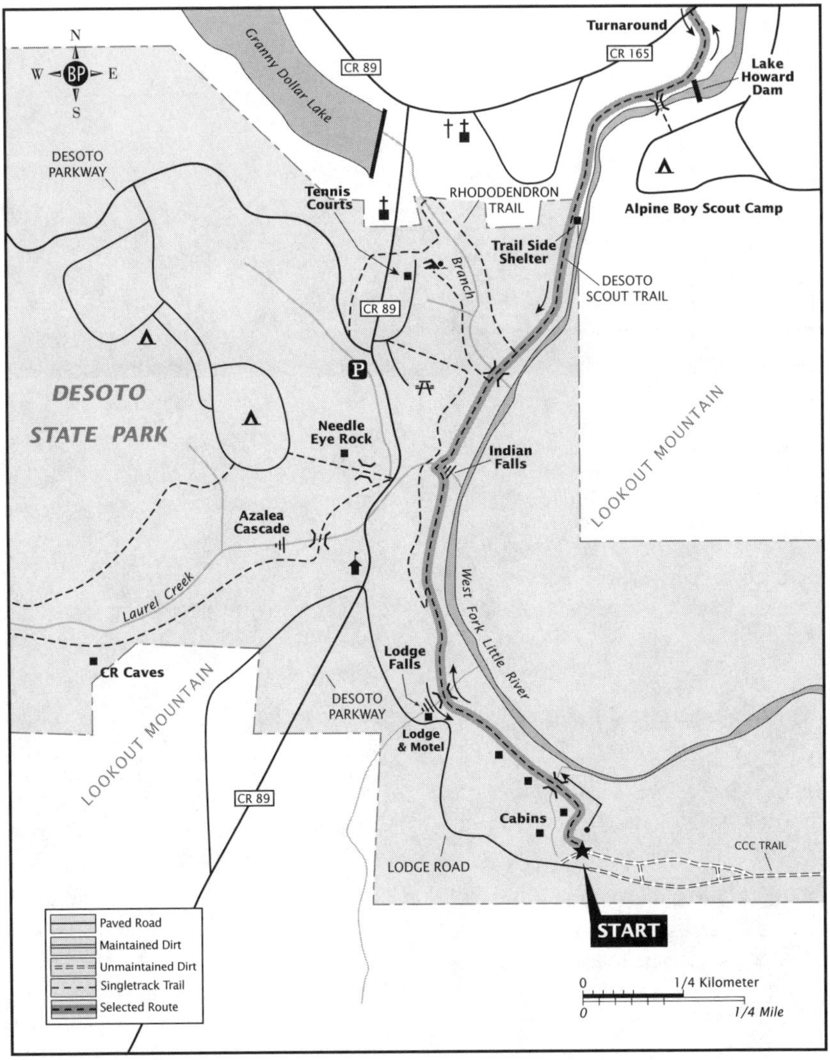

N
S
W
E
BP
Granny Dollar Lake
CR 89
CR 165
Turnaround
Lake Howard Dam
Alpine Boy Scout Camp
DESOTO PARKWAY
Tennis Courts
RHODODENDRON TRAIL
Trail Side Shelter
DESOTO SCOUT TRAIL
Branch
DESOTO STATE PARK
Needle Eye Rock
Indian Falls
LOOKOUT MOUNTAIN
Azalea Cascade
Laurel Creek
West Fork Little River
Lodge Falls
CR Caves
DESOTO PARKWAY
Lodge & Motel
Cabins
CCC TRAIL
LODGE ROAD
START
Paved Road
Maintained Dirt
Unmaintained Dirt
Singletrack Trail
Selected Route
0
1/4 Kilometer
0
1/4 Mile

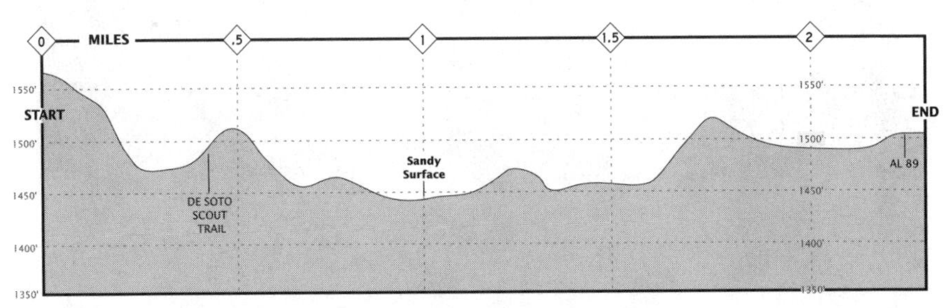

0
MILES
.5
1
1.5
2
1550'
1500'
1450'
1400'
1350'
START
END
DE SOTO SCOUT TRAIL
Sandy Surface
AL 89

The trail is much easier toward its northern end, where it travels over large, smooth rocks. The trail ends at its intersection with County Road 165.

The main wildlife to look for on this trip are the hawks that soar over the canyon and the fish in the river. Lizards dart in and out of the rocks, which also are inhabited by some snakes, including the northern black racer, northern cottonmouth, and timber rattlesnake. Along the trail are dense clusters of rhododendron bushes, plus longleaf pines.

Hike Information

Trail Contacts:
DeSoto State Park, Fort Payne, AL; (256) 845–5380 or *www.mentone.com/desoto*

Schedule:
Open year round

Fees/Permits:
No fee charged for hiking. Camping is $8 in primitive campsites, $12 at improved sites with water and electricity.

Local Information:
[See Hike 44: Eberhart Trail]

Local Events/Attractions:
[See Hike 44: Eberhart Trail]

Accommodations:
[See Hike 44: Eberhart Trail]

Restaurants:
[See Hike 44: Eberhart Trail]

Other Resources:
[See Hike 44: Eberhart Trail]

Hike Tours:
[See Hike 45: Rhododendron Trail]

Local Outdoor Retailers:
[See Hike 44: Eberhart Trail]

Maps:
USGS maps: Valley Head, AL-GA; Jamestown, AL-GA • **Brochures**—*available free of charge at the camp store*

Lost Falls Trail

Hike Summary

The Lost Falls Trail takes you to Laurel Falls, Lost Falls, and Azalea Cascade. Geological highlights include Needle Eye Rock, a boulder that has split in half, leaving an "eye." The trail also travels by the CR Caves, small cavelike overhangs cut away over the millennia by Laurel Creek.

Hike Specs

Start: From the hiker's parking lot 2.1 miles past the entrance to DeSoto State Park
Length: 3.2-mile loop
Approximate Hiking Time: 2½–3½ hours
Difficulty Rating: Mostly easy, with some moderate sections due to downed trees and limbs
Trail Surface: Dirt path; some rocky slopes
Lay of the Land: Azaleas and mountain laurel, waterfalls, unusual rock formations
Land Status: State park
Nearest Town: Fort Payne, AL
Other Trail Users: None
Canine Compatibility: Dog friendly—along this dirt footpath, with ample water; leash required

Getting There

From Fort Payne: Go east on AL 35 for about a mile and turn left onto DeSoto Parkway. Travel 5.1 miles (DeSoto Parkway turns into CR 89) to the park entrance. Continue straight for 1.6 miles. The trailhead is on the right. Go another 0.5 miles to the park headquarters and camp store. ***DeLorme: Alabama Atlas & Gazetteer:*** Page 21 G7

Water is everywhere at DeSoto State Park, with waterfalls scattered throughout the park and the Little River churning white within Little River Gorge. You'll also find lush forests and colorful wildflowers. It's no wonder the park is sometimes called the home of Mother Nature.

The park straddles the river and covers more than 5,000 acres within Little River Canyon National Preserve. While the park's DeSoto Scout Trail and Rhododendron Trail focus more on Little River, the Lost Falls Trail turns its focus on the other wonders of the park.

Lost Falls Trail is actually a combination of several different trails, each marked in its own color. It is, however, possible to get off track by mistakenly following deer trails or short, unmarked connector trails. It's generally not difficult to get back to the main path, but it's a nuisance to have to backtrack.

The gravel parking area that serves as the starting point for Lost Falls Trail is rather small, so get there early to find a spot. The trail begins on a long wooden footbridge across a marshy area. Picnic areas and gazebos along

the bridge provide opportunities to sit and view the marsh.

After the bridge, the trail heads uphill rather steeply and passes through the eye of Needle Eye Rock. The trail then weaves its way up the hillside until it tops a ridge and heads into a ravine. This portion of the trail brings you to the two largest waterfalls, Laurel Falls and Lost Falls.

Lost Falls.

The worst winter storm in decades struck this area in 1999, and this means some bushwhacking for hikers. Downed trees across the trail can be difficult to get around, and park officials say it could be some time before all of the debris is cleaned up. Just keep an eye out in the general direction of travel over these areas, and look for trail markers around the debris.

Laurel Falls is aptly named, set in a landscape filled with mountain laurel that usually blooms in mid May. A 200-foot side trail—marked by a small stone engraved with the name of the falls—takes you to the waterfall. The view is nice from the side trail, but an even better approach is to endure a little bushwhacking and hike right to the base of the falls. Layered rock forms a jagged frame around the 60-foot cascade. The area by the pool at the bottom of the falls makes a lovely spot for lunch.

Back on the main trail, another mile takes you to a second engraved stone, this one reading "Lost Falls." A short side trail goes to the 50-foot-high falls. The main trail then crosses over the head of the falls to the other side of Laurel Creek .

On the way down the trail, you'll arrive at the area known as the CR Caves, where the creek has slowly eroded the rock walls. The result is a series of rock overhangs, almost like caves, approximately 50 feet deep and four feet high.

Azalea Cascade is reached just before the trail returns to the parking lot. Surrounded by azaleas, the 30-foot-high Azalea Cascade is the smallest of the three falls along the trail. A wooden footbridge leads across the pool at the base of the falls.

Hike Information

Trail Contacts:
DeSoto State Park, Fort Payne, AL; (256) 845–0051 or *www.mentone.com/desoto*

Schedule:
Open year round

Fees/Permits:
No fee for hiking. Camping is $8 for primitive tent sites, $14 for improved with water.

Local Information:
[See Hike 44: Eberhart Trail]

Local Events/Attractions:
[See Hike 44: Eberhart Trail]

Accommodations:
[See Hike 44: Eberhart Trail]

Restaurants:
[See Hike 44: Eberhart Trail]

Other Resources:
[See Hike 44: Eberhart Trail]

Hike Tours:
[See Hike 45: Rhododendron Trail]

Local Outdoor Retailers:
[See Hike 44: Eberhart Trail]

Maps:
USGS maps: Valley Head, AL-GA; Jamestown, AL-GA • **Brochures**—*available free of charge at the camp store*

MilesDirections

0.0 START from the gravel parking lot along CR 89. Head west from the parking lot across a wooden footbridge over a marsh. To the right, steps head off into the woods. Head down the stairs, following the red paint blazes.

0.1 The Red Trail intersects another red marked trail. Continue straight. In 100 feet, reach Needle Eye Rock.

0.2 The trail appears to fork but it doesn't. This is a deer trail. Take the left fork and continue uphill.

0.3 Come up behind the RV campground and to the paved Campground Road. Turn to the left onto the road.

0.4 A sign shows the direction of the trail back into the woods. The blazes are now orange.

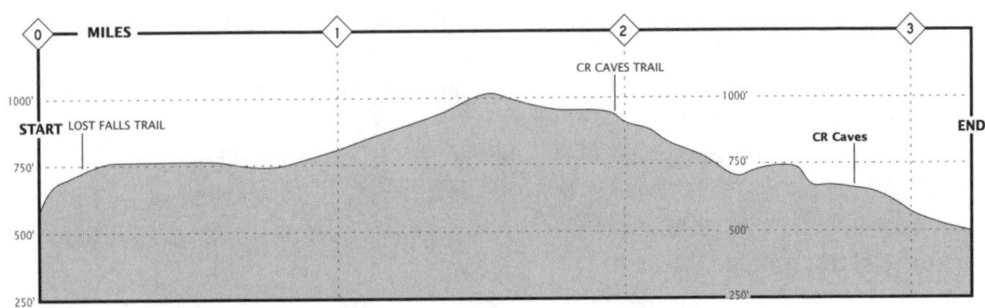

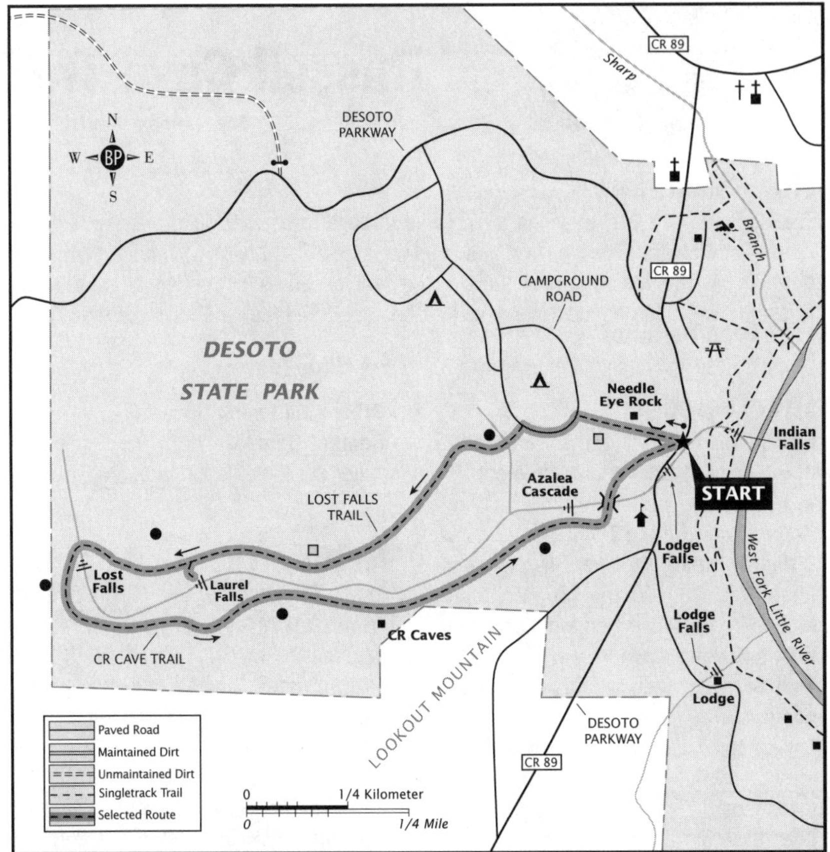

0.8 Come to a fork and go left. You're going to travel about 200 feet to a nice view of the falls and then return. A little bushwhacking will lead to the base of the falls. Be careful, though. It is extremely slippery in this area. Return to the fork by retracing steps.

0.9 Once you're back at the fork, now take the right fork on the orange-blazed trail.

1.9 Come to a fork and take the left fork. In about 100 feet you'll reach the 50-foot Lost Falls. Cross over the creek at the top of the falls. Once across, the blue paint blazes of the CR Cave Trail appear. Follow the blue blazes.

2.5 The CR Caves Trail merges with the Yellow Trail. (Yellow and blue markers are now on the trees.)

2.8 Pass the CR Caves.

3.1 Come to the top of a hill. See the park business offices through the trees. In 200 feet, the trail intersects and crosses a connector trail. Turn left and take the connector down hill. Travel over stairs formed by 4x4 timbers. The stairs end at a creek and a wooden footbridge. Cross the bridge. (To the left is the 30-foot tall Azalea Cascades.)

The bridge returns you to the parking lot.

Russell Cave Trail

Hike Summary

The Russell Cave Trail provides a nice hike through forest and wildflowers in extreme northeast Alabama. The trail first heads up the side of Montague Mountain, then winds downhill. At the foot of the mountain, the trail becomes a wooden boardwalk into Russell Cave, a large limestone cave that has sheltered humans for more than 9,000 years.

Hike Specs

Start: From the back of the visitor center at Russell Cave National Monument
Length: 2-mile loop
Approximate Hiking Time: 1½–2 hours
Difficulty Rating: Moderate due to steepness on the path up Montague Mountain; easy over the wooden boardwalk to Russell Cave
Trail Surface: Asphalt footpath; wooden boardwalk
Lay of the Land: Hickory and chestnut forest, wildflowers, and boulder-strewn landscape
Land Status: National monument
Nearest Town: Bridgeport, AL
Other Trail Users: None
Canine Compatibility: Dog friendly—water available; leash required.

Getting There

From Bridgeport: Take CR 75 west. Travel 0.5 miles from U.S. 72 to the intersection of CR 75 and CR 98. Go straight onto CR 98 and travel eight miles. The entrance to Russell Cave is on the left and is marked with a large National Monument sign. Turn left and drive to the visitor center. Park here. ***DeLorme: Alabama Atlas & Gazetteer:*** Page 20 A5

Situated near the borders of Alabama, Tennessee, and Georgia, Russell Cave National Monument has been operated by the National Park Service since 1962. The cave and surrounding landscape is said to hold the oldest and most complete archaeological records of human existence in the eastern United States.

The Russell Cave Trail includes a two-foot-wide asphalt path up the side of Montague Mountain, to an elevation of about 1,300 feet. The steep trail weaves through stands of chinquapin, hickory, and chestnut. Deep-green moss clings to rocks along the trail. Wildflowers such as bluets and white rue anemones line the path. White-tailed deer are often seen darting in and out of the brush.

Because the trail is so narrow, you can't avoid coming in contact with brush. Watch out for poison ivy. Another bit of caution: The Park Service says the area is pockmarked with hidden sinkholes and drop-offs and asks hikers to stay on the trail.

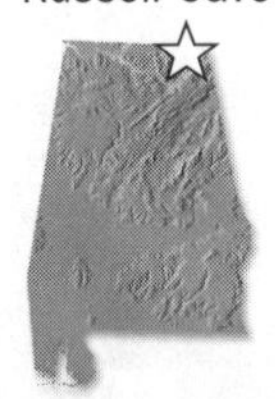

A view of the sinkhole at the start of the hike.

Dotted along the path are split-log benches, strategically placed after steeper sections of the climb. Along the trail and through the trees are views of farm pastures in the valley below and of the Bullhead, Little, and Summerhouse mountains that border the Tennessee River.

After looping the top of a ridge and returning to the base of the mountain, the trail turns onto a wooden boardwalk that takes you to Russell Cave. A park ranger will walk you down to the mouth of the cave, and along the way tell the story of the cave and its former inhabitants.

MilesDirections

0.0 START from the inside of the visitor center at the very back of the building. A sign here points to the left and reads "Cave Trail." Head out the door and turn right onto a 3-foot wide asphalt footpath. In 150 feet, a short 10-foot wooden bridge turns off of the boardwalk to the right. Turn right and head over the bridge. A short 50-foot side trail leads to a railing. From here, the "Sinkhole" can be seen. Backtrack to the asphalt footpath and continue on.

0.1 *[**FYI.** Little Mountain and Summerhouse Mountain can be seen through the trees to the right.]* Come to a fork and continue on the asphalt path.

1.2 Pass Slant Rock.

1.4 Come to a fork and go right. (The left fork is the dirt footpath passed earlier for the short nature trail.)

1.7 Pass the side trail on the right to the Sinkhole. Continue straight. The trail crosses a short bridge and rejoins the main boardwalk.

1.8 The boardwalk continues to the entrance of the cave. A park ranger will greet you and escort you to the cave. The boardwalk enters the cave for about 100 feet where it turns around and follows the same boardwalk for the return trip.

1.9 On the left, pass the hiking trail traveled earlier and continue straight.

2.0 Arrive at the visitor center.

Entrance to Russell Cave.

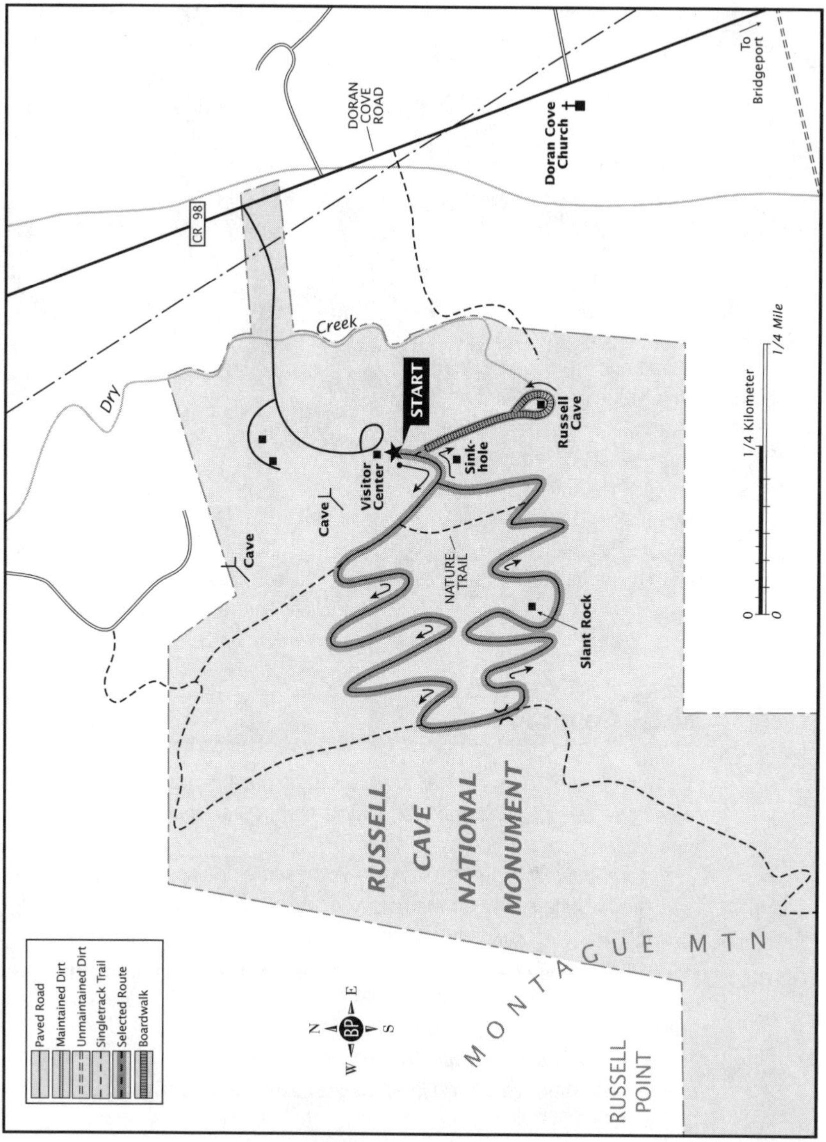

DORAN COVE ROAD
Doran Cove Church
To Bridgeport
CR 98
Dry Creek
START
Visitor Center
Sink-hole
Russell Cave
Cave
Cave
NATURE TRAIL
Slant Rock
RUSSELL CAVE NATIONAL MONUMENT
MONTAGUE MTN
RUSSELL POINT
1/4 Kilometer
1/4 Mile
0
0
N
E
S
W
BP
Paved Road
Maintained Dirt
Unmaintained Dirt
Singletrack Trail
Selected Route
Boardwalk

MILES
0
.5
1
1.5
2
1000'
750'
500'
250'
START
CAVE TRAIL
Slant Rock
Russell Cave
END

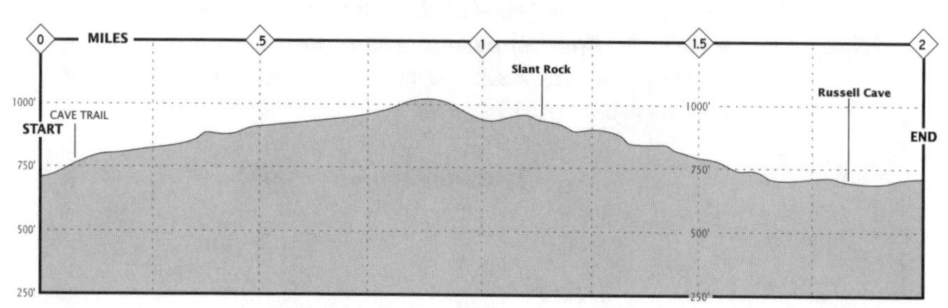

The trail passes Slant Rock.

Watch Your Step

Hiking in the South isn't all smiles. We do have our own set of annoyances to deal with. And one that affects many hikers may be right under your feet.

Picture this: You are standing in a meadow, taking in the scenery, when something starts crawling up your leg. By the time you get around to swatting at it, you feel a burning sensation. Then another. You find yourself standing in a fire ant hill.

Fire ants are ferocious little boogers who think that anything within two feet of their mound is an enemy, and they'll attack to defend their home. Their name is well deserved. The bite is painful and, for people allergic to it, it can sometimes even be fatal.

It's believed that fire ants first came to the United States on a ship from South America that docked at Mobile, Alabama, in the 1920s. Fire ants also like to use man-made roads for their travels. Road construction loosens soils, and loose soil provides an excellent base for fire ant travel. In the rapidly developing South, finding new roads is no problem. So far, the fire ant has spread to 13 southeastern states.

The limestone cave was formed when the ancient inland sea that covered this region receded. Water found its way into fissures in the limestone and began carving out the cave. The cavern roof collapsed about 11,000 years ago, creating an opening to the outside world, now the entrance to Russell Cave.

Humans first inhabited the cave about 7000 BC, at the end of the last ice age. The cave was used as a hunting camp, and carved weapons found within are on display at the monument's visitor center. Rangers give demonstrations on the construction and use of these weapons.

The public trail goes a short distance into the main chamber of the cave. Chambers and passageways farther inside the cave can be explored only after securing written permission from the park superintendent. The creek that flows into the cave is prone to flash flooding, so keep an eye on the weather when visiting.

Hike Information

Trail Contacts:

National Park Service/Russell Cave National Monument, Bridgeport, AL; (256) 495–2672 or *www.nps.gov/ruca*

Schedule:

The cave is open April–October from 8 A.M.–5 P.M. and November–March from 8 A.M.–4:30 P.M.

Fees/Permits:

No fee to hike the trail or for admission into Russell Cave National Monument. Donations are requested to help maintain the park.

Local Information:

Alabama Mountain Lakes Association, Mooresville, AL; 1–800–648–5381 or *www.almtlakes.org*

Local Events/Attractions:

Stevenson Railroad Depot/Museum, Stevenson, AL; (256) 437–3012—*Admission is free to this museum of railroad and Native American artifacts. Open December–April, Monday–Friday 9 A.M.–5 P.M., April–November Monday–Saturday 9 A.M.–5 P.M.*

Accommodations:

Hess Motor Inn, Bridgeport, AL; (256) 495–2600

Local Outdoor Retailers:

Bridgeport Sports, Bridgeport, AL; (256) 495–2312

Maps:

USGS maps: Doran Cove, AL • **Brochures**—*available free of charge at the visitor center*

Honorable Mentions

Northern Alabama

Northern Alabama gives you diverse hiking adventures, from panoramic views to breathtaking waterfalls at the geologic fall line. The following trails didn't make the top of our list, but while in the area, you may want to check them out. These hikes still provide interesting scenery and challenges. Let us know what you think about the selection. Maybe one should be upgraded to the A-list or maybe you know of a hidden trip that would make a good honorable mention.

(L) Dismals Canyon

The Dismals Canyon in northwest Alabama has been described as "one of the finest examples of ecological and geological features composing our Nation's Natural History." The area was declared a National Natural Landmark in 1975—one of 697 in the country.

The property is privately owned, with no developed camping areas in the canyon proper to keep the land pristine. The upper part of the canyon has campsites available. At the bottom of the canyon are several hiking trails that take you past a wide variety of wildflowers, as well as past waterfalls, moss covered canyon walls, and towering boulders. This region was also a hiding spot for outlaw Jesse James and was a secret ritual area for the Chickasaw Indians.

If you'd like to canoe, you can take a lazy float trip through the canyon down the lower Bear Creek or try your luck at the class I–IV rapids at upper Bear Creek.

The main attraction at the Dismals is the nightly summertime light show put on by the dismalites. Scientifically known as "Arachnocampa luminosa," these "glowworms" can only be found in New Zealand and a handful of locations on earth, the Dismals being one. It is said that at night on the canyon floor, if you were to look up, it is hard to tell where these tiny little creatures end and the stars begin. The light is used to attract food.

To get to the Dismals, go south on U.S. 43 from Russellville, and turn right on CR 8. The park will be on your left. The Dismals are open 10 A.M.–6 P.M. Sunday–Thursday and Friday and Saturday 10 A.M.–10 P.M. Special tours are held Friday and Saturday at 8:30 P.M. For more information, call (205) 993–4559 or visit *www.dismalscanyon.com.* ***DeLorme: Alabama Atlas & Gazetteer:*** Page 23 B6

(M) Black Warrior Horse Trails – Bankhead National Forest

Located within the confines of the William B. Bankhead National Forest in northern Alabama, home of the Sipsey Wilderness, the Black Warrior Horse Trails—30 miles worth—travel through some of the most beautiful canyons and rivers in the south, passing waterfalls, fast moving

rivers, towering cliffs, and deep gorges. over of trails have been designated for equestrians. These trails are primarily equestrian trails but are also open to hikers. If you plan a trip, just be cautious and courteous with the equestrians. Startling them in anyway can be dangerous to everyone around!

The forest is located about 21 miles west of the town of Cullman off U.S. 278. For more information, contact the Bankhead National Forest ranger station Monday–Friday from 7:30 A.M.–5 P.M. at (205) 489–5111. ***DeLorme: Alabama Atlas & Gazetteer:*** Page 24 B1

(N) Wheeler National Wildlife Refuge

Covering over 34,000 acres, the Wheeler National Wildlife Refuge is yet another excellent great spot for hikers to view many rare and endangered species. The refuge was established in 1938 as a "wintering ground for migratory waterfowl." Today, thanks to a series of five nature trails traveling through several "satellite" refuges, hikers can see endangered gray and Indiana bats, watercress darters, and Alabama cavefish, not to mention the hundreds of birds that call the refuge home.

There is plenty to take in at the refuge, including the wildlife observation building and interpretive exhibits. The refuge is located just outside of Decatur on AL 67 (Exit 334 off I-65). For more information call the refuge office weekdays from 7:00 A.M.–5:00 P.M. at (256) 353–7243. ***DeLorme: Alabama Atlas & Gazetteer:*** Page 18 G4

(O) Old Railroad Bed Trail – Land Trust of Huntsville

Monte Sano Mountain stands like an island amidst a rapidly developing landscape. The city and suburbs of Huntsville are continually expanding and threatening the mountain landscape. The Land Trust of Huntsville is one group who is working hard to protect our remaining treasures.

Their efforts have given us the Land Trust Loop *[see Hike 37]*. Another interesting hike at the Monte Sano Preserve is the Old Railroad Bed Trail. The trail follows the path of an old narrow gauge railroad used early in Huntsville's history and features many of the original trestles.

A brochure on the Old Railroad Bed Trail can be picked up free of charge at any Alabama Welcome Center along the interstates. Trail information can also be found online at *www.landtrust-hsv.org*. Call the Trust at (256) 534–5263 for more information. There is no charge to hike these trails. *[See Hike 37 for park directions and additional information.]* ***DeLorme: Alabama Atlas & Gazetteer:*** Page 19 D8

(P) Rainbow Mountain Trail – Land Trust of Huntsville

As already mentioned, the area around Huntsville is being heavily developed. The city, in conjunction with the Sierra Club and the Land Trust of Huntsville, set aside 65 acres of land in the Stoneridge Park area and developed 2.5 miles of trails.

The park features a unique geological landmark as its center. Balance Rock is a 75 to 100-foot boulder that resembles a toy top, and it literally stands on its point! There are other interesting rock formations around Balance Rock, including Slant Rock.

There is no charge to hike the trail. A "virtual hike" can be taken online at the Rainbow Mountain website at *www.geocities.com/Yosemite/Gorge/8186*. *[See Hike 37 for park directions and additional information.]* ***DeLorme: Alabama Atlas & Gazetteer:*** Page 19 D8

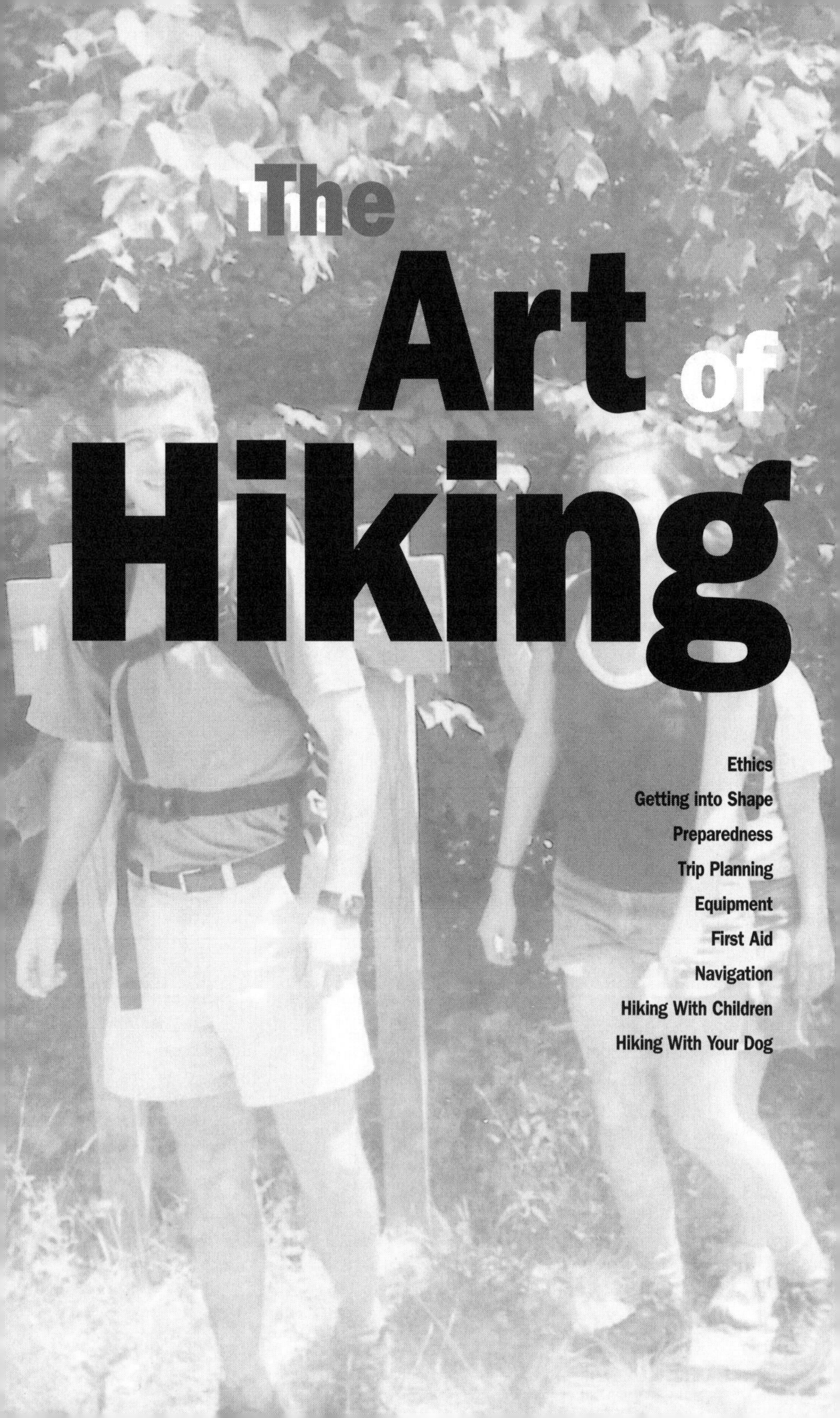

The Art of Hiking

Ethics

Getting into Shape

Preparedness

Trip Planning

Equipment

First Aid

Navigation

Hiking With Children

Hiking With Your Dog

The Art of Hiking

When standing nose to snout with a grizzly, you're probably not too concerned with the issue of ethical behavior in the wild. No doubt you're just wetting yourself. But let's be honest. How often are you nose to snout with a grizzly? For most of us, a hike into the "wild" means loading up the 4-Runner with everything North Face™ and driving to a toileted trailhead. Sure, you can mourn how civilized we've become—how GPS units have replaced natural instinct and Gortex, true-grit—but the silly gadgets of civilization aside, we have plenty of reason to take pride in how we've matured. With survival now on the back-burner, we've begun to reason—and it's about time—that we have a responsibility to protect, no longer just conquer, our wild places; that *they*, not *we*, are at risk. So please, do what you can. Now, in keeping with our chronic tendency to reduce everything to a list, here are some rules to remember.

Leave no trace. Always leave an area just like you found it—if not better than you found it. Avoid camping in fragile, alpine meadows and along the banks of streams and lakes. Use a camp stove versus building a wood fire. Pack up all of your trash and extra food. Bury human waste at least 100 feet from water sources under six to eight inches of topsoil. Don't bathe with soap in a lake or stream—use prepackaged moistened towels to wipe off sweat and dirt or bathe in the water without soap.

Stay on the trail. It's true, a path anywhere leads nowhere new, but purists will just have to get over it. Paths serve an important purpose; they limit our impact on natural areas. Straying from a designated trail may seem innocent but it can cause damage to sensitive areas—damage that may take years to recover, if it can recover at all. Even simple shortcuts can be destructive. So, please, stay on the trail.

Keep your dog under control. You can buy a flexi-lead that allows your dog to go exploring along the trail, while allowing you the ability to reel him in should another hiker approach or should he decide to chase a rabbit. Always obey leash laws and be sure to bury your dog's waste or pack it in resealable plastic bags.

Yield to horses. When you approach these animals on the trail, always step quietly off the trail and let them pass. If you are wearing a large backpack, it's a good idea to sit down. From a horse's perspective, a hiker wearing a large backpack is a scary trail monster and these sensitive animals can be spooked easily.

GETTING INTO SHAPE

Unless you want to be sore—and possibly have to shorten your trip or vacation—be sure to get in shape before a big hike. If you're terribly out of shape, start a walking program early, preferably eight weeks in advance. Start with a 15-minute walk during your lunch hour or after work and gradually increase your walking time to an hour. You should also increase your elevation gain. Walking briskly up hills really strengthens your leg muscles and gets your heart rate up. If you work in a storied office building, take the stairs instead of the elevator. If you prefer going to a gym, walk the treadmill or use a stair-master. You can further increase your strength and endurance by walking with a loaded backpack. Stationary exercises you might consider are squats, leg lifts, sit-ups, and push-ups. Other good ways to get in shape include biking, running, aerobics, and, of course, short hikes.

PREPAREDNESS

It's been said that failing to plan means planning to fail. So do take the necessary time to plan your trip. Whether going on a short day hike or an extended backpack trip, always prepare for the worst. Simply remembering to pack a copy of the *U.S. Army Survival Manual* is not preparedness. Although it's not a bad idea if you plan on entering truly wild places, it's merely the tourniquet answer to a problem. You need to do your best to prevent the problem from arising in the first place. These days the word "survival" is often replaced with the pathetically feeble term "comfort." In order to remain comfortable (and to survive if you really want to push it), you need to concern yourself with the basics: water, food, and shelter. Don't go on a hike without having these bases covered. And don't go on a hike expecting to find these items in the woods.

Water. Even in frigid conditions, you need at least two quarts of water a day to function efficiently. Add heat and taxing terrain and you can bump that figure up to one gallon. That's simply a base to work from—your metabolism and your level of conditioning can raise or lower that amount. Unless you know your level, assume that you need one gallon of water a day. Now, where do you plan on getting the water?

Preferably not from natural water sources. These sources can be loaded with intestinal disturbers, such as bacteria, viruses, and fertilizers. *Giardia lamblia*, the most common of these disturbers, is a protozoan parasite that lives part of its lifecycle as a cyst in water sources. The parasite spreads when mammals defecate in water sources. Once ingested, Giardia can induce cramping, diarrhea, vomiting, and fatigue within two days to two weeks after ingestion. Giarda is treatable with the prescription drug Flagyl. If you believe you've contracted Giardia, see a doctor immediately.

Treating Water. The best and easiest solution to avoid polluted water is to carry your water with you. Yet, depending on the nature of your hike and the duration, this may not be an option—seeing as one gallon of water weighs 8.5 pounds. In that case, you'll need to look into treating water.

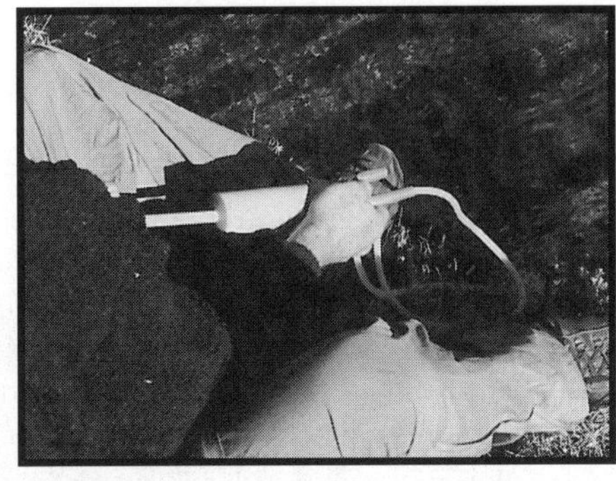

Regardless of which method you choose, you should always carry *some* water with you, in case of an emergency. Save this reserve until you absolutely need it.

There are three methods of treating water: boiling, chemical treatment, and filtering. If you boil water, it's recommended that you do so for 10 to 15 minutes. This is often impractical because you're forced to exhaust a great deal of your fuel supply. You can opt for chemical treatment (e.g. Potable Aqua) which will kill Giardia but will not take care of other chemical pollutants. Another drawback to chemical treatments is the unpleasant taste of the water after it's treated. You can remedy this by adding powdered drink mix to the water. Filters are the preferred method for treating water. Filters remove Giardia, organic and inorganic contaminants, and don't leave an aftertaste. Water filters are far from perfect as they can easily become clogged or leak if a gasket wears out. It's always a good idea to carry a back-up supply of chemical treatment tablets in case your filter decides to quit on you.

Food. If we're talking about "survival," you can go days without food, as long as you have water. But we're talking about "comfort" here. Try to avoid foods that are high in sugar and fat like candy bars and potato chips. These food types are harder to digest and are low in nutritional value. Instead, bring along foods that are easy to pack, nutritious, and high in energy (e.g. bagels, nutrition bars, dehydrated fruit, gorp, and jerky). If you are on an overnight trip, easy-to-fix dinners include rice mixes with dehydrated potatoes, corn pasta with cheese sauce, and soup mixes. For a tasty breakfast, you can fix hot oatmeal with brown sugar and reconstituted milk powder topped off with banana chips. If you like a hot drink in the morning, bring along herbal tea bags or hot chocolate. If you are a coffee junkie, you can purchase coffee that is packaged like tea bags. You can pre-package all of your meals in heavy-duty resealable plastic bags to keep food from spilling in your pack. These bags can be reused to pack out trash.

Shelter. The type of shelter you choose depends less on the conditions than on your tolerance for discomfort. Shelter comes in many forms—tent, tarp, lean to, bivy sack, cabin, cave, etc. If you're camping in the desert, a bivy sack may suffice, but if you're above the treeline and a storm is approaching, a better choice is a three or four season tent. Tents are the logical and most popular choice for most backpackers as they're lightweight and packable—and you can rest assured that you always have shelter from the elements. *[See Equipment: Tents on page 337]* Before you leave on your trip, anticipate what the weather and terrain will be like and plan for the type of shelter that will work best for your comfort level.

Finding a campsite. If there are established campsites, stick to those. If not, start looking for a campsite early—like around 3:30 or 4:00 pm. Stop at the first decent site you see. Depending on the area, it could be a long time before you find another suitable location. Pitch your camp in an area that's level. Make sure the area is at least 200 feet from fragile areas like lakeshores, meadows, and stream banks. And try to avoid areas thick in underbrush, as they can harbor insects and provide cover for approaching animals.

If you are camping in stormy, rainy weather, look for a rock outcrop or a shelter in the trees to keep the wind from blowing your tent all night. Be sure that you don't camp under trees with dead limbs that might break off on top of you. Also, try to find an area that has an absorbent surface, such as sandy soil or forest duff. This, in addition to camping on a surface with a slight angle, will provide better drainage. By all means, don't dig trenches to provide drainage around your tent—remember you're practicing minimum-impact camping.

If you're in bear country, steer clear of creekbeds or animal paths. If you see any signs of a bear's presence (i.e. scat, footprints), relocate. You'll need to find a campsite near a tall tree where you can hang your food and other items that may attract bears such as deodorant, toothpaste, or soap. Carry a lightweight nylon rope with which to hang your food. As a rule, you should hang your food at least 20 feet from the ground and five feet away from the tree trunk. You can put food and other items in a waterproof stuff sack and tie one end of the rope to the stuff sack. To get the other end of the rope over the tree branch, tie a good size rock to it and gently toss the rock over the tree branch. Pull the stuff sack up until it reaches the top of the branch and tie it off securely. Don't hang your food near your tent! If possible, hang your food at least 100 feet away from your campsite. Alternatives to hanging your food are bear-proof plastic tubes and metal bear boxes.

Lastly, think of comfort. Lie down on the ground where you intend to sleep and see if it's a good fit. For morning warmth (and a nice view to wake up to), have your tent face east.

FIRST AID

I know you're tough, but get 10 miles into the woods and develop a blister and you'll wish you had carried that first aid kit. Face it, it's just plain good sense. Many companies produce light-weight, compact first aid kits, just make sure yours contains at least the following:

First Aid

- band aids
- mole skin
- various sterile gauze and dressings
- white surgical tape
- an ace bandage
- an antihistamine
- aspirin
- Betadine® solution
- a First aid book
- Tums®
- tweezers
- scissors
- anti-bacterial wipes
- triple-antibiotic ointment
- plastic gloves
- sterile cotton tip applicators
- syrup of ipecac (to induce vomiting)
- a thermometer
- a wire splint

Here are a few tips to dealing with and hopefully preventing certain ailments.

Sunburn. To avoid sunburn, wear sunscreen (SPF 15 or higher), protective clothing, and a wide-brimmed hat when you are hiking in sunny weather. If you do get sunburn, treat the area with aloe vera gel and protect the area from further sun exposure.

Blisters. Be prepared to take care of these hike-spoilers by carrying moleskin (a lightly padded adhesive), gauze and tape, or Band-Aids. An effective way to apply moleskin is to cut out a circle of moleskin and remove the center—like a donut—and place it over the blistered area. Cutting the center out will reduce the pressure applied to the sensitive skin. Other products that can help you combat blisters are Bodyglide® and Second Skin®. Bodyglide® (1–888–263–9454) is applied to suspicious hot spots before a blister forms to help decrease friction to that area. Second Skin® (made by Spenco) is applied to the blister after it has popped and acts as a "second skin" to help prevent further irritation.

Insect bites and stings. You can treat most insect bites and stings by applying hydrocortisone 1% cream topically and taking a pain medication such as ibuprofen or acetaminophen to reduce swelling. If you forgot to pack these items, a cold compress or a paste of mud and ashes can sometimes assuage the itching and discomfort. Remove any stingers by using tweezers or scraping the area with your fingernail or a knife blade. Don't pinch the area as you'll only spread the venom.

Some hikers are highly sensitive to bites and stings and may have a serious allergic reaction that can be life threatening. Symptoms of a serious allergic reaction can include wheezing, an asthmatic attack, and shock. The treatment for this severe type of reaction is epinephrine (Adrenaline). If you know that you are sensitive to bites and stings, carry a pre-packaged kit of epinephrine (e.g., Anakit®), which can be obtained only by prescription from your doctor.

Ticks. As you well know, ticks can carry disease, such as Rocky Mountain Spotted Fever and Lyme disease. The best defense is, of course, prevention. If you know you're going to be hiking through an area littered with ticks, wear long pants and a long sleeved shirt. You can apply a permethrin repellent to your clothing and a DEET repellent to exposed skin. At the end of your hike, do a spot check for ticks (and insects in general). If you do find a tick, coat the insect with Vaseline® or tree sap to cut off its air supply. The tick should release its hold, but if it doesn't, grab the head of the tick firmly—with a pair of tweezers if you have them—and gently pull it away from the skin with a twisting motion. Sometimes the mouthparts linger, embedded in your skin. If this happens, try to remove them with a disinfected needle. Clean the affected area with an anti-bacterial cleanser and then apply triple antibiotic ointment. Monitor the area for a few days. If irritation persists or a white spot develops, see a doctor for possible infection.

Poison ivy, oak, and sumac. These skin irritants can be found most anywhere in North America and come in the form of a bush or a vine, having leaflets in groups of three, five, seven, or nine. Learn how to spot the plants. The oil they secrete can cause an allergic reaction in the form of blisters, usually about 12 hours after exposure. The itchy rash can last from ten days to several weeks. The best defense against these irritants is to wear protective clothing and to apply a non-prescription product called IvyBlock® to exposed skin. This lotion is meant to guard against the affects of poison ivy/oak/sumac and can be washed off with soap and water. Taking a hot shower after you return home from your hike will also help to remove any lingering oil from your skin. Should you contract a rash from any of these plants, use Benadryl® or a similar product to reduce the itching. If the rash is localized, create a light Clorox®/water wash to dry up the area. If the rash has spread, either tough it out or see your doctor about getting a dose of Cortisone® (available both orally and by injection).

poison ivy

poison oak

poison sumac

Snakebites. First off, snakebites are rare in North America. Unless startled or provoked, the majority of snakes will not bite. If you are wise to their habitats and keep a careful eye on the trail, you should be just fine. Though your chances of being struck are slim, it's wise to know what to do in the event you are.

If a *non-poisonous* snake bites you, allow the wound to bleed a small amount and then cleanse the wounded area with a Betadine® solution (10% povidone iodine). Rinse the wound with clean water (preferably) or fresh urine (it might sound ugly, but it's sterile). Once the area is clean, cover it with triple antibiotic ointment and a clean bandage. Remember, most residual damage from snakebites, poisonous or otherwise, comes from infection, not the snake's venom. Keep the area as clean as possible and get medical attention immediately.

If you are bitten by a *poisonous* snake, remove the toxin with a suctioning device, found in a snakebite kit. If you do not have such a device, squeeze the wound—do NOT use your mouth for suction as the venom will enter your bloodstream through the vessels under the tongue and head straight for your heart. Then, clean the wound just as you would a non-poisonous bite. Tie a clean band of cloth snuggly around the afflicted appendage, about an inch or so above the bite (or the rim of the swelling). This is NOT a tourniquet—you want to simply slow the blood flow, not cut it off. Loosen the band if numbness ensues. Remove the band for a minute and re-apply a little higher every ten minutes

If it is your friend who's been bitten, treat him or her for shock—make him comfortable, have him lie down, elevate the legs, and keep him warm. Avoid applying anything cold to the bite wound. Immobilize the affected area and remove any constricting items such as rings, watches, or restrictive clothing—swelling may occur. Once your friend is stable and relatively calm, hike out to get help. The victim should get treatment within 12 hours, ideally, which usually consists of a tetanus shot, antivenin, and antibiotics.

Now, if you are alone and struck by a poisonous snake, stay calm. Hysteria will only quicken the venom's spread. Follow the procedure above and do your best to reach help. When hiking out, don't run—you'll only increase the flow of blood throughout your system. Instead, walk calmly.

In terms of poisonous snakes, five of the six varieties found in Alabama belong to the pit viper group: the copperhead, cottonmouth, timber rattlesnake, diamondback rattlesnake, and pigmy rattlesnake. These snakes vary in color and marking but are identified by a small "pit" found between the eye and nostril. Be especially careful of where you put your hands and feet with rattlers around since they enjoy sunning themselves on rock ledges and outcroppings. The last poisonous snake found in Alabama is the rarely seen coral snake, characterized by bands of red and black, separated by narrow bands of yellow.

Dehydration. Have you ever hiked in hot weather and had a roaring headache and felt fatigued after only a few miles? More than likely you were dehydrated. Symptoms of dehydration include fatigue, headache, and decreased coordination and judgment. When you are hiking, your body's rate of fluid loss depends on the outside temperature, humidity, altitude, and your activity level. On average, a hiker walking in warm weather will lose four liters of fluid a day. That fluid loss is easily replaced by normal consumption of liquids and food. However, if a hiker is walking briskly in hot, dry weather and hauling a heavy pack, he can lose one to three liters of water an hour. It's important to always carry plenty of water and to stop often and drink fluids regularly, even if you aren't thirsty.

Heat exhaustion is the result of a loss of large amounts of electrolytes and often occurs if a hiker is dehydrated and has been under heavy exertion. Common symptoms of heat exhaustion include cramping, exhaustion, fatigue, lightheadedness, and nausea. You can treat heat exhaustion by getting out of the sun and drinking an electrolyte solution made up of one teaspoon of salt and one tablespoon of sugar dissolved in a liter of water. Drink this solution slowly over a period of one hour. Drinking plenty of fluids (preferably an electrolyte solution like Gatorade®) can prevent heat exhaustion. Avoid hiking during the hottest parts of the day and wear breathable clothing, a wide brimmed hat, and sunglasses.

Hypothermia is one of the biggest dangers in the backcountry—especially for day hikers in the summertime. That may sound strange, but imagine starting out on a hike in mid-summer when it's sunny and 80 degrees out. You're clad in nylon shorts and a cotton T-shirt. About halfway through your hike, the sky begins to cloud up and in the next hour a light drizzle begins to fall and the wind starts to pick up. Before you know it, you are soaking wet and shivering—the perfect recipe for hypothermia. More advanced signs include decreased coordination, slurred speech, and blurred vision. When a victim's temperature falls below 92 degrees Fahrenheit, the blood pressure and pulse plummet, possibly leading to coma and death.

To avoid hypothermia, always bring a windproof/rainproof shell, a fleece jacket, Capilene tights, gloves, and hat when you are hiking in the mountains. Learn to adjust your clothing layers based on the temperature. If you are climbing uphill at a moderate pace you will stay warm, but when you stop for a break you'll become cold quickly, unless you add more layers of clothing.

If a hiker is showing advanced signs of hypothermia, dress him in dry clothes and make sure he is wearing a hat and gloves. Place him in a sleeping bag in a tent or shelter that will protect him from the wind and other elements. Give him warm fluids to drink and keep him awake.

Frostbite. When the mercury dips below 32 degrees Fahrenheit, your extremities begin to chill. If a persistent chill attacks a localized area, say your hands or your toes, the circulatory system reacts by cutting off blood flow to the affected area—the idea being to protect and preserve the body's overall temperature. And so it's death by attrition for the affected area. Ice crystals start to form from the water in the cells of the neglected tissue. Deprived of heat, nourishment, and now water, the tissue literally starves. This is frostbite.

Prevention is your best defense against this situation. Most prone to frostbite are your face, hands, and feet—so protect these areas well. Wool is the material of choice because it provides ample air space for insulation and draws moisture away from the skin. However, synthetic fabrics have recently made great strides in the cold weather clothing market. Do your research. A pair of light silk liners under your regular gloves is a good trick to keeping warm. They afford some additional warmth, but more importantly they'll allow you to remove your mitts for tedious work without exposing the skin.

Now, if your feet or hands start to feel cold or numb due to the elements, warm them as quickly as possible. Place cold hands under your armpits or bury them in your crotch. If your feet are cold, change your socks. If there's plenty of room in your boots, add another pair of socks. Do remember though that constricting your feet in tight boots can restrict blood flow and actually make your feet colder more quickly. Your socks need to have breathing room if they're going to be effective. Dead air provides insulation. If your face is cold, place your warm hands over your face or simply wear a head stocking (called a balaclava).

Should your skin go numb and start to appear white and waxy, chances are you've got or are developing frostbite. Don't try to thaw the area unless you can maintain the warmth. In other words, don't stop to warm up your frostbitten feet only to head back on the trail. You'll do more damage than good. Tests have shown that hikers who walked on thawed feet did more harm, and endured more pain, than hikers who left the affected areas alone. Do your best to get out of the cold entirely and seek medical attention—which usually consists of performing a rapid rewarming in water for 20 to 30 minutes.

The overall objective in preventing both hypothermia and frostbite is to keep the body's core warm. Protect key areas where heat escapes, like the top of the head, and maintain the proper nutrition level. Foods that are high in calories aid the body in producing heat. Never smoke or drink when you're in situations where the cold is threatening. By affecting blood flow, these activities ultimately cool the body's core temperature.

NAVIGATION

Whether you are going on a short hike in a familiar area or planning a weeklong backpack trip, you should always be equipped with the proper navigational equipment—at the very least a detailed map and a sturdy compass.

Maps. There are many different types of maps available to help you find your way on the trail. Easiest to find are Forest Service maps and BLM (Bureau of Land Management) maps. These maps tend to cover large areas, so be sure they are detailed enough for your particular trip. You can also obtain National Park maps as well as high quality maps from private companies and trail groups. These maps can be obtained either from outdoor stores or ranger stations.

U.S. Geological Survey topographic maps are particularly popular with hikers—especially serious backcountry hikers. These maps contain the standard map symbols such as roads, lakes, and rivers, as well as contour lines that show the details of the trail terrain like ridges, valleys, passes, and mountain peaks. The 7.5-minute series (1 inch on the map equals approximately two-fifths of a mile on the ground) provides the closest inspection available. USGS maps are available by mail (U.S. Geological Survey, Map Distribution Branch, PO Box 25286, Denver, Colorado 80225) or you can visit them online at *http://mapping.usgs.gov/esic/to_order.html.*

If you want to check out the high tech world of maps, you can purchase topographic maps on CD-ROM. These software-mapping programs let you select a route on your computer, print it out, and then take it with you on the trail. Some software mapping programs let you insert symbols and labels, download waypoints from a GPS unit, and export the maps to other software programs. Mapping software programs such as DeLorme's TopoUSA™ (*www.delorme.com*) and MAPTECH's Terrain Navigator™ (*www.maptech.com*) let you do all of these things and more.

The art of map reading is a skill that you can develop by first practicing in an area you are familiar with. To begin, orient the map so the map is lined up in the correct direction (i.e. north on the map is lined up with true north). Next, familiarize yourself with the map symbols and try and match them up with terrain features around you such as a high ridge, mountain peak, river, or lake. If you are practicing with an USGS map notice the contour lines. On gentler terrain these contour lines are spaced further apart, and on steeper terrain they are closer together. Pick a short loop trail and stop frequently to check your position on the map. As you practice map reading, you'll learn how to anticipate a steep section on the trail or a good place to take a rest break, etc.

The Compass. First off, the sun is not a substitute for a compass. So, what kind of compass should you have? Here are some characteristics you should look for: a rectangular base with detailed scales, a liquid-filled housing, protective housing, a sighting line on the mirror, luminous alignment and back-bearing arrows, a luminous north-seeking arrow, and a well-defined bezel ring.

You can learn compass basics by reading the detailed instructions included with your compass. If you want to fine-tune your compass skills, sign up for an orienteering class or purchase a book on compass reading. Once you've learned the basic skills on using a compass, remember to practice these skills before you head into the backcountry.

If you are a klutz at using a compass, you may be interested in checking out the technical wizardry of the **GPS (Global Positioning System)** device. The GPS was developed by the Pentagon and works off 24 NAVSTAR satellites, which were designed to guide missiles to their targets. A GPS device is a handheld unit that calculates your latitude and longitude with the easy press of a button. However, the crafty defense department doesn't want civilians (or spies) to have the same pinpoint accuracy, so they have purposefully mixed the signals a bit so a GPS unit's accuracy is generally within 100 meters or 328 feet.

There are many different types of GPS units available and they range in price from $100 to $400. In general, all GPS units have a display screen and keypad where you input information. In addition to acting as a compass, the unit allows you to plot your route, easily retrace your path, track your travelling speed, find the mileage between waypoints, and calculate the total mileage of your route.

Before you purchase a GPS unit, keep in mind that these devices don't pick up signals indoors, in heavily wooded areas, on mountain peaks, or in deep valleys.

A **pedometer** is a handy device that can track your mileage as you hike. This device is a small, clip-on unit with a digital display that calculates your hiking distance in miles or kilometers based on your walking stride. Some units also calculate the calories you burn and your total hiking time. Pedometers are available at most large outdoor stores and range in price from $20 to $40.

TRIP PLANNING

Planning your hiking adventure begins with letting a friend or relative know your trip itinerary so they can call for help if you don't return at your scheduled time. Your next task is to make sure you are outfitted to experience the risks and rewards of the trail. This section highlights gear and clothing you may want to take with you to get the most out of your hike.

Day Hikes

- camera/film
- compass/GPS unit
- pedometer
- daypack
- First aid kit
- food
- guidebook
- headlamp/flashlight with extra batteries and bulbs
- hat
- insect repellant
- knife/multi-purpose tool
- map
- matches in waterproof container and fire starter
- polar fleece jacket
- raingear
- space blanket
- sunglasses
- sunscreen
- swim suit
- watch
- water
- water bottles/water hydration system

EQUIPMENT

With the outdoor market currently flooded with products, many of which are pure gimmickry, it seems impossible to both differentiate and choose. Do I really need a tropical-fish-lined collapsible shower? (No, you don't.) The only defense against the maddening quantity of items thrust in your face is to think practically—and to do so *before* you go shopping. The worst buys are impulsive buys. Since most of your name brands will differ only slightly in quality, it's best to know what you're looking for in terms of function. Buy only what you need. You will, don't forget, be carrying what you've bought on your back. Here are some things to keep in mind before you go shopping.

Overnight Trips

- backpack and waterproof rain cover
- backpacker's trowel
- bandanna
- bear repellant spray
- bear bell
- biodegradable soap
- pot scrubber
- collapsible water container (2-3 gallon capacity)
- clothing—extra wool socks, shirt and shorts
- cook set/utensils
- ditty bags to store gear
- extra plastic resealable bags
- gaiters
- garbage bag
- ground cloth
- journal/pen
- nylon rope to hang food
- long underwear
- permit (if required)
- rain jacket and pants
- sandals to wear around camp and to ford streams
- sleeping bag
- waterproof stuff sack
- sleeping pad
- small bath towel
- stove and fuel
- tent
- toiletry items
- water filter
- whistle

Clothes. Clothing is your armor against Mother Nature's little surprises. Although Alabama's weather isn't generally severe, even in the winter months, buying clothing that can be worn in layers is always a good strategy. In the winter months the first layer you'll want to wear is a "wicking" layer of long underwear that keeps perspiration away from your skin. Wearing long underwear made from synthetic fibers such as Capilene, Coolmax, or Thermax is an excellent choice. These fabrics wick moisture away from the skin and draw it toward the next layer of clothing where it then evaporates. Avoid wearing long underwear made of cotton as it is slow to dry and keeps moisture next to your skin.

The second layer you'll wear is the "insulating" layer. Aside from keeping you warm, this layer needs to "breathe" so you stay dry while hiking. A fabric that provides insulation and dries quickly is fleece. It's interesting to note that this one-of-a-kind fabric is made out of recycled plastic. Purchasing a zip-up jacket made of this material is highly recommended.

The last line of layering defense is the "shell" layer. You'll need some type of waterproof, windproof, breathable jacket that'll fit over all of your other layers. It should have a large hood that fits over a hat. You'll also need a good pair of rain pants made from a similar waterproof, breathable fabric. A fabric that easily fits the bill is GORE-TEX®. However, while a quality GOR-TEX jacket can range in price from $100 to $450, you should know that there are more affordable fabrics out there that work just as well.

Now that you've learned the basics of layering, you can't forget to protect your hands and face. In cold, windy, or rainy weather you'll need a hat made of wool or fleece and insulated, waterproof gloves that will keep your hands warm and toasty. As mentioned earlier, buying an additional pair of light silk liners to wear under your regular gloves is a good idea. They'll allow you to remove your outer-gloves for tedious work without exposing the skin.

Footwear. If you have any extra money to spend on your trip, put that money into boots or trail shoes. Poor shoes will bring a hike to a halt faster than anything else. To avoid this annoyance, buy shoes that provide support and are lightweight and flexible. A lightweight hiking boot is better than a heavy, leather mountaineering boot for most day hikes and backpacking. Trail running shoes provide a little extra cushion and are made in a high-top style that many people wear for hiking. These running shoes are lighter, more flexible, and more breathable than hiking boots. If you know you'll be hiking in wet weather often, purchase boots or shoes with a GORE-TEX® liner, which will help keep your feet dry.

When buying your boots, be sure to wear the same type of socks you'll be wearing on the trail. If the boots you're buying are for cold weather hiking, try the boots on while wearing two pairs of socks. Speaking of socks, a good cold weather sock combination is to wear a thinner sock made of wool or polypropylene covered by a heavier outer sock made of wool. The inner sock protects the foot from the rubbing effects of the outer sock and prevents blisters.

Once you've purchased your footwear, be sure to break them in before you hit the trail. New footwear is often stiff and needs to be stretched and molded to your foot.

Backpacks. No matter what type of hiking you do you'll need a pack of some sort to carry the basic trail essentials. There are a variety of backpacks on the market, but let's first discuss what you intend to use it for. Day hikes or overnight trips?

If you plan on doing a day hike, a daypack should have some of the following characteristics: a padded hip belt that's at least two inches in diameter (avoid packs with only a small nylon piece of webbing for a hip belt); a chest strap (the chest strap helps stabilize the pack against your body); external pockets to carry water and other items that you want easy access to; an internal pocket to hold keys, a knife, a wallet, and other miscellaneous items; an external lashing system to hold a jacket; and a hydration pocket for carrying a hydration system (which consists of a water bladder with an attachable drinking hose).

For short hikes, some hikers like to use a fanny pack to store just a camera, food, a compass, a map, and other trail essentials. Most fanny packs have pockets for two water bottles and a padded hip belt.

If you intend to do an extended, overnight trip, there are multiple considerations. First off, you need to decide what kind of framed pack you want. There are two backpack types for backpacking: the internal frame and the external frame. An internal frame pack rests closer to your body, making it more stable and easier to balance when hiking over rough terrain. An external frame pack is just that, an aluminum frame attached to the exterior of the pack. An external frame pack is better for long backpack trips because it distributes the pack weight better and you can carry heavier loads. It's easier to pack, and your gear is more accessible. It also offers better back ventilation in hot weather.

The most critical measurement for fitting a pack is torso length. The pack needs to rest evenly on your hips without sagging. A good pack will come in two or three sizes and have straps and hip belts that are adjustable according to your body size and characteristics.

When you purchase a backpack, go to an outdoor store with salespeople who are knowledgeable in how to properly fit a pack. Once the pack is fitted for you, load the pack with the amount of weight you plan on taking on the trail. The weight of the pack should be distributed evenly and you should be able to swing your arms and walk briskly without feeling out of balance. Another good technique for evaluating a pack is to walk up and down stairs and make quick turns to the right and to the left to be sure the pack doesn't feel out of balance.

Other features that are nice to have on a backpack include a removable day pack or fanny pack, external pockets for extra water, and extra lash points to attach a jacket or other items.

Sleeping bags and pads. Sleeping bags are rated by temperature. You can purchase a bag made of synthetic fiber such as Polarguard® HV or DuPont Hollofil® II, or you can buy a goose down bag. Goose down bags are more expensive, but they have a higher insulating capacity by weight and will keep their loft longer. You'll want to purchase a bag with a temperature rating that fits the time of year and conditions you are most likely to camp in. One caveat: the techno-standard for temperature ratings is far from perfect. Ratings vary from manufacturer to manufacturer, so to protect yourself you should purchase a bag rated 10 to 15 degrees below the temperature you expect to be camping in. Synthetic bags are more resistant to water than down bags, but many down bags are now made with a GORE-TEX® shell that helps to repel water. Down bags are also more compressible than synthetic bags and take up less room in your pack, which is an important consideration if you are planning a multi-day backpack trip. Features to look for in a sleeping bag include: a mummy style bag, a hood you can cinch down around your head in cold weather, and draft tubes along the zippers that help keep heat in and drafts out.

You'll also want a sleeping pad to provide insulation and padding from the cold ground. There are different types of sleeping pads available, from the more expensive self-inflating air mattresses to the less expensive closed-cell foam pads (e.g., Ridge Rest®). Self-inflating air mattresses are usually heavier than closed-cell foam mattresses and are prone to punctures.

Tents. The tent is your home away from home while on the trail. It provides protection from wind, snow, rain, and insects. A three-season tent is a good choice for backpacking and can range in price from $100 to $500. These lightweight and versatile tents provide protection in all types of weather, except heavy snowstorms or high winds, and range in weight from four to eight pounds. Look for a tent that's easy to set up and will easily fit two people with gear. Dome type tents usually offer more headroom and places to store gear. Other tent designs include a vestibule where you can store wet boots and backpacks. Some nice-to-have items in a tent include interior pockets to store small items and lashing points to hang a clothesline. Most three-season tents also come with stakes so you can secure the tent in high winds. Before you purchase a tent, set it up and take it down a few times to be sure it is easy to handle. Also, sit inside the tent and make sure it has enough room for you and your gear.

HIKING WITH CHILDREN

Hiking with children isn't a matter of how many miles you can cover or how much elevation gain you make in a day, it's about seeing and experiencing nature through their eyes.

Kids like to explore and have fun. They like to stop and point out bugs and plants, look under rocks, jump in puddles, and throw sticks. If you're taking a toddler or young child on a hike, start with a trail that you're familiar with. Trails that have interesting things for kids, like piles of leaves to play in or a small stream to wade through during the summer, will make the hike much more enjoyable for them and will keep them from getting bored.

You can keep your child's attention if you have a strategy before starting on the trail. Using games is not only an effective way to keep a child's attention, it's also a great way to teach him or her about nature. Play hide and seek, where your child is the mouse and you are the hawk. Quiz children on the names of plants and animals. If your children are old enough, let them carry their own daypack filled with snacks and water. So that you are sure to go at their pace and not yours, let them lead the way. Playing follow the leader works particularly well when you have a group of children. Have each child take a turn at being the leader.

With children, a lot of clothing is key. The only thing predictable about weather is that it will change. Even in Alabama the weather can sometimes be unpredictable, so you always want to bring extra clothing for your children no matter what the season. In the winter, have your children wear wool socks, and warm layers such as long underwear, a polar fleece jacket and hat, wool mittens, and good rain gear. It's not a bad idea to have these along in late fall and early spring as well. Good footwear is also important. A sturdy pair of high top tennis shoes or lightweight hiking boots are the best bet for little ones. If you're hiking in the summer near a lake or stream, bring along a pair of old sneakers that your child can put on when he wants to go exploring in the water. Remember when you're near any type of water, always watch your child at all times. Also, keep a close eye on teething toddlers who may decide a rock or leaf of poison oak is an interesting item to put in their mouth.

From spring through fall, you'll want your kids to wear a wide brimmed hat to keep their face, head, and ears protected from the hot sun. Also, make sure your children wear sunscreen at all times. Choose a brand without Paba—children have sensitive skin and may have an allergic reaction to sunscreen that contains Paba. If you are hiking with a child younger than six months, don't use sunscreen or insect repellant. Instead, be sure that their head, face, neck, and ears are protected from the sun with a wide brimmed hat, and that all other skin exposed to the sun is protected with the appropriate clothing.

Remember that food is fun. Kids like snacks so it's important to bring a lot of munchies for the trail. Stopping often for snack breaks is a fun way to keep the trail interesting. Raisins, apples, granola bars, crackers and cheese, Cheerios, and trail mix all make great snacks. If your child is old enough to carry his/her own backpack, fill it with treats before you leave. If your kids don't like drinking water, you can bring boxes of fruit juice.

Avoid poorly designed child-carrying packs—you don't want to break your back carrying your child. Most child-carrying backpacks designed to hold a 40-pound child will contain a large carrying pocket to hold diapers and other items. Some have an optional rain/sun hood. Tough Traveler® (1–800–GO–TOUGH or *www.toughtraveler.com*) is a company that specializes in making backpacks for carrying children and other outdoor gear for children.

HIKING WITH YOUR DOG

Bringing your furry friend with you is always more fun than leaving him behind. Our canine pals make great trail buddies because they never complain and always make good company. Hiking with your dog can be a rewarding experience, especially if you plan ahead.

Getting your dog in shape. Before you plan outdoor adventures with your dog, make sure he's in shape for the trail. Getting your dog into shape takes the same discipline as getting yourself into shape, but luckily, your dog can get in shape with you. Take your dog with you on your daily runs or walks. If there is a park near your house, hit a tennis ball or play Frisbee with your dog.

Swimming is also an excellent way to get your dog into shape. If there is a lake or river near where you live and your dog likes the water, have him retrieve a tennis ball or stick. Gradually build your dog's stamina up over a two to three month period. A good rule of thumb is to assume that your dog will travel twice as far as you will on the trail. If you plan on doing a five-mile hike, be sure your dog is in shape for a ten-mile hike.

Training your dog for the trail. Before you go on your first hiking adventure with your dog, be sure he has a firm grasp on the basics of canine etiquette and behavior. Make sure he can sit, lay down, stay, and come. One of the most important commands you can teach your canine pal is to "come" under any situation. It's easy for your friend's nose to lead him astray or possibly get lost. Another helpful command is the "get behind" command. When you're on a hiking trail that's narrow, you can have your dog follow behind you when other trail users approach. Nothing is more bothersome than an enthusiastic dog that runs back and forth on the trail and disrupts the peace of the trail for others. When you see other trail users approaching you on the trail, give them the right of way by quietly stepping off the trail and making your dog lie down and stay until they pass.

Equipment. The most critical pieces of equipment you can invest in for your dog are proper identification and a sturdy leash. Flexi-leads work well for hiking because they give your dog more freedom to explore but still leave you in control. Make sure your dog has identification that includes your name and address and a number for your veterinarian. Other forms of identification for your dog include a tattoo or a microchip. You should consult your veterinarian for more information on these last two options.

The next piece of equipment you'll want to consider is a pack for your dog. By no means should you hold all of your dog's essentials in your pack—let him carry his own gear! Dogs that are in good shape can carry up to 30 percent to 40 percent of their own weight.

Companies that make good quality packs include RuffWear™ (1–888–RUFF–WEAR; *www.ruffwear.com*) and Wolf Packs® (1–541–482–7669; *www.wolfpacks.com*). Most packs are fitted by a dog's weight and girth measurement. Companies that make dog packs generally include guidelines to help you pick out the size that's right for your dog. Some characteristics to look for when purchasing a pack for your dog include: a harness that contains two padded girth straps, a padded chest strap, leash attachments, removable saddle bags, internal water bladders, and external gear cords.

You can introduce your dog to the pack by first placing the empty pack on his back and letting him wear it around the yard. Keep an eye on him during this first introduction. He may decide to chew through the straps if you aren't watching him closely. Once he learns to treat the pack as an object of fun and not a foreign enemy, fill the pack evenly on both sides with a few ounces of dog food in resealable plastic bags. Have your dog wear his pack on your daily walks for a period of two to three weeks. Each week add a little more weight to the pack until your dog will accept carrying the maximum amount of weight he can carry.

You can also purchase collapsible water and dog food bowls for your dog. These bowls are lightweight and can easily be stashed into your pack or your dog's. If you are hiking on rocky terrain or in the snow, you can purchase footwear for your dog that will protect his feet from cuts and bruises. All of these products can be purchased from RuffWear™ (1–888–RUFF–WEAR; *www.ruffwear.com*).

The following is a checklist of items to bring when you take your dog hiking: collapsible water bowls, a comb, a collar and a leash, dog food, a dog pack, flea/tick powder, paw protection, water, and a First Aid kit that contains eye ointment, tweezers, scissors, stretchy foot wrap, gauze, antibacterial wash, sterile cotton tip applicators, antibiotic ointment, and cotton wrap.

First aid for your dog. Your dog is just as prone—if not more prone—to getting in trouble on the trail as you are, so be prepared. Here's a run down of the more likely misfortunes that might befall your little friend.

Bees and wasps. If a bee or wasp stings your dog, remove the stinger with a pair of tweezers and place a mudpack or a cloth dipped in cold water over the affected area.

Heat stroke. Avoid hiking with your dog in really hot weather. Dogs with heat stroke will pant excessively, lie down and refuse to get up, and become lethargic and disoriented. If your dog shows any of these signs on the trail, have him lie down in the shade. If you are near a stream, pour cool water over your dog's entire body to help bring his body temperature back to normal.

Heartworm. Dogs get heartworms from mosquitoes which carry the disease in the prime mosquito months of July and August. Giving your dog a monthly pill prescribed by your veterinarian easily prevents this condition.

Plant pitfalls. One of the biggest plant hazards for dogs on the trail are foxtails. Foxtails are pointed grass seed heads that bury themselves in your friend's fur, between his toes, and even get in his ear canal. If left unattended, these nasty seeds can work their way under the skin and cause abscesses and other problems. If you have a longhaired dog, consider trimming the hair between his toes and giving him a summer haircut to help prevent foxtails from attaching to his fur. After every hike, always look over your dog for these seeds—especially between his toes and his ears.

Other plant hazards include burrs, thorns, thistles, and poison oak. If you find any burrs or thistles on your dog, remove them as soon as possible before they become an unmanageable mat. Thorns can pierce a dog's foot and cause a great deal of pain. If you see that your dog is lame, stop and check his feet for thorns. Dogs are immune to poison oak but they can pick up the sticky, oily substance from the plant and transfer it to you.

Protect those paws. Be sure to keep your dog's nails trimmed so he avoids getting soft tissue or joint injuries. If your dog slows and refuses to go on, check to see that his paws aren't torn or worn. You can protect your dog's paws from trail hazards such as sharp gravel, foxtails, lava scree, and thorns by purchasing dog boots.

Sunburn. If your dog has light skin he is an easy target for sunburn on his nose and other exposed skin areas. You can apply a non-toxic sunscreen to exposed skin areas that will help protect him from over-exposure to the sun.

Ticks and fleas. Ticks can easily give your dog Lyme disease, as well as other diseases. Before you hit the trail, treat your dog with a flea and tick spray or powder. You can also ask your veterinarian about a once-a-month pour-on treatment that repels fleas and ticks.

When you are finally ready to hit the trail with your dog, keep in mind that National Parks and many wilderness areas do not allow dogs on trails. Your best bet is to hike in National forests, BLM lands, and state parks. Always call ahead to see what the restrictions are.

Contact Info

General State Information

Alabama Bureau of Tourism – *www.touralabama.org*
532A Perry Street, Montgomery, AL 36104
(334) 261–4169 or 1–800–ALABAMA

Alabama Live (Webpage of Alabama's major newspapers) – *www.alabamalive.com*

Birmingham Chamber of Commerce – *www.birminghamchamber.com*
2027 1st Ave. No., Birmingham, AL 35203 (205) 250–7669

Calhoun County Chamber of Commerce – *www.calhounchamber.org*
PO Box 1087, Anniston, AL 36202 (256) 237–3536

City of Mobile Department of Tourism – *www.mobile.org*
1 South Water St., Mobile, AL 36602 1–800–252–3862

Dothan Convention & Visitors Bureau – *www.dothanalcvb.com*
PO Box 8765, Dothan, AL 36304 (334) 794–6622

Eastern Shore Chamber of Commerce – *www.siteone.com/towns/chamber*
29750 Larry Dawyer Dr., P.O. Box 310, Daphne, AL 36526 (334) 621–8222

Eufaula-Barbour County Chamber of Commerce – *www.ebcchamber.org/default.htm*
PO Box 697, Eufaula, AL 36072–0697 (334) 687–6664

Fort Payne (Including information on DeSoto State Park, Little River Canyon, and Lookout Mountain) – *www.fortpayne.net/Default.htm*

Gulf Shores Area Chamber of Commerce – *www.alagulfcoastchamber.com*
3150 Gulf Shores Parkway, Gulf Shores, AL 36542 (334) 968–6904

Huntsville Convention and Visitors Bureau – *www.huntsville.org*
700 Monroe St., Huntsville, AL 35801 1–800–SPACE–4U or (256) 551–2230

Lawrence County Chamber (Including information on the Sipsey and Bankhead National Forests) – *http://homw.hiiway.net/~icc* 14220 W. Court St., P.O. Box 325, Moulton, AL 35650 (256) 974–1658

Mobile Chamber of Commerce – *www.mobcham.org*
PO Box 2187, Mobile, AL 36652 (334) 433–6951

Montgomery Chamber of Commerce – *www.montgomerychamber.org*
41 Commerce St., PO Box 79, Montgomery, AL 36101 (334) 834–5200

Saraland Area Chamber of Commerce – *www.saralandcoc.com*
939 Highway 43 S., Saraland, AL 36571 (334) 675–4444

State Government Organizations

Alabama Department of Environmental Management – *www.dcnr.state.al.us*
PO Box 301463, Montgomery, AL 36130–1463 (334) 271–7710

Alabama Environmental Council – *alenvironmentalcouncil.org/index.html*
2717 7th Ave So. Ste 207, Birmingham, AL 35233 (205) 322–3126

Alabama Forestry Commission – *www.bama.ua.edu/~foley001/index.html*
PO Box 302550, Montgomery, AL 36130–2550 (334) 240–9300

Alabama Mountain Lakes (North Alabama information) – *www.almtlakes.org*
25062 North St., PO Box 1075, Mooresville, AL 35649 1–800–648–5381

Alabama Recreation – *www.bama.ua.edu/~foley001*

Alabama State Parks – *www.dcnr.state.al.us/parks/state_parks_index_1a.html*
c/o Alabama Department of Conservation and Natural Resources –
64 North Union Street Montgomery, AL 1–800–ALAPARK

Contact Info

State Hiking and Outdoor Clubs and Organizations

Alabama Camping – (scouts) *www.sites.gulf.net/yustaga/ALCAMP.htm*
Alabama Natural Heritage Program – *ocelot.tnc.org/nhp/us/al/*
Huntingdon College Massey Hall, 1500 E. Fairview Ave., Montgomery, AL 36106-2148; (334) 834–4519
Alabama Trails – *www.alabamatrails.com*
PO Box 371162, Birmingham, AL 35237–1162
Alabama Wilderness Alliance – *www.wildlaw.org/awa-wild.htm*
PO Box 223, Mouton, AL 35650 (334) 265 6529
Alabama Wildlife Rehabilitation Center – *www.alawildliferehab.org*
1926 Hwy 31 So #101, Birmingham, AL 35244 (256) 663–7930
Anniston Outdoor Association – *www.microxl.com/vicbell/aoamain.htm*
c/o Anniston Parks and Recreation Department, PO Box 670,Anniston, AL 36202 (256) 231–7675
Appalachian Trail Club of Alabama – *sport.al.com/sport/atca*
PO Box 381842, Birmingham, 35238–1842
Atmore Chamber Of Commerce – *www.frontiernet.net/~atmoreal*
501 S. Pensacola Ave., Atmore, AL 36502 (334) 368–3305
Bama Environmental News – *www.bamanews.com*
(205) 226–7739
Birmingham Audubon Society – *http://bmewww.eng.uab.edu/bas/*
PO Box 314, Birmingham, AL 35201
Bon Secour National Wildlife Refuge – *http://southeast.fws.gov/bonsecour/index.html*
12295 St. Hwy 180, Gulf Shores, AL 36542 (334) 540–7720
Chickasabogue Park – *lyon.maf.mobile.al.us/government/local/county/county_org/chikpark.html*
760 Adlock Rd., Eight Mile, AL 36613 (334) 452–8496
Claude D. Kelley State Park – *www.dcnr.state.as.us/parks/claude_d_kelley_1a.html*
(334) 862–2511
Covington County / South Alabama Birding Association –
www.alaweb.com~kenwood/saba/birdfind/covington.htm (334) 382–2680
DeSoto State Park – *mentone.com/desoto*
13883 Co Rd 89, Ft Payne, AL 35967
Eufaula National Wildlife Refuge – *http://southeast.fws.gov/eufaula*
509 Old Hwy. 165, Eufaula, AL 36027 (334) 687–4065
Fort Conde, Mobile, AL – *www.maf.mobile/al/us/recreation/fort_conde.html*
1 So. Royal St., Mobile, AL 36602 (334) 434–7304
Georgia Pinhoti Trail Association – *www.americanhiking.org/alliance/ednowreci2.html*
(709) 291–0766
Great Outdoor Recreation Southern States (GORSS) – *gorss.com/hikingAlabama.htm*
Gulf State Park –
20115 St. Hwy 135, Gulf Shores, AL 36542 (334) 948–7275
Historic Blakeley State Park – *www.siteone.com/tourist/blakeley*
PO Box 7279, Spanish Fort, AL 35677 (334) 580–0005
Longleaf Alliance – *www.forestry/auburn/edu/la*
Crown & Colony Antiques; 26 South Section St, Fairhope, 36532 (334) 844–1020
Alabama Trail Guides by M.Lee van Horn – *public.surfree.com/Fountain/alabama.htm*

Sierra Club Cahaba (Birmingham) – *www.sierraclub.org/chapters/al/cahaba.html*
(205) 786–0622
Sierra Club Coastal Chapter – *www.sierraclub.org/chapters/al/coastal.html*
(334) 540–7496
Sierra Club East Alabama Chapter –
129 Carter St., Auburn, AL 36830–6230 (334) 821–9817
Sierra Club Mobile Chapter – *www.sierraclub.org/chapters/al/mobile.html*
(334) 655–3090
Sierra Club Montgomery Chapter –
3311 Covered Bridge Rd., Montgomery, AL 36116 (334) 277–9178
Sierra Club North Alabama (Huntsville) Chapter – *www.alabama.sierraclub.org/na.html*
Sierra Club Tennessee River (Decatur) Chapter –
(205) 685–9416
Sierra Club West Alabama Chapter – *www.sierraclub.org/chapters/al/west-al.html*
(205) 553–6748
Sipsey Wilderness – *www.montesano.com/hikeweb/sipsey.htm*
members.aol.com/sipseywilderness/
Tennessee Valley Audobon Society – *fly.hiwaay.net/~pgibson/tvas/*
Tennessee Valley Trails – *www.montesano.com/hikeweb/*
Troop 147 Camping Guide (Scout Troop page on Alabama hiking) –
www.maf.mobile.al.us/community/mob_scouts/camp/campg.html
Troop 147 c/o St. Paul's Episcopal Church, 4051 Old Shell Rd., Mobile, AL 36608
Trail of Tears – *rosecity.net/tears/*
U.S.S. Alabama Historical Trail, Inc, Mobile, AL – (334) 675–7037
Vulcan Trail Association – *www.mindspring.com/~vulcan_trail*
PO Box 19116, Birmingham, 35219–9166
(205) 982–4022
Walking and Volkssports Events – *www.ava.org/walk/alyre.htm*
AVA National Headquarters
1001 Pat Booker Rd Ste 101, Universal City, TX 78148-4147
Wild Alabama – *www.wildalabama.com*
PO Box 117, Moulton, AL 35650 (256) 974–6166
Wildflowers of Alabama – *www.auburn.edu/~deancar/*

National Hiking and Outdoor Organizations

American Hiking Society – *www.americanhiking.org*
1422 Fenwick Lane, Silver Spring, MD 20910
Ducks Unlimited – *www.ducks.org*
1 Waterfowl Way, Memphis, TN 38120 1–800–45–DUCKS
Native Forest Network – *www.nativeforest.org*
PO Box 57, Burlington, VT 05402 (802) 863–0571
National Park Service – *www.nps.gov/parklists/al.html*
USDA Forest Service – *www.fs.fed.us*
Sydney R Yates Federal Building, 201 14th St SW @ Independence Ave SW,
Washington, DC 20074
Southern Region Office (Including Alabama)
1720 Peachtree Rd. NW, Atlanta, GA 30309 (404) 347–4177
Forest Supervisor National Forests in Alabama
1765 Highland Avenue, Montgomery, AL 36107 (334) 832–4470

Talladega National Forest

District Ranger, USDA Forest Service 1001 North Street,
Highway 21 North, Talladega, AL 35150 (256) 362–2909
District Ranger, USDA Forest Service, 450 Highway 46
Heflin, AL 36264 (256) 463–2272

Bankhead National Forest

District Ranger, USDA Forest Service, P.O. Box 278, South Main Street
Double Springs, AL 35553 (256) 489–5111

Conecuh National Forest

District Ranger, USDA Forest Service, P.O. Box 310,
1100 South Three Notch Street, Andalusia, AL 36420
(334) 222–2555

Tuskegee National Forest

District Ranger, USDA Forest Service, Route 1, Box 204AA
Tuskegee, AL 36083 (334) 727–2652

Wild Law – *www.wildlaw.org*

300B Water St. Ste 214, Montgomery, AL 36104 (334) 265–6529
Email: *wildlaw@aol.com*

Wilderness Society – *www.wilderness.org*

900 7th St. NW, Washington, DC 20006–2506 1–800–THE–WILD

Index

Meet the Author

Joe Cuhaj is an Alabama transplant, having grown up in Mahwah, New Jersey, near the Harriman / Bear Mountain state parks where his love of hiking and the outdoors began.

Joe, his wife Maggie, daughter Kellie, and their two dogs, cat, and horse live in Daphne, Alabama, just east of Mobile, on the Gulf Coast. Joe is a full-time systems programmer for a local company, but finds frequent visits to area wildlife refuges, wetlands, and Oak Mountain State Park solace from the keyboard. Joe also enjoys canoeing the many rivers of the state as well as bike riding.

Author